AN
ALMANAC
OF WORDS AT
PLAY

Willard Espy, author of *The Game of Words,* is a public relations coun
sel in New York City. Reared in Oysterville, Washington, he has long
accompanied his more serious endeavors with a delight in the frivolity of
language. His light verse and serious articles have appeared in *The
Nation, The Atlantic, The New York Times Magazine, Good House-
keeping, This Week,* and *Punch.*

AN ALMANAC OF WORDS AT PLAY

Willard R. Espy

Clarkson N. Potter, Inc./Publisher NEW YORK

DISTRIBUTED BY CROWN PUBLISHERS, INC.

DEDICATION

(An Acrostic Verse in Which the Author Takes the Fifth)

For Bremen Town we're leaving now, to set us up a choir.
I, ass of asses, orchestrate. Sing, beasts of barn and byre!
Baa, randy ram! Dog, ululate! Grunt, ugsome pig! Honk, goose!
Raise brutish voices now in praise of her who let us loose!
Let anthems sound, done some in hisses, some in caws and hoots;
Let roars and mews engage in song; let peacocks sound like flutes!
Cow, aardvark, duck, and jackal, who, with camel caravanned,
In awful concord terrified a monstrous robber band—
Sing nonny nonny nonny now to her who freed us thus
(And never mind if, *entre nous,* she wanted rid of us.)

(If you would rather wait till later to start solving acrostics, simply take the first letter of the fifth word of each line, in order, and presto! the name will appear.)

Copyright © 1975 by Willard R. Espy

All rights reserved. No part of this publication may be reproduced, stored in a retrieval system, or transmitted, in any form or by any means, electronic, mechanical, photocopying, recording, or otherwise, without the prior written permission of the publisher.

Printed in the United States of America

Library of Congress Cataloging in Publication Data
Main entry under title:

An Almanac of words at play.

1. Literary calendars. 2. Word games. 3. English language—Anecdotes, facetiae, satire, etc. I. Espy, Willard R.
PN6245.A53   828'.02   74-77562
ISBN 0-517-520907 (Crown)
ISBN 0-517-524635 pbk.
    Published simultaneously in Canada by General Publishing Company Limited.
Inquiries should be addressed to Clarkson N. Potter, Inc., 419 Park Avenue South, New York, N. Y. 10016.

Second Printing, November, 1975
Designed by Ruth Smerechniak

The author's special thanks ...

To *Louise,* who meted out patience or impatience as the situation required. To *Faith* and *Ross Eckler,* whose unique publication, *Word Ways: The Journal of Recreational Linguistics,* was the source of many of these entries. To *William Cole,* the anthologist with the truffle-hound nose. To *Nina Sowers Wolfenbarger* for her card of invitation to the hanging of Lum You. To *Mignon Franco,* the only person who ever typed till 5 A.M. when I asked her to type till 5 A.M. To *Tauni de Lesseps* for painstakingly translating her visual puns from tempera to pen and ink so that I might use them in this book. To *Barbara Huston* for regularly forwarding invaluable material, and for never scathing a passage without suggesting how to improve it. To her son *Matt* for providing in all innocence the list of cowboy slang which became the starting point for one of my most indecent entries. To Jane and Lester Eldridge; Louisa and Paul Bonner; Anthony Bonner; David Pearce; Frank Johnson; Richard Edes Harrison; Ruth Bachtel; Charles F. Dery; Don Ellegood, and Don Davidson, all of whom offered useful suggestions or shared long-hoarded bits of nonsense.

To *Harper's* and *Punch* for permission to use those verses of mine that first appeared in their pages.

Above all, to God (that is, to God, above all), for permission, granted through Still Small Voice, to reprint Genesis *18, 17* and 18; Proverbs *14, 13,* and *16,* 18; Ecclesiastes *3, 2, 7, 3,* and *7, 6;* Job *8, 21* and *9, 23;* Jeremiah *5, 8;* Psalms *2, 4, 22, 7,* and *80, 6;* and John *1, 1.* Copyright © in perpetuity, God.

For arrangements made with various authors, their representatives, and publishing houses where copyrighted material was permitted to be reprinted, and for the courtesy extended by them, the following acknowledgments are gratefully made. All possible care has been taken to trace the ownership of every selection included and to make full acknowledgment for its use. If errors have accidentally occurred, they will be corrected in subsequent editions, provided notification is sent to the publisher.

"Anthologistics." From *Lyric Laughter,* by Arthur Guiterman. © 1939, E. P. Dutton. © renewed by Vida Lindo Guiterman. Reprinted by permission of Vida Lindo Guiterman. **January 8** "Rhopalic Sentence." From *Language on Vacation,* by Dmitri Borgmann, Charles Scribner's Sons. © 1965 Dmitri A. Borgmann. Reprinted by permission of Dmitri A. Borgmann. **January 11** "Doctor Emmanuel Harrison Hyde." From *The Wandering Moon* by James Reeves. © 1960, James Reeves. Reprinted by permission of James Reeves and E. P. Dutton. **January 12** "Quote or Misquote," by Peter Donchian. Reprinted by permission of *The Reader's Digest.* **January 12** "Lapsus Linguae," from *Pot Shots From Pegasus* by Keith Preston. © 1929. Reprinted by permission of Crown Publishers, Inc. **January 15** "What's Yours, Fella?" by L. R. N. Ashley. From *Word Ways.* Reprinted by permission of L. R. N. Ashley and *Word Ways.* **January 17** "Geo-metric Verses." From *Geo-metrics,* by Gerald Lynton Kaufman. © 1948, Gerald Lynton Kaufman. Reprinted by permission of A. S. Barnes & Co., Inc. **January 22** "The Pessimist, The Optimist," by Mary J. Youngquist. From *Word Ways.* Reprinted by permission of Mary J. Youngquist and *Word Ways.* **January 22** "Manicdepressant," by Kim Dammers. From *Poems One Line and Longer.* Original publication in *Gallery Series III—Poets (Levitations and Observations).* Reprinted by permission of William Cole. **January 23** "British and Scottish Pronunciation," by Darryl Francis. From *Word Ways.* Reprinted by permission of Darryl Francis and *Word Ways.* **January 25** "Edward M. Kennedy," by Leonard Miall. Reprinted by permission of Leonard Miall. **January 25** "The Lower Criticism," by John Hollander. From *Jiggery Pokery: A Compendium of Double Dactyls* edited by Anthony Hecht and John Hollander. Copyright © 1966. Anthony Hecht and John Hollander. Reprinted by permission of Atheneum Publishers. **January 28** "Le Jaseroque," by Frank Lord Warrin, Jr. © 1931, The New Yorker Magazine, Inc. Reprinted by permission.

CONTENTS

❧ ❧

Introduction   xix
A Definition of Terms   xxi

JANUARY

1 *Calendar Verse*. Jangled Janet.   1
2 *Ecology*. Caution: Living May Be Dangerous to Your Health.   2
3 *ABC Language*. An ABC Proposal Comes to 0.   2
4 *Fractured English*. Tootling in Tokyo.   3
5 *Random Rhymes*. A Man Beyond Sea-duction.   4
6 *Random Rhymes*. My S's Grow S's.   5
7 *Sex*. Fair Game.   5
8 *Rhopalics*. May Eagles Lacerate Eternally.   6
9 *Slang*. What's Yours, Fella?   6
10 *Grammar*. Suffix the Little Prefixes to Come unto Me
     (Comparatively Speaking).   7
11 *Random Rhymes*. A Squeak from Doctor Emmanuel.   7
12 *Clichés*. Clitch, Clitch, Clitch.   8
13 *Good Bad Verse*. The Muse on a Banana Skin.   9
14 *Tongue Twisters*. Rubber Baby Buggy Bumpers.   11
15 *Grammar*. One Man's Abdomen.   11
16 *American Isn't English*. Knock Up.   13
17 *Visual Wordplay*. Geo-metrics.   13
18 *Names*. Enter: Sir Benjamin Backbite.   14
19 *Homonyms, Homophones, Heteronyms*. It All Deep Ends.   15
20 *Multitudinous Nouns*. A Squirming of Snakes.   16
21 *Headlines*. Nudists Take Off.   17
22 *Equivocally Speaking*. If He Doth Love Me.   18
23 *American Isn't English*. How Do You Say Bicister, Micister?   19
24 *Hobson-Jobsons*. Ever See a Sand-Blind Titmouse?   21
25 *Higgledy-Piggledies*. Edward M. Kennedy and the Lower Criticism.   21
26 *Dialect*. Black English.   22
27 *Anagrams*. Be Friendly, Borgmann.   23

28 *Translation*. The Astonishment of Words.   23
29 *Good Bad Verse*. The Demise of the Methodist Church   25
30 *Countdown Verses*. Vile Vodka.   26
31 *Epitaphs*. Say, Who Will Write A Pun My Stone?   27

FEBRUARY

1   *Food*. What a Friend We Have in Cheeses!   29
2   *Tom Swifties*. "I'm Dying," He Croaked.   30
3   *Love*. Identity Problem in the Mammoth Caves.   31
4   *Epigrams*. Pronunciandum.   31
5   *Coined Words*. "In the Morning They Spring Up."   33
6   *Spoonerisms*. The Half-Warmed Fish.   33
7   *Pronunciation*. Telling Hearth from Earth Is Tough Stuff, Suzy.   34
8   *Malapropisms*. Many a Malapropism Has Flown under the Bridge.   36
9   *Fractured Foreigners*. Mots D'Heures: Gousses, Rames.   38
10 *Palindromes*. ¡Eva, Lave!   39
11 *Place Names*. The American Traveler.   40
12 *Presidential Prose*. The Gettysburg Address.   41
13 *Puns*. Odets, Where Is Thy Sting?   41
14 *Love*. "There Are Numerous Locutions to Express the Idea of Never."   43
15 *Grammar*. Shall I Will?   43
16 *Lipograms*. Mary Had a Lipogram.   45
17 *Dialect*. A Fraffly Well-Spoken Glossary.   46
18 *Rhymes out of Order*. Impossible Rhymes.   47
19 *Euphemisms*. Overdrawn Your Bank Account, You Negative Saver?   49
20 *Censored Fables*. Shipwreck.   50
21 *Epitaphs*. Self Service.   51
22 *Anagrams*. Washington Crisscrossing the Delaware.   52
23 *Pangrams*. Squdgy Fez, Blank Jimp Crwth Vox.   52
24 *Roman Numerals*. The Noblest City of Them All.   53
25 *Word Games for the Parlor*. The Girl I Never Saw.   54
26 *Univocalics*. Bless the Shepherd.   55
27 *Burlesque and Parody*. Rockaby Gloria.   56
28 *Acrostics*. Cats, Cats, Cats, Cats!   57
29 *Origins by Letter and Word*. The Canary, the Stallion, and the Partridge.   58

MARCH

1   *Fractured Foreigners*. The English is Coming.   59
2   *Onomatopoeia*. Chiffchaff.   60
3   *Oysterville*. Burma Shave.   61
4   *Cats*. The Cat and the Fiddle, Quaker Style.   61
5   *Clerihews*. Clerihews by Bentley.   62

6 *Visual Wordplay.* White Wine for Fish.   63
7 *The Muse Agiggle.* That Wrinkled and Golden Apricot.   65
8 *Money.* But, Honey—Are You Making Any Money?   66
9 *Sick, Sick.* Little Audrey.   66
10 *Measurements.* The Exactness of the Inexact.   67
11 *Grammar.* E Pluribus Unum.   68
12 *Abbreviations.* A Mrs. Kr. Mr.   69
13 *Horses, Frogs, and Other Insects.* A Croaking of Frogs.   70
14 *Random Rhymes.* I'd Like to Be a Corsican.   71
15 *Philosophy.* Summum Bonum.   71
16 *Fractured Foreigners.* Fairy Tales al Dante.   72
17 *Dialect.* Mr. Dooley on Christian Science.   73
18 *Onomatopoeia.* Tap Nap.   74
19 *Macaronics.* Amo, Amas, Felis-itous.   75
20 *Pow-wow.* An Eloquence of Indians.   76
21 *Biblical Bits.* A Crackling of Thorns.   77
22 *Place Names.* Ilwaco, O Ilwaco.   78
23 *Grammar.* I Sawyer Saw. Does That Make Me a Sawyer?   79
24 *Typefaces, Printing, and Typos.* Souvenir.   80
25 *Visual Wordplay.* Re: Rebuses.   80
26 *Nicknames.* Nicknames on Ticker Tape.   81
27 *Philosophy.* O Cuckoo!   82
28 *Ad Hominem.* Come Back, Little Artichoke Heart.   82
29 *Chain Words, Chain Verse.* Chain States.   83
30 *Alphabetics.* Ah, Zelda!   84
31 *Edicts.* The Mighty Fall; the Rest Just Grow Older.   85

APRIL

1 *Acronyms.* Compip, Compoop.   86
2 *Word Games.* A Hundred Words Once.   87
3 *Last Words.* As I Lay Dying.   88
4 *Anagrams.* Anagrams from Punch.   89
5 *Fractured Foreigners.* Berlitz School.   89
6 *Biblical Bits.* Biblical Fruitcake.   90
7 *Rhymes out of Order.* Single-Rhymed Verse.   91
8 *Place Names.* Spoken Like a Native.   92
9 *Origins by Letter and Word.* O.O.O. (of obscure origin, that is.)   92
10 *Euphemisms.* Rejection Slips.   92
11 *Women's Liberation.* Friedan on the Luce.   93
12 *Grammar.* The Subjunctive Rides Again.   94
13 *Mnemonics.* Off With His Foote!   94
14 *Younger Generation.* A Birthday Song for Medora.   95
15 *Univocalics.* Eve's Legend.   96

16 *Short Words.* Let Her Go. 97
17 *Hyperbole.* Hyperbole, American Style. 97
18 *Slang.* Clicket, Clicket, Clickman Toad. 98
19 *Uncommon, Improper Nouns.* Abigail to Aurora. 99
20 *Chain Words, Chain Verse.* Old Doc. 100
21 *Burlesque and Parody.* If Longfellow's "The Midnight Ride of Paul Revere" were written by Ernest Lawrence Thayer, Author of "Casey at the Bat." 100
22 *Shakespeare.* How I Lost the Race with Willy. 101
23 *Oysterville.* The Snail's on the Thorn. 102
24 *Dialect.* Let Stalk Strine. 104
25 *Metaphors.* A Tired Song of Tired Similes. 105
26 *Sick, Sick.* Little Moron. 106
27 *Slang.* The Inelegant Courtship of Pecos Chuck and Widder Nelly. 106
28 *Grammar.* Bulls from Great Pens. 108
29 *Jargon.* Ecclesiastes and George Orwell, for Instance. 108
30 *Pronunciation.* How and Why I Killed My Wife. 109

MAY

1 *Acronyms.* Acronyms of Ailment. 111
2 *Random Rhymes.* Where Did That Poisoned Pawn Come from, Mr. Fischer? 111
3 *Dialect.* When Fishermen Meet. 112
4 *Calendar Verse.* I Start My Week with Wednesday. 113
5 *Euphemisms.* When B+ = F. 113
6 *Back Slang.* Era Uoy a Diamrab? 114
7 *Logic.* Exception to the Rule. 115
8 *Random Rhymes.* Poor Paralyze Can't Lift a Finger. 116
9 *Visual Wordplay.* Sticks and Stones May Break My Bones. 117
10 *Love.* Should She Have the Baby? 118
11 *Fractured English.* "¡Wellcome, To the Caves of Arta!" 119
12 *Younger Generation.* Finding Your Thing. 120
13 *Word Games for the Parlor.* Redundance. 121
14 *Pronunciation.* Bird and Behemoth. 122
15 *Dialect.* Harpin' Boont in Boonville. 123
16 *Origins by Letter and Word.* Schizophrenic Words. 124
17 *Reflections.* At 39,000 Feet. 125
18 *Multitudinous Nouns.* House of Horrors. 127
19 *Graffiti.* Jesus Saves, Moses Invests. 128
20 *The Younger Generation.* The Copper and the Jovial Undergrads. 129
21 *Measurements.* Measure for Measure. 130
22 *Jargon.* Like Hell We'll Pray for Him! 131
23 *Homonyms, Homophones, Heteronyms.* Four Kate, Won Eye a Door. 131
24 *Short Words.* Words with One Syllable Work. 133
25 *Clichés.* Time on Your Feet. 133

26 *Random Rhymes.* Foot-Notes. 134
27 *Fractured English.* Mark Twain's Portuguese Find. 135
28 *Random Rhymes.* Kind of Four of a Kind. 136
29 *Echoes, Echoes.* Echoing Sentence, Echoing Rhymes. 137
30 *Younger Generation.* Eletelephony. 139
31 *Grammar.* Curtailed Words. 139

JUNE

1 *Food.* Menu Madness. 141
2 *Sex.* Shiver, Tickle, Sneeze. 142
3 *Haiku.* Haiku Prove I.Q. 143
4 *Cats.* A Cat's a Cat for A' That. 144
5 *Abbreviations.* When Baby Gurgles Guam and Georgia. 144
6 *Homonyms, Homophones, Heteronyms.* Now Here We Are Alone, My Dear.
7 *Dialect.* Doggerel in Loggerel. 146
8 *Clichés.* It Stands to? Reason. 147
9 *Symbols and Signs.* I Love You to OO ($\pm$ A°). 148
10 *American Isn't English.* The British Crossword Labyrinth. 150
11 *Spoonerisms.* Cynarae, Hot Woe! 150
12 *Place Names.* We Canal Praise the Streets of New Orleans. 151
13 *Names.* Praisegod Barebone—I Begin with E! 152
14 *Grammar.* The Jealous Governes. 153
15 *Shakespeare.* He Beat You to That One, Too. 154
16 *American Isn't English.* Britannia Rules of Orthography. 155
17 *Dialect.* Balamer Is In Murlin. 155
18 *Word Games for the Parlor.* Rosencrantz and Guildenstern. 156
19 *Random Rhymes.* Kipling Rudyards. 158
20 *Good Bad Verse.* Oysterville, O Oysterville! 158
21 *Grammar.* Like, Wow, Man! 159
22 *Hidden Words.* Part of Adam Is Mad. 160
23 *Malapropisms.* Petersonese. 161
24 *Uncommon, Improper Nouns.* Midsummer Madness. 161
25 *Horses, Frogs, and Other Insects.* The Centipede, the Water Beetle, and the Praying Mantis. 162
26 *Women's Liberation.* To Ms or Not to Ms. 163
27 *Word Games for the Parlor.* Point of View. 164
28 *Translation—Limerick Division.* Spring in the Fall? Nein! Nicht Möglich! 164
29 *Ambiguity.* Confound Your Words, Your Looks, Your Handwriting! 165
30 *Onomatopoeia.* Töf-töf, Doki-doki. 166

JULY

1 *Sex.* The Hard-boiled Seduction of a Soft-boiled Egg. 167

2 *Dictionaries and Encyclopedias*. Encyclopedic Chant.   168
3 *Headlines*. Crush vs. Whip.   169
4 *American Isn't English*. Fanny by Any Other Name.   171
5 *Long Words*. Sesquipedalia, Hold On! I'm Coming!   171
6 *Alphabetics*. Cockney Alphabet.   172
7 *Ecology*. Remember Cyclamates? Maybe They Weren't So Harmful
      after All.   173
8 *Palindromes*. He Goddam Mad Dog, Eh?   174
9 *Labels*. Those Terrible Russian Winters.   175
10 *Place Names*. Omak Me Yours Tonight.   176
11 *Fractured Foreigners*. The French Don't Talk like You and Me.   179
12 *Dictionaries and Encyclopedias*. Scrawny Cag-Mag Sheep.   179
13 *Women's Liberation*. Funsky with Strunsky.   180
14 *Grammar*. Punctuation (Parenthetical).   180
15 *ABC Language*. Last Request.   181
16 *Visual Wordplay*. Equational Communication.   182
17 *Random Rhymes*. The Akond of Swat.   183
18 *Edicts*. Office Rules and Regulations.   184
19 *Love*. O Some May Promise Riches.   185
20 *Jargon*. Journal de la Mère Oye.   186
21 *The Muse Agiggle*. Hallelujah, Hermit!   186
22 *Names*. All in the Family.   187
23 *Dialect*. Newspeak and Nadsat.   188
24 *Metaphors*. Gay's Gay New Song of Gay New Similes.   189
25 *Love*. A Windy Love Song, Annotated.   189
26 *Shaped Verse*. More Geo-Metrics.   191
27 *Palindromes*. Palindromes of Number.   192
28 *Names*. Hitchcock Steers a Bull.   192
29 *Clichés*. Young Johnny and Ugly Sal.   193
30 *Nicknames*. The Nicknaming of States.   194
31 *History*. The Gentle Witch.   195

AUGUST

1 *Fractured Foreigners*. Fifty English Emigrants.   197
2 *Younger Generation*. Aris Old Tot.   197
3 *Word Games for the Parlor*. Word Ways' Ways with Words.   198
4 *Jargon*. Mnemonics into Jargon.   199
5 *Countdown Verse*. Drinking Song of a Hard-Hearted Landlord.   200
6 *Dialect*. The Showman's Courtship.   201
7 *Onomatopoeia*. Sounds of Oysterville.   202
8 *Hobson Jobsons*. A Brew of Brewer.   203
9 *American Isn't English*. Salisbury, Colquhoun, and Cuchulain.   204
10 *Censored Fables*. The Comtator and the Door.   205
11 *Fractured Foreigners*. For the Common Market.   206

12 *Two-line Verse*. Poem Composed in Rogue River Park.   207
13 *Ecology*. Coleridge on Cologne   207
14 *Grammar*. Sentences Askew   208
15 *Puns*. In Vino Veritas.   209
16 *Biblical Bits*. A Reasonable Reply to John Ball.   210
17 *Sick, Sick*. Lizzie Borden and Her Playmates.   211
18 *Riddles*. High Flight Highlights.   211
19 *Dictionaries and Encyclopedias*. The Thesaurus and the Muse.   213
20 *Word Games for the Parlor*. Word Belt.   214
21 *Philosophy*. The Web Retangled.   215
22 *Tom Swifties*. Swiftly Speaking.   215
23 *Fakes and Frauds*. Some Mad Young Wags.   216
24 *Pronunciation*. The Susurrant Schwa.   217
25 *Palindromes*. Professor Otto R. Osseforp.   218
26 *Typefaces, Printing, and Typos*. Printing Was Difficult at Fust.   218
27 *Origins by Letter and Word*. Had Darwin Dug Up Fossil Words.   219
28 *News*. Mystery News.   220
29 *Dialect*. Fraffly Fine Poetry.   221
30 *Dictionaries and Encyclopedias*. Anthon's Classical Dictionary.   222
31 *Cats*. Cat Words.   223

SEPTEMBER

1   *Good Bad Verse*. A Teacher Looks at Oysterville.   225
2   *Dialect*. The Yellow Prose of Texas.   226
3   *Abbreviations*. The Conversational Reformer.   227
4   *Anagrams*. A Chronology of Anagrams.   227
5   *Jargon*. The Profundity Kit.   228
6   *Limericks*. A Lewdness of Limericks.   229
7   *Multitudinous Nouns*. The Venereal Game.   230
8   *The Muse Agiggle*. A Gaggle of Giggles.   231
9   *Random Rhymes*. Please, Please Keep Coming.   232
10 *American Isn't English*. English Is Unamerican.   233
11 *Dialect*. Amos 'n' Andy.   234
12 *Metaphor*. I Dreamed the Devil's Wife Proposed a Game.   235
13 *Eskimos*. Eskimo Recipes.   236
14 *Origins by Letter and Word*. The Fable of the H[1] and the Stupid but
        Persistent A[2].   237
15 *Typefaces, Printing, and Typos*. Reas'ning but to Err.   238
16 *Grammar*. The Naughty Preposition.   240
17 *Rhopalics*. I into My Mirror Peeked.   241
18 *Rhymes out of Order*. Sight Rhymes, Slight Rhymes.   241
19 *Malapropisms*. Much Ado About Malapropisms.   242
20 *Word Games for the Parlor*. Nameplay.   243
21 *Grammar*. I Saw a Peacock with a Fiery Tail.   243

22 *Palindromes*. Word and Line Palindromes.   244
23 *Place Names*. Address Unknown.   244
24 *Long Words*. Chemicals and Other Big Ones.   245
25 *Clerihews*. Take 5 Tsp Auden; Add 1 Tsp Listerine.   246
26 *Abbreviations*. The Hrglphs f th Nw Yrk Tms.   247
27 *Sex*. About That Cow . . .   248
28 *Biblical Bits*. King David and King Solomon.   248
29 *Grammar*. The Rein in Spain Reigns Mainly in the Rain.   249
30 *Dialect*. Mr. K*A*P*L*A*N's Dark Logic.   250

OCTOBER

1   *Spoonerisms*. Ballade of Soporific Absorption.   252
2   *Ad Hominem*. Pinking the Politician.   253
3   *Dialect*. Strine Revisited.   253
4   *Grammar*. Singular Plurals.   254
5   *Ciphers*. How Not to Solve a Cipher.   255
6   *Slang*. Where Is the Slang of Yesteryear?   255
7   *Eskimos*. Lo, the Frolicsome Eskimo.   257
8   *Opposites*. Opposite Proverbs.   257
9   *Word Games for the Parlor*. What Is the Question?   258
10 *Burlesque and Parody*. The Mad Round Robin.   259
11 *Place Names*. Streets in Old London.   261
12 *Grammar*. "Hark to the Mewsicians of Bremen!" Mewed the Caterpillar.   262
13 *Typefaces, Printing, and Typos*. Sim Ines.   262
14 *Slang*. The Variety of Abel Green.   263
15 *Women's Lib*. Fallen Women.   264
16 *Grammar*. A Collection of Crocks.   264
17 *Homonyms, Homophones, Heteronyms*. Colloquy between a Devout Man
        and His Wicked Echo.   265
18 *Folk Etymology*. Mini, Minu.   266
19 *Grammar*. Forgotten Positives.   266
20 *Younger Generation*. Alexander's Number One.   267
21 *Metaphors*. Lerner's Mixed Lerning.   268
22 *Word Games for the Parlor*. Stinky-Pinkies.   268
23 *Philosophy*. Upon October Twenty-third.   269
24 *Names*. Surf Bird, Shore Bird.   269
25 *Clichés*. We Interrupt Our Program for a Word from Mr. McLuhan.   270
26 *Homonyms, Homophones, Heteronyms*. Polish Up Your Polish, Zywacki!   271
27 *Higgledy-Piggledy*. Above All That?   271
28 *Short Words*. Love Is a Four-letter Word.   272
29 *Word Games for the Parlor*. Caught in the Middle.   272
30 *Fractured Foreigners*. A Fracture of French, an Omelet of Afrikaans,
        and an Indiscretion of Italian.   273
31 *Random Rhymes*. Dipping for Apples.   273

NOVEMBER

1 *Word Games for the Parlor*. Page-flipping in a Daybook. 275
2 *Dirges*. A Tolling of Bells. 276
3 *Slang*. Bloody. 277
4 *American Isn't English*. There's Nothing Funny about Falling into the 'Ay Cutter. 278
5 *History*. Extracts from 1066 and All That. 279
6 *Grammar*. Just Because . . . 281
7 *Epigrams*. Epigrammatic Espy. 281
8 *Love*. Lay of the Deserted Influenzaed. 282
9 *Measurements*. I'd Walk 1.6093 Kilometers for a Camel. 283
10 *Cats*. The Naming of Cats. 283
11 *Clichés*. Pandora Opens a Can of Worms. 284
12 *Drink*. The Drunkard's Conceit. 285
13 *Visual Wordplay*. Notpoems. 287
14 *Dialect*. Dialects, Various. 288
15 *Word Games for the Parlor*. Double Duty. 289
16 *Grammar*. Let the Ball Lay Where It Was Flang. 289
17 *Multitudinous Nouns*. A Flock of Ships. 290
18 *Anagrams*. The Strange Case of the Surplus Anagrams. 291
19 *Dialect*. You Know Me, Al. 291
20 *Presidential Prose*. Eisenhower's Address at Gettysburg. 293
21 *Good Bad Verse*. Big and Little Slips from Big and Little Slippers. 294
22 *Place Names*. Lines to Miss Florence Huntingdon. 295
23 *Philosophy*. The Egg That Hen Belonged To. 295
24 *Slang*. Winchellese. 296
25 *Typefaces, Printing, and Typos*. Jenson with Scotch in Hand. 298
26 *Puns*. A Zoological Romance. 299
27 *Oxymorons*. Faultily Faultless. 300
28 *Chain Words, Chain Verse*. Truth and Such. 301
29 *Ad Hominem*. The Venom of Contented Critics. 302
30 *Dialect*. "Biby's" Epitaph. 303

DECEMBER

1 *Dictionaries and Encyclopedias*. A Delight of Dictionaries. 304
2 *Word Games for the Parlor*. Friend in the Middle. 305
3 *Opposites*. Pseudo-opposites. 305
4 *Random Rhymes*. Ambivalence in the Oyster Beds. 306
5 *Food*. Alimentary Canals Abroad. 306
6 *Random Rhymes*. Agape and Cupid. 307
7 *Word Games for the Parlor*. Ounce Dice Trice. 308
8 *Names*. Stop Hissing, Belinda! 309
9 *Dialect*. Mama's Advice. 310

10 *Fractured English*. Da, One Jellyfish to Go, Tovarich   311
11 *Birthdays*. We Men of Sagittarius.   311
12 *Equivocally Speaking*. Triple Platform.   312
13 *Anagrams*. ********** Drank for 969 Years.   313
14 *Philosophy*. The Quodlibets of Tom Aquinas.   314
15 *Homonyms, Homophones, Heteronyms*. Holey, Holey, Holey, Holed Sox
    Almighty.   315
16 *Onomatopoeia*. Kew, Kew, Si Si Si.   316
17 *Word Games for the Parlor*. Games for Insomniacs.   316
18 *The Muse Agiggle*. One Last Giggle.   317
19 *Dialect*. Da Wheestlin' Barber.   319
20 *Visual Wordplay*. Antics.   321
21 *Tom Swifties*. One Last Croak.   321
22 *Dialect*. Cajun Night Before Christmas.   322
23 *Origins by Letter and Word*. Nay, Nay, Neigh Not, Neighbor Bob.   324
24 *Visual Wordplay*. A Visit from St. Nicholas.   325
25 *Acrostics*. Take Back That Powdered Rhinoceros Horn, Santa!   326
26 *Rhymes out of Order*. Spark in the Dark.   326
27 *Grammar*. The Assination of English.   327
28 *Visual Wordplay*. More Notpoems.   328
29 *Horses, Frogs, and Other Insects*. The Kentucky Thoroughbred.   329
30 *Pidgin English*. Papa Belong Me-Fella, Nipee Off Her Nose.   330
31 *Fare Well to Wits and Wags*. Fee, Fi, Fo, Fum—I Smell the Blood of
    Frank Sullivan, Etc.   330
Answers and Solutions   333
Index   357

INTRODUCTION

The verbal vagaries in this book are designed to last you for a year. They include examples of all the hidden apparel you would find if a proper young bride permitted an improper inspection of her person:

> *Something old; something new;*
> *Something borrowed; something blue.*

Old? I cast back to the time of Jeremiah, when young men neighed like hay-fed horses after their neighbors' wives.* New? This introduction is not yet even written. Borrowed? Half of the pages that follow are either borrowed, begged, or stolen.

As to something blue . . . well, my Aunt Dora, who had a tolerant ear for blue jokes (indeed, she could pay no higher compliment to one of her sex than to describe her as a "fine, upstanding, double-breasted woman"), would have refused to condemn the ancient Egyptian beauty who for a price entertained "both pygmies and giants."† She would have slapped her knee over "The Hard-boiled Seduction of a Soft-boiled Egg."‡ But it is a relief to know that her sister Susie will never read those particular passages. Aunt Susie had a nose for brimstone.

An Almanac of Words at Play is something of a three-ring circus of words: words clowning; words walking tightropes; words venturing their heads into the mouths of lions; words cleaning up after the elephants.

I can recall only one other passion so consuming as my lifelong passion for words . . . and that one did not last. It occurred in my fourteenth year, when I commuted to and from high school in a bus that was irradiated by the presence of the daughter of the driver—a girl whose hair was the color of a goldfinch. She was perhaps two years older than I, and I worshiped her; she is the only member of her sex whom I still remember having a halo around her head. Through that whole school year, though, she showed no awareness of my existence. My closest approach to her came when I dreamed she was standing at a sunlit window, while I sat mournful in the shadows. After a long pause she turned to me—but only in the dream—put her soft hand on my head, and whispered, "I never knew you cared."

Some days words, too, may whisper in my ear, "I never knew you cared." But I am not taking bets. Words choose their lovers arbitrarily. They may bestow their affections on some seedy characters, but they are never seduced against their will. (In fact, I suspect they are most relaxed among themselves. Notice what happens the next time you leave your unabridged dictionary open near the front or back. The pages

---

* 23 December.
† 6 September
‡ 1 July

will begin quietly to turn by themselves: *ablate,* perhaps, calling on *fermentation,* or *yodel* visiting *perspicuity.*)

Words are self-centered; they like best what Isaac Disraeli described as "veneration of words and indifference to sense." I suspect they have never forgiven Democritus for calling them "but the shadow of actions," or Shakespeare for his slighting comment:

> *'Tis well said again;*
> *And 'tis a kind of good deed to say well;*
> *And yet deeds are not words.*

I wrote this book to amuse, not to frustrate. If some passage is confusing, just look up the answer in the back—or, better yet, skip to the next entry.

Treat words as a Victorian gentleman treated a lady: as his superior, certainly, but not his equal. Cosset them. Defer to them. Tell them how beautiful they are. Give them your seat in the subway. But don't let them break your heart as I have let them break mine. Don't take them seriously.

Rather, emulate Russell Baker, who knows that a deep question deserves a frivolous answer. Or Beverly Nichols, whose goal is to disseminate entertainment uncluttered with enlightenment. Treat words the way such wise men as Lewis Carroll, W. S. Gilbert, Ogden Nash, and Cole Porter treated them: as a gorgeous joke.

"I can't help thinking," said philosopher-scientist Claude Levi-Strauss, "that science would be more appealing if it had no practical use." Words, too.

Which is why I for one, though I may not be able to resist the temptation to write, at least have the common sense not to say anything.

OYSTERVILLE
31 December, 1974

A DEFINITION OF TERMS

Since some of the rhetorical devices in this almanac may be unfamiliar to you, I define them here:

ABC LANGUAGE. A substitution of like-sounding letters, digits or symbols for words or parts of words: U R YY 4 me.

ACRONYM. A word formed from the initial letters of a name, as WAC from Women's Army Corps; or by combining parts of series of words: *radar* for *radio detecting and ranging*.

ACROSTIC. A composition, usually in verse, in which one or more sets of letters, as the initial or final letters of the lines, taken in order, form a word or words.

ANAGRAM. A word or phrase formed by reordering the letters of another word or phrase: *opts, pots, tops, stop, spot, post.*

CLERIHEW. A humorous, unscanned quatrain about a person who is generally named in the first line. The inventor was Edmund Clerihew Bentley.

DOUBLE-DACTYL (also called Higgledy-Piggledy, Niminy-Piminy, etc.). A verse invention of Paul Pascal and Anthony Hecht. It consists of eight double-dactyl lines with a strict composition and rhyme scheme.

ÉQUIVOQUE. A passage which, according to the way it is read, can have two or more meanings. If the second meaning is risqué, an équivoque is also a double entendre.

HOBSON-JOBSON. A folk-etymological alteration of a borrowed word. "Shame-faced," for instance, has nothing to do with "face" at all; it is from Old English *sceamfest,* "bound by shame."

HOMONYM, HOMOPHONE. A word having the same pronunciation as another, but differing from it in origin, meaning, and, often, in spelling. There is a distinction between the meanings of the two words that I cannot keep in my head.

LIPOGRAM. A composition lacking a certain letter or letters. The *Odyssey* of Tryphiodorus had no a in the first book, no b in the second, and so on. The fifty-thousand-word novel *Gadsby,* by E. V. Wright, has no e.

MACARONICS. See Pig Latin.

MALAPROPISM. A grotesque and unintentional misuse of one word for another of similar sound: *pretend* for *portend, fortuitously* for *fortunately.*

MNEMONICS. A system to improve or develop the memory. It is named for the goddess Mnemosyne, mother of the Muses.

ONOMATOPOEIA. The formation of words in imitation of natural sounds; words so formed. *Buzz* and *hiss* are onomatopoeic words.

OXYMORON. A conjunction of incongruous or contradictory terms, generally for rhetorical effect: *cruel kindness, nasty politeness*.

PALINDROME. A word, phrase, verse, or sentence that reads the same forward as backward: Madam, I'm Adam.

PANGRAM. A verse, sentence, phrase, or the like, containing all the letters of the alphabet. Pangrammatists are still trying unsuccessfully to use each letter only once and make sense.

PATCHWORK VERSE (also called Cento or Mosaic). A verse consisting of lines, often incongruous, borrowed from other poems.

PIG LATIN. A jargon in imitation of Latin, as *og-day atin-lay* for Dog Latin. If you mix vernacular words with Latin-sounding words, you have *macaronics*.

REBUS. A riddle composed of symbols or pictures that suggest visually the sound of the words or syllables to be deciphered. $\frac{\text{Paid}}{\text{He}}$ ("He is underpaid") is a rebus.

RHOPALIC. A snowballing line or passage in which each successive word has one more syllable (or letter) than the last.

SPOONERISM. An unintentional transposition of sounds (as, *Let me sew you to your sheet* for *Let me show you to your seat*). Named after William A. Spooner, English clergyman.

STINKY PINKY. A noun modified by a rhyming adjective: drunken punkin.

UNIVOCALIC. A writing containing only one vowel: "Persevere, ye perfect men; ever keep the precepts ten."

Anthologistics

Since one anthologist put in his book
Sweet things by Morse, Bone, Potter, Bliss and Brook,
All subsequent anthologists, of course,
Have quoted Bliss, Brook, Potter, Bone and Morse.
For, should some rash anthologist make free
To print selections, say, from you and me,
Omitting with a judgment all his own
The classic Brook, Morse, Potter, Bliss and Bone,
Contemptuous reviewers, passing by
Our verses, would unanimously cry,
"What manner of anthology is this
That leaves out Bone, Brook, Potter, Morse and Bliss!"

—ARTHUR GUITERMAN

JANUARY

1 JANUARY

Jangled Janet

The following old rhyming calendar should get you through this year, but apparently not through next:

JANET WAS QUITE ILL ONE DAY

JANet was quite ill one day.
FEBrile troubles came her way.
MARtyr-like, she lay in bed;
APRoned nurses softly sped.
MAYbe, said the leech judicial,
JUNket would be beneficial.
JULeps, too, though freely tried,
AUGured ill, for Janet died.
SEPulchre was sadly made;
OCTaves pealed and prayers were said.
NOVices with many a tear
DECorated Janet's bier.
—*Author Unknown.*

The verse below is for anyone who may have awakened with a headache this New Year morning:

JANGLE BELLS

JANgle bells, jangle bells, jangle all the way!
FEBrifuge, aspirin, start this New Year's day.
MARk me down for a clown— I had the whole gang over;
APRicot brandy's what left me with this hangover.
MAYbe I erred to try whiskey laced with rum;
JUNiper potions were drunk *ad libitum.*
JULep's sinful when a skinful has a vodka chaser;
AUGht of saki leaves me rocky the ensuing day, sir.
SEPtic all alcohol is—the stuff of devils:
OCTopods, elephants, joined my New Year revels.
NOVelties from D.T.'s pall; I end my lay
DEClaiming I shall stay dry this whole New Year's day.
—*W.R.E.*

1

2 JANUARY

Caution: Living May Be Dangerous to Your Health

After counting my pulse and reading Stephen Leacock, I conclude that this may be a risky year.

"Just think of it," wrote Leacock, "a hundred years ago there were no bacilli, no ptomaine poisoning, no diphtheria and no appendicitis. Rabies were little known and imperfectly developed. All of these we owe to medical science. Even such things as psoriasis and peritonitis and trypanosomiasis, which are now household names, were known only to the few and were quite beyond the reach of the great mass of the people."

Medical science has stridden since Leacock's time. Nowadays life's risks include glue on postage stamps, hormones in chicken, antibiotics in beef, dyes in lipstick, plastic falsies, mercury in fish, radiation from TV, cranberries, cyclamates, the mist from lubricating oil, and the lining of tin cans.

Jogging causes heart attacks in the elderly, and slipped disks in the young; bed rest encourages blood clots; eat horse meat, my sister Dale says, and you will get the trots; the drinker is headed for cirrhosis, and the nondrinker for a nervous breakdown; coffee leads to gout; tea is constipating; eggs clog the arteries. If you bib wine, expect cancer of the larynx. If you sleep, you dream, and an exciting dream may wind up in a coronary occlusion.

To cap the climax, as advocates of birth control might put it, semen has been charged with responsibility for cancer of the cervix. ("This is carcinogenic, dear," ejaculated Tom anticlimactically.)

Wilbur Cross understood. "Caution!" he cried. "Living may be dangerous to your health!"

3 JANUARY

An ABC Proposal Comes to O

My brother Edwin used to say I was so lazy I was bound to wind up as a minister, Ironically, it turned out to be Ed who devoted his life to religion, and Ed is one of the hardest-working men I know. But he was right; few people are lazier than I. When I approach a revolving door, I wait for someone to give the first push.

ABC is a lazy man's language. One digit or one letter of the alphabet can replace a whole word. Take this ABC love song:*

---

* The original of this has disappeared from my files, and I fear my reconstruction may have some errors

A PROPOSAL

O FE dear, what XTC
I MN8 when U IC!
Once KT 1 me with her I's;
2 LN I O countless sighs.
'Twas MLE while over Cs.
Now all 3 R nonNTTs,
4 U XL them all U C
U suit me FE 2 a T.
          —*Louise J. Walker*

This ABC passage is elegant:

U O a O but I O U;
O O no O but O O me;
O let not my O a O go,
But give O O I O U so.
          —*William Whewell*

The sense begins to emerge when you reflect that an O may be just that; or oh; or owe; or a cipher; or a zero; or an aught; or a naught.

Having mastered Whewell, you will find the following octet as simple as, say, ABC.

Oy OO thO he O
2 On an OO. OO bO
An OO but he never thO
He'd O the OO dealer O
For the OO OO bO.
Say, has OO's OO brO
OO O that OO sO?
OO's OO's good for nO.
          —*W.R.E.*

O I C

I'm in a 10der mood today
  & feel poetic, 2;
4 fun I'll just — off a line
  & send it off 2 U.

I'm sorry you've been 6 o long;
  Don't B disconsol8;
But bear your ills with 42de,
  & they won't seem so gr8.
          —*Anonymous*

4 JANUARY

Tootling in Tokyo

A translation of certain Japanese traffic regulations for the benefit of English-speaking drivers:

When a passenger of the foot heave in sight, tootle the horn, trumpet at him melodiously at first, but if he still obstacles your passage, tootle him with vigor, express by mouth the warning Hi, hi! Beware the wandering horse that he shall not take fright as you pass him by. Do not explode the exhaust box at him. Go soothingly by. Give big space to the festive dog that shall sport in the roadway. Go soothingly in the grease-mud as there lurks the skid-demon. Avoid the tanglement of the dog with your wheel spokes. Press the braking of the foot as you roll round the corner to save collapse and tie-up.

(It was a Japanese who in an English court said of a shady entrepreneur: "He has a finger in every tart.")

5 JANUARY

A Man Beyond
Sea-Duction

(To fully appreciate the truth of the following verse, you must understand that I was reared in a tiny Washington state hamlet named, with good reason, Oysterville. When I tell you I find oyster beds uncohabitable I know whereof I speak.)

I
Do not roister
With an oyster
I
Like my
Bed dry
An oyster
Moister
The wetter
The better
I
Find wet beds uncohabitable
Which is why
The moist
Oyst
And the dry
I
Are incompatible.

          —W.R.E.

6 JANUARY

My S'S Grow S'S

Some words ending in s change to quite unrelated words if another s is added:

"My s's grow s's, *alas!*" cried *a lass;*
"My *handles* turn *handless,* my *bras* turn to *brass.*
A girl who *cares* deeply is quick to *caress;*
She dreams of the *posses* whose love she'd *possess;*
An *as* with an s is an *ass,* and no less
When *asses* add s's, those *asses assess.*
Add s's to *mas* and they worship at *mass;*
Add s's to *pas,* and the pas make a *pass.*

          —W.R.E.

The verse below, one of the most famous of puzzles, takes advantage of the s plus s oddity. The word involved is one of those I have cited.

A word there is of plural number
Foe to ease and tranquil slumber.
Any other word you take
And add an s will plural make;
But if you add an s to this
So strange the metamorphosis:
Plural is plural now no more
And sweet what bitter was before.

          —George Canning

7 JANUARY

Fair Game

In 1930, in Paris, I bought an unexpurgated edition of *Lady Chatterley's Lover,* but courage failed me when it came time to smuggle the book into the United States. It was finally published here in 1959, to mixed notices. *Field and Stream,* a magazine devoted to outdoor pursuits, was disappointed:

Although written many years ago, *Lady Chatterley's Lover* has just been reissued by the Grove Press, and this pictorial account of the day by day life of an English gamekeeper is full of considerable interest to outdoor-minded readers as it contains many passages on pheasant-raising, the apprehending of poachers, ways to control vermin and other chores and duties of the professional gamekeeper.

Unfortunately one is obliged to wade through many pages of extraneous material in order to discover and savor those sidelights on the management of a Midland shooting estate, and in this reviewer's opinion the book cannot take the place of J. R. Miller's *Practical Gamekeeping*.

8 JANUARY

May Eagles Lacerate Eternally

Rhopalon is Greek for a club which thickens from the handle to the head. A rhopalic verse is composed of lines in which each successive word has more syllables than the one before:

> May eagles lacerate eternally
> Your liver, overproud Prometheus!
> Your fiery offering, predictably,
> Has rendered humankind vainglorious.
> —*W.R.E.*

Remove the limitations imposed by meter and rhyme, and rhopalics can swell to the size of the club that Theseus used to kill Procrustes. This example by Dmitri Borgmann adds letters instead of syllables:

I do not know where family doctors acquired illegibly perplexing handwriting; nevertheless, extraordinary pharmaceutical intellectuality, counterbalancing indecipherability, transcendentalizes intercommunications' incomprehensibleness.

9 JANUARY

What's Yours, Fella?

This is hash-house vocabulary. The more terms you recognize, the more deplorable your eating habits.

1. Draw one!
2. Gimme a shimmy!
3. Side of French!
4. Mickey with a wreath!
5. Mike and Ike!
6. Chocker hole and murk!
7. Arizona!
8. Clean the kitchen, red lead!

9. One on the city!
10. A Coney Island!
11. Garibaldi!
12. BLT, hold the mayo!
13. Whistleberries and hounds, a pair!
14. Bossy in a bowl!
15. Stir two! Wheat!
16. Black and white!
17. Straight Kelly!
18. Eighty-one!
19. Novy on a B!
20. Adam and Eve on a raft!

—*Leonard R. N. Ashley*

10 JANUARY

Suffix the Little Prefixes to Come unto Me (Comparatively Speaking)

Stop, Esther, stop! I quite concur:
Comparatives are suffixed *er*.
Comparative of *cow* is *cower*;
Comparative of *bough* is *bower*.

And I agree it's manifest
Superlatives are suffixed *est*.
Digest means "*dig* excessively,"
And *zest* is maximum of *z*.

Yet *er* can prefix, too, my doe;
Thus, *ergo* means "one up on *go*;"
And *ermine's* easy to define:
"Another's fur that's more than *mine*."

As prefix, *est* retains its touch;
Estate comes out as "*ate* too much."
You, *Esther* dear, I long have prized
As "woman apotheosized."

—*W.R.E.*

11 JANUARY

A Squeak from Doctor Emmanuel

Edith Wharton once remarked that if only you stopped trying to be happy, you could have a pretty good time. If you stop insisting words should make sense, they can tell you quite a bit. Two senseless examples:

DOCTOR EMMANUEL

Doctor Emmanuel Harrison-Hyde
Has a very big head with brains inside.
I wonder what happens inside the brains
That Doctor Emmanuel's head contains.

—*James Reeves*

This is from "Amateur Orlando":

> A squeak's heard in the orchestra
> As the leader draws across
> Th' intestines of the agile cat*
> The tail of the noble hoss.
> —*George T. Lanigan*

1 2 JANUARY

Clitch, Clitch, Clitch

Complained England's Ernie Bevin of England's Aneuran Bevan: "All 'e ever says is clitch, clitch, clitch, clitch."

Cliché, which started life as a printer's term for a stereotype plate,† has come to mean "a phrase that has lost precise meaning by iteration." Yet communication in the absence of clichés is as inconceivable as breathing without air. If we had to freshen every utterance, most of us would be unable to communicate at all—with a few exceptions such as Bill here:

AN ORIGINAL CUSS

> A real original, I think,
>   My friend Bill can be termed;
> A smoker, not inveterate,
>   A drinker, not confirmed,
> A hail fellow, but not well met,
>   A realtor, but no Babbitt;
> I never knew a cuss like Bill
>   For cutting loose from habit.
>   —*Keith Preston*

I give you some run-of-the-mill (cliché!) clichés. If you can develop fresher expressions that make the point better, please send them to me.

Go the whole hog	There's the rub
A pretty kettle of fish	His own worst enemy
The acid test	A foregone conclusion
Move heaven and earth	He sank like a stone
Beauty is only skin deep	It is not all black or white

---

* It is not known that the intestines of cats were ever used for violin strings. The tradition probably arises from the fact that there was formerly a kind of small violin called a *kit*.
† For that matter, see what happened to stereotype!

His heart was in his mouth	May the best man win
He drank like a fish	A tower of strength
Root and branch	Castles in the air
Lock, stock, and barrel	Hit the ceiling

And there are some clichés that nobody ever gets quite right. Peter Donchian, who composed the list below, says that to have even three of them right is something of an accomplishment, whereas to get them all you need to be a pedant.

1. Pride goeth before ————.
2. To ———— the lily.
3. A little ———— is a dangerous thing.
4. A penny for your ————.
5. Music hath charms to soothe a ————.
6. Imitation is the sincerest ———— flattery.
7. Ask me no questions, and I'll tell you no ————.
8. Give him an inch, he'll take ————.
9. Variety's the ———— of life.
10. ———— is the root of all evil.
11. Water, water, everywhere, ———— drop to drink.
12. I only regret that I have but ———— for my country.

13 JANUARY

The Muse on a Banana Skin

"Good bad verse," say D. B. Wyndham Lewis and Charles Lee in *The Stuffed Owl*, "has an eerie, supernal beauty. It is devilishly pleasing." The good bad verse they savor most is a pratfall of the poetic great (or of those who consider themselves great), a plunge being more noteworthy from a cliff than from a cushion. Among the immortals quoted in Lewis and Lee's book are Dryden, Goldsmith, Chatterton, Burns, Southey, Hunt, Byron, Wordsworth, Keats, Emerson, Poe, Elizabeth Barrett Browning, Longfellow, and Tennyson.

But they whoo into lesser owls, too, and with a will. "When the poet assumes the cothurnus,* the chlamys, and the mask to announce that it will rain tomorrow because his corns are shooting," they say, "he becomes a candidate for this book, whoever he may be."

The thirteenth is a good bad day to ration out some good bad verse. Try these for starters:

---

* The cothurnus was a high laced boot worn by ancient actors; the chlamys, a short oblong mantle fastened with a clasp at the front or at the shoulder.

ADVICE TO THE STOUT

The languid stomach curses even the pure
Delicious fat, and all the race of oil;
For more the oily aliments relax
Its feeble tone; and with the eager lymph
(Fond to incorporate with all it meets)
Coyly they mix, and shun with slippery wiles
The woo'd embrace. The irresoluble oil,
So gentle late and blandishing, in floods
Of rancid bile o'erflows: what tumults hence,
What horrors rise, were nauseous to relate.
Choose leaner viands, ye whose jovial make
Too fast the gummy nutriment imbibes.
                                    —*John Armstrong*

ADDRESS TO MY INFANT DAUGHTER (excerpt)

—Hast thou then survived—
Mild offspring of infirm humanity,
Meek Infant! among all forlornest things
The most forlorn—one life of that bright star,
The second glory of the Heavens?—Thou hast.
                                    —*William Wordsworth*

LORD BYRON'S LIFE (excerpts)

"Lord Byron" was an Englishman
    A poet I believe,
His first works in old England
    Was poorly received.
Perhaps it was "Lord Byron's" fault
    And perhaps it was not.
His life was full of misfortunes.
    Ah, strange was his lot.

Sometimes again "Lord Byron"
    Was censured by the press,
Such obloquy, he could not endure,
    So he done what was the best.

He left his native country,
    This great unhappy man;
The only wish he had, " 'tis said,"
    He might die, sword in hand.

He had joined the Grecian Army,
    This man of delicate frame;
And there he died in a distant land,
    And left on earth his fame.
"Lord Byron's" age was 36 years,

Then closed the sad career,
Of the most celebrated "Englishman"
Of the nineteenth century.
                              —*Julia Moore*

14 JANUARY

Rubber Baby Buggy Bumpers

I murmured to myself:

"If I fell on a felon feloniously,
Who's the felon—the felon I fell on, or me?"

In the first flush this seemed a passable tongue twister, but of course it is not—it's too easy to say. By contrast, try to say rapidly, "The sixth sick sheik's sixth sheep's sick."

If your memory goes back as far as Prohibition, this snatch from a tongue-twisting verse by Newman Levy may strike a nostalgic chord:

If you stick a stock of liquor in your locker,
   It is slick to stick a lock upon your stock,
Or some joker who is slicker's going to trick you of your liquor . . .
   If you fail to lock your liquor with a lock.

Martin Gardner's collection of tongue twisters includes "rubber baby buggy bumpers," "bug's bad blood," and "the sinking steamer sunk." He adds: "Also well known is the skunk that sat on a stump; the skunk thunk the stump stunk, but the stump thunk the skunk stunk. Some are on the blue side, such as the curious cream-colored cat that crept into the crypt, crapped, and crept out again. It is said that a famous radio actor once refused a detective role when he learned that one of his lines would be 'Show me the chair Schmidt sat in when he was shot.' 'Whip gig, whip gig, whip gig' and 'troy boat, troy boat, troy boat' are both exceedingly difficult to repeat many times. An amusing children's catch is to challenge someone to recite 'Betty Boop, Betty Boop, Betty Boop' rapidly. After about the fifth 'Betty Boop,' wave your hat and shout, 'Heigh ho, Silver!'"

15 JANUARY

One Man's Abdomen

My mother initiated a boy into certain nuances of the English language. Years later, a man grown, he returned to town and thanked her. "For one thing, Mrs. Espy," he said, "you made me realize how important pronouncination is."*

Pronouncination is important indeed to WQXR, the radio station of *The New York Times*. If you apply for an announcing job there, be prepared to read this passage aloud, and correctly:

> The old man with the flaccid face and dour expression grimaced when asked if he were conversant with zoology, mineralogy, or the culinary arts. "Not to be secretive," he said, "I may tell you that I'd given precedence to the study of genealogy. But, since my father's demise, it has been my vagary to remain incognito because of an inexplicable, lamentable, and irreparable family schism. It resulted from a heinous crime, committed at our domicile by an impious scoundrel. To err is human . . . but this affair was so grievous that only my inherent acumen and consummate tact saved me."

WQXR's pronunciation of the disputable words (and how do you pronounce "disputable," WQXR?):

flaccid	FLACK-sid	inexplicable	in-EX-plic-able
dour	DOO-er	lamentable	LAM-entable
grimaced	gri-MACED	irreparable	ear-REP-arable
conversant	KON-ver-sant	schism	SIZ-m
zoology	zoh-OL-o-ji	heinous	HAY-nus
mineralogy	miner-AL-o-ji	domicile	DOMM-i-sil
culinary	KEW-li-ner-y	impious	IM-pee-yus
secretive	see-KREE-tiv	err	ur
precedence	pre-SEED-ens	grievous	GREEV-us
genealogy	jan-e-AL-o-ji	inherent	in-HERE-ent
demise	de-MIZE	acumen	a-KEW-men
vagary	va-GAIR-y	consummate	kon-SUMM-it
incognito	in-KOG-ni-toe	(adj.)	

If you made only four or five mistakes you may (or may not) be hired. But wait a minute: Even if you pronounced all the words wrong, you may be just as right as WQXR is.

Forget the myth that the pronunciation a dictionary lists first is any more acceptable than those it lists second and third. They are all correct.

Webster's unabridged dictionary, the second edition, says it is all right to pronounce dour DOW-er, culinary CULL-i-neri, precedence PRESS-e-dens or PREE-se-dens, genealogy jen-e-AL-o-ji or jee-ne-AL-o-ji (Jan-e-AL-o-ji, the WQXR choice, is not given. A misprint, perhaps?) Webster's recognizes in-cog-NEE-toe, and puts va-GARR-i before va-GAIR-i. The American Heritage Dictionary likewise accepts

---

* Which reminds me that I read long ago (where? in *St. Nicholas? The Youth's Companion? The Saturday Evening Post?*) this couplet:

> *The boy who calls a creek a crick*
> *Was sick for three whole days last wick.*

DOW-er, CULL-i-ner-i and PRESS-e-dens. It accepts either jee-ne-AL-o-ji or jen-e-AL-o-ji, and blesses the pronunciation of the AL as ALL.

It approves of pronouncing grimace GRIM-is, conversant con-VER-sant, inexplicable in-ex-PLIK-able, lamentable la-MEN-table, schism SKIZ-m, mineralogy min-er-ALL-ogy, secretive SEE-kre-tiv, domicile dom-i-SILE or dome-i-SILE, vagary VAY-gar-y. (Va-GAIR-i, bet on by WQXR [and me] does not win, place, or show.)

So not to worry when you don't sound like WQXR. One man's AB-do-men is another man's ab-DOUGH-men.*

16 JANUARY
∽

Knock Up

"The use of this term by Englishmen in America is fraught with danger," says Norman W. Schur, "like the use of fanny† by Americans in England. A respectable American will take great pains to avoid knocking up a lady friend, as he understands the term, because in his country it is an indelicate expression for getting a lady into a delicate condition. In England [it] is a far less serious matter. All it means there is to *wake* people *up*."

But not quite all. He adds that *knock-up* in England also may be the equivalent of American *warm-up* (in sports), and of throw together, as in "Come along to lunch, we can always *knock* something *up* in a hurry."

He does not, however, mention *knocked-up* as a synonym for exhausted, common in nineteenth-century England and, I believe, still extant. Says Jane Austen in *Mansfield Park:* "This will be a bad day's amusement for you, if you are to be knocked up" . . . "And but for Mr. Crawford and the beauty of the weather, [she] would have been knocked up now" . . . "The first division of their journey occupied a long day, and brought them, almost knocked up, to Oxford."

Knock up can also mean to accumulate. *The Listener* tells of people going reluctantly into the world "to knock up a bank balance."

17 JANUARY
∽

Geo-Metrics

Ever since people began writing, they have been shaping verses into crosses, wine glasses, hourglasses, and so on, according to the subject. They have had a lot of fun

* How often have you caught others, or been caught yourself, on the pronunciation of polopony?
† See 4 July.

doing it. The following examples are by Gerald Lynton Kaufman:

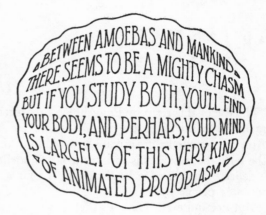

CELLARITHMETIC

THIS SKETCH HAS BEEN COMPOSED TO TELL A PARADOX ABOUT A CELL RELATING TO A SUBTLE TRICK IT USES IN ARITHMETIC: SO GAZE UPON ITS TINY SIZE AND THINK HOW WHEN IT MULTIPLIES IT SOLVES WITH EFFORTLESS PRECISION. A MAJOR PROBLEM IN DIVISION

AMOEBA-VERSE

Micro-picto-graphic rhymes
Enlarged 100,000,000 times

BETWEEN AMOEBAS AND MANKIND THERE SEEMS TO BE A MIGHTY CHASM BUT IF YOU STUDY BOTH, YOU'LL FIND YOUR BODY, AND PERHAPS, YOUR MIND IS LARGELY OF THIS VERY KIND OF ANIMATED PROTOPLASM

18 JANUARY

Enter: Sir Benjamin Backbite

To "mull," in English dialect, is to muddle or fumble. The Berry Brothers, still notable London wine merchants, in the eighteenth century sent the dramatist Richard Brinsley Sheridan—too promptly to please him—a "mulled up" bill. He wrote back:

> You have sent me your Bilberry,
> Before it is Dewberry.
> This is nothing but a Mulberry,
> And I am coming round to kick your Rasberry
> Until it is Blackberry
> And Blueberry.

In Sheridan's dramas he employed surnames to let the audience know whether it was expected to cheer, boo, or ridicule his characters. *The School for Scandal* featured such as Sir Peter Teazle, Sir Oliver Surface, Sir Harry Bumper, Sir Benjamin Backbite, and Lady Sneerwell, not to mention Careless, Snake, and Crabtree. Congreve's *The Way of the World,* in the same spirit, starred Fainall, Witwould, and Petulant.

The manservant was Waitwell; the woman servant, Foible. John Gay populated *The Beggar's Opera* with such as Peachum, Lockit, Filch, Jimmy Twitcher, Crooked-fingered Jack, Mrs. Coaxer, Mrs. Vixen, Betty Doxy, Jenny Diver, and Suky Tawdry.

The verses below refer to characters from three Restoration plays:

The Beaux' Stratagem (Farquhar, 1707)

Sullen's a sorehead, and Scrub does the hall;
  Aimwell and Archer throw darts at the wall;
Gibbet's a highwayman; Bagshot's the same;
  Cherry's been plucked, and requires a new name.

Love for Love (Congreve, 1695)

Pray tell me, Foresight (gullible old male!) if
  Tattle still would wed his Mrs. Frail if
Her fondness for the other sex were tattled
  By Scandal, who beneath the rose has prattled
That Valentine will have to go to jail if
  Sir Sampson Legend won't pay Snap the bailiff?
(Foresight does not reply; the old man's rattled.)

The Provok'd Wife (Vanbrugh, 1697)

Who's that man in a woman's suit?
  Sir John Brute!
What is Heartfree thinking of?
  Falling in love!
Constant's constant; yet he thrives
  Wooing wives.
Treble is singing and Rasor is shaving;
Bully and Rake are the ones misbehaving.

—W.R.E.

19 JANUARY

It All Deep Ends

English contains homonyms by the thousands—caul and call, hail and hale, pear and pair, and the like. Many words have inner homonyms as well. They sound like a series of shorter words strung together, the parts having no relationship in meaning to the whole. Words-within-words may make an eerie kind of sense:

• Come, passion • Purr, puss • No bull • Gas so lean • Die a tribe • Deep lore •
Grew some • Fall turd • Judge meant • Free dumb • Junk shun, miss shun, sex shun

• Loan sum • Shall owe • King dumb, seek king, kick king, croak king • Promise sorry • Pole light • Whore id • Vow well • Tack tile • Sexed aunt • Suck core • Thor axe.

Break up your syllables as suits you best. *Fertilize* translates as *fur till eyes, fur till lies,* or *fertile eyes* (only the last of the three is worth keeping); *depart* becomes either *deep art* or *deep part,* and so on.

You might enjoy seeing how many words you can find that change in sound and sense if you separate them into two or more parts: *warbled* into *war bled, areas* into *are as,* etc.

You may find ten, or a hundred, or a thousand. It all deep ends.

20 JANUARY

A Squirming of Snakes

My brother Edwin, running barefoot across newly mown hay, found himself surrounded by a squirming of snakes—scores of the things, long and black and thick, with narrow yellow or red stripes running down their backs. They were harmless enough in all conscience, but nightmarish to a ten-year-old boy. He was too terrified even to call out, and several minutes passed before our father, riding the haymower, glanced over his shoulder and saw the boy frozen in place. Pop unhitched a horse, leaped astride, and galloped to the rescue, sweeping his son to safety with one arm.

One evening Ed encountered a stinking of skunks. He was pitching hay down from the mow under the barn roof, intending to distribute it among the cows enstanchioned below, when his fork thrust into live flesh. From the smell of him when he arrived home, a whole family of skunks must have been benighted in that hay mow.

"A squirming of snakes" and "a stinking of skunks" are improvised examples of the application of collective nouns to beasts.* Such collectives (called also venereal nouns, Venus having been goddess of the hunt) have found permanent niches in the English language. Though there can be swarms of either bees or flies, for instance, and herds of cattle, whales, or seal, there can be a kindle only of kittens, and a litter only of pups. Each of the following collectives is limited to a single family of animals:†

1. A shrewdness of ———
2. A rout of ———
3. A sounder of ———
4. A brood (or clutch) of ———
5. A cete of ———
6. A flock (or flight) of ———

* See 18 May, 8 September, 17 November. And be sure to read James Lipton's delightful *An Exaltation of Larks.*
† Except as noted in the answer section.

7. A leap of ———
8. A nye of ———
9. A sloth of ———
10. A doylt of ———
11. A school (or shoal) of ———
12. A clowder of ———
13. A drove of ———

14. A down of ———
15. A troop of ———
16. A skulk of ———
17. A muster of ———
18. A gaggle of ———
19. A covey of ———
20. A pod of ———

21 JANUARY

Nudists Take Off

Headlines that linger:

• On the death of Abdul Abzis: ABDUL ABZIS AS WAS

• On Poet Laureate John Masefield's refusal to prepare an official poem: KING'S CANARY WON'T CHIRP

• On the death of Ernest Hemingway: PAPA PASSES

• On a harassed nudist group that climbed high into the hills to find a hideaway: NUDISTS TAKE OFF

I doubt whether the *New York Times* meant to be funny when in 1912 it headlined an imminent hotel workers' strike this way: MAIDS ALL TO GO OUT WITH HOTEL WAITERS

Write headlines for each of the following news stories and see how yours match those of the professional headline writers:

1. (picture caption) U. S. Open Champion Lee Trevino's wife holds door for him as they prepare to leave El Paso Hospital where Lee seems to have beaten bronchial pneumonia.

2. China's second great purge in five years could leave the country wide open to chaos when its present handful of aging leaders die.

3. The Great Panda Squabble was settled yesterday when the White House announced that President and Mrs. Nixon had decided the rare, teddy-bear-like animals will go to the Washington National Zoo.

4. The Oregon Game Fowl Breeders Association is asking the Jackson County Circuit Court to determine that two statutes concerning cruelty to animals do not apply to gamecock contests, since "it is customary and traditional to provide the birds with steel gaffs and often these contests end in the death of one of the combatants."

Your competition is given at the back of the book.

2 2 JANUARY

If He Doth Love Me

A curious rhetorical device is the équivoque, in which one radically changes the meaning of a passage by the shift of as little as a comma.* Take this example:

> If he doth love me, then no more
> He dreams of others' kisses.
> If he doth love me, then no more
> He misses other misses.

Re-position the commas, and a darker view emerges:

> If he doth love me then no more,
> He dreams of others' kisses.
> If he doth love me then no more,
> He misses other misses.
> —*W.R.E.*

I saw this two-column headline in the sports section of *The New York Times*:

> JOHNSON, ON HIS RETURN,
> SORRY FOR LEAVING GIANTS

Then I spread the page, and discovered that the full headline took up three columns and read:

> RANDY JOHNSON, ON HIS RETURN,
> NOT SORRY FOR LEAVING GIANTS

The second of the two poems below says the opposite of the first, purely through changes in punctuation:†

THE PESSIMIST

> That deep red rose—I see its thorn.
> I just ignore the scent that's borne.
> To me it's nothing. I deplore
> Those scratches that I got before.
> I just complain about the pain.
> A lot I think of beauty's gain!

THE OPTIMIST

> That deep red rose I see;
> Its thorn I just ignore.

---

* For other équivoques, see 12 December.
† For an acrostic équivoque, see 28 February.

The scent that's borne to me—
It's nothing I deplore!

Those scratches that I got—
Before I just complain
About the pain a lot,
I think of beauty's gain.
                    —*Mary Youngquist*

The following verse might be termed a Freudian équivoque:

MANICdepressant

SOMETIMES I'M HAPPY
sometimes i'm sad,
SoMeTiMeS i'M HsAaPdPY.
                    —*Kim Dammers*

2 3 JANUARY

How Do You Say Bicister, Micister?

The second Earl of Leicester sat silent in the House of Lords for sixty-seven years; the third, for thirty-two; the fourth, for twenty-three. The fifth and present earl, Thomas William Edward Coke, held his silence for twenty-two years and then made his maiden speech, as follows: "I hope we shall use safer chemicals in place of those which have devastated the countryside."

Gabby Tommy, his family calls him.

It is an astonishment to an American that any Englishman dares open his mouth at all. The proper names alone should be sufficient to tongue-tie him. Lord Drogheda, head of the *Financial Times,* is called *Droyda;* Beauchamp Street is *Beetcham;* the Marquess of Cholmondeley is *Chumbley;* Magdalen College is *Maudlen;* and St. John is *Sin-jon.* Herbert Mayes tells me Alnwick is pronounced *Anick,* Hargham *Haarfan,* Terfilian *Treveelan,* and Zwill, most unaccountably, *Yool.*

Darryl Francis reports these English and Scottish pronunciations:

THE ENGLISH PLACE NAME	THE ENGLISH PRONUNCIATION
Abergavenny	aber-genny
Leominster	lem-ster
Cirencester	sis-e-ter
Churchtown	chow-zen
Uttoxeter	uck-ster
Godmanchester	gum-sister or gon-shister
Wymondham	win-dum

Jervaulx	jar-vis
Amotherby	amer-by
Pontrefact	pom-fret
Lympne	lim
Mousehole	moo-zel
Ulgham	uff-am
Ulverston	oo-ston

THE SCOTTISH PLACE NAME	THE SCOTTISH PRONUNCIATION
Kircudbright	ker-koo-bree
Balquhidder	bal-widder
Dalziel	dee-ell
Borrowstounness	bo-nes

Robert Benchley remarked that even the most incompetent English actor "gives forth a sound so soft and dulcet as almost to be a bar of music." And he provided examples:

Wotjuthinkofrehddie?

Hesbeanofflyapsehtletly

Eheaidehntneh-hehesentehnyfethleft

The only difficulty, he said, was that few Americans could understand the *words*. In Shaw's *Major Barbara,* for instance, the young man who played Cusins recited in the key of C♯, with a range from B to G♯ in an almost continuous cadenza. But what did he *say?*

Eetsnottth'sao ehvmeh seuhl thett trehbles meh; Eh hev seuhld et teuh efften teh care abeht thett. Eh hev seuhld et fereh preuhfessorshep. Eh hev seuhld et tescep beinempressoned feh refusin t'peh texes fer hengmen's reuhps end ehnjust wehrs end things thet ehabbeuh. Wot es ehl humen cehnduct beht th'daioy end heurhly sao of ehur sehuls f'trehfles? Wot ehem neu seoinet feh is neither meneh eh pesition nehr kemfet, bet freelity and fpeuher

24 JANUARY

Ever See a Sand-Blind Titmouse?

Many are sand-blind who never saw sand; the prefix corrupts the obsolete prefix *sam-,* meaning "half." The humble in "humble pie" was once *umble,* the umbles being the less attractive meats of a slain deer—heart, liver, and entrails. *Purlieu* derives not, as would seem reasonable, from French *lieu* (place), but from Old French *pour allée.* Rosemary is used as if it meant the "rose of Mary," but its source is *ros marinus* (sea-dew). London's Rotten Row is a distortion of *route du roi.* The spade in your bridge hand is no spade, but a sword; it comes from Spanish *espada.* The sire of bully is not bull, but Dutch *boel* (a lover):

> I kiss his dirty shoe, and from my heart-strings
> I love the lovely bully.
> *—Twelfth Night*

The titmouse, from *tit* meaning "small," and *mase,* a variety of bird, is no rodent, nor is it mammalian. Nitwits may lack wits but whether they have nits is an open question; the word comes from Dutch *niet wit* (I don't know). Slughorn, a battle trumpet, results from Chatterton's erroneous reading of Gaelic *slogan.* "The big cheese" comes from Hindi *chiz,* meaning "thing."

All these are *hobson-jobsons*—foreign or forgotten expressions assimilated to familiar English words. For instance:

• *Cleopatra's needle* (brought to the Thames Embankment from Alexandria in 1878) was found in the capital of the Egyptian queen, but is otherwise unconnected with her; it was originally set up by Thothmes III 1500 years before she was born.

• *Ventriloquism* derives from the mistaken notion that the voice of the ventriloquist proceeds from his stomach.

• *Blindworms* can see, and they aren't worms; they are legless lizards.

• *Dutch clocks* were first of German, not Dutch manufacture.

• *India ink* originated in China.

• *Turkeys* are native not to Turkey but to North America.

• *Guinea pigs* are not pigs, but cavies from South America. (No, Virginia, *Guinea* is in Africa; *Guiana* is in South America.)

25 JANUARY

Edward M. Kennedy and the Lower Criticism

The first line of a higgledy-piggledy is usually double-dactyl nonsense; the second line, a double-dactyl name; the sixth, a one-word double dactyl; the third, fifth, and seventh, any sort of double dactyl; and the fourth and eighth, rhyme lines. Thus:

EDWARD M. KENNEDY

Tiddely Quiddely   Pleas of amnesia
Edward M. Kennedy   Incomprehensible
Quite unaccountably   Possibly shattered
Drove in a stream.   Political dream.
                            —*Leonard Miall*

THE LOWER CRITICISM

Higgledy-piggledy   Where (though I hate to seem
Dorothy Richardson   Uncomplimentary)
Wrote a huge book with her Nothing much happens and
Delicate muse.   Nobody screws.
                            —*John Hollander*

26 JANUARY

Black English

Linguist J. L. Dillard asserts that Black English, usually considered a by-product of illiteracy, is in fact a legitimate dialect, with a syntax based on West African languages. *Themself* is correct in Black English because the *them* establishes plurality; "He a nice little girl" is correct, because Black English does not differentiate between genders of pronouns. An implicit verb can go unmentioned, and tenses can be ignored if not needed for clarity. The following Black English verse (which I present with some hesitancy, since I find the rules of the language obscure), is an adaptation of a passage from an experimental reading book for the ghetto:

LA VERNE AND THE WATER BUG

Ollie big sister (La Verne she call),
She grown up now, she ain't scared at all
Of nobody, but that don't mean to say
She don't never be scared. The other day
She start to screaming when she in the house;
Didn't nobody know if she be seeing a mouse,
Didn't nobody know what the matter be,
So Big Momma run to the bedroom to see.
Guess what Big Momma she find on the rug?
One of them big black water bug!
Ugh.
                            —*W.R.E.*

27 JANUARY

Be Friendly, Borgmann

An English writer, juggling the letters of *Spiro Agnew*, discovered he had written *grow a penis. Dame Eleanor Davies,* a prophetess in the reign of Charles I, was anagrammed into *never so mad a ladie*, and *Queen Victoria's Jubilee* became *I require love in a subject*. Puzzlemaker Dmitri Alfred Borgmann anagrammed his name in the best and worst of lights: first *grand mind, mortal fibre!*; then *damn mad boring trifler*. The best I could do with Willard Richardson Espy was *airs children's wordplay*, though *riddlers always chirp on* is not bad.

The elegance of an anagram lies in its aptness: *angered—enraged*, for instance. What are apposite anagrams of the words on the following lists?

1. Agitator
2. Constraint
3. Determination
4. French revolution

5. Misanthrope
6. Parliament
7. Train

—*J. Newton Friend*

1. The United States of America
2. The eyes
3. Is pity love?
4. Abandon hope all ye who enter here
5. A sentence of death
6. A shoplifter
7. Circumstantial evidence
8. Spring, summer, autumn, winter
9. The countryside

10. Anagrams
11. Lawyers
12. Punishment
13. Compassionateness
14. Conversation
15. Desperation
16. Endearments
17. Negation
18. Panties

—*Dmitri A. Borgmann*

28 JANUARY

The Astonishment of Words

I have a tin ear for languages; I read the subtitles of foreign films.

But even with my kitchen-French and pig-German, I was able to get gloriously drunk on Victor Proetz's book of familiar English poems side by side with translations in French and German.

"How do you say 'Yankee Doodle' in French," wondered Mr. Proetz, "in case you can? Does 'The snail's on the thorn' get to be about an escargot? How do they say 'Houyhnhnm' and 'Cheshire Cat' and things like that in German? How can you keep a phrase like 'La Belle Dame sans Merci' in a French translation of the poem from being lost in the surrounding French? And how, in God's name, can you possibly say 'There she blows.' "*

Mr. Proetz went to and fro in the earth collecting translations, and mewed them into *The Astonishment of Words,* which he did not live to see in print. But he did discover something joyous:

"The complete success of some of these translations is incredible. They have weathered all the agony of change and have come through it in full bloom. A few, a very few . . . have actually improved on their way through hell."

Some examples:

FROM "JABBERWOCKY"

English:
> One, two! One, two! And through and through
>> The vorpal blade went snicker-snack!
> He left it dead, and with its head
>> He went galumphing back.
>> —*Lewis Carroll*

French:
> Un, deux, un, deux, par le milieu,
>> Le glaive vorpal fait pat-à-pan!
> La bête défaite, avec sa tête
>> Il rentre gallomphant.
>> —*Translated by Frank L. Warrin, Jr.*

German:
> Eins, Zwei! Eins, Zwei! Und durch und durch
>> Seins vorpals Schwert zershnifersnück.
> Da blieb es todt! Er, Kopf in Hand,
>> Gelaumfig zog zurück!
>> —*Translated by Dr. Robert Scott*

FROM "TO A MOUSE"

English:
> Wee, sleekit, cowrin, tim'rous beastie,
>> O, what a panic's in thy breastie!
> Thou need na start awa sae hasty
>> Wi' bickering brattle!
> I wad be laith to rin an' chase thee,
>> Wi' murdering pattle!
>> —*Robert Burns*

French:
> Petite bête lisse, farouche et craintive
> Oh, quelle panique dans ton sein!

---

* One dubious French solution: "Elle siffle!"

Tu n'as pas besoin de te sauver si vite
  Et d'un pas si précipité!
Je me répugnerais de courir après toi
  Avec le cuvoir meurtrier!
      —*Translated by Leon de Wailly*

German:
  Klein, furchtsam Tierchen, welch ein Schrecken
  Erfüllt dein Brütschen, so durch Hecken
  Und Furchen dich zum Lauf zu strecken?
    Bleib! Nicht so jach!
  Nicht setz ich mit dem Pflügerstecken
    Grausam dir nach!
      —*Translated by Ferdinand Freiligrath*

FROM "THE TIGER"

English:
  Tiger, tiger, burning bright
  In the forests of the night,
  What immortal hand or eye
  Could frame thy fearful symmetry?
      —*William Blake*

French:
  Tigre, tigre, brûlant éclair
  Dans les forêts de la nuit,
  Quel oeil, quelle main immortelle
  A pu ordonner ta terrifiante symétrie?
    —*Translated by M. L. and Philippe Soupault*

German:
  Tiger, Tiger, lohendes Licht,
  Das durch die Nacht der Wälder bricht,
  Welches Auge, welche unsterbliche Hand
  Hat dich furchtbar in dein Ebenmass gebannt?
      —*Translated by Mela Hartwig*

29 JANUARY

The Demise of the Methodist Church

Awhile back I mentioned my fondness for good bad verse. My feeling probably stems from the fact that in Oysterville, my boyhood home, there was a good bit of such verse around, as I imagine there must be in many small towns. One example, lamenting the destruction of the Methodist Church in a hurricane, follows, and I expect to uncover others as the year goes along:

> Volunteers erected the pile,
> Working it out in a Methodist style.
> Upon its spire a gilded cross,
> A beacon of light in a mantle of white.
> How many is the tale its bell could tell,
> Ringing for the living, or tolling a knell.
> Where some came to sing, and others to pray,
> And where Santa held forth on Christ's sanctified day.
> It was a guide to the mariner out in a fog,
> As well as some wayward half full of grog,
> A blushing young bride just taking a vow,
> Or the sanctified shepherd settling a row.
> All creeds and all classes, both the rich and the poor,
> Were extended a welcome from its wide open door.
> But the church, like its parishioners,
> Having its year and its day,
> When a storm, like a demon
> From Hell, rose and fell,
> When a peal from its throat
> In one last silvery note,
> And such is the story, historically true,
> Of the little white church and the bell we all knew.
> —*Author Unknown*

A line or two seems to have gone AWOL. But it's a great poem.

30 JANUARY

Vile Vodka

This quatrain will show you how countdown verses work:*

> Who of vodka distilled from potoooooooot† partake,
>   Heed this warning;
> You'll be jolly at night, but ooooooooooo when you wake
>   In the morning.

The first line is easy to decipher: eight o's are lined up there, so clearly the word

* See also 5 August.
† There was once an English racehorse named Potooooooo.

you are after is, by sound, *potatoes*. But what about those eleven o's in the second line? Well, eleven is a greater number than eight, is it not? So:

> Who of vodka distilled from potatoes partake,
>   Heed this warning:
> You'll be jolly at night, but morose when you wake
>   In the morning.
>   —*W.R.E.*

This is a cross between a countdown verse and an ABC verse:

FAREWELL, A LONG FAREWELL TO ALL MY PROTESTANT ETHIC

> Day-day mis-tune-tune-tune-tune John ignores, 2 8
> Morrow-morrow joys, which he CCCC as great;
> Get-get-get-get that if his TTTT were a curse,
> His TTTTTTT and TTTTTTTT must be worse.
> The future he tell-tell-tell-tell sounds fine; but he
> Go-go-go-go it-it-it-it sake present XTC—
> Bid-bid-bid-bid himself all actions apt to please.
>
> *My* rule is this: Time's lock-lock-lock-lock meant CC.
> What's here UUUU I mean UU; I reach
> 4 surf that phosSSSS on the beach
> No less than sweet AAAA and aging-aging-aging-aging;
> All are YYYY men's use EE life's stings.
> John's sight-sight-sight-sight not 4 me; I give my praise
> Pleasure-pleasure not morrow-morrow but day-day.
>   —*W.R.E.*

MITIGATION

> So der der der der der der der der der der the night,
> So der der der der der der der der der der the voice of
>   the dove,
> Who can blame the young wight
> If he der der der der der der der der der der his lady
>   his love?
>   —*W.R.E.*

31 JANUARY

Say, Who Will Write a Pun My Stone?

On this day in 1902, my home county of Pacific carried out its only formal capital sentence. It hanged by the neck until dead one Lum You, a Chinese laborer who, the preceding August, for reasons unrecorded, had shot and killed a certain Oscar Bloom. The sheriff, a sociable man, sent favored citizens invitations to the festivities. This example has survived:

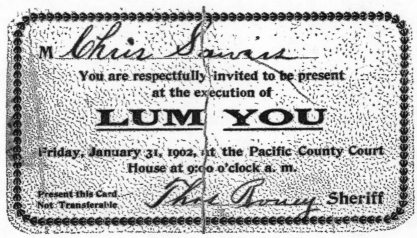

If you know where Lum You is interred, tell me; I'd like to raise money for a headstone. It might bear this legend:

> I LUM YOU (1873–1902).
> WHY YOU NO LUM ME?

Not all mourners are prevented by grief from punning on the name of the dear departed. A headstone for John Rose and family, for instance, bears the legend "This Grave's a Bed of Roses." Other punning epitaphs:

ON ARCHBISHOP POTTER

Alack, alack and well-a-day;
Potter himself is turned to clay.

ON JOHN CAMDEN HOTTEN*

Hotten
Rotten
Forgotten.
                    —*George Augustus Sala*

ON EMMA AND MARIA LITTLEBOY

Two littleboys lie here.
Yet strange to say
The littleboys
Are girls.

ON A MUSIC TEACHER

Stephen and time
Are now both even:
Stephen beat time
Now time's beat Stephen.

ON MRS. NOTT

Nott born. Nott dead.
Nott christened.
Nott begot.
Lo here she lies
Who was
and who was Nott.

* An English book publisher termed a "pirate" by Mark Twain.

FEBRUARY

❦ ❧

1 FEBRUARY
∽

What a Friend We Have in Cheeses
"Poets have been mysteriously silent on the subject of cheeses."
—*G. K. Chesterton*

What a friend we have in cheeses!
For no food more subtly pleases,
Nor plays so grand a gastronomic part;
Cheese imported—not domestic—
For we all get indigestic
From the pasteurizer's Kraft and sodden art.

No poem we shall ever see is
Quite as lovely as a Brie is,
For "the queen of cheese" is what they call the Brie;
If you pay sufficient money
You will get one nice and runny,
And you'll understand what foods these morsels be!

How we covet all the skills it
Takes in making Chèvre or Tilset,
But if getting basic Pot Cheese is your aim,
Take some simple kurds and wheys, a
Bit of rennet—Lo! you've Käese!
(Which is what, in German, is a cheese's name.)

Good lasagna, it's a-gotta
Mozzarella and Ricotta
And a lotta freshly grated Parmesan;
With the latter *any* pasta
Will be eaten up much faster,
For with Parmesan you'll find a charm is on.

Ask Ignacio Silone
What he thinks of Provolone,
And the very word will set his eyes aflame;
Then go ask the bounteous Gina
Her reaction to Fontina—
If you raise your eyes, you'll see she feels the same!

A Pont-l'Évèque *au point!* What ho!
How our juices all will flow!
But don't touch a Pont-l'Évèque beyond that stage,
For what you'll have, you'll surely find
Is just an overfragrant rind—
There's no benefit to this *fromage* from age.

Claret, dear, not Coca Cola,
When you're having Gorgonzola—
Be particular to serve the proper wines;
Likewise pick a Beaune not Coke for
Pointing up a Bleu or Roquefort—
Bless the products of the bovines and the vines!

Ave Gouda! Ave Boursault!
Ave Oka even more so!
Ave Neufchatel, *Saluto* Port Salut!
And another thing with cheeses—
Every allied prospect pleases—
Ah timbale! Ah Welsh Rabbit! Ah fondue!

And we all know that "Say cheese" is
How a cameraman unfreezes
A subject in a stiff, or shy, or dour way;
There's no other food so useful,
So bring on a whole cabooseful
Of the stuff of life! The cheeses of the gourmet!
—*William Cole*

2 FEBRUARY

"I'm Dying," He Croaked

Croakers, invented and named by Roy Bongartz with the help of his wife and selected friends, are Tom Swifties in which a verb rather than an adverb supplies the pun. Some Croakers supplied by Mr. Bongartz to the *Saturday Review:*

- "We've taken over the government," the general cooed.
- "My experiment was a success," the chemist retorted.
- "You can't really train a beagle," he dogmatized.
- "That's no beagle, it's a mongrel," she muttered.
- "You ought to see a psychiatrist," he reminded me.
- "That's my gold mine!" he claimed.
- "But it was mine!" he exclaimed.
- "And I used to be a pilot," he explained.

- "The fire is going out," he bellowed.
- "Bad marksmanship," the hunter groused.
- "Another plate of steamers all around," he clamored.
  Mr. Bongartz also introduces double-worded Croakers:
- "I've got a new game," mumbled Peg.
- "I spent the day sewing and gardening," she hemmed and hawed.
- "I was in a riot in Paris," he noised abroad.
- "My bicycle wheel is melting," he spoke softly.

3 FEBRUARY

Identity Problem in the Mammoth Caves

O pendant stalactite,
  Deposit crystalline,
Insensate troglodyte
  Shaped of accreted brine,

Aspire you still to pierce
  That upright stalagmite
Who in a million years
  Your love cannot requite?

And if indeed your drip
  With ardor one day fill her,
And bring you lip to lip,
  And make you two one pillar . . .

Still, how can you be sure,
  O pendant stalactite,
If you are you, or her—
  An upright stalagmite?

—W.R.E.

4 FEBRUARY

Pronunciandum

In Sir David Lyndsay's *The Exactions and Delays of the Law,* a farmer who went to court about the loss of his horse laments:

Of *pronunciandum* they made me wonder fain;
But I gat ne'er my gude grey meir again.

Is that an epigram? As "a short poem, treating concisely and pointedly of a single thought"—yes. Otherwise—perhaps. The classic epigram is not a mosquito bite, which smarts awhile and goes away; it is a bee sting with the stinger left in, and it smarts forever.

Here, first-come-first-served, are some familiar epigrams:

When late I attempted your pity to move,
    What made you so deaf to my prayers?
Perhaps it was right to dissemble your love,
    But why did you kick me downstairs?
                            —*Isaac Bickerstaff*

Earth labored, and lo! man lay in her lap—
She murmured "homo" . . . and then added "Sap!"
                            —*Justin Richardson*

This humanist whom no beliefs constrained
Grew so broad-minded he was scatter-brained.
                            —*J. V. Cunningham*

I am unable, yonder beggar cries,
To stand or move; if he say true, he lies.
                            —*John Donne*

Don't steal. Thou'lt never thus compete
Successfully in business. Cheat.
                            —*Ambrose Bierce*

Ah! what avails the classic bent
And what the cultured word
Against the undoctored incident
That actually occurred?
                            —*Rudyard Kipling*

Treason doth never prosper; what's the reason?
For if it prosper, none dare call it treason.
                            —*Sir John Harington*

The crucified martyr made light of his loss
Till he spotted another on a higher cross.
                            —*Author unknown*

On Rabelais

Censors in the custom house treat him rather shabbily
By cutting out the better bits of Master Francis Rabelais.
                            —*Morris Bishop*

5 FEBRUARY
∾

"In the Morning They Spring Up . . ."

To sell his mythical perpetual motion machine, John W. Keeley made up more than 1500 meaningless but plausible-sounding words designed to impress the nineteenth-century layman. As far as I know, none has survived. Of the 1700 words said to have been coined by Shakespeare, on the other hand, hundreds have become fixtures. A few attributed to him:*

> Assassination, suspicious, barefaced, bump, castigate, critical, countless, denote, dwindle, eventful, foppish, fretful, gnarled, hurry, impartial, lapse, laughable, lonely, leapfrog, misplaced, monumental, sportive.

Alexander Pope appropriated "bathos" ("depth" in Greek) to use for a sudden descent from the sublime to the you-know-what. Keats loved to invent words, but most of his offspring—"upblown" and "needments" are two unhappy examples—failed to outlast him. "Nihilist" first appeared in Ivan Turgenev's *Fathers and Sons*.

Gelett Burgess coined "bromide" and "blurb." British aviators in World War II originated "gremlin," a small goblinesque creature accused of playing tricks upon propeller, flaps, wings, engine, tail rudder, and other sensitive areas of the airplane.

Radar, flak, gestapo, soccer, kodak are all coined words. If you keep an eye out, you will soon find hundreds more.

6 FEBRUARY
∾

The Half-Warmed Fish

Whether Dr. Spooner made all the accidental sound transpositions attributed to him is doubtful; Bergen Evans credits him with only one spoonerism: "half-warmed fish" for "half-formed wish." Still, he has the name, and may as well have the game. Some of his alleged transgressions:

• Calling on the dean of Christ Church, he inquired, "Is the bean dizzy?"

• To a group of farmers, he began, "I have never before addressed so many tons of soil."

• Visiting a friend who had just acquired a country cottage, he congratulated him on his "nosey little cook."

• He hailed the "tearful chidings" of the gospels, and asked the congregation to sing with him "From Iceland's Greasy Mountains."

H. Allen Smith† cites the following spoonerisms by TV and radio announcers:

* See also 15 June.
† Charles F. Dory brought Mr. Smith's collection of spoonerisms to my attention.

• One announcer asked, "Why not try Betty Crocker's poo seep?" and another said the fog was "as thick as sea poop." ("Soo peep" is a splendid spoonerism, too.)

• Milton Cross described the "Prince of Pilsen" as "the Pill of Princeton"; Jerry Lawrence said, "You will know the King and Queen have arrived when you hear a twenty-one-sun galoot"; an emcee, introducing Walter Pidgeon, said, "Mr. Privilege, this is indeed a Pidgeon"; a Los Angeles announcer wanted his audience to "get the best in bread," but transposed; Fred Hoey opened a broadcast with "Good afternoon, Fred Hoey, this is everybody speaking"; a cooking expert started her recipe for vichyssoise with "first you take a leek" (a fake spoonerism, but too delicious to ignore).

Other spoonerisms in the Smith collection:

• "I'm getting my soles half-shoed after I have a cough of cuppee." . . . "The thot plickens" . . . "The Indian died and went to the happy grunting hound" . . . "Give me a jar of oderarm deunderant."

Says Mr. Smith of the last-quoted item: "That's what I call a snooperism!"

7 FEBRUARY

Telling Hearth from Earth is Tough Stuff, Suzy

The verse below, called to my attention by Jean Libman Block, was devised by a group of Britishers after World War II to help the multination personnel of NATO pronounce English properly. Since some of the examples were so British that they would puzzle an American as much as any other foreigner, I have made a few changes.

Dearest creature in creation,
Spelling's not pronunciation.
Hear, my Suzy, how diverse
Corpse from *corps* sounds, *horse* from *worse!*
Trip *among* my *songs, young* dear;
Tear your hair, and shed a *tear*
As I keep you, *Suzy, busy,*
Till your *heated head* grows *dizzy*
Saying *heart,* and *beard,* and *heard;*
Dies and *diet; lord* and *word.*

Rounded like to *wounded*'s written;
Sword to *sward; retain* to *Britain.*
What? Do *early, dearly,* plague you?
They're no worse than *vague* and *ague,*
Lose, ooze, use. Since you must speak,
Say *break* and *steak,* but *bleak* and *streak;*

Cloven, oven; how, but *low;*
Rowed, but *plowed; shoes, does,* and *toe.*
Watch for Anglo-Saxon trickery
In *daughter, laughter; chores, Terpsichore;*
In *scour, tour, pour;* in *measles, aisles,*
Exiles, similes, reviles;
Amen and *stamen; war,* and *far;*
Scholar, solar, and *cigar;*
Anemone, and *bone,* and *one;*
Lichen, richen, benison;
Scene; Melpomene.

                                    Say *signed*
But *signet; wind,* but *mind.*
Billet's right, but so's *ballet,*
Wallet, mallet, and *chalet.*
Say with me *blood, flood, food, stood;*
Bull, and *dull,* and *mould,* and *should;*
Toward and *forward, cowed* and *owed;*
Viscous, viscount; broad, and *load;*
Petal, penal; grieve, and *sieve;*
Friend, and *fiend; alive,* and *live.*
Say, too, *Rachel; moustache; ache;*
Seven; Heaven; heave. Now make
Note of *hallowed* and *allowed;*
Of *people, leopard; towed,* and *vowed.*

Mark how lightly "o" shifts over
From *move* to *love,* and so to *clover.*
Say *leeches, breeches; wise, precise;*
Chalice, but *police* and *lice.*
Unstable, constable are plain;
So *certainly* and *ascertain.*

Principle, disciple form;
Chair, chaise, chaos; worm and *storm;*
Ivy, privy; query, very;
Famous, clamour; fury, bury;
River, rival; tomb, bomb, comb;
Doll and *roll* and *some* and *home;*
Demise and *premise; stranger, anger;*
Dour and *four; devour* and *clangour.*

The short for *Geoffrey* must be *Geoff.*
Say *zephyr, heifer, chef,* and *deaf.*
In *actual* and *interdict*
And *verdict,* use the c; you're licked,
Though, if you use it in *indict.*

In this, as *victual*, c's not right.
Remember: utter *gaunt*, but *aunt;*
Font, front, wont; want, grand, grant.
Say *finger, singer, ginger;* pause
O'er words like *gauge* and *mauve* and *gauze.*
Toss back and forth in badinage
Age, and *foliage*, and *mirage.*

Rhyme not *alien* with *Italian,*
Or *dandelion* with *battalion;*
Or *sea, idea, guinea, area;*
Rhyme not *Maria* with *malaria.*
Say *rally*, but *ally*, say *fever*,
But *ever; leisure, skein, deceiver;*
Canary, granary; preface, efface;

Phlegm, phlegmatic; glass, and *bass;*
Say *large;* say *target; gin, give, verging;*
Say *ear*, but *earn*, and *scour*, but *scourging;*
Youth, south, southern; cleanse, and *clean;*
Doctrine, turpentine, marine;
Scenic, Arabic, landau,
Science, conscience, Arkansas;
Monkey, donkey.
                                    Say *endeavor,*
Asp, grasp, wasp; say *fever, sever.*

Suzy, though you've studied so,
You must take one final blow.
Is the proper rhyme for *tough*
Though, through, plough, cough, or *enough?*
Hiccough has the sound of *cup.*

Suzy, better give it up.

8 FEBRUARY

Many a Malapropism
Has Flown under the Bridge

In *Tom Brown at Oxford* an old farmer, bruised by a fall from a ladder, reports the verdict of the doctor who examined him:

"A zem'd to zay as there wur no bwones bruk—ugh, ugh—but a couldn't say wether or no there wasn't some infarnal injury—"
"Etarnal, Simon, etarnal!" interrupted his wife; "how canst use such words afore the young ladies?"

And again:

> "Wut's to hinder thaay tryin' ov 'un, if thaay be minded to't? That's
> wut I wants to know."
> " 'Tis wut the counsellors call the Statut' o' Lamentations."
> "Wutever's Lamentations got to do wi't?"
> "A gurt deal, I tell 'ee. What do's thou know o' Lamentations?"
> "Lamentations cums afore Ezekiel in the Bible."

Malapropisms continue their merry way. Some are apocryphal, as is, I suspect, the
story of the landowner who said he proposed not to plant his property, but to measure
it by leaps and bounds. His wife asked the gardener to put in a bed of saliva. "Fine,"
he agreed; "and while I'm at it I'll plant spittoonia for the border."

But many a malapropism is genuine. James Thurber's cook said one of her brothers
"works into an incinerator where they burn the refuge"; a second brother had just
passed his "silver-service eliminations"; and her sister got "tuberculosis from her
teeth and it went all through her symptom."

A newspaper refers to the Duchess of Windsor as a "grievous widow." Another
says that Isaac Asimov, author of more than a hundred books, "attributes his prof-
ligacy to the fact that he can type 90 words a minute." A Democratic politician, asked
whether he is encouraging Teddy Kennedy to run for President, replies, "I haven't
made any ovations to him, and he hasn't made any to me." Pierre Salinger describes
John F. Kennedy as "a vociferous reader." Andrei Gromyko of Russia tells *The New
York Times* that "a lot of water has flown under the bridge since the war." A wife
says proudly, "My husband is a marvelous lover . . . he knows all the erroneous
zones."

As IRS commissioner, Johnnie Walters cut the word "spouse" from his income tax
instructions because too many people thought he was talking about a water fountain.

Some malapropisms from the collection of columnist Don Duncan: "He communi-
cates to work"; "No phonographic pictures allowed"; "We arrived at our predestina-
tion"; "she apologized affluently"; "relapse and enjoy it."

Norton Mockridge collected thousands of the monsters in *Fractured English*. A
dip-in:

> The English language is going through a resolution. . . . I was so sur-
> prised you could have knocked me over with a fender. . . . Now that we
> have teen-agers, we've been renegaded to the back seat. . . . Everything
> is going to rot and ruin. . . . A wealthy typhoon. . . . He's a busy-
> buggy. . . . He treats me like the dirt on his feet. . . . It sure is good to
> be back on terra cotta again. . . . My father is retarded on a pension. . . .
> White as the dripping snow. . . . He uses millinery brushes, and my sister
> uses massacre on her eyes. . . . I rode an alligator to the top of the Empire
> State Building. . . . Frances has beautiful hands, and some day I'm going
> to make a bust of them. . . . He used biceps to deliver the baby.

After a radio interview with sportscaster Jack Buck, Yogi Berra received a twenty-
five-dollar check as an honorarium. "How the hell long have you known me, Jack?"
he grumbled. "How could you spell my name like that?" The check was made out to
"Bearer "

9 FEBRUARY

Mots d'Heures: Gousses, Rames

My daughter Joanna, working for a book publisher, brought home a forty-page volume, *Mots d'Heures: Gousses, Rames,* explaining that it was in an extinct French dialect, and that she knew I was interested in that sort of thing. Well, I could make neither head nor belly nor tail of that book. I could not even understand the title, much less the verses inside. They certainly *looked* like French, but that was as far as it went. And though the elaborate annotations were in English, I could make no sense of them either.

Only when I tried reading the verses aloud did I realize that there was a familiar ring to them. At last the answer came like a *coup de tonnerre.* "Mots d'Heures Gousses Rames:" Mother Goose rhymes! Of course! How obvious!*

In self-defense I will say that I have shown that book to dozens of friends, and only one of them realized without prompting that the verses consisted of French words arranged so as to approximate English sounds.†

I give you two of these *rames,* with the original notes. Read them *à haute voix,* with an accent as bad as mine, and you will realize that you have known them all your life:

OH, LES MOTS D'HEUREUX BARDES

Oh, les mots d'heureux bardes
Où en toutes heures que partent.[1]
Tous guetteurs pour dock à Beaune.[2]
Besoin gigot d'air
De que paroisse paire.[3]
Et ne pour dock, pet-de-nonne.[4]

1. Minstrels were no doubt a happy lot, and it is not surprising that France, a cradle of wit and culture, could turn them out in such numbers that they came and went on an almost predictable schedule. As one came in by the portcullis another left by the oubliette.

2. Beaune. Town in the Côte-d'Or, 11,000 pop., famed for its wines and mustard. It is not a port, therefore, why should everyone watch its docks? Certainly it does not have any particular renown as a center of contraband.

3. This must refer to the Côte-d'Or, a peerless parish indeed. Rich in some of the finest vintages of France and, if we are to believe the previous line, a great lambing country.

4. Pet-de-nonne. An extremely light and fluffy pastry. Although any decent housewife would ask for them without hesitation at her favorite pâtisserie, delicacy forbids a direct translation here.

---

* When the author, Luis d'Antin Van Rooten, died, his obituary failed even to mention that he was author of this intricate Franglish jape.

† Matt Huston, a twelve-year-old without a word of French, glanced at the title and understood it instantly.

ET QUI RIT DES CURÉS D'OC?

Et qui rit des curés d'Oc?[1]
De Meuse raines,[2] houp! de cloques.[3]
De quelles loques ce turque coin.[4]
Et ne d'ânes ni rennes,
Écuries des curés d'Oc.[5]

1. Oc (or Languedoc), ancient region of France, with its capital at Toulouse. Its monks and curates were, it seems, a singularly humble and holy group. This little poem is a graceful tribute to their virtues.

2. Meuse, or Maas, River, 560 miles long, traversing France, Belgium, and the Netherlands; Raines, old French word for frogs (from the L., *ranae*). Here is a beautiful example of Gothic imagery; He who laughs at the curés d'Oc will have frogs leap at him from the Meuse river and

3. infect him with a scrofulous disease! This is particularly interesting when we consider the widespread superstition in America that frogs and toads cause warts.

4. "Turkish corners" were introduced into Western Europe by returning crusaders, among other luxuries and refinements of Oriental living. Our good monks made a concession to the fashion, but N.B. their Turkish corner was made of rags! This affectation of interior decorating had a widespread revival in the U.S.A. at the turn of the century. Ah, the Tsar's bazaars' bizarre beaux-arts.

5. So strict were the monks that they didn't even indulge themselves in their arduous travels. No fancy mules nor reindeer in *their* stables. They just rode around on their plain French asses.

10 FEBRUARY

¡Eva, Lave!

PUERTO VALLARTA, Jalisco—I have come to Mexico to rest on the sand of the Gulf of California for a few days and watch for whales mating. To spy on mating whales must be the epitome of voyeurism. So far, though, I have seen nothing but a pair of mongrel dogs copulating on the cobblestones outside my hotel. There is no sadder sight than the expression on the face of a copulating dog.

My presence in a Spanish-speaking country emboldens me to copy down here a few of the Spanish-language palindromes given me by Anthony E. Bonner,* currently a resident of Spain. If you know no Spanish, skip.

* Tony also sent me a book of French wordplay called *Oulipo*. Most of it is not French to me; it is Greek. Thank me for not quoting here a French palindrome which runs to more than 5,000 letters.

Allí ves a Sevilla.
Se van sus naves.
Oirás orar a Rosario.
Anita lava la tina.
¿Subo tu auto o tu autobus?
Nada por ropa dan.
Allí trota la tortilla.

I am also emboldened to report a translation from Spanish into English by the officials of an international automobile race in Mexico City. According to Joseph Coolidge, they handed out the following instructions to the English-speaking drivers: "The drivers will defile themselves on the Plaza at 10 A.M. They may relieve themselves on each other's convenience."

11 FEBRUARY

The American Traveler

Robert H. Newell wrote this verse around the time of the Civil War. I have dropped fourteen stanzas that deal with places in states other than Maine.

To Lake Aghmoogenegamook,
    All in the State of Maine,
A man from Witteguergaugaum came
    One evening in the rain.

"I am a traveler," said he,
    "Just started on a tour,
And go to Nomjamskillicock
    Tomorrow morn at four."

He took a tavern-bed that night,
    And with the morrow's sun,
By way of Sekledobskus went,
    With carpet-bag and gun.

A week passed on; and next we find
    Our native tourist come
To that sequester'd village called
    Genasagarnagum.

* * * * * *

So back he went to Maine straightway,
    And there a wife he took,
And now is making nutmegs at
    Moosehicmagunticook.

1 2 FEBRUARY

~

The Gettysburg Address

The unkindest thing you can do to a fine piece of writing is to proclaim it as a model, thus antagonizing some people and frightening the rest. The fate of a model, said Simeon Strunsky, is to be edited as a classic, "with twenty pages of introduction and I don't know how many foot-notes." He speculates that somewhere in the high schools or the colleges this is what the young soul finds in the Gettysburg Address:

Four score and seven years[1] ago our fathers[2] brought forth on this continent[3] a new nation,[4] conceived in liberty, and dedicated to the proposition[5] that all men are created equal.[6] Now we are engaged in a great civil war,[7] testing whether that nation,[8] or any nation so conceived and so dedicated,[9] can long endure. We are met on a great battlefield[10] of that war.

1. i.e., eighty-seven years ago. The Gettsyburg Address was delivered Nov. 19, 1863. Lincoln is here referring to the Declaration of Independence.

2. Figuratively speaking. To take "fathers" in a literal sense would, of course, involve a physiological absurdity.

3. The western continent, embracing North and South America.

4. "A new nation." This is tautological, since a nation just brought forth would necessarily be new.

5. "Proposition," in the sense in which Euclid employs the term and not as one might say now, "a cloak and suit proposition."

6. See the Declaration of Independence in Albert Bushnell Hart's "American History Told by Contemporaries" (4 vols., Boston, 1898–1901).

7. The war between the States, 1861–65.

8. i.e., the United States.

9. See Elliot's Debates in the several State Conventions on the adoption of the Federal Constitution, etc. (5 vols., Washington, 1840–45).

10. Gettysburg; a borough and the county seat of Adams Co., Pennsylvania, near the Maryland border, 35 miles southwest of Harrisburg. Pop. in 1910, 4,030.

1 3 FEBRUARY

~

Odets, Where Is Thy Sting?

If I pun inadvertently, I take the credit. This is only fair, since so many of my advertent puns miscarry. I once brought into a conversation that an Arab would always win in a camel race against a Jew, because no matter how good a camel driver the Jew was, the Arab would be a Bedouin. Once, did I say? I maneuvered my way into that pun a score of times before I admitted it was a born loser. "Bedouin! Bedouin!" I would say, punching my hapless listener with my elbow. "Don't you get it?" No one would admit that he did. I had better luck with "Watch where European," but that *bon mot* has to be saved for special occasions.

A Congressman, I am told, has proposed a constitutional amendment to ban puns; but Prohibition should have taught him that such evils as drinking, gambling, whoring, and punning cannot be eliminated by edict. When New York seemed on the verge of losing a prestigious brewery, how did a shocked citizenry respond? With puns, as in this deplorable letter from Edward E. Brown to *The New York Times:*

> "A. Sock's suggestion [letter Jan. 22] that the Mayor plant an Anheuser Busch in memory of a departing brewery, and A. H. Green's riposte [letter Jan. 30] to the effect that the failure of the brewer Busch to realize profits from such an act would leave him sadder Budweiser provoked in me a sudden Piel of laughter.
>
> "Should I ever have the good fortune to meet either or both of these gentlemen, I would certainly invite them over for a cold beer or two, and perhaps ask them to Schaefer dinner."

Even commerce pays credit to the clout of the pun. A New York fish store is called "Wholly Mackerel."

Addison worried lest the British "degenerate into a race of punsters." Eachard wondered "Whether or no Punning, Quibbling, and that which they call Joquing, and such other delicacies of Wit, highly admired in some Academick Exercises, might not be very conveniently omitted."

Charles Lamb, on the other hand, worshiped puns the way unregenerate Hebrews worshiped the golden calf. "The puns which are most entertaining," he said, "are those which will least bear an analysis. Of this kind is the following recorded with a sort of stigma in one of Swift's *Miscellanies:*

> An Oxford scholar, meeting a porter who was carrying a hare through the streets, accosts him with this extraordinary question: 'Prithee, friend, is that thy own hare, or a wig?'

"There is no excusing this," Lamb concluded, "and no resisting it."

One man's Mede, as punsters have reported *ad nauseam,* is another man's Persian. Individuals trying to remove spilled oil from seagulls reported that they "left no tern unstoned." William Safire thought this among the best of recent puns; yet it does not touch my funnybone* at all. Were those people throwing rocks at the seagulls? Or feeding them LSD? The wordplay is over my head.

"Edna St. Vincent Malaise," muttered a jealous poet. "Housman's knee," sneered another. "Puberty is a hair-raising experience," reflected John Wildman. "Armageddon sick of it," cried Robert A. Henlein. Norman Corwin, permitting Joe Julian to answer a call of nature during rehearsal, said, "I always want my actors to mind

---

* *Humerus* is Latin for the upper armbone.

their pees and cues." Bob Bendiner warned a young lady who was backing into two candles on a sideboard, "Watch out—you'll burn your end at both candles." Franklin P. Adams punned about Columbus:

> Oh, I should like to see Columbus's birthplace,
> And then I'd write a fine, authentic poem,
> And critics, none of whom would read it through,
> Would say, "At last we have the Genoan article."

Dedicated punsters sometimes go to inordinate lengths to set the stage. In the nineteenth century George Augustus Sala, hearing that a prominent watchmaker was to be knighted, rode his horse twenty miles to the man's home in order to shout, as the clock struck twelve, "Watchman, what of the knight?"

Someone once told me who first said, "Odets, where is thy sting?" But I have forgotten the name, and, besides, I don't believe anybody said it first. These weeds spring simultaneously in many fields.

14 FEBRUARY

"There Are Numerous Locutions to Express the Idea of Never"

When all the world grows honest;
When the Yellow River's clear;
When Calais meets with Dover,
Do you suppose, my dear,

I shall forget I've lost you? . . .
Not until St. Tib's Eve,
Not for a year of Sundays
Shall I forbear to grieve—

Till noon strikes Narrowdale; till
Latter Lammas dawns;
Till Queen Dick reigns; till Fridays
Arrive in pairs like swans;

Till the Greek calends, and the
Conversion of the Jews.
I'll mourn you till the coming
Of the Cocqcigrues.

—W.R.E.

15 FEBRUARY

Shall I Will?

An English teacher, trying to explain the difference between shall and will, told her class that a would-be suicide swam out to sea, crying as he went, "I will drown—no one shall help me!" He passed an unfortunate, going down for the third time, whose last words were, "I shall drown! No one will help me!"

We are all occasional solecists (I know a Harvard man who says "between you and I"), and I seldom tax others with their grammatical failings lest they tax me with my own.

Yet it is astonishing that grammatical errors are so common in formal writing. Carelessness is the usual excuse; but even this implies that the transgressors, when they do not stop to think, find the wrong word more natural than the right one.

Examples of common grammatical blunders:

• "Dalling lay in the middle of it, prone on his back and finished." Ross McDonald knows perfectly well that, being on his back, Dalling lay not prone but supine. Just as Edward S. Aarons knows it is tautological to say "The junk puttered along at only a few knots per hour."

• "The campus fires have been stoked on such issues." Rabbi Norman Frimer meant to say the fires have been banked.

• "It is only when they run into a sentence that mysteriously fails to track that they reach for an authoritarian handbook." Authoritative, not authoritarian, unless the writer was being funny.

• "Romney had already promised a full-scale review of the project, noting that one important criteria of HUD's program is the impact of proposed low-income projects." There can be no fewer than two criteria (maybe one and a half) and no more than one criterion.

• "Look at the top of the page, where it tell you what to do." This is from the teacher's directions in the New York Metropolitan Achievement Tests. Perhaps a typographical error?

• "Both were considered talented and capable, and each promised to support whomever won." (That is, whomever was the one whom won.)

• In similar vein, Anatole Broyard, the book critic, wrote, or his typesetter did, "Though the Duchess or her publisher—it is not clear whom—seems to feel . . ." And George Steiner remarked of Edmund Wilson, "He wanted to do a book on the Hungarian poet Petofi, whom he had convinced himself was of a stature with Pushkin . . ."

• "Senator George McGovern is the plain-spoken son of a country preacher who now sports $15 Gucci ties." Are you sure it is the father who sports those $15 ties, Time? Isn't it the son?

Certain grammatical dilemmas cannot be resolved; they can only be avoided. One not avoided by *The Public Interest:* "There is not one but two." Another, not avoided by James Reston: "They will be able to agree on regulations at least as effective, and probably more so, as those in effect since the last World War."

The Wall Street Journal editorialized, much, I am sure, to its own astonishment: "The great body of Americans do not want Detroit to suffer, does not expect the impossible, and will make accommodations along the way . . ."

Some grammatical sphincter should have spared Grace Glueck from this bemusing peristaltic slip in a *New York Times* book review: "He deducts . . . that she defecates."

He didn't deduct at all *She* did

16 FEBRUARY

Mary Had a Lipogram*

R. Ross Eckler re-created "Mary Had a Little Lamb" six times, excluding in turn the letters s, h, t, e, and a. In the final verse he used just half of the alphabet: e, t, a, y, n, c, l, d, m, r, h, i, and p.

The original verse

Mary had a little lamb,
 Its fleece was white as snow,
And everywhere that Mary went
 The lamb was sure to go;
He followed her to school one day,
 That was against the rule;
It made the children laugh and play
 To see a lamb in school.

The verse without h

Mary owned a little lamb,
 Its fleece was pale as snow,
And every place its mistress went
 It certainly would go;
It followed Mary to class one day
 It broke a rigid law;
It made some students giggle aloud,
 A lamb in class all saw.

The verse without s

Mary had a little lamb,
 With fleece a pale white hue,
And everywhere that Mary went
 The lamb kept her in view;
To academe he went with her,
 Illegal, and quite rare;
It made the children laugh and play
 To view a lamb in there.

The verse without t

Mary had a pygmy lamb,
 His fleece was pale as snow,
And every place where Mary walked
 Her lamb did also go;
He came inside her classroom once,
 Which broke a rigid rule;
How children all did laugh and play
 On seeing a lamb in school!

The verse without a

Polly owned one little sheep,
 Its fleece shone white like snow,
Every region where Polly went,
 The sheep did surely go;
He followed her to school one time,
 Which broke the rigid rule;
The children frolicked in their room
 To see the sheep in school.

The verse without e

Mary had a tiny lamb,
 Its wool was pallid as snow,
And any spot that Mary did walk
 This lamb would always go;
This lamb did follow Mary to school,
 Although against a law;
How girls and boys did laugh and play,
 That lamb in class all saw.

* Michael Gartner says he always thought a lipogram was a nasty rejoinder sent via Western Union.

Finally, the verse without half the letters of the alphabet

Maria had a little sheep,
  As pale as rime its hair,
And all the places Maria came
  The sheep did tail her there;
In Maria's class it came at last,
  A sheep can't enter there;
It made the children clap their hands,
  A sheep in class, that's rare.

—*A. Ross Eckler*

17 FEBRUARY

A Fraffly Well-Spoken Glossary

Says Professor Afferbeck Lauder, whom some confuse with Alistair Morrison:

"Fraffly, the language spoken in the West End of London, takes its name from the expression 'Fraffly caned a few,' meaning 'Frightfully (i.e., very) kind of you,' and from the many variants of this expression, such as 'Fraffly caned a fume shore' and 'Fraffly nacer few.'

"A characteristic feature of Fraffly is that it is thought, not only by those who speak it, but also by those to whom it is spoken, to be English. This is not an unusual phenomenon; Australians, who speak Strine, also think they are speaking English; and a similar misapprehension exists in America."

Some fraffly fine definitions by Professor Lauder:

A. Ashel; Ashered. I shall; I should, as in "This food's a disgress; ashel bring it op in the House." or "Ashered of thotty would hef bin myrrh kretful."

B. Blemmer; Blemmin. Blame her (or him), as in "Wong con blemmer, relleh, when one nerzer bare crond."

C. Chozz; Chozzle (sometimes also Chairs). Your good health! Cheers! As in: "Nozz the tem frolgered men to compter the edda the potty. Chozzle man! Chozz!"

E. Earce. Yes, as in "Earce, earce, thairk yaw;" "Earce and nir;" "Earce, of koss"; etc.

F. Fay. Very, as in "Shiss fay caned, and fay swit; Aim fay fawn torfa."

H. Hunts. Hunts are the terminal portion of the human *oms*. They are specially modified by having fingers and thumbs, for *grosping,* and for wearing rings of *dammonds and droopies.* Many songs and poems have been written about hunts, including "Pell hunts aloft" and "Mimmeh, your tanny hunts are quet chilleh."

N. Nairflet. (sometimes: Yoom snairflet.) Prefix, corresponding to the English "never let," to which various suffixes may be added, e.g., chaw, chom, sko, ter, tit, etc. As in "Nairfletchaw way-feet peas with a naif;" "Nairfletchom mostosh be calm and tangled in the coffee grindah."

O. One. In Fraffly one says not I but one, even though this may sometimes result in something that sounds like nonsense; like "One thought one had won one, and one had won one, too." Ordinarily, however, the meaning is clear enough, e.g., "One knows when one zop stezz"; or "One was jolleh depressed."

P. Poncer. Pardon, sir, as in "Ah peck your poncer, but mairn trop choofra merment?"

R. Revving. Talking as though in a delirium, as in "Miss Jenny is a revving beauty," meaning that she is beautiful but mad. As "revving" also means "revolving," it could mean that she is "off her rocker and rolling." Perhaps it means "mad spinning Jenny."

S. Sweller's Bing. As well as being, as in "Sweller's bing a memmerer pollerment, zolso a fay keen burtwotchah"; or "Sweller's bing a jollickered spot, yolso plessy organ."

T. Tin Etcher. A young person (specifically, aged thirteen to nineteen years) of either sex, whose clothes, habits, and attitudes to life are a constant source of anxiety and criticism to those who are thirty or more years older and wish they weren't.

W. War Snebble. Was not able, as in "War snebble to mecket." Related phrases include hoozar nebble, shomp yebble, quettar nebble, ear snebble, probblier nebble, werp yebble, noughtshorrivizebble, and sensi skaned regodze but regretzy czar nebble.

18 FEBRUARY

Impossible Rhymes

Silver is a hard word to rhyme. Here is the way Stephen Sondheim managed it:

> To find a rhyme for silver
> Or any "rhymeless" rhyme
> Requires only will, ver-
> bosity and time.

Mr. Sondheim's rhyme, in the correspondence column of *Time,* prompted this from Ira Levin:

> A woman asked me to rhyme a penguin.
> I said, "Does the erstwhile Emperor Eng win?

If not, I'll send a brand-new tractor
To "Big Boy" Williams, cinemactor;
On the card attached, a smiling penguin
Will say, "You're truly a man among men, Guinn."

"All right," she said, "so now rhyme silver."
But I left, because I'd had my filver.

Speonk, a town on Long Island, offers a minor challenge:

WEE-ONKS ARE EXPECTED SOON

If a masculine porker's a he-onk,
The feminine must be a she-onk;
  When the gal meets the guy
  In a Long Island sty,
They're a he-onk and she-onk in Speonk.
                              —W.R.E.

Victorian writers did some ingenious rhyming:

VELOCITY

Having once gained the summit, and managed to cross it, he
Rolls down the side with uncommon velocity.
                              —R. H. Barham

INTELLECTUAL

Ye lords of ladies intellectual,
Come tell me, have they not hen-pecked you all?
                              —Lord Byron

CARPET

Sweet maid of the inn,
'Tis surely no sin
To toast such a beautiful bar pet;
Believe me, my dear,
Your feet would appear
At home on a nobleman's carpet.
                              —Author Unknown.

MONTH

How many weeks in a month?
Four, as the swift moon runn'th.
                              —Christina Rossetti

If I were a cassawary
  On the plains of Timbuctoo,
I would eat a missionary,
  Cassock, band, and hymn-book too.
                              —Samuel Wilberforce

In the 1920s, F. P. A. rhymed Massachusetts this way:

Of tennis I played one or two sets
On a court at Richmond, Massachusetts.

Nigel Nicolson says Vita Sackville-West's grandfather, "Old Lionel," composed a saying about a girl named Rosamond Grosvenor: Rosamond Grosvenor / got nearly run ovner. This bothered Vita, then in her teens, "because she could not see how he got it to rhyme properly."

My report closes, as it began, with a rhyme for silver:

TO VERONA

> If Pegasus
> Were but a bus
> That any man could board,
> I might distil Ver-
> ona's silver
> Beauty in a word.
> —*W.R.E.*

19 FEBRUARY
∽

Overdrawn Your Bank Account, You Negative Saver?

If someone were to tell you that he was in the REUSED METAL PRODUCTS INDUSTRY, it would probably take you a while to figure out that he was a *junk dealer*. "Super titles" are becoming increasingly prevalent as the lust for a burnished image dominates any interest in the substance it obscures.

Sometimes, super-titling is simple euphemism, wherein the distasteful becomes acceptable, as in UNDERFASHIONS for *underwear* (itself a euphemism). In this way, *sexual intercourse* emerges as CONJUGAL RELATIONS. We can soften the harshest realities, such as *nuclear missiles,* simply by calling them FACTORS OF PEACE (for the good guys) or INSTRUMENTS OF AGGRESSION (for the bad guys). The super title may be totally unrecognizable without its referent by its side, as when we call a *bar of soap* a BEAUTY CAKE.

In a recent issue of *The New Yorker* there was a story about a man hired by an oil company to take complaints over the telephone. On his first day, he jotted down a customer's complaint about an oil burner that had exploded. It was his boss who then exploded: "You won't get far in this business until you learn that we do *not* have explosions. We have PUFFBACKS." It is this sort of mentality that gives us MEMORIAL GARDEN for *graveyard,* HOME ENTERTAINMENT CENTER for *radio-phonograph combination,* and PRESENTATION SESSION for *class.*

The death industry is especially replete with super titles. MORTICIANS[1] place LOVED ONES[2] in CASKETS[3] for INTERMENT[4]. (Incidentally, and quite beside the point, there is an Indianapolis undertaker who advertises that his coffins come with a "lifetime guarantee"!)

---

1. undertakers; 2. dead persons; 3. coffins; 4. burial.

People, in the hands of bureaucrats, become PERSONNEL, who don't live anywhere, but are DOMICILED. *Old People* have become SENIOR CITIZENS, and the *poor,* when they are mentioned at all, are merely UNDERPRIVILEGED. We are no longer *fired* from our jobs; we are TERMINATED.

Just as the *undertaker* elevates himself to a MORTICIAN, so does the *gardener* become a LANDSCAPE TECHNICIAN, the *tax collector* a REVENUE AGENT, the *plumber* a WATER SYSTEMS SPECIALIST, and the *film projectionist* a MULTIMEDIA SYSTEMS TECHNICIAN. We no longer have *janitors;* we now employ SANITATION MAINTENANCE SUPERINTENDENTS. If a limb of one of your trees is sagging, don't bother to look in the Yellow Pages for a *tree trimmer;* look rather under HORTICULTURAL SURGEONS. Remember when Art Carney used to get a laugh on the Jackie Gleason Show by describing himself as a SUBTERRANEAN SANITATION TECHNICIAN? It's no laughing matter any more; just call City Hall some time and ask for the help of a *sewer worker*—they won't know what you're talking about.

While you're on the line to City Hall, you might ask about the *dogcatcher:* you'll learn that he's now the CANINE CONTROL OFFICER. And did you know that policemen no longer carry *clubs?* No sirreebob! That long, wooden, blunt instrument is a NIGHT BATON! Joining the *dogcatcher* in oblivion is the *barber;* in his place we now have a HAIR STYLIST. Should your stomach start to turn on your next plane trip, don't bother looking for the old *vomit bag,* because you won't find it; in its stead is something called an AIR SICKNESS CONTAINER. . . . Oh, yes—the next time you are in the market for a *used car,* be careful. Some newspapers are advertising PRE-OWNED VEHICLES.

NASA's rocket fuel workers at Cape Kennedy recently wondered why the supply depot no longer carried *portable field showers,* needed to wash off the rocket fuel. It was probably due to the fact that the quartermaster had redesignated the showers as ROCKET PROPELLANT PERSONNEL NEUTRALIZERS.

—*Temple G. Porter*

2 0 FEBRUARY

Shipwreck

I refer in the following verse to the shipwreck that ultimately accounts for us all. One three-letter combination, dropped into the blanks, makes the meaning all too clear.

> ***, ***, *** your boat
>   Till the p*** go down;
> Fie on him who bor***s sor***:
> All must sink and d***n tomorrow;
>   All must sink and d***n.
>
> Let no wailing c***d your throat;
>   Bar your b*** from f***n;

Bare your breast to Cupid's ar***,
Gnaw the bone and suck the mar***,
  Ere you sink and d***n.

Pluck the blossoms life has g***n,
  Wear them as a c***n;
Many a c*** shall fly from spar***,
Many a lad his *** shall har***
  Ere you sink and d***n.
               —*W.R.E.*

21 FEBRUARY

Self Service

M. Piron wrote the following epitaph for himself after his rejection by the French Academy:

Ci-gît Piron, qui ne fut rien,
  Pas même académicien.

Shakespeare called down a curse on anyone who might disturb his grave:

Good frend, for Jesus' sake forbeare
To digg the dust enclosed heare;
Blest be ye man y^t spares thes stones,
And curst be he y^t moves my bones.

Wrote John Gay:

The world's a joke, and all things show it.
I thought so once, and now I know it.

Benjamin Franklin's self-written epitaph was gentler:

The body of
Benjamin Franklin, printer,
Like the cover of an old book,
Its contents worn out
And stript of its lettering and gilding,
Lies here food for the worms.
Yet the work itself shall not be lost,
For it shall, as he believes,
Appear once more,
In a new
And more beautiful edition,
Corrected and amended
        By the Author.

Thomas Fuller said: "Here lies Fuller's earth."

Gossip columnist Walter Winchell wrote: "If only when my epitaph is readied, they will say, 'Here is Walter Winchell with his ear to the ground—as usual.'"

2 2 F E B R U A R Y

Washington Crisscrossing the Delaware

Not only is each line that follows an anagram of "Washington Crossing the Delaware," but the poem originally contained at least eight more lines, which have not come down to us, or at least not to me. This is a tour de force, though imperfect in some lines. It appeared November 10, 1890, in a New York magazine called *The Boys' Champion*.

> A hard, howling, tossing winter scene;
> Strong tide was washing hero clean.
> "How cold!" Weather stings as in anger.
> O silent night shows war ace danger!
> The cold waters swashing on in rage,
> Redcoats warn slow his hint engage.
> When across General wish'd train t'go,
> He saw his ragged continentals row.
> He stands while crew sit, an oar going
> And so this general watches rowing.
> He hastens—winter again grows cold;
> A wet crew gain Hessian stronghold.
> George can't lose war with 's hands in;
> He goes astern—Alight, O crew, and win!
> —*Skeezix*

2 3 F E B R U A R Y

Squdgy Fez, Blank Jimp Crwth Vox

The quality of existing pangrams is unsatisfactory. Augustus Morgan's nineteenth-century "I, quartz pyx, who fling muck beds," ignored v and j, recent arrivals on the alphabetical scene. "Cwm fjord-bank glyphs vext quiz" makes room for the v and j, but is not likely to become a common remark even among geologists. Claude E. Shannon wrote, "Squdgy fez, blank jimp crwth vox," which has something to do with wearing a squashed Turkish hat and muting a Welsh violin.

If you are willing to fudge by repeating a few letters, the problem of including all twenty-six letters in a single passage becomes more manageable. For instance:

"The five boxing wizards jump quickly." (31)

"Pack my box with five dozen liquor jugs." (32)

"Jim just quit and packed extra heavy bags for Liz Owen." (44)

If you wish to use each letter twice, your goal is a sentence of fifty-two letters. The nearest to this I have run into is Mary Youngquist's "Sylvan plight: five jinxed wizards jump, weigh quartz, mock quick baby fox." (60)

Darryl Francis found in *Webster's New International Dictionary,* second edition, three words totaling thirty-nine letters and including all the twenty-six letters of the alphabet. The words are *quick-flowing, semibolshevized,* and *juxtapyloric.* The following verse is a *lipogram,** since it lacks the letter e, and also a *pangram,* since it contains all the other letters of the alphabet:

> Quixotic boys who look for joys
> Quixotic hazards run.
> A lass annoys with trivial toys
> Opposing man for fun.
> —*Author unknown*

24 FEBRUARY

The Noblest City of Them All

ROME, Ides of March—Despite doomsayers' forecast of the end of the western part of the Roman Empire in this year A.D. 476, a survey by Danielus Yankelovicius, a leading public opinion research organization, found that two-thirds of those questioned thought that Rome would not decline or fall.

Only e pluribus unum, Bibbonius by name, believed that the city's long-term outlook was bleak.

Following are some of the key findings of the survey: XC percent felt that in Rome you do as the Romans do, that it was not built in a day, and that all roads lead to it.

Rome was the home by choice of LIV percent of those interviewed, who apparently felt strongly that the city had much going for it. They held that Rome had grandeur —though not the glory that was Greece—unmatchable bread and circuses and interesting rostrums and that in education no other municipality could match its declensions and conjugations.

What do Romans do on a holiday? They like to stroll through the Forum, despite fallen arches, to see the toga and sandal shops, to soak in the Baths of Caracalla (XX percent would like to have opera there, too). They enjoy going to the Colosseum and

* See 16 February.

cheering until the vox cracks—the Colosseum is more popular with pagans than with Christians.

Here are the statistical results of answers to the question, "How would you rate Rome?"

	Nice Place to Visit	Wouldn't Want to Live There
Friends	XXX	LXX
Romans	LXX	XXX
Countrymen	L	L

An overwhelming majority of Romans—rich and poor, patrician and plebeian, slave and free—consider the barbarian invasion the worst problem they face.

Asked, "Have you taken any steps to protect yourself or your family?" XIV percent stated they would put a Cave Canem sign on their janus post, while XL percent said they would take to the VII hills.

Questioned about commuting, XV percent said philosophically, "sic transit gloria," and called for subsidia to keep the XXXV denarii fare.

Some were thinking of moving to Constantinople.

—*Nanette E. Scofield, Lionel Casson*

25 FEBRUARY

The Girl I Never Saw

The frustration I recall most bitterly occurred during a period when I was theoretically studying philosophy at the Sorbonne. Since I had no marketable skills, my principal source of income was my reddish, curly beard, which appealed to Left Bank artists. One of these paid me a few francs to pose for a painting of a seedy-looking fellow—me—sitting across what I took to be a parlor table from a comely nude. Between us stood an almost empty bottle of wine and an almost burned-out candle.

There was one drawback to the assignment: the artist never posed the girl and me together. Each time I arrived, I would see her there on the canvas, still pinker and more Renoirish than the time before. She looked at me with a speculative expression that never changed, but mine did; with each sitting it grew more ravenous. I pleaded with the artist, I embraced his knees, I offered to waive my pittance of a fee if only he would permit me to sit with that girl once in the flesh. Before the final sitting he agreed. But men are deceivers ever. When I arrived that last day, on the run, he announced that he considered the painting finished. I never did see that girl. I still don't know whether the small brown mole on the underslope of her left breast was real. Some day, in some gallery . . . in some attic . . . perhaps overpainted with an oil of a cow grazing beside a pond . . . a collector will find me still sitting, staring in hopeless longing at a girl I never saw . . . .

What parlor games she and I might have played! They are too numerous for a full listing, but I give you two:*

1. Choose a letter to be the first letter of a noun. Then make a list of adjective-noun combinations, each noun starting with the key letter, while the adjective linked to the first noun starts with a, the adjective for the second noun with b, and so on through the alphabet. (Skip x and z.) The first person to finish wins. For instance: Aged sweetheart, bitter sea, curious spaniel, drugged swan, enticing siren, frozen stream, golden silence, hideous sight, idle striker, juicy salad, etc.

2. The first player gives two commonly associated words. His opponent makes the second word the first word of another familiar combination, and so back and forth until one or the other gives up. A sampler: Gang saw, saw horse, horse fly, fly guy, guy rope, rope ladder, ladder truck, etc.

In parlor games of this sort there are forfeits. I am afraid that when I wake at night to consider the games that that girl and I might have played, I spend more time working out the forfeits than working out the games.

26 FEBRUARY

Bless the Shepherd

This sestet uses only the vowel e:

> Bless the shepherd,
> Bless the sheep,
> Bless the shepherdess.
> Ewe, Bellwether,
> Sheltered keep:
> Send them blessedness.
> —*W.R.E.*

By inserting i at appropriate intervals, you can complete the nineteenth-century quatrain below:

APPROACH OF EVENING

> dling, st n ths mld twlght dm,
> Whlst brds, n wld, swft vgls, crclng skm.
> Lght wnds n sghng snk, tll, rsng brght,
> Nght's Vrgn Plgrm swms n vvd lght!
> —*Author Unknown*

* William and Mary Morris told me about these.

Decide for yourself the vowel to be inserted (thirty-nine times) in the quatrain below:

INCONTROVERTIBLE FACTS

Dll hmdrm mrmrs lll, bt hbbb stns.
Lclls snffs p msk, mndngs shns.
Pss prrs, bds brst, bcks btt, lck trns p trmps;
Bt fll cps, hrtfl, spr p njst thmps.

—Author unknown

27 FEBRUARY

Rockabye Gloria

A parodist exaggerates a writer's peccadilloes of style and attitude as a caricaturist might enlarge his nose or chin. The examples that follow are from a collection by Dwight Macdonald:

(An anonymous summary of a court decision awarding eleven-year-old Gloria Vanderbilt to her aunt during the week and to her mother on weekends)

Rockabye baby,
Up on a writ,
Monday to Friday, mother's unfit.
As the week ends, she rises in virtue;
Saturday, Sunday,
Mother won't hurt you.

THE MAN WITH A HOE

"The Man with a Hoe," Edwin Markham's poem inspired by Millet's painting, became a journalistic sensation in the United States in the 1890s. Its first four lines:

Bowed by the weight of centuries he leans
Upon his hoe and gazes on the ground,
The emptiness of ages in his face,
And on his back the burden of the world.

A poem so oozy is fair game, and parodies popped up like thistles in spring. This is the start of one about a Boston bicycle rider:

Bowed by the drooping handle-bars he leans
Upon his bike and gazes at the ground;
His back is humped and crooked and his face
Is strained and agonizing in its looks.
Who made him sit upon a wheel like this?

—Author Unknown

28 FEBRUARY

Cats, Cats, Cats, Cats!

These two monosyllabic acrostics* are verbally identical; yet they present two separate rhyme schemes. Acrostically speaking, they separate cat lovers from dog lovers.

CATS, CATS, CATS, CATS!   CHASE 'EM, SCAMP, GO ON!

Cats come with mews,   Cats come with mews, all
All have sharp claws,   Have sharp claws, they
They air their views,   Air their views, stray
Stray soon from laws,   Soon from laws, climb wall.
Climb wall. Each tom
And each mog†—grand   Each tom and
Thieves—munch meal from   Each mog—grand thieves—munch
Scamp's‡ lunch. Scamp planned . . .   Meal from Scamp's lunch.
      Scamp planned . . .
Chain off, he might
Aim at a rout,   Chain off, he might aim
Touch mogs and bite   At a rout, touch
Such prime bits out!   Mogs and bite such
Chance came. Grey dawn.   Prime bits out. Chance came.
At once left mat.
The deuce! On lawn—   Grey dawn. At
Scamp loose—no cat!   Once left mat. The deuce!
      On lawn—Scamp loose—
      No cat!

                          —*J. A. Lindon*

Mr. Lindon's tour de force reminds me that I have seen no verses that use whole words instead of letters for acrostic purposes. This omission is repaired herewith:

FORECAST: CHILLY

Time befriends   *Looks must fade,*
For brief space—   *Like or not.*
Warm days sends;
Clothes in grace   One is not here
      Long, my chums;
Man and maid.   Cold from hot, here
This I wot: Winter comes.

                          —*W.R.E.*

* See also Dedication and 25 December.
† In English slang, pussy cat.
‡ One assumes Scamp to be the house dog.

29 FEBRUARY

~

The Canary, the Stallion, and the Partridge

A *canard*, said someone who did not mind reaching, is something one canardly believe. I canardly believe that a word meaning female duck could turn into one meaning false, unfounded story, but that is what happened. From the meaningless quacking of a duck, do you suppose?

Duck itself comes from the place you would expect—old English *duce*, to duck or dive. The origins of some animal names are more surprising. For instance:

> *Canary* comes from *dog,** as *stallion* from
> The *stall* where he is daily combed and brushed.
> And *partridge* comes from *fart*—because its thrum
> Vhen it is flushed sounds just like . . . being
> flushed.†
>
> —*W.R.E.*

The goose laid a much prettier word than the duck. I get pleasurable goose pimples when I reflect that gossamer was once *goose summer*.

---

* Canaries once abounded in the Canary Islands, so called for the wild dogs (canus, dog (L.)) found there by the first settlers.

† It was a joy to discover this presumably inadvertent pun in the Appendix of *The American Heritage Dictionary*, under *Perd-*, to fart.

MARCH

1 MARCH

The English Is Coming

"When I was little," says Jean Cocteau, "I believed that foreigners could not really talk at all, but were only pretending."

Yet even in M. Cocteau's childhood a strong west wind was blowing English words across the channel into France. Today he must be as familiar as any Englishman with "management," "le weekend," "le grand rush," "le beesness," "le whisky," "le leadership," "blugines" (with the spelling Frenchified), "le cocktail," and "le golf." (Says one confused Parisian: Les Français aiment les gadgets—en anglais, les gizmos.")

The French government tries to blow the English words back home. Recently 350 of them were exiled at a stroke. "Flashback" was ordered to yield to "retrospectif;" "hovercraft" to "aeroglisseur;" "ferry boat" to "transbordeur;" "tanker" to "navire citerne;" "hit parade" to "palmarès."

But it is doubtful whether English will fall back for long, in France or anywhere else. In Germany, for instance—where fashion advertisements ask "Was ist IN, was ist OUT?"—English words are IN. The Germans have adopted "appeasement," "escalation," "rollback," "comeback," and "no comment." A German official who had resigned his post insisted that "Mein Walkout war richtig!" German members of "das Establishment" are served on airplanes by "Stewardesses" and "Purserettes." They may call for "a long drink." And if a business deal goes sour, they feel "frustriert."

Of course, the thing sometimes works the other way. Marshall Davidson once sat on a New York grand jury, which was hearing a French witness. The District Attorney asked, "Were you at such a place at such a time?" The translator turned the sentence into French, and the witness replied, "Yes, zat ees true." Said the translator to the jury: "Elle dit, 'Oui, c'est vrai.' "

There is no telling how far this homogenizing of languages will go. With Britain and Germany now bundling in the Common Market, says a London paper, both countries may be using these automotive terms by 1984:

- Bonnet (Hood): Der Fingerpinsher.
- Exhaust Pipe: Das Spitzenpopper Bangentuben.
- Speedometer: Der Egobooster und Lineschootinbackeruppen.
- Air Horns (Klaxons): Die Vhatderhellvosdat Klaxenfanfaren.
- Puncture (Flat tire): Das Pflatt mit Dammundblasten.

- Learner Driver: Dumkopf Elplatt.
- Estate Car (Station Wagon): Der Schnoginwagon mit Bagzeroomfurrompin inderback.
- Mini (Compact): Der Buzzboxen mit Traffiksveerinfistshaker underfinger raisen.
- Petrol (Gasoline): Das Koslijozze fur Geddinsegreezeoffendentrousen.
- T Junction: Das dontgostraitonnenkorner.
- Power Brakes: Die Shtoppinworks mit edbangenon der vindscreen.
- Juggernaut (Outsized truck): Das Damgreatvagen mit das Hausenshaken.

2 MARCH

Chiffchaff

George Oppenheimer had dinner with Lillian Gish last night, and she told him a curious story. She said that on a sailboat in the Aegean she met a couple who owned a pet sea gull. This sea gull loved to sit on Miss Gish's lap (as who wouldn't?), but was uncomfortably heavy. "How heavy?" asked George. "Five pounds? Ten pounds?" "Oh, no," said Miss Gish firmly; "at least forty pounds. The problem, though, was that they had to give it four times its weight in food every day."

Let us say Miss Gish's estimate was generous. Perhaps the sea gull really weighed only twenty-five pounds. Four times twenty-five is a hundred. That sea gull, which had grown far too lazy to fish for itself, consumed a hundred pounds of protein a day. Let's stop blaming human irresponsibility for all those famines. Let's blame the sea gulls.

Birds may be responsible, too, for the persistent misunderstandings among nations. You would think that a bird in Argentina, say, would speak the same way as its cousin in New Guinea. But not at all. Roger Peterson went through *A Field Guide to the Birds of Britain and Europe* for renditions in various languages of the call of the chiffchaff (a European warbler),* and here is what he came up with:

> *English:* chiff, chaff, chiff, chiff, chaff
> *Finnish:* til, tal, til, til, tal
> *German:* zilp, zalp, zilp, zilp, zalp
> *French:* tyip, tsyep, tyip, tyip, tsyep
> *Dutch:* tjif, tjaf, tjif, tjif, tjaf
> *Swedish:* tji, tju, tji, tji, tju
> *Spanish:* sib, sab, sib, sib, sab
> *Italian:* ciff, ciaff, ciff, ciff, ciaff
> *Icelandic:* tsjiff, tsjaff, tsjiff, tsjiff, tsjaff
> *Danish:* tjif, tjaf, tjif, tjif, tjaf

* For further observations on bird calls, see 16 December.

3 MARCH
~

Burma Shave

During my college years, the Espys drove every September from Oysterville, Washington, to Redlands, California, fifteen hundred miles away, returning every June. These were not uneventful journeys. Roads and automobiles were equally unreliable. Flat tires were as common as detours. Engines overheated; so did brakes. I remember that on one side trip to Crater Lake, Oregon, we parked, like everyone else, on the rim of the crater. As we came to a halt, a mother returned to the sedan next to us and removed her sleeping infant. She had scarcely picked up the child and slammed the door behind her when the brakes of her sedan let go; it rolled over the rim and plummeted two hundred and fifty feet into the lake. On another occasion I remember seeing a horse's head poke from the side window of a passing car; how the great beast had been compressed into the tiny aft-space of a passenger car remains a total mystery to me.

Advertisers frequently painted their messages on barns by the road. One common message, the slogan of a flour company, was "Pure as drifted snow." I found this message particularly thought-provoking because it was often half-concealed by a hill of manure shoveled from the barn window.

The one assured and unalloyed pleasure on those trips was the Burma Shave signs. In the late 1920s these shaving-cream advertisements speckled the highways of the entire west coast and, I suppose, of the nation. Burma Shave signs, spaced a hundred feet apart, were designed to be read from cars traveling thirty or forty miles an hour; if you drove faster, you lost the continuity. Hence: SLOW DOWN, PA / SAKES ALIVE / MA MISSED SIGNS / FOUR AND FIVE.

There was often a drama compressed into a series of signs: BEN / MET ANNA / MADE A HIT / NEGLECTED BEARD / BEN-ANNA SPLIT. Or philosophy: IF HARMONY / IS WHAT YOU CRAVE / THEN GET / A TUBA / BURMA SHAVE. At times there was the sorrow of the ages: MY JOB IS KEEPING / FACES CLEAN / AND NOBODY KNOWS / DE STUBBLE I'VE SEEN.*

4 MARCH
~

The Cat and the Fiddle, Quaker Style

I thought I had quite finished with cats, when I suddenly remembered that inexplicable little verse about a cat and a fiddle:

---

* If you would like to read all the Burma Shave verses, look up *The Verse by the Side of the Road*, by Frank Rowsome. Stephen Greene Press published it in 1965.

Hey diddle diddle,
    The cat and the fiddle,
The cow jumped over the moon;
    The little dog laughed to see such sport,
And the dish ran away with the spoon.

A very peculiar jingle, very peculiar indeed, in fact nonsensical; and so the Quakers thought, for they tried to amend it. They tried to turn it into reasonable sense, which is the last thing that any child desires. Rearranged by the Quakers, this is how the old rhyme came out:

Hey diddle diddle,
    The cat and the fiddle,
(Yes, thee may say that, for that is nonsense,)
    The cow jumped over the moon.
(Oh no, Mary, thee mustn't say that, for that is a falsehood; thee knows a cow could never jump over the moon; but a cow may jump under it; so thee ought to say,
    The cow jumped *under the* moon.)
    The little dog laughed . . .
(Oh, Mary, stop! How can a little dog laugh? Thee knows a little dog can't laugh. Thee ought to say,
    The little dog barked . . .)
And the dish ran after the spoon . . .
(Stop, Mary, stop! A dish could never run after a spoon. Thee had better say . . .)
But let us desist. Mary has been sufficiently snubbed.

—*V. Sackville-West*

5 MARCH

Clerihews by Bentley

A clerihew is the ideal put-down—gentle, compassionate, unanswerable. These are by Mr. Clerihew himself:

1. Geoffrey Chaucer
   Took a bath (in a saucer)
   In consequence of certain hints
   Dropped by the Black Prince.

2. The only occasion when Comte
   Is known to have romped
   Was when the multitude roared *"Vive
   La Philosophie Positive!"*

3. "Susaddah!" exclaimed Ibsen,
   "By dose is turdig cribson!
   I'd better dot kiss you.
   Atishoo! Atishoo!"

4. The digestion of Milton
   Was unequal to Stilton.
   He was only feeling so-so
   When he wrote *Il Penseroso.*

5. What I like about Clive
   Is that he is no longer alive.
   There is a great deal to be said
   For being dead.

6. When Alexander Pope
   Accidentally trod on the soap,
   And came down on the back of his
        head—
   Never mind what he said.

   —*E. C. Bentley*

6 MARCH

White Wine for Fish . . .

It is hard to believe that Ferdinand de Lesseps, who was born in 1805 and dug the Suez Canal in the 1860s, could have a granddaughter alive today, but there she is on East 86th Street—Tauni de Lesseps, young as Peter Pan and beautiful as a sunrise. She is a superbly talented sculptor with a particular flair for skeletal horses; she creates endlessly; and she releases her fey sense of humor in such pictorial nonsense as she has given me here:

"Always drink White Wine with Fish"

"Chevrolet"

"Always drink Red Wine with Beef"

7 MARCH

That Wrinkled and Golden Apricot

Many a serious poet could have risen to be a fine light rhymester if he had worked at it. Swinburne and Housman were comic poets manqués. Samuel Butler, Samuel Taylor Coleridge, William Cowper—yes, and e. e. cummings, Walter de la Mare, and T. S. Eliot too—wrote some of the funniest lines in English.

It is too bad that we remember Oliver Goldsmith for

> When lovely woman stoops to folly

but not for

> The needy seldom pass'd her door,
>   And always found her kind;
> She freely lent to all the poor—
>   Who left a pledge behind.

One grows in fondness for Edith Sitwell on reading

> "Tra la la—
>   See me dance the polka,"
> Said Mr. Wagg like a bear,
> "With my top hat
> And my whiskers that
> (Tra la la) trap the Fair."

I had always liked her brother Sir Osbert, but I liked him even better after reading "Elegy for Mr. Goodbeare," which ends:

> Do you remember Mr. Goodbeare,
> Mr. Goodbeare who never forgot?
> Do you remember Mr. Goodbeare,
> That wrinkled and golden apricot,
> Dear, bearded, godfearing Mr. Goodbeare
> Who remembered remembering such a lot?
>
> Oh, do you remember, do you remember,
> As *I* remember and deplore
> That day in drear and far-away December
> When dear, godfearing, bearded Mr. Goodbeare
> Could remember
> No more!

(Sir Osbert once recalled that while he was attending Eton a classmate committed suicide. At the memorial service, the headmaster asked the boys whether they could give any hint as to why so well-liked and highly regarded a lad should have done away with himself. A moment of silence. Then the proverbial boy in the back timidly waved his hand: "Do you suppose, sir, it might have been the food?")

8 MARCH

ᴈ

But, Honey—Are You Making Any Money?

There are few sorrows, however poignant, in which a good income is of no avail.

—LOGAN PEARSALL SMITH

I mentioned at lunch today that I had never had money, never expected to have money, and assumed I would always go on living as if I had money. Someone, probably Octave Romaine, asked how this was possible, and I replied that it is all a matter of practice; the Espys have been doing it for generations. But I have to say that my two brothers-in-law, both investment bankers, are of very little help. On my sixtieth birthday one of them gave me a child's brass bank shaped like a nineteenth-century mail drop box. "You have had to listen to us talk about banking so much," said the accompanying note, "that I thought you might like to have a bank of your own." Unfortunately, he made no deposit; I shook the bank hard, but there was nothing inside, not even a nickel.*

My views on money accord with those below.

> As I sat in the café I said to myself,
> They may talk as they please about what they call pelf,
> They may sneer as they like about eating and drinking,
> But help it I cannot, I cannot help thinking
>   How pleasant it is to have money, heigh-ho!
>   How pleasant it is to have money . . .
> —*Arthur Hugh Clough*

> I'm tired of love, I'm still more tired of rhyme,
> But money gives me pleasure all the time.
> —*Hilaire Belloc*

"A feast is made for laughter, and wine maketh merry; but money answereth all things."†

—*Ecclesiastes*

9 MARCH

ᴈ

Little Audrey

Little Audrey is the girl who just laughed and laughed at disaster to her family, her friends, and herself. She was regularly killed, only to reappear as lively as ever in another Little Audrey story:

---

* The song I remember best from the Depression had as its refrain, "But, honey—are you making any money? That's all I want to know."
† See 21 March.

Once upon a time Little Audrey got lost on a desert island. Along came a big bunch of black cannibals and kidnapped her. They tied her up to a tree and started their pot to boiling. Little Audrey knew they were going to make stew of her; so she looked around at those lean, hungry cannibals and counted them. There were nineteen. Little Audrey just laughed and laughed 'cause she knew she was not big enough to make enough stew to go around.

Little Audrey and her mama and papa and her little brunette sister were sitting at the dinner table. Papa said, "Little Audrey, pass the cream, please." So Little Audrey passed the cream to her papa, and he poured some into his coffee. Then he put the pitcher down, and Little Audrey noticed that right on the tip end of the spout there was a little drop of cream all ready to fall. Little Audrey just laughed and laughed, 'cause she knew all the time that the little cream pitcher couldn't go *sniff, sniff*.

One day Little Audrey was standing on the corner just a-crying and a-crying, when along came a cop who said, "Little Audrey, why are you crying?" And Little Audrey said, "Oh, I've lost my papa!" The cop said, "Why, Little Audrey, I wouldn't cry about that. There's your papa right across the street leaning against that bank building." Little Audrey was overjoyed; without even looking at the traffic she started across the street. Along came a big two-ton truck that ran over Little Audrey and killed her dead. The cop just laughed and laughed. He knew all the time that that was not Little Audrey's papa leaning against the bank building.

One day Little Audrey was playing with matches. Mama said, "Ummm, you better not do that." But Little Audrey was awful hard-headed; she kept right on playing with matches, and after a while she set the house on fire, and it burned right down to the ground. Mama and Little Audrey were looking at the ashes, and mama said, "Uh, huh, I told you so! Now, young lady, just wait until your papa comes home. You certainly will catch it!" Little Audrey just laughed and laughed. She knew all the time that papa had come home an hour early and had gone to bed to take a nap.

10 MARCH

The Exactness of the Inexact

Edwin was a meticulous boy. He went to count the cows, and returned with a figure of twenty-four and a half. "Why not twenty-five?" asked my father. "Daisy was partly behind a blackberry bush," said Edwin.

Which leads me to the matter of Adam's off ox:

Many of you have no doubt heard a person say that he didn't know someone else from Adam's off ox, but you may not have stopped to consider the peculiar aptness of this folk expression. Of Adam's two oxen, the near ox is better known than the off ox for two reasons: first, he is nearer the driver, and, second, the sight of him is unobstructed. We can say, then, that the off ox is less known than the near ox, who in turn is less known than Adam, who is not known at all. This expression illustrates one method of making the inexact exact: the unknown or inexact is divided into the parts which it must logically possess.

The common folk have long known and used this method. Their expressions often particularize the unparticularable, both to lend the drama of the concrete to what would otherwise be abstract and to gain credence by adding minute detail. One might indicate height by saying a thing is knee-high to a half-grown jack-rabbit, length by saying it is as long as a short piece of rope, or depth by saying it is hip-deep to a tall Indian.

Those of us who say that a person is ugly enough to stop an eight-day clock use this principle of exactness, although we may never have stopped to verbalize it. Just as there are obvious differences in clocks, so there are obvious differences in ugliness, and, if it takes x-ugliness to stop a twenty-four-hour clock, it must be $8x$-ugliness to stop the eight-day kind. This is assuming, of course, that the progression is arithmetic, not geometric.

One of the sayings reported in the *Publications of the American Dialect Society* is that a girl was so buck-toothed that she could eat a pumpkin to the hollow through a crack in a board fence. We must of necessity admire the truthfulness, the courage, and the discrimination of the speaker, for he has obviously divided buck-toothedness into at least three categories—that by which one can eat only the inner rind, that by which one can eat to the hollow, and that by which one can eat the whole pumpkin. Is it conceivable that a man who is so precise in his statements could be lying?
—*James N. Tidwell*

11 MARCH
∾

E Pluribus Unum

I abhor the smell of uncooked fish. There is an excellent fish store in the next block, and between one step and the next as I pass by—the exact place varies from day to day, so it is no use holding my breath—a nauseous whiff, for just one instant, invades my nostrils. Erasmus had a worse problem; he could not stand fish raw or cooked; the Lenten season was torture to him. "My heart is Catholic," he mourned, "but my stomach is Lutheran."

Which has nothing to do with the following verse, except that one of the creatures mentioned in it is an eel. The point is that the words species, congeries, shambles, and kudos, all ending in s, are identical in their singular and plural spellings:*

> The drunken Species homeward reels,
> Or reel; it sets the mind ajar
> That Species is and Species are.
>
> A Congeries of conger eels
> Is either are or is a bunch;
> Are either is or are for lunch.
>
> A Shambles of new-slaughtered seals
> Is either are or is deplorable;
> Are either is or are abhorrable.
>
> No Kudos for this verse, one feels,
> Is either are or is in view;
> Nor is, are, it, he, she, they, due.
> —W.R.E.

12 MARCH

A Mrs. Kr. Mr.

In my sixteen years at *Reader's Digest,* a continuing assignment was to prepare the cover essay—a brief article, approved and signed by some person of note, which by coincidence always wound up with a kind word for the *Digest.* (When I sent Groucho Marx his essay with the agreed-upon payment, he replied, "I hope your check is better than your copy.")

My usual procedure was to visit the prospective signator, come to an agreement on the thrust of the article, study his speech mannerisms, and then try to make the piece sound the way *he* sounded to me.

I particularly enjoyed this assignment, because it gave me a chance to talk on an unusually personal basis with celebrities ranging from popes to Presidents and from poets to polar explorers—people whom otherwise I would never have met at all. (Albert Einstein was my favorite, first because he was a saint, and second because he wore no socks.)

All this comes to mind because today I lunched with a man who was in my department at the *Digest,* but whom I have seldom seen since I left the magazine in 1957. He told me something I should dearly love to believe, though I have no independent memory of it. He says that when I was writing those cover essays I *became* the person in whose name I was writing. He says when I was General Marshall I walked like

---

* Ralph Beaman has written a verse featuring words of French origin—gardebras, corps, précis, faux pas, rendezvous—which, besides being identical in singular and plural spellings, share another oddity: the final s, mute in the singular, is pronounced in the plural.

the General and snapped at my associate if he did not salute. When I was Winston Churchill, I took brandy before lunch and frequently mumbled, "This is an impertinence up with which I will not put." And when I was Richard Nixon, I began every second sentence with "Let me make one thing perfectly clear."

By way of thanks, I gave my friend a piece of excellent advice. I told him the *Digest* editors have not taken the concept of condensation nearly far enough. They should condense the individual words as well as the articles. I gave him this poem—inspired by a limerick I read somewhere—as a style guide, and you may expect to see the *Digest* written in abbreviations any month now:*

> The Mrs. kr. Mr.
> Then how her Mr. kr.!
> He kr. kr. kr.
> Until he raised a blr.
> The blr. killed his Mrs.
> Then how he mr. krs.!
> He mr. mr. mr.
> Until he kr. sr.
> He covered her with krs.
> Till she became his Mrs.
> The Mrs. kr. Mr.
> (and so on and on)
> —*W.R.E.*

13 MARCH

A Croaking of Frogs

OYSTERVILLE—The frogs are making loud communal love in the marshes today. May all their troubles be tadpoles! The time has come for two of my favorite frog verses:

THE FROG

> What a wonderful bird the frog are—
> When he stand he sit almost;
> When he hop, he fly almost.
> He ain't got no sense hardly;
> He ain't got no tail hardly either.
> When he sit, he sit on what he ain't got almost.
> —*Anonymous*

Come to think of it, that is not exactly a verse. But this is:

* See 26 September for a similar suggestion to *The New York Times*.

THE FROG

Be kind and tender to the Frog,
　And do not call him names,
As "slimy-skin" or "Polly-wog,"
　Or likewise, "Ugly James,"
Or "Gape-a-grin," or "Toad-gone-wrong,"
　Or "Billy Bandy-knees."
The frog is justly sensitive
　To epithets like these.

No animal will more repay
　A treatment kind and fair.
At least, so lonely people say
Who keep a frog (and, by the way,
　They are extremely rare.)

—*Hilaire Belloc*

14 MARCH

*I'd Like to Be a Corsican**

Every male Corsican thinks he is Napoleon Bonaparte.
—*Travel article.*

I'd like to be a Corsican,
A coarsey, horsy Corsican,
And do the deeds a Corsican,
Or even those his horsican,
　His horsican, his horsican.

When weary grows the Corsican
Of wedded intercoursican
Arrange a quick divorcican
And trot off on his horsican,
　His horsican, his horsican.

With oaths and curses coarsican
Take courtesans by forcican
And if his throat grows hoarsican
Tap out his oaths in Morsican,
　In Morsican, in Morsican.

The Corsican, of Corsican
Take any course, that Corsican,
Of Corsican, of Corsican,
Of course, of course, of Corsican . . .
　I'd like to be a Corsican . . .
—*W.R.E.*

15 MARCH

Summum Bonum

What is the chief excellence of man? What is the highest possible good? There are
as many answers as there are philosophers. Bentham and Mill, for instance, voted
for the greatest happiness of the greatest number, while Spencer's ultimate was those

* To be read aloud—the louder the better.

actions which best tend to the survival of the individual and the race. Here, adapted from Brewer, are some other points of view:

> Come summer, come winter, come meadow, come wood,
> *Seek ever the highest obtainable good.*
> Squat Socrates' precept for some may suffice:
> "For *knowledge*, read *virtue;* for *ignorance, vice."*
> Helvetius taught one to diddle one's friend,
> *Self-interest* being man's ethical end.
> The good most belov'd by the great Aristotle
> Was *happiness,* meaning a babe and a bottle.
> Which Browning boiled down, and I think said it best,
> To the *kiss of one girl,* and the hell with the rest.
>
> —*W.R.E.*

16 MARCH

Fairy Tales al Dante

I have been trying unsuccessfully for more than a year to locate the author of the following stories. First, I propose to shake his hand. Second, to see if his English sounds the way the stories read.

DI TRI BERRESE

Uans appona taim uas tri berres; mamma berre, pappa berre, e beibi berre. Live inne contri nire foresta. NAISE AUS. No mugheggia. Uanna dei pappa, mamma, e beibi go bice, orie e furghetta locche di dorra.

Bai enne bai commese Goldilocchese. Sci garra natingha tu du batte meiche troble. Sci puscia olle fudde daon di maute; no live cromma. Den sci gos appesterrese enne slipse in olle beddse.

Bai enne bai commese omme di tri berres, olle sannebrone enne send inne scius. Dei garra no fudde; dei garra no beddse. En uara dei goine due to Goldilocchese? Tro erre aute inne strit? Colle pulissemenne?

Fatta Cienza!

Dei uas Italian Berres, enne dei slippe ona florre.

Goldilocches stei derre tri uicase; itta aute ausenomma bicose dei esch erre tu meiche di beddse sci sei "go tu elle," enne runne omme craine tu erre mamma, tellenerre uat sanimabicese di tri berres uer.

Uatisue? Uara iu goine du? Go compleine sittiolle?

—*Bob Belviso*

GIACCHE ENNE BINNESTAUCCHE

Uans appona taim usse disse boi. Neimmese Giacche. Naise boi. Live uite ise mamma Mainde da cao

Uane dei, di spaghetti ise olle ronne aute. Dei goine feinte fromme no fudde. Mamma soi orais, "Oreie Giacche, teicche da cao enne traide erra forre bocchese spaghetti enne somme uaine."

Bai enne bai commese omme Giacche. I garra no fudde, i garre no uaine. Meichese misteicche, enne traidese da cao forre bonce binnese.

Giacchasse!

Mamma scise engri. Giompe appe enne daon craine, "Uara iu, somme caine creisi?" Den csi tro olle binnese aute da uindo.

Necchese dai, Giacche luchhese aute enne aura iu tink? Ise si disse binnestaucche uate rice appe tru di claodese.

Somme uide!

Giacche gos appe da binnestaucche. Ise si disse ogghere! Ise menne nainti sicchese fit taulle uite tri grin aise! En i garra ghuse uate leise ghoide egghese!

Giacche ielle "Giao!" Den ise grabbe da ghuse enne cuiche claime daon fromme da binnestaucche. Ise go cioppe cioppe uita da acchese. Da nainti sicchese futte menne ise faulle enne breicche de necche.

Auce!

Mamma giompese fromme gioie. Meicchese naise ghuse cacciatore.

Bai enne bai, dei garra no morre fudde. Dei goina dai! Uatsa iuse? Uara iu goine du uene iore ghuse ise cucchedo?!

—*Bob Belviso*

17 MARCH

Mr. Dooley on Christian Science

In 1893, when the sound of Irish was loud in the land, Finley Peter Dunne wrote his first "Mr. Dooley" piece for the Chicago *Evening Post*. Since the Irish dialect was automatically the mark of the clown, Mr. Dooley was as free as any of Shakespeare's jesters to attack sacred cows, and did so with a savagery that would have made his sketches unpublishable if they had been written in everyday English. Both the brogue and the issues that exercised Mr. Dooley are dusty memories now, but if you read him today you will still find yourself laughing aloud, unaware that your throat has been cut.

Take Christian Science, for instance:

"What's Christyan Science?" asked Mr. Hennessy.

"T is wan way iv gettin' th' money," said Mr. Dooley.

"But what's it like?" asked Mr. Hennessy.

"Well," said Mr. Dooley, "ye have somethin' th' mather with ye. Ye have a leg cut off."

"Th' Lord save us!" exclaimed Mr. Hennessy.

"That is, ye think ye have," Mr. Dooley went on. "Ye think ye have a leg cut off Ye see it goin' an' says ye to yeer'self: 'More expinse. A wooden leg.' Ye think ye have lost it. But ye're wrong. Ye're as well as iver ye was. Both legs is attached to ye, on'y ye don't know it. Ye call up a Christyan Scientist, or ye'er wife does. Not manny men is Christyan Scientists, but near all women is, in wan way or another. Ye'er wife calls up a Christyan Scientist, an' says she: 'Me husband thinks he's lost a leg,' she says. 'Nonsense,' says th' Christyan Scientist, she says, f'r she's a woman too. 'No wan iver lost a leg,' she says. 'Well, 't is shtrange,' says th' wife. 'He's mislaid it, thin,' she says, 'f'r he has n't got it,' she says. 'He on'y thinks he's lost it,' says th' Christyan Scientist. 'Lave him think it on again,' she says. 'Lave him raymimber,' she says, 'they's no such thing in the wurruld,' she says, 'as pain an' injury,' she says. 'Lave him to put his mind hard to it,' she says, 'an' I'll put mine,' she says, 'an' we'll all put our minds to it, an' 'twill be all r-right,' she says. So she thinks an' th' wife thinks an' ye think th' best ye know how, an' afther a while a leg comes peepin' out with a complete set iv tootsies, an' be th' time th' las' thought is expinded, ye have a set iv as well-matched gambs as ye iver wore to a picnic. But ye must n't stop thinkin' or ye'er wife or th' Christyan Scientist. If wan iv ye laves go th' rope, th' leg'll get discouraged an' quit growin'. Manny a man's sprouted a limb on'y to have it stop between th' ankle an' th' shin because th' Christyan Scientist was called away to see what ailed th' baby."

18 MARCH

Tap Nap

Wind droops. Sloop stops.
Flopping onto my bunk, I hear
Waves slap the side. I ride
A slight chop, while sleep nears.

Nearer, though, in dank dark
Waterdrops from tank tap
Drip, one by one, to drum
On top of tin cups, draining
Upside-down in sink; ric-
Ochet to spank zinc, and slip
Down slope past slops to lip
Of trap, which greedily drinks
Them up, with gurgling, slurping suck.

Curse the luck! Tin din
Of tap's cantankerous talk plucks
My nerve joints like banjo strings:
Plink, plankety, plonk—a blank,
Unsyncopated ping-pong game,
A singsong thing gone wrong.
Can a leaky tap speak?
Utter bunk . . . I think, but,
Weakening, I begin to link
Honky-tonky tinkle tunes
Oblique to a junky theme.

Thus a wonky toggle takes
Shape, joining the shank of prank-
Ish tap's dribbling claptrap
To drip-happy me. I sink
Thankfully into dreams.
                    —*Ormonde de Kay, Jr.*

19 MARCH

Amo, Amas, Felis-itous

AMO, AMAS

Amo, amas,
I love a lass,
As cedar tall and slender;
Sweet cowslip's grace
Is her nominative case,
And she's of the feminine gender.

CHORUS

Rorum, corum, sunt di-vorum,
  Harum, scarum, divo;
Tag-rag, merry-derry, periwig and
  hatband,
  Hic, hoc, horum genitivo.

Can I decline a nymph so divine?
  Her voice like a flute is dulcis;
Her oculus bright, her manus white
  And soft, when I tacto, her pulse is.

Chorus (Rorum, corum, etc.)

O how bella, my puella
  I'll kiss in secula seculorum;
If I've luck, sir, she's my uxor,
  O dies benedictorum.

Chorus (Rorum, corum, etc.)

—*O'Keefe*

VERY FELIS-ITOUS

Felis sedit by a hole,
Intente she, cum omni soul,
  Predere rats.
Mice cucurrerunt trans the floor,
In numero duo tres or more,
  Obliti cats.

Felis saw them oculis,
"I'll have them," inquit she, "I guess,
  Dum ludunt."
Tunc illa crepit toward the group,
"Habeam," dixit, "good rat soup—
  Pingues sunt."

Mice continued all ludere,
Intente they in ludum vere,
  Gaudenter.
Tunc rushed the felis into them,
Et tore them omnes limb from limb,
  Violenter.

MORAL.

Mures omnes, nunc be shy,
Et aurem praebe mihi—
  Bensigne:
Sic hoc satis—"verbum sat,"
Avoid a whopping Thomas cat
  Studiose.

—*Green Kendrick*

This is not macaronics, but it does stem from Latin:

A CLASSICAL EDUCATION

The Latin teacher's explicating
  Amo, amas
To Latin students conjugating
  Right in class.

—*W.R.E.*

Now, back to macaronics:

THE ELDERLY GENTLEMAN

Prope ripam fluvii solus
A senex silently sat
Super capitum ecce his wig
Et wig super, ecce his hat.

Blew Zephyrus alte, acerbus,
Dum elderly gentleman sat;
Et a capite took up quite torve
Et in rivum projecit his hat.
—*J. A. Morgan*

20 MARCH

An Eloquence of Indians

There were not many Indians left in Oysterville—smallpox had done most of them in a generation before—and they were not noted for their eloquence.* They spoke mostly in grunts, and in those but rarely. So I find it astonishing that there is a long tradition of eloquence among Indians. William Jennings Bryan would have met his match in Speckled Snake, a Creek Indian who in 1829, having passed his hundredth year, spoke to his tribesmen as follows:

"Brothers! I have listened to many talks from our great father. When he first came over the wide waters, he was but a little man . . . very little. His legs were cramped by sitting long in his big boat, and he begged for a little land to light his fire on . . . But when the white man had warmed himself before the Indians' fire and filled himself with their hominy, he became very large. With a step he bestrode the mountains, and his feet covered the plains and the valleys. His hand grasped the eastern and the western sea, and his head rested on the moon. Then he became our Great Father. He loved his red children, and he said, 'Get a little further, lest I tread on thee . . .'

"Brothers, I have listened to a great many talks from our great father. But they always began and ended in this—'Get a little further; you are too near me.'"

Often, and justifiably, Indian eloquence was bitter. But there was humor, too, as in this reply from Indians of the Six Nations who, in 1744, were invited to send youths to William and Mary College:

"We know that you highly esteem the kind of learning taught in those Colleges, and that the Maintenance of our young Men, while with you, would be very expensive to you. We are convinced that you mean to do us Good by your Proposal; and we thank you heartily. But you, who are wise, must know that different Nations have

---

* Our Indians were called *Siwashes.* Years later I discovered, to my astonishment, that the name is a corruption of French "sauvage," "savage."

different Conceptions of things and you will therefore not take it amiss, if our ideas of this kind of Education happen not to be the same as yours. We have had some Experience of it. Several of our young People were formerly brought up at the Colleges of the Northern Provinces; they were instructed in all your Sciences; but, when they came back to us, they were bad Runners, ignorant of every means of living in the woods . . . neither fit for Hunters, Warriors, nor Counsellors, they were totally good for nothing.

"We are, however, not the less oblig'd by your kind Offer, tho' we decline accepting it; and, to show our grateful Sense of it, if the Gentlemen of Virginia will send us a Dozen of their Sons, we will take Care of their Education, instruct them in all we know, and make Men of them."

21 MARCH

A Crackling of Thorns

The festival Purim, which celebrates the deliverance of the Jews from Haman, is an occasion of joy and laughter. Since Purim falls around this time of year, I have turned to the Old Testament to see how laughter fared there. I find that it fared poorly. Seldom does the word connote joyousness and merriment (two exceptions— "A time to weep, and a time to laugh"; "till he fill thy mouth with laughing, and thy lips with rejoicing").*

Commonly, laughter in the Old Testament is *at* someone:

"He will laugh at the trial of the innocent." "He that sitteth in the heavens shall laugh; the Lord shall have them in derision." "All they that see me laugh me to scorn." "Thou makest a strife unto our neighbors, and our enemies laugh among themselves."

Abraham and Sarah laughed even at Jehovah's assurances: "Then Abraham fell upon his face, and laughed, and said in his heart, Shall a child be born unto him that is an hundred years old? . . . Sarah laughed within herself, saying, after I am waxed old shall I have pleasure, my lord being old also? . . . Then Sarah denied, saying, I laughed not; for she was afraid. And he said Nay; but thou didst laugh."

To those old Jews, laughter was bogus, or at least suspect:

"Even in laughter the heart is sorrowful; and the end of that mirth is heaviness." "I said of laughter, it is mad; and of mirth, what doeth it?" "Sorrow is better than laughter; for by the sadness of the countenance the heart is made better."

A generally sensible columnist recently asked how any sensitive person dared laugh in a world of wickedness. To laugh, he appeared to be saying, was to condone the wickedness. By that argument, all laughter should have stopped on the day that Adam and Eve ate the apple—the same day, I am told, that Pandora opened her box. Somebody should slip up behind that columnist and tickle him.

Other critics of laughter make an exception for the mordant sort evoked in the

* See 8 March

Christian era by such as Swift and Rabelais, and in our post-Christian time by such as Heller and Vonnegut. These are writers who put social warts (large enough to begin with) beneath a magnifying glass, and laugh at what they see. They rattle their typewriters at the universe, and laugh when the universe ignores them.

Still others will permit you to laugh as long as you do so in the tradition of Pagliaccio the clown, to hide a breaking heart. Here laughter is no sword to spit evil, but a breastplate to deflect it. To put the idea another way, it is a baby thrown off the sled to delay the onrushing wolves.

And yet I venture that some laughter is neither aggressive nor defensive, neither sword nor shield. Rather than deploring the universe, this laughter glories in it. Often—shocking thought!—the source from which it bubbles is sheer animal spirits. It recognizes that people, by and large, are dearly, wonderfully funny, and that many of their actions are dearly, wonderfully funny as well.

If I were the devil, and two angels were coming after me with broadswords, it would not be the one howling maledictions who concerned me. It would be the one laughing; for the devil can neither laugh nor withstand laughter.

So I shall not cease laughing, even when you point your finger at me and quote from Ecclesiastes:

"For as the crackling of thorns under a pot, so is the laughter of the fool."

22 MARCH

Ilwaco, O Ilwaco

The place names of my native state of Washington lend themselves to punning.* "An Oysterville solace your Tumtum," I murmured this morning, not meaning it at all. Whereupon the following play on Washington place names (which you are to sing to the tune of the hymn "I Need Thee Every Hour") descended on me from Heaven like a dove:

Leland Ilwaco, dear,
   Tacoma to you;
Ilwaco and I'll swim De-
   watto too.

Tillicum, Attalia
   Alava you;
I Wauna you to Lummi
   The way I do.

CHORUS

Ilwaco, O Ilwaco;
   Tacoma to you Ilwaco;
Across Leland Ilwaco
   Tacoma to you.

—W.R.E.

Just in case you are unfamiliar with "I Need Thee Every Hour," here is the score of the chorus:

* See 10 July.

swim De-wat-to too.
Il-wac-o O Il-wac-o; Ta-coma to you
Lummi; A-lav-a you.
Il-waco; a-cross Leland Ilwaco Ta-coma to you! A-MEN.

23 MARCH

I Sawyer Saw. Does That Make Me a Sawyer?

If you grant that:

A man sawing wood in the woods is a sawyer
While a second man, following law, is a lawyer

It follows that:

A crab has a claw, so a crab is a clawyer;
The rodent that gnaws at my cheese is a gnawyer;
A crow, since it caws, is correctly a cawyer.

I now apply this reasoning to your own situation:

If your gem has a flaw, then your gem is a flawyer;
If your yawl tends to yaw, then your yawl is a yawyer;
If your baby Charles baws, he will be a Charles Boyer;
If you suck up your tea with a straw, you're a strawyer.

Which leads irresistibly to this doleful conclusion:

Do these helpful lines stick in your craw?—You're a crawyer.
Do I hear you say pshaw?—Pshaw to you too, you pshawyer.

—*W.R.E.*

24 MARCH

SOUVENIR *

Louisa Bonner sent me a blurred copy of this typeface tarradiddle, and John Speziali, who has printer's ink in his veins, went from shop to shop to find the faces required to re-create the poem.

A **Spartan Bookman** in his **Cloister**

Thought the **Antique** world his oyster.

Times Roman were his great delight,

Italian Old Style girls the height

Of **Radiant** beauty. What a shame

No 𝔚𝔢𝔡𝔡𝔦𝔫𝔤 𝔗𝔢𝔵𝔱 will he declaim.

Instead he's **Stymied** in his **Tower**

𝕊𝕙𝕒𝕕𝕠𝕨 like and wondering how or

When he'll find a **Lydian** pal.

A *Cursive Legend* of a gal.

He yearns to be befriended

By **Venus Bold Extended**

—*Christopher Reed*, in *The Browser*,
Harvard University Press

25 MARCH

Re: Rebuses

My thanks to Paul E. Manheim for these two rebuses:
1. Inscription on an envelope which was delivered by the Post Office to the right recipient:

WOOD
JOHN
MASS

* The title type is "Souvenir." See also 25 November.

2. This rebus is to be rendered as a descriptive phrase:

bĕd

Mary J. Youngquist prepared these word rebuses:

1.	3.	5.
ADO	E	ONE ANOTHER
ADO ADO	M	ONE ANOTHER
0	A	ONE ANOTHER
ADO ADO	R	ONE ANOTHER
ADO	F	ONE ANOTHER
		ONE ANOTHER

2.   4.

WORLAMEN   ONALLE

6.

M E
A L

26 MARCH

Nicknames on Ticker Tape

The tradition that nicknames pay tribute to Old Nick, as Christian names honor our Lord, is etymologically baseless. Still, it seems fitting that Wall Street, surely the very Pandemonium of Old Nick, applies disrespectful names to highly respectable companies. *Business Week* says a floor broker will call Asamera Oil *Asthma;* Disney Productions *Mickey Mouse;* Montgomery Ward *Monkey.* Ticker tape symbols supply endless inspiration. KLR (Kleinert's) becomes *Killer;* DEV (Devon Apparel), *Devil;* MNY (Management Data), *Money;* KO (Coca Cola), *Knockout;* IGL (International Minerals & Chemicals), *Igloo.* "Be careful," warns *Business Week,* "if someone says he's buying *Heavy.* He might mean Harvey's Stores, HVY on the Amex, or High Voltage Engineering, HVE on the Big Board. Or he might just mean 'heavily.' "

The girls' names *Fanny Mae, Becky, Maggie, Jennie,* and *Pamela,* stand respectively for Federal National Mortgage Association (FNM), Beckman Instruments, Magnavox, General Telephone and Pamida.

Nicknames having nothing to do with ticker symbols have been applied to the three Wilson companies spun off by LTV Corporation. What do the floor brokers call the meatpacking Wilson & Company? *Meatball,* of course. Wilson Pharmaceutical & Chemical? *Goofball.* Wilson Sporting Goods Company? *Golfball.*

Why is General Instrument (GRL), *Gorilla* rather than *Girl?* What naughty fellow decided to turn Holiday Inns (HIA) into *Hot Beds,* or Simmons (SIM), the mattress makers, into *World's Playground?*

Some nicknames are even raunchier. You will have to figure out for yourself what traders call SHS (Shaer Shoe), AAS (Associated Spring), TTI (Technical Tape), and FKM (Fluke Manufacturing Company).

27 MARCH

O Cuckoo!

When William Wordsworth asked,

> O Cuckoo! shall I call thee Bird
> Or but a wandering Voice?

his self-searchings were not very profound, and they deserved the irony of the wit who mocked,

> State the alternative preferred,
> With reasons for your choice.

But what the mock shows (it comes from *Punch* and not, as was said, A. E. Housman) is precisely that the questions of poetry cannot be answered in the formula of the examination room.

—*J. Bronowski*

28 MARCH

Come Back, Little Artichoke Heart

Time carries a letter to the editor headed "What's in a Word?" It says:

> If "jew" as an epithet of opprobrium is successfully banned from the *Oxford English Dictionary*, there are plenty of other people who might like a chance at revising the language. The gypsies and the Welsh will want to excise the verbs *gyp* and *welsh*. The Vandals are no longer around to complain of *vandalism*, but the *Slavs* and the *Bulgarians* will surely object to *slavery* and *buggery*. Here in America the Indians can militate against *Indian giver*. There are enough words in the dictionary to offend anyone who likes to take offense.

A number of animals and plants might take similar offense. Gary Jennings in *Personalities of Language* lists some of them:

To be called a "turtle" by a Chinese is the vilest of insults; the belief in China is that the turtle commonly practices incest. The French call a miscreant a "camel," a pimp a "mackerel," and a whore a "hen." An "April fool" in France is an "April fish." The Germans call a villain a "pigdog" (Schweinhund). Botanical metaphors are also universally employed. English slang includes "pansy," "seedy," "wall flower," etc. The Spaniard calls a policeman a "hot pepper." To the French a dunce is a "sauerkraut-head." The jilted Frenchman accuses his inconstant mistress of having an "artichoke heart" (easily peelable, one assumes).

But it takes an Irishman really to call names. This way:

A GLASS OF BEER

The lanky hank of a she in the inn over there,
Nearly killed me for asking the loan of a glass of beer;
May the devil grip the whey-faced slut by the hair,
And beat bad manners out of her skin for a year.

That parboiled ape, with the toughest jaw you will see
On virtue's path, and a voice that would rasp the dead,
Came roaring and raging the minute she looked at me,
And threw me out of the house on the back of my head!

If I asked her master he'd give me a cask a day;
But she, with the beer at hand, not a gill would arrange!
May she marry a ghost and bear him a kitten, and may
The High King of Glory permit her to get the mange.

—*James Stephens*

29 MARCH

&

Chain States

Wyoming is in Kent County, Delaware;
Delaware is in Southampton County, Virginia;
Virginia is in Kitsap County, Washington;
Washington is in Knox County, Maine;
Maine is in Coconino County, Arizona;
Arizona is in Burt County, Nebraska;
Nebraska is in Jennings County, Indiana;
Indiana is in Indiana County, Pennsylvania;
Pennsylvania is in Mobile County, Alabama;

Alabama is in Genesee County, New York;
New York is in Santa Rosa County, Florida;
Florida is in Houghton County, Michigan;
Michigan is in Osage County, Kansas;
Kansas is in Seneca County, Ohio;
Ohio is in Gunnison County, Colorado;
Colorado is in South Central District, Alaska;
Alaska is in Mineral County, West Virginia;
West Virginia is in St. Louis County, Minnesota;
Minnesota is in Colquitt County, Georgia;
Georgia is in Lamar County, Texas;
Texas is in Baltimore County, Maryland;
Maryland is in East Baton Rouge County, Louisiana;
Louisiana is in Pike County, Missouri;
Missouri is in Brown County, Illinois;
Illinois is in Sequoyah County, Oklahoma;
Oklahoma is in Daviess County, Kentucky.
—*Darryl Francis*

30 MARCH

Ah, Zelda!

Amoral angel,
Bifurcate bawd;
Coyly capricious
Duopod . . .

Eyelids embellished;
Flirtily frocked;
Glittering gewgaws
(Handily hocked) . . .

Impishly innocent,
Jaunty, jejune,
Kissably kittenish,
Loveable loon:

Marry me! Make me
Notably nowed—
Overjoyed . . . osculant . . .
Peacockish proud!

Quinquagenarian
Randily roused;
Skippetyskippeting,
Tenderly toused.

* * * *

Unsanctified
Venus vied
With wanton wick
*Xenogenic;**

Yielding ye,
Zestfully,
Zelda Z.:

Amoral angel . . . (repeat)
—*W.R.E.*

* Xenogenous, really; but I needed the rhyme.

3 1 MARCH

The Mighty Fall; The Rest Just Grow Older

Try as I may, I can think of only two events of world significance that have taken place since 1935. The first is that I have grown forty years older. The second is that the former Emperor Haile Selassie of Ethiopia no longer can enforce such edicts as this one, issued to fight off the invading Italians:

Addis Ababa. Issued by His Highness Heili Selasie in 1935 Conscription Act.

All men able to carry a spear go to Addis Ababa.

Every married man will bring his wife to cook and wash for him.

Every unmarried man will bring any unmarried woman he can find to cook and wash for him.

Women with babies, the blind, and those too aged to carry a spear are excused.

Anyone who qualified for battle and is found at home after receiving this order will be hanged.

APRIL

1 APRIL

Compip, Compoop

Newsmen developed shorthand references for predictable phrases in the speeches of former Governor Wilson of New York. One such, written either COMPIP or COM-POOP, stood for: "The hallmark of this administration will be compassion for people, within a framework of government economy." Mr. Wilson's predecessor, Governor Rockefeller, became known for BOMFOG, shorthand for the "brotherhood of man and the fatherhood of God."

These are nonce acronyms. Snafu is more likely to endure; I don't need to tell you what *that* stands for. But did you know that Mafia abbreviates *"Morte Ai Francesi gl'Italiani Anelo"* (a thirteenth-century Sicilian battle cry);* or that ASS condenses the respected Association of Sociologic Scientists; or that AEIOU, the device adopted by Emperor Frederick III of Austria in 1440, stands for *Archidux Electus Imperator Vivat?*

I pass on a few more acronymic jottings from my daybooks: The letters of some acronyms must be separately pronounced: F.F.V. ("first families of Virginia"); G.P.U. (abbreviating the former name of the Soviet secret police). Other acronyms are pronounced like words: WAC (Women's Army Corps); SWEB (South Western Electricity Board); ENSA (Entertainment National Service Association); jeep (an acronym by sound for G.P., "general purposes" vehicle).

Acronyms can take over existing words. Women's Royal Naval Service is WREN; Defense of the Realm Act is DORA; Electronic Random Number Indicating Equipment is Ernie; National Economic Development Council is Ned. "Clio," the name signed to certain Addison papers in the *Spectator,* was derived, supposedly, from the initial letters of the towns in which the papers were written: *C*helsea, *L*ondon, *I*slington, and *O*ffice.

The *basic* in "basic English" puts together the initials of *B*ritish, *A*merican, *S*cientific, *I*nternational, and *C*ommercial. *Nazi* stands for *Nati*onal-So*zi*alist.

Acronyms from English history:

Hempe. "When Hempe is spun England is done." Brewer says Bacon "heard this prophecy when he was a child, and he interpreted it thus: Hempe is composed of the initial letters of *H*enry, *E*dward, *M*ary, *P*hilip, and *E*lizabeth. At the close of the last reign 'England was done,' since the sovereign no longer styled himself 'King of England' but 'King of Great Britain and Ireland.' "

* But Brewer's Dictionary says it is apparently an Arabic word meaning "place of refuge." No acronym there at all.

Tip. In the eighteenth century, customers, arriving at inns and roadhouses, would hand the waiter coins and a paper bearing the letters *T.I.P.*—"to insure promptness."

Limp. This word, used as a Jacobite toast in the time of William III, is formed from the initials of Louis (XIV), James (II), his wife Mary (of Modena), and the Prince (of Wales). In those days "j" and "i" were interchangeable.

Cabal. Said to come from *C*lifford, *A*shley, *B*uckley, *A*rlington, and *L*auderdale, ministers under Charles II; but actually from Hebrew *cabala,* "an occult theosophy, full of hidden mysteries."

Amectymnuus. The name of this anti-Episcopal tract, published in 1641 in answer to Bishop Hall's Humble Remonstrance, puts together the initials of the authors (with a bit of poetic license): *S*tephen *M*arshall, *E*dward *C*alamy, *T*homas *Y*oung (once Milton's tutor), *M*atthew *N*ewcomen, and *W*illiam *S*purstow.

The following familiar words are real or spurious acronyms:

> ABRACADABRA
> ICHTHYS
> HIP! HIP! HURRAH!
> NEWS
> PAKISTAN

R. W. Charleston wrote to *Playboy* or *Penthouse* or *OUI* or some similar magazine that "In Old England, when two people were convicted of fornication, the bailiff would enter in his book the words For Unlawful Carnal Knowledge. This entry became abbreviated to F. U. C. K. Thence our word." Intentionally or not, Mr. Charleston was pulling his readers' legs; *f---* goes back to the German *fichen*, to strike, and probably even further, to Latin *futuere* and Greek φυτερω.

2 APRIL
∽

A Hundred Words Once

Challenged to write a composition of 100 words without repeating a single word, a high school English class put their heads together and came up with this:

> Let's go! The challenge is to write a composition without using any word more than once. Do you think that it can be done? If not, give one reason for doing this. While we are sitting here in English class at Pompton Lakes High School, Lakeside Avenue, New Jersey, all of us figure out something which makes sense. Mrs. Feldman helps her pupils because another teacher said they couldn't accomplish such tasks. Nobody has fresh ideas right now. Goal—100! How far did students get? Eighty-five done already; fifteen left. "Pretty soon none!" says Dennis O'Neill. Gary Putnam and Debra Petsu agree. So there!

Congratulations to the students of Pompton Lakes High School—and to Pearl L. Feldman, their teacher. Now how about you?

3 APRIL

ᔧ

As I Lay Dying

The last words of James Croll, the teetotalling Scots physicist, were, "I'll take a wee drop o' that. I don't think there's much fear o' me learning to drink now."*

Dr. Croll's farewell fittingly rounded off his life; and I treasure several other death-bed statements for the same reason. Thus Dr. Joseph Green, a surgeon, said to his physician, "Congestion." He then took his own pulse, murmured, "Stopped," and died. As professional to the last was the Swiss physiologist Albrecht, who checked his pulse and said, "Now I am dying. The artery ceases to beat."

Dominique Bonhours, the grammarian, commented, "I am about to—or I am going to—die; either expression is used."

Wilhelm Hegel, the philosopher, also stayed in character. "Only one man understood me," he sighed . . . "and he didn't understand me."

Less admirable, but equally apt, were the last words of Dylan Thomas: "I've had eighteen straight whiskies. I think that is the record."

Asked whether he would prefer to have his niece or his nurse spend the night by his bedside, the playwright Sir Henry Arthur Jones replied: "The prettier. Now fight for it!"

I like Arthur Roth's list of apocryphal last words:

> A judge: "I have no precedent for this."
> A believer in reincarnation: "Intermission time already?"
> A lawyer: "My final brief."
> A mortician: "I'm off on a busman's holiday."
> A childless railroad conductor: "End of the line."
> A philosopher: "No cogito, ergo no sum."
> An atheist: "I was kidding all along."
> A student: "I fail."
> A bridge player: "I pass."
> A gossip: "I'm just dying to tell someone."
> An elevator operator: "Going up?"
> My wife: "I'm not ready yet, give me another five minutes."

---

* He was more flexible than my father, who told me: "At twenty-one I took my first swallow of whiskey. I had heard whiskey was an acquired taste, but I liked that first drink so much I thought it best never to take another." And he never did.

4 APRIL

Anagrams from Punch

For a while I wrote a weekly anagram verse for *Punch*. Then a new editor took over. I am told that he started to hang up his hat, paused, and said to his secretary, "No—first, get rid of Espy."

I still don't see what he could have against verses like these:

ANIMAL FARE

Each beast that in this ****** moos
(Or ******, or quacks, or honks,
    or coos),
Must grace our ******, cleaned and
    dressed.
This shows which beast is ******.

PRE-PARENTAL PLAINT

When I ******* to be a father,
You ******* my willingness to bother.
Now I *******, for I foresee
You'll leave the ******* to me.

A CLERIC OF ANTIC
On a diet to cure him of gripes,
A ****** ate the ****** of ******,
Which altered him oddly;
He was no longer godly,
But a ****** who danced playing the
    pipes.

GASTRONOMICALLY, CRANES ACT COMICALLY

A crane inside a ***** is mewed
To see how cranes ***** to food.
Cooks ***** to his every wish.
The meals are a la *****; each dish
Is flavored* with a ***** of fish.

MAKE THAT GHOST STOP PEEKING, HONEY!

***** tonnere!" bold François cried,
"No ghost shall ***** me from my
    bride!
Who ***** if we make am'rous moans
In ***** haunted by dry bones,
And love where ancient ***** died?"

ROYAL PICK-ME-UP

One ***** *****, swiftly drained,
May make a monarch addle-brained.
But if his queen is feeling grim,
Her ***** ***** will sober him.

—*W.R.E.*

5 APRIL

Berlitz School

A professional linguist complained that I set back linguistics a hundred years by saying a Viennese might mistake the sound of "Donkey field mice" for "Danke viel

---

* *Punch* of course wrote "flavoured."

mals," meaning "Thank you very much." The six verses that follow should set linguistics back at least six hundred years more:

1. "So" 's Italian for "I know,"
   While, in Spanish, it means "Whoa;"
   "Stupid" to the French, I think;
   "Lock" to robber-conscious Chink;
   "Be afraid" in Vietnamese;
   "Face" to Zulus climbing trees;
   To the Fijian housewife toiling,
   "Scrape the skins off yams ere boiling."
   In Japan they have it pat:
   "So," to us and them, 's
                    "Like that."

2. Since One is "itchy" in Japan;
   Since Two is "knee;"
   Since Four is "she;"
   Since Five is "go" . . . pray tell me, man,
   What word is Three?

3. "Who stole the till?" I asked the Swede.
     And he shot back:
   "Who stole the till may err, my friend."
   A Swedish crack.

4. An enthusiastic Russian in the very front row
   Impeded my enjoyment of the horror show.
   Each time I got well horrified, he'd cry, "Oho!
     O horrible, O horrible, O horror show!"

5. The Spaniard called me yellow, so I brought him some ice;
   He muttered, "Meant ta kill ya," and I buttered him twice.
   "Eso si que es!" said he, and quicker than a fox
   I figured out his spelling, and I brought him some socks.

6. A poet spoke in Kenya, at a terrible cost:
   As soon as he said "Simile," the Kenyans got lost.

—W.R.E.

6 APRIL

Biblical Fruitcake

Loretta Harold 'phoned this recipe for fruitcake to Ellen Kimball's talk show in Boston and Ellen kindly passed it on to me:

1. 4½ cups I Kings 4:22
2. 1½ cups Judges 5:25
3. 2 cups Jeremiah 6:20
4. 2 cups I Samuel 30:12
5. 2 cups Nahum 3:12
6. 1 cup Numbers 17:8
7. 2 tbs I Samuel 14:25

8. 6 articles Jeremiah 17:11
9. Pinch of Leviticus 2:13
10. 1 tsp Amos 4:5
11. Season to taste with II Chronicles 9:9
12. Add citron, and follow Solomon's advice for making a good boy
(Proverbs 23:13, 14)

Bake in 300° oven temperature for 2–2½ hours

According to my Concordance, by the way, the Bible makes no mention whatever of lemons. This surprises me. I had always assumed that the fruit offered Eve was really a lemon, not an apple at all.

Returning to the ingredients in the recipe: I count six Bible verses referring to flour; ten to butter; two to sugar (cane); four to raisins; forty-nine to figs, fig leaves, and fig trees; five to almonds; twenty-nine to honey (and nine to honeycomb); seven to eggs (including cockatrice eggs, which might not help the fruitcake); twenty-four to salt; seventeen to baking soda (leaven); and twenty-nine to spices (not counting "spice beds," "spiced wine," and so on).

Use the recipe at your own risk.

7 APRIL

Single-rhymed Verse

SONNET WITH A DIFFERENT LETTER AT THE END OF EVERY LINE*

O for a muse of fire, a sack of dough,
Or both! O promissory notes of woe!
One time in Santa Fe, N. M.,
Ol' Winfield Townley Scott and I . . . but whoa.

One can exert oneself, *ff,*
Or architect a heaven like Rimbaud,
Or if that seems, how shall I say, *de trop,*
One can at least write sonnets, apropos
Of nothing save the do-re-mi-fa-sol
Of poetry itself. Is not the row
Of perfect rhymes, the terminal bon mot,
Abeisance enough to the Great O?

"Observe," said Chairman Mao to Premier Chou,
"On voyage à Parnasse pour prendre les eaux.
On voyage comme poisson, incog."
                                        —*George Starbuck*

* And just one rhyme.

8 APRIL

Spoken like a Native

Here, according to Bob Considine, are the names of a number of countries and cities as pronounced by their inhabitants. See if you recognize them:

1. Pyee-Daung-Su Myanma Nainggan-Daw
2. Sri Lanka
3. Chung-hua Min-kuo
4. Chung-hua Jen-min Kung-ho Kuo
5. Po
6. Vasileon Tis Ellados
7. Lydveldid Island
8. Keshvare Shahanshahiyeiran
9. Daehan-Minkuk
10. Choson Minchu-Chui Inmin Konghwaguk

9 APRIL

O. O. O.

(Of obscure origin, that is.)

What is the provenance of catawampus, conniption, cub, culvert, curmudgeon, dander, dollop, larrup, moniker, moola, mosey, nincompoop, crick? Don't be embarrassed if you don't know; nobody else knows, either.

The following quatrains give clues to two words whose origins are lost:

1. Douse erring wives in clabber, as
    Is Yorkshire farmers' custom.
   Since Yorkshire "a"s are broad, you
       have
   Another word for "bust 'em."

2. Were I the fisher, you the fish,
    You'd find it rather rum
   If I should grind you into bait
    And then should call you "———"

—*W.R.E.*

10 APRIL

Rejection Slips

A manuscript of mine was returned in the mail this morning. It was too specialized, said the editor, adding, "Thank you, however, for lightening our day." Day, hell—he had had it 120 days! Oliver Herford spoke wry truth when he called a manuscript something that is submitted in haste and returned at leisure. A few editors, though, do try to soften the blow. Frank Crowninshield of *Vanity Fair* once rejected a contribution of Paul Gallico's with the following note:

> My dear Paul, this is superb. A little masterpiece! What color! What life! How beautifully you have phrased it all! A veritable gem!—Why don't you take it around to *Harper's Bazaar*?

11 APRIL

Friedan on the Luce

Clare Boothe Luce's birthday falls this week. Herewith my felicitations:

HAPPY BIRTHDAY, CLARE BOOTHE LUCE!*

Unnumbered years ere Women's Lib
Turned into MS both Miss and Madam,
This prototype of Adam's rib
Was ribbing Adam.

When Adam yielded in that war,
Clare tarried nor to gloat nor grieve,
But launched the still more ticklish chore
Of ribbing Eve.

Next, Rome was ribbed by that rib bone
With ribaldry long overdue;
From whence she went to Washington
And ribbed it too.

Upon this birthday, Clare Boothe Luce,
Your subjects raise a glass in trib-
     ute to your unexampled use
Of Adam's rib.

—W.R.E.

Betty Friedan's birthday was in February, but I have written a verse for her anyhow. Here you are, Betty:

SAID BETTY FRIEDAN

Said Betty Friedan
     To Germaine Greer,
"I've met a man
     Who's rather a dear."

"If he's a deer†
     He can't be a man,"
Said Germaine Greer
     To Betty Friedan.

—W.R.E.

* In a minority report, detective story writer Rex Stout said he moved from New York to Connecticut in 1930 because "I didn't want Hamilton Fish as my Representative, so instead I got Clare Boothe Luce." Mrs. Luce, author of the Broadway hit *The Women*, was United States Ambassador to Italy and later a congresswoman.

† Deer and men have this in common: some are muleys, and some wear horns.

12 APRIL

The Subjunctive Rides Again

The subjunctive will soon be as dead as the dodo, the carrier pigeon, and yesterday's newspaper. This has been an article of faith among grammarians for years. "The subjunctive has almost disappeared from English speech," wrote Wilson Follett, "and is retreating, though more slowly, from written prose." Ernest Gowers said, "The subjunctive is dying." H. W. Fowler went further: "The subjunctive," he announced, "is, except in isolated uses, no longer alive."

Well, these distinguished gentlemen forgot to tell the subjunctive. It is as indestructible as dandelions. In almost any magazine or newspaper you will come across subjunctives like these:

"He insisted that Hanoi agree . . ."

"The judge recommended that the convicted man serve fifteen years of his life sentence."

"My doctors' advice is that I not involve myself in any extensive campaigning."

"I advised Senator Eagleton that I have been under intense pressure that he withdraw from the ticket."

"Mr. Mitchell resigned as President Nixon's campaign manager after his wife had issued a public ultimatum that he leave politics or she would leave him."

If the deaths of the dodo and the carrier pigeon are as exaggerated as that of the subjunctive, I might look out my window right now and see those extinct beasts cavorting there.

But yesterday's newspaper is dead, all right.

13 APRIL

Off with His Foote!

Mnemosyne, mother of the muses, was big on memory. It is her fault that many of us still try to recall things as well forgotten, from discontinued telephone numbers to the date of the battle of Hastings.

Mnemonics is the art of reenforcing the memory, generally through associational or rhyming devices. "Spring forward, fall back" is supposed to tell you how to set your clock when daylight saving time comes and goes. We all have been exposed to

> Thirty days hath September,
> April, June, and November.
> All the rest have thirty-one
> Excepting February alone . . .

As Browning said before me, I forget the rest. Anyhow, here is a mnemonic verse for carrying pi (the ratio of the circumference of a circle to its diameter) to twenty decimal places:

PI

Now I sing a silly roundelay
Of radial roots, and utter, "Lackaday!
Euclidean results imperfect are, my boy . . .
Mnemonic arts employ!"

—W.R.E.

But mnemonics can be counterproductive. A Mrs. Hummock gave her church a stained-glass window to commemorate her late husband, and the vicar, to be sure he credited her properly, rhymed her name in his mind with "stomach." It was perhaps inevitable that in his thanks from the pulpit she came out as "our beloved patroness . . . Mrs. Kelly."

The eighteenth-century actor Charles Macklin was reputedly able to memorize any passage at a single reading. But no mnemonic system could help him when Samuel Foote gave him this:

So she went into the garden to cut a cabbage leaf to make an apple pie, and at the same time, a great she-bear coming up the street pops its head into the shop. What! No soap! So he died; and she very imprudently married the barber; and there were present the Picninninies, and the Joblilies, and the Garyulies, and the grand Panjandrum himself, with the little round button at top. And they all fell to playing the game of catch as catch can, till the gunpowder ran out of the heels of their boots.

14 APRIL

A Birthday Song for Medora, of the Sixth Generation to Bear That Name

Medora bore a-
nother Medora
(This story, Medora,
Is true);
Who bore encore a-
nother Medora,
Who opted for a-
nother Medora,

Who raised the score a-
nother Medora.
Now who's once more a-
nother Medora?
It's you, Medora,
It's you!

—W.R.E.

1 5 APRIL

∾

Eve's Legend

In the following, no vowel is used but *e:*

Men were never perfect; yet the three brethren Veres were ever esteemed, respected, revered, even when the rest, whether the select few, whether the mere herd, were left neglected.

The eldest's vessels seek the deep, stem the element, get pence; the keen Peter when free, wedded Hester Green—the slender, stern, severe, erect Hester Green. The next, clever Ned, less dependent, wedded sweet Ellen Heber. Stephen, ere he met the gentle Eve, never felt tenderness: he kept kennels, bred steeds, rested where the deer fed, went where green trees, where fresh breezes greeted sleep. There he met the meek, the gentle Eve; she tended her sheep, she never neglected self; she never needed pelf, yet she heeded the shepherds even less. Nevertheless, her cheek reddened when she met Stephen; yet decent reserve, meek respect, tempered her speech, even when she shewed tenderness. Stephen felt the sweet effect; he felt he erred when he fled the sex, yet felt he defenseless when Eve seemed tender. She, he reflected, never deserved neglect; she never vented spleen; he esteems her gentleness, her endless deserts; he reverences her steps; he greets her:

"Tell me whence these meek, these gentle sheep,—whence the yet meeker, the gentler shepherdess?"

"Well bred, we were eke better fed, ere we went where reckless men seek fleeces. There we were fleeced. Need then rendered me shepherdess, need renders me sempstress. See me tend the sheep, see me sew the wretched shreds. Eve's need preserves the steers, preserves the sheep; Eve's needle mends her dresses, hems her sheets; Eve feeds the geese; Eve preserves the cheese."

Her speech melted Stephen, yet he nevertheless esteems, reveres her. He bent the knee where her feet pressed the green; he blessed, he begged, he pressed her.

"Sweet, sweet Eve, let me wed thee; be led where Hester Green, where Ellen Heber, where the brethren Vere dwell. Free cheer greets thee there; Ellen's glees sweeten the refreshments; there severer Hester's decent reserve checks heedless jests. Be led there, sweet Eve."

"Never! We well remember the Seer. We went where he dwells—we entered the cell—we begged the decree—

'Where, whenever, when, 'twere well
Eve be wedded? Eld Seer, tell!'

"He rendered the decree; see here the sentence decreed!" Then she presented Stephen the Seer's decree. The verses were these:

'Ere the green be red,
Sweet Eve, be never wed;
Ere be green the red cheek,
Never wed thee, Eve meek.'

The terms perplexed Stephen, yet he jeered them. He resented the senseless credence, "Seers never err." Then he repented, knelt, wheedled, wept. Eve sees Stephen kneel, she relents, yet frets when she remembers the Seer's decree. Her dress redeems her. These were the events:

Her well-kempt tresses fell: sedges, reeds beckoned them. The reeds fell, the edges met her cheeks; her cheeks bled. She presses the green sedge where her cheeks bleed. Red then bedewed the green reed, the green reed then speckled her red cheek. The red cheek seems green, the green reed seems red. These were the terms the Eld Seer decreed Stephen Vere.

HERE ENDETH THE LEGEND.

—*Lord Holland*

16 APRIL

Let Her Go

On the dubious theory that the less said the better, I set out to write a love poem in words of no more than three letters. But though I am well known as an idealist, not to say sentimentalist, the poem came out with a disagreeably cynical timbre to it. The next time I go wooing I shall use longer words.

Let her go;	You can get
She is no	A new pet—
Use to you	Let me say
Now.	How:
Do not pay	*For a lie*
For the hay	*You can buy*
Of a dry	*Any new*
Cow.	*Vow.*

—*W.R.E.*

17 APRIL

Hyperbole, American Style

Foreigners tell us that in America even nature hyperbolizes. As you would guess, the passage that follows was written by an Englishman.

When we lived in the American Middle West, things did seem rather larger than life. The summers were sizzling hot, with spectacular thunderstorms, and the winters were below zero. The robins were the size of thrushes, one king-size beefburger was food enough for the family, and the giant economy size of soap powder looked like a five-gallon jerry can. I found it hard to believe that one shop really did sell sixty-four different varieties of doughnut.

The trend, it seems, continues. I have received a kind invitation to a Washington University, St. Louis, Medical Alumni Social Hour. It is from 6 to 8 P.M.

18 APRIL

Clicket, Clicket, Clickman Toad

My attention has been called to a curious volume of eighteenth century colloquialisms, slang, and cant,* including a number to warm the cockles of the heart. "Cockles" itself is an example; to "cry cockles" is "to be hanged; perhaps from the noise made whilst strangling."

The usages least suited to polite society naturally caught my interest first. I liked "apple dumplin shop" for the female bosom, and "bushel bubby" for a particularly full-breasted woman; "bob tail" for "a lewd woman, or one that plays with her tail"; "to box the Jesuit" for masturbation ("a crime, it is said, much practiced by the reverend fathers of that society"); "commodity" for "the private parts of a modest woman, and the public parts of a prostitute;" "face making" for begetting children, and "buttock ball" for amorous congress. Some more detailed definitions:

• *Carvel's ring.* "The private parts of a woman. Hans Carvel, a jealous old doctor, being in bed with his wife, dreamed that the devil gave him a ring, which, so long as he had it on his finger, would prevent his being made a cuckold; waking, he found he had got his finger the Lord knows where."

• *Belly plea.* "The plea of pregnancy, generally adduced by female felons capitally convicted, which they take care to provide for previous to their trials; every gaol having, as the Beggar's Opera informs us, one or more child-getters, who qualify the ladies for that expedient to procure a respite."

• *Clicket.* "A copulation of foxes; and thence used, in a canting sense, for that of men and women; as, The cull and the mort are at a clicket in the dyke; the man and woman are copulating in the ditch."

But to restrict my quotations to the bawdy is to do Captain Grose's compilation a serious injustice. It is ridiculous; it is outrageous; it is packed with astonishing information. If ever I knew, I had quite forgotten, for instance, that the word "bull,"

---

* *A Classical Dictionary of the Vulgar Tongue,* by Captain Francis Grose. It was reissued in 1931 in an edition of 551 copies by the Scholartis Press, London.

for a blunder,* comes "from one Obadiah Bull, a blundering lawyer of London, who lived in the reign of Henry VII; by a bull is now always meant a blunder made by an Irishman."

Another of the Captain's accounts I beg leave to doubt. "Cockney," he says, "is a nickname given to the citizens of London, or persons born within the sound of Bow Bells, derived from the following story: A citizen of London, being in the country, and hearing a horse neigh, exclaimed, Lord! how that horse laughs! A by-stander telling him that the noise was called *neighing,* the next morning, when the cock crowed, the citizen to show he had not forgot what was told him, cried out, Do you hear how the *cock neighs?*"

My favorite definition so far (I am still in the f's) is the following:

• *Clickman toad.* "A watch; also an appellation for a West-countryman, said to have arisen from the following story: A West-countryman, who had never seen a watch, found one on a heath near Pool, which, by the motion of the hand, and the noise of the wheels, he concluded to be a living creature of the toad kind; and, from its clicking, he named it a clickman toad."

19 APRIL

Abigail to Aurora

Certain familiar words—sandwich, lynch, and cardigan, for example—were once proper names. I have collected about a thousand such words, and some day, if I can find a publisher, I am going to present them, with the stories of their origins, in a slim, elegantly designed volume. Meanwhile, as a teaser, I give you a few uncommon, improper nouns starting with *a.* How many of the origins do you know?

Why do we refer to a lady's maid as an *abigail?* A school as an *academy?* A fungus as an *agaric?* A variety of gypsum or calcite as *alabaster?* A type of overshoe as an *alaska?* A twelve-syllable verse as an *alexandrine?* A pale blue color as *alice blue?* A certain flower as *amaryllis?* A stately dance as *allemande?* A strong woman as an *amazon?* A soft velvet hat as an *alpine?* A pungent gas as *ammonia?* A pale dry sherry as *amontillado?* An electric measurement as an *ampere?* A short account as an *anecdote?* A kind of bitters as *angostura?* A tidy as an *antimacassar?* A Paris gangster as an *apache?* A stimulus to sexual desire as an *aphrodisiac?* A handsome young man as an *apollo?* An ornate design as an *arabesque?* A spider as an *arachnid?* Rustic and peaceful as *arcadian?* An antiaircraft gun as an *archie?* A large group of islands as an *archipelago?* A fleet of vessels as an *argosy?* A pheasant with eyelike spots in its tail feathers as an *argus?* A kind of pattern and sock as an *argyle?* A rich tapestry fabric

* See 28 April.

as an *arras?* A type of well as *artesian?* A scarf as an *ascot?* An analgesic as *aspirin?* A political killer as an *assassin?* A kind of lamb fur or skin as an *astrakhan?* A literary club as an *atheneum?* A volume of maps as an *atlas?* A poisonous alkaloid as *atropine?* The part of a building just below the roof as the *attic?* The dawn as *aurora?*

2 0 APRIL

Old Doc

Each word of the following passages begins with the last letter of the preceding word:

Old Doc came even nearer, revealing gold dentures, smiling grimly. "You understand, Delbert, that the extra assistance each hour requires seven, not two, operators," said Doc. "Can't this stop permanently?" "Yes," said Delbert, taking great time enlightening good Doc Carey, "Yes, surely."

—A. Ross Eckler

WINTER REIGNS

Shimmering, gleaming, glistening glow—
Winter reigns, splendiferous snow!
Won't this sight, this stainless scene,
Endlessly yield days supreme?

Eyeing ground, deep piled, delights
Skiers scaling garish heights.
Still like eagles soaring, glide
Eager racers; show-offs slide.

Ecstatic children, noses scarved—
Dancing gnomes, seem magic carved—
Doing graceful leaps. Snowballs,
Swishing globules, sail low walls.

Surely Year-end's special lure
Eases sorrow we endure,
Every year renews shared dream,
Memories sweet, that timeless stream.

—Mary Youngquist

2 1 APRIL

If Longfellow's "The Midnight Ride of Paul Revere" Were Written by Ernest Lawrence Thayer, Author of "Casey at the Bat"

It looked extremely rocky for the Colonists that night;
The British were attacking with no hope of help in sight;

So, with villages in danger from the enemy so near,
They had to send a warning, and they called on Paul Revere.

There was ease in Paul's demeanor as he climbed upon his mare;
There was pride in Paul's expression as he sat so tall and fair;
And then the horse grew skittish, and she gave a sudden jump,
And Paul fell from his saddle, landing smack upon his rump.

With a smile of Yankee courage, Paul rose smartly to his feet,
And once again upon the saddled mare he took his seat;
But as he gripped the reins, she made a sudden turn around,
And once again Paul plummeted onto the dusty ground.

The smile has vanished from Paul's face, his eyes burn with a glare;
He grips the bridle fiercely as again he mounts the mare;
And now he tells the horse to gallop, in an urgent tone,
And now the air is shattered as the horse takes off—alone;

Oh, somewhere in this war-torn land the people safely know
That Redcoats are invading, taking captives as they go;
And somewhere people are prepared to flee the British force,
But there's no hope for New England—

> Paul Revere can't ride a horse!
> —*Frank Jacobs*

22 APRIL

How I Lost the Race With Willy

This is probably Shakespeare's birthday, but nobody knows for sure. Indeed, nobody knows for sure how he spelled his surname; family records show forty-four different versions.

Similarly, no one knows why in my undergraduate days I took for granted that I was to become a second Shakespeare. The only certainty is that I did. I even fell deeply in love with* a girl named Ann Hathaway. The sole flaw in her perfection was that she did not spell the Ann with an e.

Disillusion set in one year when I was studying at—well, attending courses at—the Sorbonne. A young Parisienne of my acquaintance worked for the Sûreté, the Paris police department, as a handwriting expert. At a critical point in our relationship she decided that before matters went farther she should analyze my handwriting. She did, and found that it revealed many excellent qualities. But nowhere in my fist, she declared, was there a sign of creative imagination.

In a race with Shakespeare, a man without imagination would be carrying too

---

* It did not last. She knew from the start that I was no Shakespeare.

much weight, it seemed to me; so I decided to abandon creative writing for journalism and advertising. They are two fields where you need no imagination. You only need to know how to lie.

One Shakespearean reference—just because this *is* probably his birthday. Scholars have long puzzled over a line in Hamlet describing the Dane as "fat and short of breath." Surely no actor has ever played him as a fat man! Comes now Patricia R. Welch and deposes roughly as follows:

> The mystery was solved by a Shakespearean scholar who stopped for a drink of water in a remote area of southern England where something akin to Elizabethan English is still spoken. A farm woman said: "You are fat," meaning: "You are perspiring." "Aha!" said the scholar (who was far from fat): *"that's* what Shakespeare meant, and *that's* why the Queen said, 'Take my napkin, rub thy brows.' Hamlet was sweating!"

2 3 APRIL

The Snail's on the Thorn

Entranced by a tour of English gardens, I resolved to create my own rhododendron-banked croquet lawn at Oysterville. Since I am not there often, the garden has emerged slowly. In the first year I uprooted the gorse and the evergreen blackberry bushes that held squatters' rights on the plot I had selected.* In the second year I uprooted the squatters again. In the third year, as I was about to begin planting, I was reminded that winter tides regularly inundate the plot, and would drown rhododendrons and lawn alike. So I trucked in loam from the marsh to raise the ground level, muttering all the while J. A. Lindon's burlesque:

MY GARDEN

With a Stern Look at T. E. Brown

A garden is a *lovesome* thing? What rot!
Weed plot,
Scum pool,
Old pot,
Snail-shiny stool

In pieces; yet the fool
Contends that snails are not—
Not snails! in gardens! when the eve is
    cool?
Nay, but I see their trails!
'Tis very sure *my* garden's full of snails!

---

* "I" is misleading. J. Harold Clarke, an authority on rhododendrons, designed the garden and selected the plants. Johnny Morehead, with assists from Bob Meadows and Ollie Oman, did the work.

The fourth year came around, and I plowed, disked, harrowed, rolled, dragged, fertilized, and sowed. In the fifth, I found the lawn still to be a concatenation of bumps and hollows, so I scraped off the grass and started all over. In the sixth year— only a few weeks ago—I tipped in the rhododendrons. And this morning I looked out my north window to behold—rhododendrons in white bloom! The sun itself is blooming, albeit in a watery sort of way! I shall stride the countryside today, face to the sky, bellowing this hymn of praise from "Pippa Passes":*

> The year's at the spring,
> And day's at the morn;
> Morning's at seven;
> The hill-side's dew pearl'd;
> The lark's on the wing
> The snail's on the thorn;
> God's in His heaven—
> All's right with the world!
> —*Robert Browning*

One language is not enough on a day like this. I'll bellow in French too:

> L'année est au printemps;
> Le jour est au matin,
> Le matin à l'aurore;
> Le flanc de la colline est imperlé de rosée,
> L'alouette a pris son essor;
> L'escargot rampe sur l'aubépine;
> Dieu est au ciel . . .
> Tout est bien en ce monde!
> —*Translated by Jules Guiraud*

And in German:

> Das Jahr, wenns fruhlingt,
> und der Tag wird geborn
> morgens um sieben,
> der Hang, taubeperlt [sic]
> die Lerche beschwingt,
> die Schecke am Dorn:
> Gott in Seinem Himmel—
> Gut stehts um die Welt!
> —*Translated by*
> *Alexander von Bernus*

* See 28 January.

24 APRIL

Let Stalk Strine

A dictionary of Strine (Australian English), may be out by the time this book is published. It contains 1,800 pages and 100,000 dinkum Aussie words.

The new dictionary is not really needed, though. All the phrases that might confuse you or me are already defined in *Let Stalk Strine,* a definitive study by Professor Afferbeck Lauder, head of the Department of Strine Studies at the University of Sinny. Take a dekko:

A. **Air Fridge.** A mean sum, or quantity; also, ordinary, not extreme. As in: The air fridge person; the air fridge man in the street.

B. **Baked Necks.** A popular breakfast dish. Others include emma necks; scremblex; and fright shops.

C. **Cheque Etcher.** Did you obtain. As in: "Where cheque etcher hat?" or "Where cheque etcher dim pull, son? Where cheque etcher big blue wise?"

D. **Doan Lemmyaf.** I do not want to have to. As in: "Arn jew kids in bare jet? Emeny times die affter tellyer. Now doan lemmyaf to speak dear Ken."

E. **Egg Jelly.** In fact; really. As in: "Well, there's nothing egg jelly the matter with her. It's jess psychological."

F. **Flares.** Blooms, blossoms; e.g., corn flares, wile flares, etc., as in: Q. Wet cheque etta flares? A. Glaria sarnthay. I gom airtat Sairf Nils.

G. **Garbler Mince.** Within the next half hour. Also Greetings. As in: "I'll be with you in a garbler mince," or "With the garbler mince of the Gem of Directors."

H. **Harps.** Thirty minutes past the hour. As: Harps two; harps four; harps tait; etc. Related words are: Fipes; temps; corpse. As: Fipes one; temps two; corpse four.

J. **Jess Tefter; Lefter.** It is necessary to. As in: "She'll jess tefter get chews twit," or "You lefter filner form."

L. **Letty Mare Fit.** Let him have it. As in: "Letty mare fit tiffy wonsit. Zarf trawly zonier kid."

M. **Mare chick.** Effects produced by the assistance of supernatural powers. As: Black mare chick; mare chick momence; "Laugh, your mare chick spell is airfree ware."

N. **Numb Butter; Jessa** (Synonyms). Only. An in: "They're numb butter buncher drongoes," or "He's jessa no-hoper."

O. **Orpheus Rocker.** Psychopathic; neurotic; psychotic; slow; quick; eccentric; absentminded; unstable; excitable; imaginative; introspective; creative; or in any way different.

P. Puck, Charlie Charm. A whimsical character in Strine folklore, about whom many amusing anecdotes are told. Charlie Puck is famous for having introduced the popular sport of sheep-stealing. Mentioned in the national anthem ("Where sat Charlie Charm Puck you've got in your tucker bag?")

R. Retrine. Making an effort. As in: How to speak Strine without retrine.

S. Sex. Large cloth bags used as containers for such things as potatoes, cement, etc. As: sex of manure, corn sex, etc.

T. Tiger. Imperative mood of the verb to take. As in: "Tiger look at this, Reg, you wooden reader battit," or "Tiger perrer spargly guys."

U. Uppendan. To and fro; backward and forward. As in: "She walked uppendan Flinner Street farairs an then she finey got a cabbome to Cannerbry."

W. Would Never. Do not have. As in: "You would never light woodgermite?" or "Ar would never glue."

Z. Zarf Trawl. Because, after all. As in: "Zarf trawl Leica nony doomy Bess," or "Zarf trawl wee rony flesh and blood wennit Saul boiled down."

25 APRIL

A Tired Song of Tired Similes

As mute as a mackerel, darling, I am;
Yet fit as a fiddle, dear, gay as a lamb;
As clean as a whistle, as ugly as sin;
As fat as a hog and as neat as a pin;
As brave as a lion, but deaf as an adder;
As brown as a berry, as mad as a hatter.

While you, my own darling, the love of my life,
Are free as the wind, and as sharp as a knife;
As blind as a bat and as sly as a fox,
As pert as a sparrow, as dumb as an ox;
As plump as a partridge, as red as a rose,
As flat as a flounder, as plain as my nose.

So come, let us marry!—and we shall be twain
As merry as crickets, and righter than rain!
Our days will be brighter than rainbows are bright;
Our hearts will be lighter than feathers are light.
Our love will be surer than shooting is sure,
And poorer we'll be, dear, than churchmice are poor.
                                        —*W.R.E.*

26 APRIL
ᗡ

Little Moron

On my arrival home, perhaps slightly tiddly (this was a long time ago), I noticed there was no light under my door. I remember thinking, "Too bad—he doesn't seem to be back yet." Thus life imitates art; I was being a Little Moron. Herbert Halpert collected the following Little Moronisms:

Two morons joined the cavalry and got horses and couldn't tell them apart; so one said he would cut the mane off his. That was O.K. till it grew back in. So then the other said he would cut the tail off his, and that was O.K. till it grew back in. They decided to measure them by hands then, and the black one was two hands higher than the white one.

•

The little moron wrote himself a letter and when asked what it said, replied, "I don't know; I won't get it until tomorrow."

•

The little moron said he was glad his mother had named him Willy 'cause all the kids at school called him that.

•

The little moron was waiting for a 'phone call and couldn't wait any longer; so he took the receiver off the hook and left a note.

•

The little moron lost his watch on top of a hill, but wouldn't go back for it. He knew it would run down.

•

The little moron wrote letters to his girl very slowly. He said she couldn't read very fast.

•

The little moron went to a show and was asked whether he wanted to sit up in the balcony or on the main floor. He said, "What's playing upstairs?"

27 APRIL
ᗡ

The Inelegant Courtship of Pecos Chuck and Widder Nelly

Joe Julien's grandfather, a storekeeper in cowboy country, was asked to set aside a pair of boots. When two years passed with no sign from the purchaser, Mr. Julien resold the boots. (The pun is inadvertent.) The first purchaser showed up the next day, was informed his boots had been sold out from under him (see how wordplay feeds on itself!), and without a word shot Joe's grandfather dead.

Western movies had made me aware of this violent streak in oldtime cowboys Until Matthew Huston gave me a book about cowboy slang, though, I was unaware that they must also have possessed the filthiest tongues in Christendom. For the verse below I have selected perhaps the least unappetizing of their expressions; but if you have a sensitive stomach, I advise you to skip.

The morning Pecos Chuck set out to nicker fer a squaw
The cows was giving icicles, the weather was so raw.

"Hey, Chuck," says Widder Nelly, "won't you plow my dry weeds under?"
"No ma'am; with one more varmint you could start a school, by thunder!"

"I figger you have just the rake to gather up my crop."
"Yore center's ripe for rakin', but yo're porely at the top."

"The fellers in the grubhouse say I'm purty as a linnet."
"Yore butt must be a gold mine, there's been so much diggin' in it."

They both were gettin' sore now, and they traded crack for crack;
Nell labeled Chuck a "lyin' bean, as talks behind yore back."

"Yo're useless as a horsin' mare," the Widder Nelly spits;
"You'd put yore milk pails under bulls; you'd milk a boar pig's tits!"

"What once you done all night," she says, "you take all night to do.
You're limper than a neck-wrung rooster!"
                                    . . . He says, "Nell, ain't you?"

Them words changed somethin' 'twixt them. Says Widder Nelly then:
"Yo're whiffy on the lee side, Chuck, but so is other men.

I guess our cinches both is frayed, we're draggin' on our rope—
We're old for suckin', mebbe, but not too old to hope.

Don't have your haunches spurred, Chuck, by no farmer's drip-nosed daughter;
They may be cute as heifers, but their coffee's weak as water.

They couldn't teach a settin' hen to cluck inside its shed;
They couldn't find a cow if she was calvin' in their bed.

Now, I've got wrinkles on my horns; I'm smarter than a weasel;
If you was hot as ruttin' elk, I'd still take down your pizzle."

* * * * * *

Then Chuck he cried "A-tisket!" and Chuck he cried "A-tasket!
I bet us two will get along like two pups in a basket!"

And Nelly cried "A-tasket!" and Nelly cried "A-tisket!
Our love will use the hide, the horn, the beller and the brisket!"

And thicker than calf-splatter were that chuckleheaded pair
Till, hanging each from hempen rope, they climbed the Golden Stair.

—W.R.E.

28 APRIL

Bulls from Great Pens

Irish bulls are amusing verbal blunders. No writer, however skilled, is exempt from them. For instance:

> So the *pure limpid* stream, when *foul with stains*
> Of rushing torrents and descending rains.
> *—Addison*

The astonished Yahoo, smoking, as well as he could, a cigar, *with which he had filled all his pockets.*
—Samuel Warren

Every monumental inscription should be in Latin; for that being a *dead* language, it will always *live.*
—Samuel Johnson

> Turn from the glittering bribe your scornful eye,
> Nor sell for gold *what gold can never buy.*
> *—Shakespeare*

> When first young Maro, in his noble mind,
> A work *t' outlast immortal Rome designed.*
> *—Pope*

In his Dictionary, Dr. Johnson defines a *garret* as "a room on the highest floor in the house," while a *cockloft* is "the room over the garret."

29 APRIL

Ecclesiastes and George Orwell, for Instance

Children make a game of finding unfamiliar words for familiar facts, as in "My gastronomical satiety admonishes me that I have arrived at a state of deglutition inconsistent with dietetic integrity." This is supposed to be longhand for "I've had too much to eat."

Adults sometimes play the same game. *Word Ways* turned a familiar proverb into the following incomprehensible stew:

> While bryophytic plants are typically encountered on substrata of earthly or mineral matter in concreted state, discrete substrata elements occasionally display a roughly spherical configuration which, in the presence of suitable gravitational and other effects, lends itself to a combined translatory and rotational motion. One notices in such cases an absence of the otherwise typical accretion of bryophyta.

Sociologists, environmental scientists, business schools, and personnel management experts are perhaps the worst jargoneers of all. What gets into them? Bruce Fraser, editor of Ernest Gowers' *The Complete Plain Words,* thinks they still feel outside the academic community. In their own language, "The indeterminate nature of sociology within the context of academic esteem is probably one of the most pervasive determinants of the linguistic environment within which sociologists must work and their readers' needs must be ignored."

A casebook example of limpid English is this from Ecclesiastes:

> I returned, and saw under the sun that the race is not to the swift, nor the battle to the strong, nor yet favor to men of skill; but time and chance happeneth to them all.

In jargon, said George Orwell, the passage would go like this:

> Objective consideration of contemporary phenomena compels the conclusion that success or failure in competitive activities exhibits no tendencies to be commensurate with innate capacity, but that a considerable element of the unpredictable must invariably be taken into account.

Jargon has been known to produce laughter. In laughter, said George Van Ness Dearborn, a neuropsychiatrist, "there occur . . . chronic spasms of the diaphragm in number ordinarily about 18 perhaps . . . while the skin at the outer canthi of the eyes is characteristically puckered . . . a marked proper flexion of the trunk for its relief . . . the eyes often slightly bulge forwards and the lachrymal gland becomes active . . ."

That passage is not jargon. It is funny because the deadpan scientific terminology is so incongruous with the usual idea of what laughter is all about. But these remarks by Professor James M. Jones, who teaches humor at Harvard, are definitely jargon:

> The relative contribution of motivational and cognitive factors is difficult to ascertain since there is always a covariation of these variables in the humor stimulus. It should, however, be possible to arrange a large set of humor stimuli so that cognitive and motivational aspects of these stimuli are orthogonally represented. If such independence is not possible to create, that would be interesting too.

Could Professor Jones have written this with tongue in cheek? Who has the last laugh here, anyway?

30 APRIL

Why and How I Killed My Wife

I have mentioned before, and expect to again, that pronunciation is a highly personal matter. Like bridge, croquet, and back-seat driving, it may cause arguments between husband and wife. Few of these, fortunately, issue so tragically as the incident described below.

"Nancy," I said, "I would not retail
  Your faults; and yet I cannot fail
To make some mention of a detail—"
  But she corrected me—"detail!"

"My dear," I said, "you're mine, you're
    my Nance;
  You may correct me, when, by chance,
I err with reference to finance—"
  And Nancy smiled and said—
    "finance!"

"Or when," said I, "I fail to fill a straight,
  When undue odds my purposes
    frustrate,
Correct me, if with oaths I illustrate—"
  She shook her head and said—
    "illustrate!"

"Correct my manners or my waggeries,
  But though my accent's not the berries,
Spare my pronunciation's vagaries—
  To that she merely said—"vagaries!"

"Yes, when you dine," I said, "or when
  you wine,

And I grow talkative, why then you
  win,
For you correct my words so genuine—"
  She said with condescension—
    "genuine!"

"Think! Every journey, every sea-tour
  Has end; and every ill its cure;
It's a long road that has no detour!"
  Her only comment was—"detour!"

The blood within my veins ran riotous,
  I cried: "No more shall grammar
    cheat us!
Take from my vengeful fist your
    quietus!"
  She moaned in agony—"quietus!"

I whammed her on the cerebellum
  Her beating brain to overwhelm;
I hung her body on an elm*—
  And as she died she whispered—
    "elm!"

—*Morris Bishop*

* Pronounced ellum, one assumes.

MAY

1 MAY

Acronyms of Ailment

Profanity, obscenity, and violence are slipping into medical terminology and phraseology unobtrusively through the back door of the acronymal abbreviation. When quoted as an acronym, *c*oronary *a*rtery *d*isease becomes an insulting "CAD," *s*econdary *c*arcinoma of the *u*pper *m*ediastinum turns into "SCUM," *t*hyroid *u*ptake gradient transforms into "THUG," and *r*ight *a*trial *p*ressure *e*levation transmutes into "RAPE." Medical papers abound in such vulgarisms as "GIP" (*g*onorrheal *i*nvasive *p*eritonitis), "HOG" (*h*epatic *o*utput of *g*lucose), "IMP" (*i*diopathic *m*yeloid *p*roliferation) and "HOOD" (*h*yperbaric *o*xygen *o*ngoing *d*elivery).

Even if not downright offensive, some acronyms can provoke depression by unpleasant association. "TAX" (*t*ubular *a*scending *x*anthomatosis), "POX" (*p*eriorbital *x*anthelasma), "DUMP" (*d*iffuse *u*ncontrolled *m*onotonal *p*eristalsis) and other abbreviations of similar ilk are hardly conducive to good cheer. Nor do politically tainted acronyms such as "RED" (*r*apid *e*rythrocyte *d*isintegration) and "PINKO" (*p*apillomatous *in*vasive *k*eratosis *o*culi) inspire confidence.

Not all, of course, is in bad taste in the acronymic ambit. There are sweet words like "PIE" which stands for *p*ulmonary *i*nfiltration with *e*osiniophils, friendly words like "AMI" which represents *a*cute *m*yocardial *i*nfarction, or "PAL" which epitomizes *p*yogenic *a*bscess of the *l*iver. "ALAS" (*a*mino *l*evulos *a*cid *s*ynthetase), they are the exception rather than the rule.

—*S.V.*

2 MAY

Where Did That Poisoned Pawn Come from, Mr. Fischer?

Bobby Fischer, the bad boy of chess, was sued by his lawyer for alleged nonpayment of legal fees. The New York *Post*'s headline on the story:

NEXT MOVE IS FISCHER'S

His Lawyer Quits & Seeks Check

Mr. Fischer would not think the chess moves below make sense, but if you translate the symbols into their standard English equivalents you will find that the verse rhymes, and even scans.*

> The match begins; the breaths are bated.
> Will Black resign? Will White be mated?
> White's Ruy Lopez circumvents
> Black's Nimzo-Indian defense.
> Now White (intent) and Black (intenter)
> Maneuver to control the center.
>
> White moves. Too bold? Perhaps from whiskey?
> NxB!?
> Now Black, to plaudits from the ringside,
> Correctly O-O.
> QxQ (White's ranks are thinning)
> !!
>
> The mating net is drawing tight:
> PxP, RxN.
> White, backed against his R wall
> In vain seeks check perpetual.
> Of Q, R, B, P bereft,
> He—to right, he—to left.
>
> *Poor White in Zugzwang sealed his fate;*
> *His Fianchetto came too late.*
> *He pondered a Maroczy Bind,*
> *Could see no future, and resigned.*
>
> —W.R.E.

3 MAY

When Fishermen Meet

Bill Brougher submitted the following colloquy to *Inport,* the in-house publication of the Port of Seattle. Read it, and you will know a fisherman the next time you hear one:

"Hiyamac"	"Cuplours"
"Lobuddy"	"Cetchanenny?"
"Binearlong?"	"Goddafew"

* A. Ross Eckler says, "I doubt that even a chess expert can reconstruct some of the lines you give." Feel free to consult the answers.

"Kindarthay?"	"Fishanonaboddum?"
"Bassencarp"	"Rydononaboddum"
"Ennysizetoom?"	"Whatchadrinkin?"
"Cuplapowns"	"Jugajimbeam"
"Hittinhard?"	"Igoddago"
"Sordalike"	"Seeyaroun"
"Wahchoozin?"	"Yeahtakideezy"
"Gobbawurms"	"Gudluk"
	—Author unknown

4 MAY

I Start My Week with Wednesday

There is only one day of the week I dislike, and that is Tuesday, for the good reason given here:

I start my week with Wednesday, for it is easy to find words beginning with WED—
Well, three: Wed, itself; Wedding, and Wedge. The next day, THUR,
Gives Thurber, as well as two incense-words: Thurible, and Thurify. FRI
Is no problem either—Fricassee and Frizzle are good ones that day—and as for SAT,
Why, there are dozens of SAT words, some rather ugly: Satan, Saturnine, Satyriasis,
    for instance. SUN
Yields Sunder, Sundry, and Sunk, while MON
Is as rich in words as Sat; of these, Money* is my favorite. But TUE
Is a stopper; I know no words beginning with TUE but Tuebor, "I will defend," the
    motto of Michigan, and Tueiron, a pair of blacksmith tongs.
... Which is why I start my week with Wednesday.

                                                                —*W.R.E.*

5 MAY

When B+ = F

In 1940, I applied for work on *Time*. An editor gave me a story to rewrite, and scored me B+. Not aware that a *Time* B+ was the equivalent of a college F, I celebrated by naming my new Scotty pup B+. At this point I had just fathered twins, and B+ wetted on the lap of a white-uniformed nursemaid I was interviewing. One

* See 9 March.

would think nursemaids would be accustomed to such slips, but this one left in a wet huff. One may call an F a B+, but it is hard to pretend that a wet lap is dry.

The art of treating a wet lap as if it were dry is a form of *euphemism*—the lifeblood of social intercourse.

Bulls in my grandfather's time were called male cows. Harlots became fallen women, while breasts, whether fallen or not, became bosoms. Ass was bowdlerized to donkey; castrate to alter; give suck to nurse; go awhoring to go astray; pregnancy to interesting condition; rape to assault. In our own time a Boston newspaper reported that a man "knocked a girl down, dragged her down the cellar steps, beat her with an iron pipe, and then assaulted her."

Spiro Agnew was wrong to call a fat Jap a fat Jap, and to say that once you have seen one slum you have seen them all. Both statements were true enough, but, damn it, a gentleman doesn't talk that way. We prefer to call a poor man "underprivileged," a madman "disturbed," a common man a "gentleman," and syphilis a "social disease."

"Don't call *me* a senior citizen," fumed one reader of *The New York Times*. "Just call me a little old lady."

These euphemisms from school are reported by Peggy Bainbridge:

What the Parent Hears	*What the Teacher Means*
George's social adjustment has not been quite what we hoped.	The kids all hate George.
Debby is overly interested in the work of other children.	Debbie copies every chance she gets.
Bruce doesn't always respect the property of others in the class.	Bruce steals like crazy.
Jane is exceptionally mature socially.	Jane is the only girl in fifth grade with pierced ears, eye shadow, and dates.

6 MAY

Era Uoy a Diamrab?

In back slang, man is pronounced nam and curious turns to suoiruc. A backward boy is a yob, which inspired the first of the two back-slang verses here.

> 1. A DIAMRAB fell in love,
>   and wed her TSEUG.
>   Of all Earth's NERDLIHC
>   Theirs were the TSE.

2. Era uoy sa gnuoy saw I nehw
Etihw metsys eht delb I
Slevon dna esrev gnidaer nehw
Thgir eht morf gnitrats yb

Ma I sa dlo era uoy nehw
Tfereb yllauqe dna
Od I sa neht trofmoc ekat . . .
By reading right from left.
—W.R.E.

I have read that the Tifinagh alphabet, used by the Tuaregs of the Sahara desert, can be written either from right to left or left to right, and vertically either up or down. A sample from "Believe It or Not":

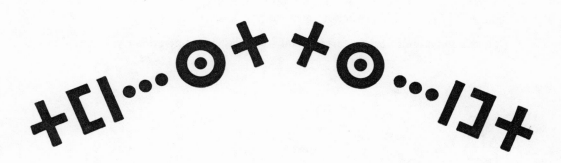

7 MAY

Exception to the Rule

David L. Silverman got to brooding awhile back, and dredged from his mind a paragraph of profundities about rules and exceptions. This is the way it goes:

Is the old maxim true about there being an exception to every rule? Well, no doubt we can all think of rules that appear to have no exceptions, but since appearances can be deceiving, perhaps the old maxim is true. On the other hand, the maxim itself is a rule, so if we assume that it's true, it has an exception, which would be tantamount to saying that there is some rule that has no exception. So if the maxim is true, it's false. That makes it false. Thus we know at least one rule that definitely has an exception, viz. "There's an exception to every rule," and, although we haven't identified it, we know that there is at least one rule that has no exceptions.

I sometimes wish my mind could attain the abstraction of David's. I tend to feel rather than think. This is particularly true in human relations, and most particularly true in my relations with the female of the species. Here I have one special female in mind:

EXCEPTIONS PROVE THE RULE? THEY DO

Exceptions prove the rule? They do;
    But *no* exceptions prove it too;
Though maids have oft held men in thrall,
    Your rule o'er me's exceptional.
There's no exception to the rule
    Of you, the queen, o'er me, the fool.
Yet I the rule's exception prove:
    You cannot rule, except I love.

(There's something Shakespearean about those last two lines, don't you think?)

8 MAY

Poor Paralyze Can't Lift a Finger

Two suffixes undergoing considerable abuse these days are -wise and -ize. Misuse of the first flashes a clear signal that the speaker is no more than half-educated, be he an eighth-grade dropout or the holder of a *summa cum laude* degree. The fraternities of finance and advertising are infiltrated with *-wise*crackers, *-wise*nheimers, and others who do not know a prefix from a suffix: *marginwise,* they say; *saleswise, depreciation-wise, profitwise, losswise, percentagewise.* "Until the rage abates," comments Wilson Follett, "a sensible writer will resort to such coinages in *-wise* only to make fun of them, as S. J. Perelman does when he speaks of *what was going on, prosewise, from 1930 to 1938.*"

So too with *-ize.* Orchestras *concertize;* procedures are *uniformized,* and agreements *finalized.* Let me *emphasize* that there are no such barbarisms in the verse below; the problem besetting the eyeless questioner is that he has no background enabling him to separate the sense of the words from the sounds.

An eyeless beggar at my door
Inquired what Realize are for,
And swore he would not let me by
Till I twelve times had answered Why:

Why Summarize are decked with leaf,
   While Winterize are bare;
Why Legalize prepare a brief,
   While Tranquilize don't care;

Why Malthus dreaded Fertilize;
   Why Sterilize won't sprout;
Why there's no pa for Bastardize;
   Why Vocalize sing out;

Why Idolize don't answer prayer;
   Why Catalyze are dumb;
Why Fossilize give stony stare,
   And Vulgarize chew gum.
                    —W.R.E.

9 MAY

Sticks and Stones May Break My Bones

If this book has a message, Mr. Schulz has caught the whole of it here:

© 1972 United Feature Syndicate, Inc.

10 MAY
∾

Should *She Have The Baby?*

My study telephone rang a few minutes ago. When I answered, a sultry voice, sounding as if spoken by an olive tree, said, " 'Allo, darling?" The following conversation ensued:

Me: Hello—who is this?
Her: It's me, darling.
Me: Are you sure you have the right number?
Her: Of course, darling. Darling—
Me: Yes?
Her: Darling, I'm pregnant.
Me: Oh, really? How nice!
Her: But I'm pregnant by you, darling.
Me: Are you sure you have the right number?
Her: Don't be silly, darling. What do you think—should I have an abortion, or should I have the baby?
Me: Why, I think to have the baby would be very nice, don't you?
Her (something in Spanish, then): What did you say, darling?
Me: I said I think to have the baby would be very nice, don't you?
Her (something in Spanish, then): Are you going to tell your wife?
Me: I don't suppose I have much choice, do I?
Her: Oh, you are cruel! (She hangs up with a bang.)

I swear that is exactly how the exchange went; I wrote it down at once, while every word was still trembling in my ear. What was that girl up to? Though it is true that I was recently in Mexico, it is a long while since I have ventured even to hold the hand of any girl down there. At first I suspected a practical joke. Then her apparently real confusion when I suggested having the baby made me think I might be the object of a shakedown. She perhaps found my name on the mailing list of a massage parlor. I now believe she was so distraught she failed to realize she had dialed the wrong number and was talking to the wrong man. Poor creature.

Hm. Perhaps it's just that I have forgotten. It is curious how these trifles can slip one's mind, once one is no longer in love. Could I have been enamored of some Spanish beauty as recently as . . . say, six weeks ago? I was hopelessly in love for several days with the girl who is the subject of the verse below. Let me see . . . what was her name, anyhow?

WHEN I FOR LOVE OF YOU LAY ILL

> When I for love of you lay ill,
>   Fal-lal-lal-lay,
> You doled out kisses like a pill,
>   Three times a day.
> The kisses cured—whence I deduce,
> In love, placebos have their use;

Or else that any lover
Will nearly die, till some excuse
Permits him to recover.
Fal-lal-lal-lay,
Fal-lal-lal-lal-lal-lay.
—*W.R.E.*

The lightest frost can nip the tender roots of budding love, as we see here:

ON RETURNING YOUR RING

You drove me daft
When you laughed
Both fore and aft.
—*W.R.E.*

11 MAY
〜

"¡Wellcome, to the Caves of Arta!"

"They are hollowed out in the see-coast at the municipal terminal of Capdepera at nine kilometers from the town of Arta in the Island of Mallorca, with a suporizing infinity of graceful columns of 21 meters and by downward, which prives the spectator of all animacion and plunges in dumbness. The way going is very picturesque, serpentine between style mountains, til the arrival at the esplanade of the vallee called 'The Spiders.' There are good enlacements of the railroad with autobuses of excursion, many days of the week, today actually Wednesday and Saturday. Since many centuries renown foreing visitors have explored them and wrote their elegy about, included Nort-American geoglogues." [From a tourist guide.]

Such subtile filigranity and nobless of construccion
    Here fraternise in harmony, that respiracion stops.
While all admit their impotence (though autors most formidable)
    To sing in words the excellence of Nature's underprops,
Yet stalactite and stalagmite together with dumb language
    Make hymnes to God wich celebrate the stregnth of water drops.

¿You, also, are you capable to make precise in idiom
    Consideracions magic of ilusions very wide?
Already in the Vestibule of these Grand Caves of Arta
    The spirit of the human verb is darked and stupefyed;
So humildly you trespass trough the forest of the colums
    And listen to the grandess explicated by the guide.

From darkness into darkness, but at measure, now descending

You remark with what esxactitude he designates each bent;
"The Saloon of Thousand Benners," or "The Tumba of Napoleon."
"The Grotto of the Rosary," "The Club," "The Camping Tent,"
And at "Cavern of the Organs" there are knocking strange formacions
Wich give a nois particular pervoking wonderment.

¡Too far do not adventure, sir! For, further as you wander,
The every of the stalactites will make you stop and say
Grand peril amenaces now, your nostrills aprehending
An odour least delicious of lamentable decay.
Was it some poor touristers, in the depth of obscure cristal,
Wich deceased of their emocion on a past excursion day.
                                        —*Robert Graves*

12 MAY

Finding Your Thing

He said he had liked my poems before all poetry began to give him bad vibrations, and he had dropped in because he happened to be passing by. He was like on the road and he was trying to find himself. In paraphrase, as I soon gathered, that meant his psyche had no time left over for holding down a job. It had its consciousness to expand and its thing to find. Finding its thing was directly related to finding something called "Allness." Not only was it necessary to find both its thing and Allness's thing, but then Allness and its thing had to be related to the psyche's thing.

"On equal terms?" I asked.

"Like flower to sun, man. The sun's bigger and older and way out there and goes on like to infinity. And the flower is only like now, this instant, but in the infinity of the instant they are like equal, like one *from* the other and *to* the other, and *in* the other. Like essence, man. And when this instant is over, right behind it comes another instant as infinite as every other instant. And even if everything now was closed, I mean like without being an infinite, it would still take all of infinity like to think about it, I mean to get really with it."

I had a notion about where all this was leading, but can you ask a man who is arm-wrestling the universe to take a job? "The examined life," I said aloud.

"Oh, wow, yes, man, that's it! Essence! The examined life! Just those three words, but like turning on the lights! A mind-blower!"

"What Wallace Stevens called 'the main of things, the mind.'"

"Go, man, go!"

"A holiday in reality."

"A holy day in ultimate reality!"

"All those slobs out there," I said, "blacking out from nine to five, then home, all

numbed out by habit, too dragged for anything but square togetherness with a mortgage on it. Not an infinite flower to sit to and too late for the sun." I was enjoying
the game.

"No identity, man," he said.

"OK," I said, "I get the picture."

"Man, for a square you get the big picture, and in Day-glo!"

"How much?" I asked.

"Well, fifty?"

"Say again."

"Twenty?"

"I'll take a chance," I said. . . . "You're a flower man; I'll go twenty bucks for a
weeded rose bed."

"But weeding, man," he said, "that's like pulling up life, roots and all! . . . I
mean a weed—that's part of the Allness."

"In the rose bed, alas, it's most of the Allness. We've been away and the weeds
got ahead of us. . . ."

"I can't do it. It's not my thing."

"I thought you were a flower man. Why isn't it your thing to help roses grow?"

"Killing makes nothing grow. How can I reach to Allness with bloody hands?"

"There are always a few scratches, but I'll give you some canvas gloves."

"Man, just give me the twenty and I'll split."

"That," I told him, "is not my thing."

—John Ciardi

13 MAY

Redundance

French wits play a word game called Redundance. The idea is to strip a poem of all
except the last few words of each line, and still retain, or even enhance, its original
sense. I have never seen this game played in English. Here is what might happen
with Hamlet's most famous soliloquy:

> The question:
> . To suffer
> Fortune,
> Troubles? . . .
> . To sleep,
> End shocks?
>
> Consummation: . . .
> To sleep?
> *The rub*
> *May come*
> *Off this mortal coil.*

Respect
Long life,
Contumely,
Delay,
The spurns
The unworthy takes.
Make,
Bear
Weary life.

Of something after death,
Whose bourn
Will have
Of
Us all
Resolution,
Thought,
Moment . . .
Turn awry.
　　　　　　　　—W.R.E.

I am not sure this game works very well in English. Too bad.

14 MAY

Bird and Behemoth

That some words have more than one correct pronunciation is a nuisance when one has to make a choice, but it is a boon for wordplayers. Without that eccentricity of the language, Lord Kennet could not have written:

A BIRD IN THE BUSH

I live in hope some day to see
The crimson-necked phalarope;
(Or do I, rather, live in hope
To see the red-necked phalarope?)

"Behemoth" has not two but three accepted pronunciations, an oddity considered here·

BEHOLD NOW BĒHĔMOTH (BĒHEMŎTH? BĔHEMŌTH?)

Behold now! By the Jordan dreameth
That beast by scholars called bē-hē′-moth;

Though scholars of another cloth
I understand say bĕ'-he-mŏth;
While others still, rejecting both,
Refer to him as bĕ-he-mōth'.

The beast is one, the sound trichotomous;
The fact is, he's a hip-pō-pot'-a-mus.
                                    —W.R.E.

15 MAY

Harpin' Boont in Boonville

Boontling, one of the oldest invented languages in the United States, is a creation of the isolated Northern California hamlet of Boonville, pop. (1969) 1,003. A *Time* report on Boontling is abbreviated here:

> One day in '92, sitting around the Anytime saloon, Reg and Tom Burger and the Duff brothers started putting some of their old Scotch-Irish dialect words together with some on-the-spot code words into a language that the enemies—be they womenfolk, their rivals, their elders, their children—could not possibly understand. It caught on rapidly, losing its value as a code; soon "boontlingers" and their friends were eagerly trying to shark (con) each other with new inventions.
>
> It was more fun to call coffee zeese instead of coffee, because it recalled old J.C., a cook who made coffee so strong you could float an egg in it. Or to call working *ottin'*, after an industrious logger named Otto. To call a big fire in the grate a *jeffer*, because old Jeff Vestal always had a big fire going. To say *charlie ball* for embarrass, because old Charlie Ball, an Indian, was so shy he never said a word. To say *forbes*, short for four bits, and *tubes*, for two bits. To call a phone a *buckywalter* after Walter Levi, known back then for having a phone at home. To say *ball* for good, because the old standard of quality was the Ball-band shoe, with the red ball on the box.
>
> Other words came right out of old Scotch-Irish dialect—*wee* for small, *kimmie* for man, *tweed* for young man, *deek* for look at. Still other words were borrowed from the Pomo Indians, who moved off to a reservation after an early settler set up his general store in the middle of their camping ground. A few words are corruptions of French, like *gorm* (gourmand) for eat.
>
> Then there were the code names for *nonch* (not-nice) subjects. To go to bed with a girl was to *burlap* her, because one day in the 1890s someone walked into the general store, found no clerk, checked the storeroom

and found him making love to a young lady on a pile of sacks. The word caught on, although it got competition from *ricky-chow,* an onomatopoeic description of the twanging bedsprings in the Boonville Hotel's honeymoon suite.

Some of the language was developed to cushion tragedy; everybody feared having their sheep frozen or starved by a sudden change in the weather. That was too big a disaster just to report baldly, so they would say "That frigid perel [cold rain, which resembles little pearls] made many white spots [dead lambs]. There'll be nemer croppies [no more sheep, which crop the grass] come boche season [*boche,* meaning deer, is derived from a Pomo word]."

Now Boontling is spoken by only a minority of Boontners. They have a club that meets every other week in one of the members' houses to *harp* (speak). There are twenty members, though more like two hundred harp and understand. Mack Miller, in his sixties, drives down from Ukiah, a larger town on the coast, "because I'm tonguecuppy [sick] when there's nemer to harp Boont with."

But *codgiehood,* their word for old age, is overtaking most of the Boontlingers. The oldtimers—Wee Ite and Buzzard, and Fuzz and Deekin', Wee Tumps and High Pockets, and Iron Mountain, Skeeter, and Sany—are dwindling. They are saying their last sayings in Boont: "A dom in the dukes is baller than dubs in the sham [bush]." A couple of dude ranches have sprung up in the valley, and just a year ago, for the first time ever, a bank dared open a branch in once-woolly Boonville. The end is near.

—*Timothy Tyler*

1 6 MAY
∽

Schizophrenic Words

Depending on their context, some words change their meanings, even turn them inside out. *Sanction,* for instance, may be either authoritative approval or penalty for noncompliance. If you say I am *imposing,* you may mean either that I am impressive or that I am taking unfair advantage of you. To *stem* from is to develop from, but to *stem* is also to block—that is, to stop the stemming. To *cleave* is either to adhere or to split in two. If you are *fast* you may be quick, loose-living, or tied up; and in the last case you will have to *fast* unless someone comes along to feed you.

Some words have reversed meaning over the years. *Bully** is a bully example. To *ban* once meant to summon. *Let,* meaning to permit, meant to hinder in the old law term "without let or hindrance."

---

* See 24 January.

When you dress a chicken you are removing its feathers, but when you dress yourself you are putting yours on; you trim a Christmas tree to embellish it, but a fat cut of meat to disembellish it; when you trip you may be either moving nimbly or stumbling; "weather" means both to wear well and to wear out; "overlook," both to inspect and to neglect; "cavalier" to be either gallant and gentlemanly, or haughty and ungentlemanly; "to think better of," to like a person better or to like his suggestion less. And both "best" and "worst" mean "to defeat."

"Deduction" as noun form of the verb "deduct" means "subtraction," while as noun form of the verb "deduce" it means "a logical inference." Similarly, "revolution" as noun form of "revolt" means "total change"; as noun form of "revolve," it means "orbital motion about a point."

What does *mean* mean? Well, it means *mean:* "I mean it." It means *mean:* "I mean you're a *mean* man." It means *mean:* "I mean you're a mean man of *mean* estate." And it means *mean:* "I mean you're a mean man of mean estate who hews to the golden *mean.*"

17 MAY

At 39,000 Feet

I am 39,000 feet above sea level, on my way to Boise to see my cousin Joan. My first transcontinental flight, back in 1932, also ended, though inadvertently, at Boise. The Ford tri-motor aircraft left Newark in the morning, but night had caught us by the time we crossed the Rocky Mountains, and the landscape below was washed in brilliant moonlight which left only the canyons as meandering rivers of indigo. Like a rampaging elevator, the Ford tri-motor alternately plunged vertically toward the waiting canyons and shot vertically toward the moon. I took the occasion to hold the stewardess's hand.

The Ford was headed for San Francisco and I for Portland, so at Salt Lake City I transferred to a single-engine plane. I was the only passenger. The night was bitter cold, but by pulling a lever at my feet I could let in warmth from the manifold. The warm air was nine-tenths gasoline fumes, however, tolerable for no more than a couple of minutes at a time. I would let the lever go, the cold would rush in, my hands would begin to tingle and my teeth to chatter, and I would pull the lever again. So it went until, thank goodness, a snow storm over the Cascades forced the flight to abort at Boise, and I took a Pullman the rest of the way.

Ordinarily an airplane flight for me is simply a blank space between what has been and what is to be. Three flights, however, I shall never forget:

• En route from Montreal to Vancouver in 1947, we sat down in Calgary, where a wire from my boss changed my itinerary and I deplaned—the only passenger to do so. The plane proceeded, and vanished in the sloughs around Vancouver. As far as I know, the wreckage was never found.

• Finding it difficult to sleep on overnight flights, I asked my wife to put a sleeping pill in my bag. At takeoff I strapped myself in, took out the pill, called for a cup of water to wash it down, raised it to my mouth, glanced at the pill one last time, and realized I was about to swallow the dog's worm medicine. What a night that would have been!

• In 1954, I flew from New York to San Francisco with my eighteen-month-old son Jefferson. When I opened my bag at the hotel I found on top not the heaps of diapers I had so carefully packed, but a shiny, meticulously folded tuxedo. What must have gone through the mind of the man who had traded bags with me, when he went to put on his dinner jacket and found diapers instead!

With no such lively matters to distract me now, I am free to engage in verbal doodling, like this:

LOVE SONG FROM ONE NEUROTIC TO ANOTHER

Had you been my psychiatrist,
I think we two had never kissed.
You never would have held my hand
Had I been your analysand.

—W.R.E.

Herbert Hoover was honored at the Dutch Treat Club on his eightieth birthday. Asked whether he resented those who had vilified him during his Presidency, Mr. Hoover replied: "You remind me of the minister who asked his congregation whether any of them could honestly say he had no bitterness in his heart toward anyone. One ancient creaked slowly to his feet. 'Ah,' cried the minister, 'how inspiring it is to see a man without malice of any kind! Sir, how did it happen?' Replied the ancient: 'I outlived the sons of bitches.' "

MY AMNESTY TO ALL, EXCEPT . . .

My amnesty to all
The poor, imperfect throng,
Excepting just one pest:
The man who has the gall
To say, when things go wrong,
"I meant it for the best."

—W.R.E.

Though thousands of Americans can brag of relatives high in governmental circles who were jailed in the wake of the Watergate scandals, no one can take from me the fact that my grandmother Richardson's cousin, Albert Fall, as President Harding's secretary of the interior was the very first cabinet official ever to be convicted and imprisoned—all for a puny half-million-dollar bribe. Which goes to show that everybody can find something in his background to be proud of, if he looks hard enough.

THE MAN OF THOUGHTS PROFOUND

The man of thoughts profound resents
Us silly, superficial gents.
We do not care to hang around
The man who thinks his thoughts profound.
—*W.R.E.*

18 MAY

House of Horrors

Here assembled, unscanned, are a number of venereal terms (how apt the collective!) applied to ladies of the night.

He asked, as he had asked before,
How much is horror more than whore?
Do flautists set aside their flutes
And listen when a prostitutes?
He said, who is that lively group
Of laughing ladies on a stoop?
Pray tell me, friends, pray tell me, teachers,
What shall I call the pretty creatures?
Their answers, as such answers do,
Involved subjective points of view:

An orchestra conductor led:
  "A flourish of strumpets, lad," he said.
Another phrase the butcher coins:
  "A pride . . . of loins."

In ringing tones the campanilist knells:
  "A peal . . . of Jezebels."
Responds a teacher of domestic arts:
  "A jam . . . of tarts."

The dietician weighs the giddy bawds:
  "An expanse . . . of broads."
A jeweler assays the self-same maids:
  "A ring . . . of jades."

"To me," said the dancer, "a wiggle of wenches."
  "To me," said the chemist, "a beaker of stenches."
"A cargo of baggages"—such was the guess
  Of Henry, who drives the Railway Express.

(His English teacher said, "Who knows?
An essay of trollops? An anthology of pros?")

He asked, as he had asked before,
How much is horror more than whore?
Do flautists set aside their flutes
And listen when a prostitutes?

—*W.R.E.*

1 9 MAY

Jesus Saves, Moses Invests

Webster's says a graffito is "a rudely scratched inscription, figure drawing, etc." The word is from Italian *graffio,* "a scratching." Most men's-room graffiti reflect sexual and excretory fantasies:

- Merry syphilis and a happy gonorrhea!

The graffiti that recently swarmed over the buses and subway cars of New York City, sometimes beautifully drawn, are mostly initials, street numbers, and gang codes—a way of asserting identity and immortality, like the handprints of motion picture stars in the sidewalk before Grauman's Chinese Theater in Hollywood.

Recorded in some locations are such intellectual scribblings as

Nietzsche is pietsche
But Sartre is smartre.

A visitor to the Caribbean came home with this translation from the French: "Do not throw cigarettes in the pissoir. It makes them soggy and difficult to light."

In the French student revolt of 1968, graffiti provided part of the intellectual and philosophical rationale: "Il est interdit d'interdire," said a scribble on the wall of Nanterre University.

Norton Mockridge, in "The Scrawl of the Wild," put together one of the liveliest collections of graffiti around. These are a few of the messages he has preserved:

- Death is nature's way of telling you to slow down.
- Help a nun kick her habit.
- My mother made me a homosexual.
  (Immediately under this, in a different hand:)
  If I get her the wool, will she make me one?
- Old soldiers never die—just young ones.
- God is dead—Nietzsche.
  (And under it:)
  Nietzsche is dead—God.
- The Lord giveth and the Lord taketh away.
  (Underneath:)
  Indian Giver be the name of the Lord.

- Support your local police station—steal.
- George Washington lives and makes coffee.

Below a scrawl reading, "Legalize mental telepathy!" claims Barbara Huston, was "I knew you were going to say that!"

Seeing on a wall the affirmation, "I love grils," a punctilious fellow scratched out "grils" and substituted "girls." Next day a line had been added: "What's wrong with us grils?"

How could Norton get a whole book out of graffiti when I can barely eke out one page?

2 0 MAY

The Copper and the Jovial Undergrads

One Night three Well-Bred Young Men, who were entertained at the Best Houses wherever they went, started out to Wreck a College town.

They licked two Hackmen, set fire to an Awning, pulled down many Signs, and sent a Brick through the Front Window of a Tailor Shop. All the Residents of the Town went into the Houses and locked the Doors; Terror brooded over the Community.

A Copper heard the Racket, and saw Women and Children fleeing to Places of Safety, so he gripped his Club and ran Ponderously, overtaking the three Well-Bred Young Men in a dark part of the Street, where they were Engaged in tearing down a Fence.

He could not see them Distinctly, and he made the Mistake of assuming that they were Drunken Ruffians from the Iron Foundry. So he spoke harshly, and told them to Leave Off breaking the Man's Fence. His Tone and Manner irritated the University Men, who were not accustomed to Rudeness from Menials.

One Student, who wore a Sweater, and whose people butt into the Society Column with Sickening Regularity, started to Tackle Low; he had Bushy Hair and a Thick Neck, and his strong Specialty was to swing on Policemen and Cabbies.

At this, his Companion, whose Great Grandmother had been one of the eight thousand Close Relatives of John Randolph, asked him not to Kill the Policeman. He said the fellow had made a Mistake, that was all; they were not Muckers; they were Nice Boys, intent on preserving the Traditions of dear old *Alma Mater*.

The Copper could hardly Believe it until they led him to a Street Lamp, and showed him their Engraved Cards and Junior Society Badges; then he Realized that they were All Right. The third Well-Bred Young Man, whose Male Parent got his Coin by wrecking a Building Association in Chicago, then announced that they were Gentlemen, and could Pay for everything they broke. Thus it will be seen that they were Rollicking College Boys and not Common Rowdies.

The Copper, perceiving that he had come very near getting Gay with our First

Families, Apologized for Cutting In. The Well-Bred Young Men forgave him, and then took his Club away from him, just to Demonstrate that there were no Hard Feelings. On the way back to the Seat of Learning they captured a Night Watchman, and put him down a Man-Hole.

Moral: *Always select the Right Sort of Parents before you start in to be Rough.*

—George Ade

21 MAY

Measure for Measure

THE I-DON'T-CARE SCALE

2 jots	=	1 tittle
3 tittles	=	1 continental
2 continentals	=	1 tinker's dam
4 tinker's dams	=	1 damn

POLITICAL OPPONENT'S MEASURE

2 nincompoops	=	1 fathead
2 fatheads	=	1 incompetent
3 incompetents	=	1 opportunist
2 opportunists	=	1 machiavelli

LINEAR MEASURE

2 hops	=	1 skip
2 skips	=	1 jump
24 jumps	=	1 stone's throw
3 stone's throws	=	1 piece
12 pieces	=	1 way-the-hell-and-gone

ALCOHOLIC BEVERAGE MEASURE

2 fingers	=	1 tot
2 tots	=	1 shot
2 shots	=	1 slug
4 slugs	=	1 snootful
2 snootfuls	=	1 night in jail

APPLAUSE SCALE

2 salvos	=	1 accolade
2 accolades	=	1 triumph
3 triumphs	=	1 ovation (sitting)
4 ovations	=	1 lionization
2 lionizations	=	1 outtasight

ALTERCATION SCALE

2 tussles	=	1 fray
3 frays	=	1 fracas
2 fracases	=	1 skirmish
2 skirmishes	=	1 fight

PAPRIKA MEASURE

2 dashes	=	1 smidgen
2 smidgens	=	1 pinch
3 pinches	=	1 soupçon
2 soupçons	=	too much paprika

HISTORICAL INVECTIVE SCALE

2 scamps	=	1 rascal
3 rascals	=	1 knave
2 knaves	=	1 varlet
4 varlets	=	1 scoundrel
2 scoundrels	=	1 charlatan

—Joe Ecclesine

22 MAY

Like Hell We'll Pray for Him!

Language almost doesn't mean anything anymore. (A recent guest in the Senate remarked, "The only person I understood during the whole afternoon was the guard at the door who said, 'Take your hat off!' ")

And foggery can even lead to fame! Mention Ezra Pound and you'll hear, "A great talent." Here's a sample of it:

SUBILLAM

Cumis ego occulis meis
sleeping under a window:
  pray for me,
withered to skin and nerves
  tu theleis
respondent illa
apothanein; pray for me gentlemen.

Like hell we'll pray for him, at least not until he sticks to one language at a time.

—*J. M. Hickerson*

23 MAY

Four Kate, Won Eye a Door

You may wonder whether the verses below are composed of homophones or homonyms, but don't ask me. I can't tell the difference.

ANT SONG

Necks tweak coffer mere Rome ants
Holed mead ants and ants and ants
Ants sir ants sir ants Urdu
Lettuce turnip pay sore too.

ANN DREW

Ann drew ann drew ann drew drew ann
Ann drew drew ann ann drew ann drew

A CYST ME TWO

A cyst me two purse you ewe Kate;
My cent tea meant four yew is grate.

My heart is melon colic, Kate;
Ah, wood that eye mite German eight
In ewe all so this can't sir, Kate!
Ah, wood that eye mite in cull Kate
Eye doll a tree of me in Kate!
When icey yew my I's die late.
Yet ewe a peer in viol eight;
Two know a veil do eye play Kate
Ewe Kate.
My purr puss four yew eye reel late
And men shun how eye dale lea weight
Four ewe bee four yore man shun gait;
But this a noise ewe, four yew hate
Roam ants, deer Kate.
In cents eight oh pals chorus Kate
And sin till late
Know more than ewe, in hew man Kate.
Die earn a lee eye sup lick Kate
Ewe Kate,
My car is mat tick Kate.
O Kate, a bait
My sore did state!
Deep lore my fate!
Come Munich Kate
Affect shun, Kate!
Bee knot can tanker us, deer Kate—
Cap it you late!
Say yew will bee my candy date
For mat tree moan knee all estate.
Prey, ant sir, Kate!

KNOT TWO KNOT FOUR WON EYE A DOOR

'Tis not a miss a miss two fined
With prom miss sinner glance, sir;
If miss with miss stir bee come bind,
Then miss chief is the ant, sir.

Alas two idle eyes ice ought
In sum seek lewd dead sex shun;
The no bull ass a lass wood knot
Axe seed too my affect shun.

If few sum made den wood a choir
She may a void dew wall so;
All ads are freak went lea a fire,
All asses soft tar fall so.

—W.R.E.

2 4 MAY

Words with One Syllable Work

I propose shortly to put in a few long words for long words.* Now, however, I present the case for words of one syllable:

> When you come right down to it, there is no law that says you have to use big words when you write or talk.
>
> There are lots of small words, and good ones, that can be made to say all the things you want to say, quite as well as the big ones. It may take a bit more time to find them at first. But it can be well worth it, for all of us know what they mean. Some small words, more than you might think, are rich with just the right feel, the right taste, as if made to help you say a thing the way it should be said.
>
> Small words can be crisp, brief, terse—go to the point, like a knife. They have a charm all their own. They dance, twist, turn, sing. Like sparks in the night they light the way for the eyes of those who read. They are the grace notes of prose. You know what they say the way you know a day is bright and fair—at first sight. And you find, as you read, that you like the way they say it. Small words are gay. And they can catch large thoughts and hold them up for all to see, like rare stones in rings of gold, or joy in the eyes of a child. Some make you feel, as well as see: the cold deep dark of night, the hot salt sting of tears.
>
> Small words move with ease where big words stand still—or worse, bog down and get in the way of what you want to say. There is not much, in all truth, that small words will not say—and say quite well.
>
> —*Joseph Ecclesine*

2 5 MAY

Time on Your Feet

Russell Baker once entered a bill of particulars against clichés connected with time. Why, he asked, should time not hang light on one's feet, instead of heavy on one's hands? Try one's body, instead of one's soul? Run long, instead of short, and in, instead of out? Jump up and down noisily instead of standing still? Bus or drive, instead of flying? Why is time money, but never credit? Ripe, but never green? Why does one have the time of one's life, but never of one's day or week? Why does one

* See 5 July.

arrive in the nick of time, but never in the slash? And is not time not just the great healer but the great sickener of all things?

26 MAY
∽

Foot-Notes

What! Never heard of Edward Edwin Foot, poet laureate of Her Majesty's customs? Why, the footnote was named after him—or should have been. "No English poet before or since," assert two of his bedazzled admirers, "has ever taken such pains to make his meaning clear and to guarantee the authenticity of his statements. As one example out of a hundred we may take his poem on the Lover's Leap, the beauty-spot on the Dart, which the Prince Consort visited in 1852. The Prince, sings the poet:

> —— turned around anew
> And bade the lovely spot adieu,
> Expressing pleasure at the glorious scene.

"To which he adds in a footnote: 'This is stated on the authority of Mr. G. Sparkes, of Ashburton, who had the honour of conducting His Royal Highness and suite through this part of the journey.'"

Two more examples of Foot's footling:

DISASTER AT SEA

> The captain scans the ruffled zone,[1]
>   And heeds the wind's increasing scope;
> He knows full well, and reckons on
>   His seamanship, but God's his hope . . .
>
> Look, look ye down the plumbless deep,
>   See,[2] if ye can, their lifeless forms!—
>
> Here laid, poor things! across a steep,
>   An infant in its mother's arms;
>
> There, it may be, a man and wife,
>   (Embracing either now as when
> They went to rest, at night, in life)
>   Are resting in a turbid glen.

[1] A figurative expression, intended by the Author to signify the horizon.
[2] Imagine.

A LISP IN NUMBERS

Altho' we[3] mourn for one now gone,
And he—that grey-haired Palmerston,[4]
We will give God the praise,—
For he, beyond the age of man,[5]
Eleven years had over-ran
Within two equal days.

27 MAY

Mark Twain's Portuguese Find

New Guide of the Conversation in Portuguese and English, a classic of translation, was discovered a hundred years ago by Mark Twain. "One cannot open this book anywhere and not find richness," said Twain. "To prove that this is true, I will open it at random and copy the page I happen to stumble upon."

Here is what he copied:

DIALOGUE 16

FOR TO SEE THE TOWN

Anthony, go to accompany they gentilsmen, do they see the town.

We won't to see all that is it remarquable here.

Come with me, if you please, I shall not folget nothing what can to merit your attention. Here we are near to cathedral; will you come in there?

We will first to see him in oudside, after we shall go in there for to look the interior.

Admire this master piece gothic architecture's.

The chasing of all they figures is astonishing indeed.

The cupola and the nave are not less curious to see.

What is this palace how I see youder?

It is the town hall.

The streets are very layed out by line and too paved.

What is the circuit of this town?

Two leagues.

---

[3] The nation.

[4] The Right Honourable Henry John Temple, Viscount Palmerston, K.G., G.C.B., etc. (the then Premier of the British Government), died at "Brockett Hall," Herts., at a quarter to eleven o'clock in the forenoon of Wednesday, 18th October, 1865, aged eighty-one years (all but two days), having been born on the 20th October, 1784. The above lines were written on the occasion of his death.

[5] Scriptural limitation.

There is it also hospitals here?
It not fail them.
What are then the edifices the worthest to have seen?
It is the arsnehal, the spectacle's hall, the Cusiom-house, and the Purse.
We are going too see the others monuments such that the public pawn-broker's office, the plants garden's the money office's, the library.
That it shall be for another day; we are tired.

DIALOGUE 17

TO INFORME ONE'SELF OF A PERSON

How is that gentilman who you did speak by and by?
Is a German.
I did think him Englishman.
He is of the Saxony side.
He speak the french very well.
Though he is German, he speak so much well italyan, french, spanish and english, that among the Italyans, they believe him Italyan, he speak the french as the Frenches himselves. The Spanishmen believe him Span-ishing, and the Englishes, Englishman.
It is difficult to enjoy well so much several languages.

28 MAY
∽

Kind of Four of a Kind

I suppose it is too much to expect day-and-night adulation. There must be some brief moment when somebody says to himself that even Richard Nixon was not perfect; can Willard Espy be? I hear overtones of such criticism:

THEY SAY

They say though I'm
A rhyming man,
From time to time
My verse don't scan;

And what is worse,
From time to time
They say my verse
Don't even rhyme.

I can reply to these cynics only that when I was seven or eight years old, a verse of mine opposing bolshevism was printed in the county paper. I even remember that it rhymed "stitches" with "ditches." And surely I have improved since then. I must admit, though, in the doggerel hereunder the improvement is not striking:

1.   ## FOR THE GRAVESTONE OF THE LATE
        ## JOHN SHALLOW, ESQ.

When young, preferring books to sleep,
    I read by midnight tallow;
My teachers said that I was deep,
    But I knew I was Shallow.

When old, I lay till sunrise cheep
    Awaiting Death's low hallow.
The grave that holds me now is deep,
    And I no longer Shallow.

2.   ## WHEN HOMER SMOTE THE STRINGS

When Homer smote the strings, and told
    Of men and gods on fire,
The stable boys yelled, "Hear that old
    Blind liar beat that lyre!"

3.   ## A VERY CLEVER COMMENT

How very clever you would be
    If you were cleverer than me!
And I'd be very clever too
    If I were cleverer than you.

4.   ## WILLIAM'S DECLINE

At twenty-one or such
    Of William Little, lover,
No girl could ask too much,
    For he was stuffed with clover.

Now, sixty winters through him
    And snow along his jaw,
Their first wink would undo him,
    For William's stuffed with straw.
                            —W.R.E.

29 MAY

Echoing Sentence, Echoing Rhymes

One can play on the echoing quality of words in a number of ways. In this sentence from *Word Ways,* the first syllable of each word repeats the last syllable of the word preceding it·

Jackson's sons are Arthur (thirsty!), Steven (vender), Dermot (motors), Orson (on air), Errol, Roland and Andrew.

Other echoes:

GO WEST, YOUNG MAN!

Go west, go west! And when thou goest,
Take west my low esteem—my lowest!
Owe west of here the bills thou owest!
Throw west of here the bull thou throwest!
No estimable man thou knowest
But joins me in, "Go west, pest! *Go* west!"

—*W.R.E.*

DYNASTIC TIFF

Oh I am the King of Siam, I am!
  With cunning I rule from Bangkok!
The King of Bagdad is a sham, a sham,
While *I* am the King of Siam. (I am.)
All others I gladly goddam, Goddam
  The worthless contemptible flock!
Oh, I am the King of Siam, I am!
  With cunning I rule from Bangkok.

Oh I am the King of Bagdad, egad!
  To Hell with the King of Siam!
His ruling is merely a fad, a fad,
While *I* am the King of Bagdad, egad!
His manners, moreover, are bad, quite bad,
  What can you expect from a ham?
Oh I am the King of Bagdad, egad!
  To Hell with the King of Siam!

—*Geoffrey Hellman*

JUST DROPPED IN

*Secretary of State John Foster Dulles conferred today with Burmese Premier U Nu.
He said later he had come here neither to woo neutral Burma nor to be wooed. . . .
His reception was studiously polite.*—The New York Times.

He did not come to woo U Nu,
And there wasn't much of a state to–do,
And they sat around and talked, those two,
And there isn't a doubt that they mentioned Chou.

When reporters asked, "A political coup?"
He waved them aside with a light "Pooh-pooh."
But he didn't just come to admire the view,
Which he certainly knew *you* knew, U Nu.

—*William Cole*

30 MAY

Eletelephony

I reached my apogee at the age of six. Nothing was beyond my power then, though I did have a little difficulty tying my shoe laces in a double bow. I was delighted to be no longer five, and had no desire to become seven. I knew that once seven I'd wish to be eight, and so on until the tide turned, so that at thirty I'd prefer to be only twenty-nine.

There is no age to match six, and there is no verse to match a six-year-old-oriented verse like this one:

> Once there was an elephant,
> Who tried to use the telephant—
> No! No! I mean an elephone
> Who tried to use the telephone—
> (Dear me! I'm never certain quite
> That even now I've got it right.)
>
> Howe'er it is, he got his trunk
> Entangled in the telephunk;
> The more he tried to get it free,
> The louder buzzed the telephee—
> (I fear I'd better drop the song
> of elephop and telephong!)
> —*Laura Elizabeth Richards*

31 MAY

Curtailed Words

We tend to shorten some words as they become old chums, just as William, once we know him better, becomes Bill. Some of these curtailed words, says Fowler, "establish themselves so fully as to take the place of their originals or to make them seem pedantic; others remain slangy or adapted only to particular audiences." The jingle below contains several of each sort.

DEAR PERAMBULATOR, HOW THIN YOU'VE GROWN!

> Do you recall, as I do,
>   When words before anointment
> Were weighed upon a hay-scale
>   To prove their embonpointment?

When words, like Gibson girls, were
  Strategically plump,
And won their beauty contests
  By girth of bust or rump?

Ah, how I loved to watch them
  Come waddling down the lane:
Quadrangle! Mobile Vulgus!
  Fanatic! Aeroplane!

And *Zoologic Garden!*
  Stenographer! Raccoon!
Stool Pigeon! Schizophrenic!
  Detective! Pantaloon!

Vice President! and *Doctor!*
  Biopsy! Autobus!
Professional! And *Mamma!*
  And *Stradivarius!*

Tricycle and *Bicycle,*
  Perambulator too,
And even *Spatterdashes*
  Hove grandly into view.

* * *

But now the style's to diet;
  The pounds fall one by one;
Lo! yesterday's Fat Lady's
  Today's Live Skeleton:

The gaunt high-fashion model,
  The wraith of a gazelle;
What's in is see-through costumes
  And see-through words as well.

Fan, Mob, Quad, Dick, and *Stooly;*
  Plane, Steno, Zoo, and *Bike;*
Coon, Pants, Pro, Bus, and *Bio;*
  Zoo, Doc, Ma, Strad, and *Trike.*

Dear, plump *Perambulator*
  Has shrunk to *Pram,* and what
Remains of *Spatterdashes?*
  For me, one lonely *Spat.*
                              —W.R.E.

JUNE

1 JUNE

Menu Madness

WASHINGTON—Al, Nick, Pete, and Quentin went to an expensively decorated restaurant for lunch. The food was just as expensive as the décor and almost as tasty.

"The chef here isn't much," Al confided as they sat down, "but they've got the best menu writer on the East Coast. It cost them a fortune to hire him. He'd been in New York writing book-jacket blurbs for Gothic novels."

A waiter took their drink orders, distributed four menus, and departed.

After studying his menu a few minutes, Nick said he was thinking of ordering the tender chunklets of milk-fed veal, lovingly dipped in the slightest hint of aromatic herb sauce and served in an iron casserole rushed fresh from the famed forges of France.

"That's a little too metallic for my literary taste," Al said. "Personally, I recommend the lumps of luscious backfin crabmeat delicately wrapped in light French crêpes to retain the sealed-in flavors and savory juices, baked and covered with sauce Mornay in a delightful sprinkling of parmesan cheese redolent with memories of sunny Naples."

Pete said he was watching his weight, but found it hard to resist the refulgent green lightness of gelatine quivering on an emerald bed of crisp crunchy lettuce born of the mating between sparkling sunshine and cool, clear water in the golden valleys of old California.

Quentin said he didn't see anything on the menu that didn't need editing and thought he'd just have a hamburger, medium rare.

"You can't just ask for a hamburger in a place like this," Al whispered.

"The author would be insulted," said Nick.

"In France, where food really counts for something," said Pete, "men have been shot for less."

"I want a hamburger!" insisted Quentin, who tended to stubbornness. "Medium rare."

"Quent, old boy," said Al, "why not try the Seafood Symphony?"

"Because," said Quentin, consulting the menu, "I don't want succulently clustered clumps of crabmeat, jumbo shrimp, tender lobster meat and fresh saltwater fish sautéed in butter with mushrooms and shallots, blended with thick luscious cream and flavored with shimmeringly shadowed sherry wine to create a symphony in seafood, served in casserole."

The waiter, noting tensions at the table, eased within eavesdropping range.

"Have a Cowpuncher's Dream," urged Nick.

"No steaks," said Quentin.

The waiter, who had overheard, came over. He was miffed.

"Our waiters do not traffic in steak," the waiter said. "Steak is for illiterates."

This put Quentin's back up. "I demand to see the author," he said.

Some time later an overpaid man stuffed with succulent juicy adjectives presented himself. "Hamburger?" he repeated.

"Hamburger," said Quentin. "Medium rare."

The writer wandered to the water cooler, washed his hands, looked up the weather report, made some unnecessary phone calls, looked at his tongue in a mirror for symptoms of fatal disease and, when he had at last exhausted methods of killing time, went to his typewriter.

Returning to Quentin, he asked, "Is the creation you have in mind a magnificently seared thickness of sizzling goodness that has been reduced by grinders of rarest Toledo steel to mouth-watering palate-tantalizers of Kansas City beef beaded with rich ruby globules served on a farm-fresh roll and laced lavishly with great oozing lashings of rarest mustards and onions from faraway Spain?"

"Enough! Enough! Stop!" cried Quentin. "I can't listen to another bite."

The menu writer smiled in triumph and left. The waiter returned. "Are you gentlemen ready to order?" he asked.

"Yes," said Al. "Four coffees."

"And," said Nick, "send our compliments to the author."

Quentin burped with contentment.

—*Russell Baker*

2 JUNE
∾

Shiver, Tickle, Sneeze

On certain subjects I am a frozen Conservative—what you might call an Ill Liberal. I believe, for instance, that my seven-year-old grandson has not thought twice, or even once, about orgasms, unless his parents discuss them in his presence, which is unlikely. Yet I have before me a full-page advertisement for a children's book on sex which says, *inter alia:* "How should you explain an orgasm to your seven-year-old child? Compare it with a shiver, a tickle, or a sneeze."

So that's all it amounts to! My darling, I hasten to pass the word along:

> Shiver, tickle, sneeze . . .
> Which of these
> Fuses me to you?
> Achew!

Tickle, sneeze, shiver . . .
  When the planets quiver,
What doth then occur?
  Brrr!

Shiver, sneeze, tickle . . .
  Muckle now is mickle.*

See the lovers wriggling . . .
  Giggling.
                    —W.R.E.

3 JUNE

Haiku Prove I.Q.

The Japanese haiku is a verse-form consisting of seventeen syllables—five each in the first and third lines, seven in the second—to which the reader adds his own associations and imagery. Here is one:

Oh! I ate them all
And oh! What a stomachache—
Green stolen apples!
                    —Shiki

I have few associations to add to haikus (you will see in a moment my reason for spelling the plural variantly), so I am not particularly fond of them. Or I was not until I discovered this splendid American example:

THE TRADITIONAL GRAMMARIAN AS POET

Haiku, you ku, he,
She, or it kus, we ku, you
Ku, they ku. Thang ku.
                    —Ted Hipple

Now, there, I said to myself, is a haiku that is worthwhile. And if Ted Hipple can do it, so can I:

Haikus show I.Q.'s.
High I.Q.'s like haikus. Low
I.Q.'s—no haikus.†
                    —W.R.E.

---

* Fowler says "muckle" is simply a variant of "mickle." As far as I am concerned, many a mickle still makes a muckle.
† William Cole says it's the other way around.

4 JUNE

A Cat's a Cat for A' That

"The name for cat is the same in most languages," says V. Sackville-West; "it is really difficult to believe that cat should be *cattus* in Latin, *katts* in Byzantine Greek, *katt* in Saracenic, *katti* in Finnish, *cath* in Welsh and Cornish, and just plain *cat* in Gaelic." A cat is likewise *Katze* in German, *chat* in French, and *gato* in Spanish.

In some ways cats seem to be more interwoven with humans than dogs are. We say "Scat!" for "Get away, cat!" Why don't we say "Sdog!" for "Get away, dog"? *

A writer for the lamented "Topics" column of *The New York Times* caught the ambivalence of mankind's attitude toward cats in a bloodcurdling little tale, the original of which I have long since lost. Denying that he either idolized or anathematized the creatures, he insisted that he only wished to sweep away the superstitions about them. "One of these superstitions," he said (in effect), "is that cats always land on their feet. Now the last thing I do before going to bed is to toss my cat down the cellar steps, and I have discovered that by giving it a certain twist I can make it land on its head every time."

5 JUNE

When Baby Gurgles Guam and Georgia

Two-letter abbreviations for all states of the United States were introduced only in 1963, and I am not used to them yet. So I quickly lost the thread this morning when I heard the Oysterville postmistress singing, as she popped the letters of the day into their boxes, something that sounded like this:

When baby gurgles GUAM and GEORGIA,
Then how I NEVADA baby's PENNSYLVANIA,
ARIZONA slapping NEBRASKA with loud huzzah
He sings INDIANA KENTUCKY OREGON cries, "Hurrah!
MICHIGAN tad's OKLAHOMA OHIO tra LOUISIANA LOUISIANA!"

---

* Said Sidney Smith: "A lady asked me once for a motto for her dog Spot. I proposed, 'Out, damn Spot,' but strange to say she did not think it sentimental enough."
  Said David McCord:

> Shoo to a fly,
> Scat to the cattypus.
> What is the cry
> For a duckbill platypus?

But when the sound is WASHINGTON WASHINGTON WASHINGTON
He loudly shouts, "Where ARKANSAS you MASSACHUSETTS?
Our ALASKA is ILLINOIS OHIO pish OHIO bah!
The MARYLAND's off at baccarat!
OHIO MASSACHUSETTS go HAWAII you INDIANA our cah
And fetch him to MAINE, near OREGON fah!"
Then I don't NEVADA PENNSYLVANIA at a'.

"But that makes neither meter nor sense," said I.
"It certainly does," said the postmistress; "here, I'll write it out for you."
This is what she wrote:

> When baby gurgles GU and GA,
> Then how I NV baby's PA,
> AZ slapping NE with loud huzzah
> He sings IN KY OR cries, "Hurrah!
> MI tad's OK OH tra LA LA!"
> But when the sound is WA WA WA
> He loudly shouts, "Where AR you MA,
> Our AL is IL, OH pish, OH bah!
> The MD's off at baccarat!
> Oh MA go HI you IN our cah
> And fetch him to ME, near OR fah!"
> Then I don't NV PA at a'.
>
> —W.R.E.

6 JUNE

Now Here We Are Alone, My Dear

The insertion or deletion of a space or two changes some phrases remarkably—often for the worse. Or spelling and sense may change without changing sound, as in J. A. Lindon's

> Healthy parlourmaid's inconstancy:
> Hell, the parlour made sin constant, see?

A typesetter corrupted Leo Rosten's innocent "therapists say" to "the rapists say." Dmitri Borgmann mused that if a boy and girl were *amiable together,* the boy might wonder, "Am I able to get her?"

The answer to Mr. Borgmann, if we can trust the verse that follows, is "no."

> *Now here* we are alone, my dear,
> With none to spy or interfere.
> But where's a kiss to show you care?
> *Nowhere.*

You still pretend you find *bed evil*
Beyond retrieval?
Forget such bedside prudishness!
Bedevil me no more! Undress!
                                    —W.R.E.

7 JUNE

Doggerel in Loggerel

In the wonderful world of the legendary lumberjack, a donkey engine was a power-driven apparatus that took in and let out wire cable, thus raising or lowering the log to which the cable was attached. The donkey driver tightened or slackened line in accordance with shouts from the men manhandling the log—a long "hooooooo," perhaps, followed by a curt "hoo." The problem about these signals was that the donkey engine was sometimes located a quarter of a mile or more from the log, and voices don't carry well at that distance. So there used to be someone called a whistle punk, stationed between the log and the engine, who relayed the message.

If the engineer misheard the signal—if he treated a short as a long, say—he might slacken or tauten the wrong cable. This was sometimes fatal. I know because I was a whistle punk one summer. The punk before me had misread a shout, with the result that six men were squashed to wood pulp beneath a dropping log. So I refused to relay any shout the first time around; I waited until it had been repeated two, three, or four times. The delay did not make me popular, but nobody got squashed.

No outsider could have known the meaning of "hoooooo hoo hoo" as opposed to "hoo hoo hoooooo." Similarly, no outsider could be expected to catch the point of this story:

> "Nurse," said an injured logger, "let me tell you how it happened. I was setting chokers on the candy side and was just hooking onto a big blue butt, when the rigging slinger says to let her go. The booker yelled, 'Hi!' to the punk, the punk jerked the wire, the puncher opened her wide and . . . well, Nurse, here I am."
>
> "But I don't understand," said the nurse. The logger sat up in his cot. "Damned if I do either," he exclaimed, "unless that haywire rigging slinger was crazy."

The loggerel doggerel that follows is dedicated to all whistle punks.

IF SHE-STUFF IS YOUR WEAKNESS

> If she-stuff is your weakness
> And you are under-hung,
> Beware, beware Hamburger Flats,
> Lest you should lose your Pung;

Beware its Tonsil-polish,
   Its Snow-plows and their pox;
Stay home beside your Bush Wren
   Until the Top Push knocks.

You and your War Department
   He'll take to town to feast
With Chokerman and Bull Cook,
   Car Toad and Timber Beast;

With Gyppo Man and Faller;
   With Punk and Eagle Eye;
With Bull Buck and Cat Skinner.
   The Hasher will supply

Gut Heater for a starter;
   Or Cougar Milk instead;
Or Spotted Dog or Chokem
   May make a tasty spread.

Try Spool Stuff; try a Klondike Spud.
Try Belly Pad washed down with Mud.
But hold the Cougar Milk to size,
Or next day you'll be Counting Ties.
                       —W.R.E.

8 JUNE

It Stands to? Reason

(With a bow to Frank Sullivan, cliché-killer)

To everything its what? *Its season.*
This statement stands to what? *To reason.*

  What is crushing? *Cost.*
  What is temper? *Lost.*

What is commentary? *Wry.*
  And wit? *Dry.*

What are pathways? *Winding.*
  And snowstorms? *Blinding.*

What does absence render us?
  Conspicuous.

A miss is good as what? *A mile.*
  What is durance? *Vile.*

What's the street of writers? *Grub.*
There is what? *The rub.*

If you have a life, you *Bet it.*
If an appetite, you *Whet it.*

Conscientious to a? *Fault.*
I am grinding to a? *Halt.*

—W.R.E.

9 JUNE

I Love You to ∞ *(+A°)*

Back beyond my memory, my father raised sheep. The iron he used to brand them is still around. It is a reverse HA*E, standing for Harry Albert Espy.

When I was a child, we sliced the tip off the left ear of newborn calves to indicate they were our property. Other ranchers used various notches and holes for the same purpose.

Our cattle's notched ears were the lineal descendants of such brand marks as these, all familiar in the old West:

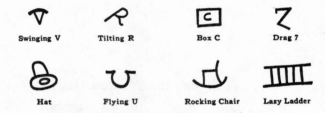

| Swinging V | Tilting R | Box C | Drag 7 |
| Hat | Flying U | Rocking Chair | Lazy Ladder |

Every discipline, from aeronautics to astronomy, from the church to electricity, from money to physics, from punctuation to stamp collecting, has its arbitrary signs and symbols. For instance:

AN ' TO MY FRIEND JOHN

Friend John, whose : was removed,
  When asked why he had lately proved
So free of caution and of fear,
  Said, "I've no *, my dear."†

—W.R.E.

---

† I thought this pun was original with me, but I should have known better. R. Robinson Rowe says he heard it more than forty years ago, and see what William Cole has done with it on the next page.

I LOVE YOU TO ∞ (±A°)

I am ♂ and you are ♀ ;
Am'rous war shall rage between us—
War in which, as ♋ , my *f*
Is to orbit toward ♂ ,
While ℛ you pretend,
And ○° to my end.
A ♀ knows dissatisfaction
A ⇌
Since (as always in these wars)
♀ ⟶ at last to ♂ :
My Σ of love you'll give again
✕ eight or ten.

—W.R.E.

INTERGENERATIONAL QUERY

If parents showed less ε,
Would children show less ρ?

—W.R.E.

This bit of symbol-play arrived in today's mail:

"I've missed my . ," said Stella.
Mark Colon was annoyed. "— it all!"
"I heard your ! ," she said. "It's not funny. Just remember it's my * !"
"Then have the baby," Mark said. "It will be a little ; ."
"Oh, no it won't. It'll be a : . A *full* : ."
"What are you getting @ ?"
"Marriage; I've got your #."
"Jesus," Mark groaned in ( ). Do I have to marry this o?"
"All things being = , yes," she snapped back.
"OK. It makes ¢ ."
"There's no ? that it does," she said firmly.
"May I get married in my +4s ?" he asked.
"Don't be ,cal," she replied.
So they went ¼ and she became his better ½.

—William Cole

Finally this:

♂ AND ♀

The glabrous girl and hispid boy
Make all the roses dance with joy
The hispid wench and glabrous youth
Make even roses seem uncouth
So to your proper sexes flee:
Glabrosity, hispidity.

—W Craddle

10 JUNE

The British Crossword Labyrinth

Several of my friends have taken up residence in London, saying nasty things over their shoulders about the deteriorating quality of life back in the States. Their return to the womb carries with it a curious self-abasement before all things British. This reverses the attitude of fifty years ago, when Britishers existed for Americans principally as a subject for bad jokes.

One thing that Londoners do better than New Yorkers is to verbalize. The conversation of what was once called the upper classes is frequently civilized and even elegant.

This preoccupation with words is reflected in their crossword puzzles. Turn to the crossword puzzle in the *Times* of London, and you will find what Anthony Lewis describes as "a mass of maddening puns and in-jokes":

> "Far from benign in a saint of citrus associations" is the clue: the word turns out to be "inclement." Why? You have to know the old nursery rhyme about St. Clement Dane's Church: "Oranges and lemons says the bells of St. Clement's."
> Or try "distraught intent air of Melmoth, for instance." The answer is "itinerant." Why? "Intent air" is an anagram of the answer. And there was a gothic novel by Charles Maturin called *Melmoth the Wanderer*.

But even the *Times* cannot match the clues that Shipwinkle used to put out in the *New Chronicle*. Take this one: "In church, in short; short measure, at your pleasure; that twisted chin provokes the solver's grin." All that, and the answer is "inch."

Neither at home nor in school do Americans live in such heady companionship with words. An Englishman named Roy Dean solved before millions of television viewers, in three and three-fourths minutes, a London *Times* puzzle that I could not have solved in three and three-fourths days.

My guess is that before long these expatriated Americans will come slinking back home. The crossword puzzles here are easier.

11 JUNE

Cynarae, Hot Woe!

Once you start spoonerizing well-known verses, you can go on forever, but the joke grows stale after the first few lines. So I manfully refrain from entering here more than the first stanza of my spoonerized Cynarae:

> Mast light, ah, nesterbight, letwixt her yips and nine
> There shell thy fadow, Cynara! thy sheath was bred

Umon sy pole wetween the bisses and the kine;
And I was pesolate and dick of a gold assion.
Yea, I was hesolate and dowed my bed;
I have thin baithful to fee, Cynara! in fy mashion.
         —*W.R.E., after Ernest Dowson*

The best spoonerisms are those in which the altered words make an eerie sort of sense:

A: Hot woe, Barley Chinks!
B: Hot woe, Chilly Bass!
A: Blocking showy, Miss Thorning.
B: Glowing a bale.
A: Porter on the willows? Tut-tut!
B: Mad for the bite. Cuddles on the pot.
A: A very washy splinter.
B: All blood and mowing.
A: Here's to spray in the Ming!
B: Sadsome glummer! 'Ware fell!
A: Low song!

         —*J. A. Lindon*

12 JUNE

We Canal Praise
the Streets of New Orleans

The cartoonist John Chase wrote a book about New Orleans streets, listing three of them in his title: "Frenchmen, Desire, Good Children." Other New Orleans streets are capitalized in the quartet of quatrains below:

Streets! where all ABUNDANCE win
   Through eager INDUSTRY!
Streets! aSWAMP in PEACE and
      LOVE,
   In LAW and PIETY!

Where LAFITTE are not of clay!
   Where no mouth need pucker!
(If you CHEW a LEMON, pray
   OUR LADY OF PROMPT
      SUCCOR!)

Where e'en MADMAN lives in HOPE,
   And NUNS in CHURCH shoot
      CRAPS;
Where CROSSMAN yields to
      HARMONY,
   And VIRTUE sighs, "Perhaps . . ."

Streets! where GREATMEN praise
      DELORD,
   And PIRATES dread the PITT!
Where the POETS' final word
   Is, "AMEN, boys! That's it!"

         —*W.R.E.*

13 JUNE

Praisegod Barebone—I Begin with E!

Among the Christian names in my family register, my favorite is Seaborne, given to a girl born in the middle of the Atlantic ocean in the middle of the seventeenth century. If my home were in Texas I would surely cast my vote for a politician there, Barefoot Sanders, on account of his first name alone. If Jeff Nightbyrd and Tom Turnipseed were in my district, I would vote for them too.

The Dictionary of National Biography told *Webster's Biographical Dictionary,* which told Anna Peirce, who in turn told me, that Praisegod Barebone (after whom the 1653 "Barebone's Parliament" was named) reportedly had two brothers christened (1) Christ-came-into-the-world-to-save Barebone, and (2) If-Christ-had-not-died-thou-hadst-been-damned Barebone, the latter shortening to Damned Barebone.*

Flie-fornication is among the names in English parish registers. A Texas farmer born as recently as 1883 was christened Daniel's-wisdom-may-I-know, Stephen's-faith and-spirit-choose, John's-divine-communion-seal, Moses's-meekness, Joshua's-zeal, Win-the-day-and-conquer-all Murphy—Dan, for short.

Anna Peirce also mentioned that a number of her colonial forebears were christened Freelove, the name presumably referring to Agape† rather than Eros.‡

Some generations back, kinfolk of Louisa Bonner named their first boy Walter. He died, and they named their next Walter Restored. He too passed away, and they named their third Walter Restored Twice—Walter R. T. Jones.

More recently, an oil man—and a successful one—named his son Carbon Petroleum Dubbs. Since names represent us to the outside world, it is not surprising that we should be sensitive about them. "To think," mourned my Great-aunt Shae, "that I should have lived to address a daughter 'Mrs. Jones, Hayfork!'" My own family briefly modified its surname. In the 1880s my grandfather had accumulated what appeared to be enough money to start a dynasty. His children (my father alone dissenting) feared that E-s-p-y looked too much like the name of pig farmers (which indeed the seventeenth-century Ulster Espys probably were). So they persuaded grandpa to change the spelling to "Espey," which they thought had a rather Norman shine to it. Unfortunately, my grandfather later lost in gold most of what he had

---

* The Greek word for name is *onoma,* and an onomasticon is a collection of names. Members of the Sunday department of *The New York Times* once suggested such cognates as *onomasticate,* to chew over funny names; *onomaster,* one who onomasticates superbly, and *autonomast,* one who enjoys his own funny name. But in what way does *onoma* connote anything funny?

† 6 December has more on Agape.

‡ A quatrain about busts and bosoms, mentioned by me in an earlier book as of unknown origin, was written by Anna Peirce's late father, Waldo, the painter. The correct title was "To My Mother-in-law's Breastworks," and I had the words wrong. The verse should have read:

> Breasts and bosoms have I known
> Of varied shapes and sizes,
> From poignant disappointments
> To jubilant surprises

made from oysters, whereupon the family reverted to the old spelling. If you ever find me spelling my name Espey, you will know there has been an oil strike in our oyster beds.

"As his name is, so is he," says I Samuel, and there is something to that. I am lucky to have a surname beginning with E. If my name began with M, says the Council for Alcoholism,* I should be eight times more prone to alcoholism than the average drunk. If my name began with any letter from S through Z (this according to the British Medical Association), I should have twice the usual susceptibility to ulcers, and be three times as subject to heart attacks. The frequency of neuroses in us A-R types is half that of you S-Z people, and our life expectancy is twelve years greater.

But I don't feel too well, at that.

14 JUNE

The Jealous Governes

Daisy Ashford, at the age of nine, wrote that scintillant comedy of manners *The Young Visiters*. Her sister Angela, at an even earlier age—eight, to be exact—wrote a novel of her own. It was called *The Jealous Governes or The Granted Wish*. Angela was perhaps not quite so mordant a social critic as Daisy, but her spelling was even worse.

I do not propose to tell you the plot or the outcome of *The Jealous Governes*—it is a tragic tale—but here, at least, is the beginning:

Chapter 1
Wishing

One evening late in Sep: Mr. Hose sat in his armchair reading a news paper. His wife sat in an other looking at the "Strand" Magerzine. Mr. Hose sudonly looked up at his wife; "Elizabeth" he said "one thing I have been wishing for, ever since we were married is a baby, would not you like to have one looking at her seariously "Yes indeed I should" ansed his delicate wife with a sigh.

I soud like to adobt one continued Charlie, I would like to have one of my own said Elizabeth I dont like adopting babys, well you cant do it any other way if you dont get one. Besides if it was a boy what name have you got for it if it was a boy it should be named Charlie after you dear, and if it was a girl I suppose you would call it Elizabeth and liza for short would not you said Charlie, well yes she said beginning to read her magazine.

Chapter 2
The New Baby

When the clock had just struck half past six they heard a ring at the

---

* Glasgow, Scotland.

door bell and within a few minutes the maid servant came hurrying up
stairs and said the Dr. had arrived with a box under his arm and he would
like to see Mrs. Hose she said. "Oh well, will you show him up to this
bedroom" said Mrs. Hose turning to her husband and saying "you don't
mind him coming up, do you dear?" Mary went out of the room grinning,
closing the door quietly behind her.

In a few minutes the Dr.'s bold step was heard at the door and then a
loud knock and with a "come in" from Mrs. Hose he entered the room.

"Oh I say Mrs Hose" he began taking off his hat "I have heard you have
been wishing for a baby, so I have brought you one and your wish is
granted."

"Oh hurrah" said Mrs. Hose "Is it a boy or a girl?"

"Well I don't know" said the Dr. *quite,* but I'll leave you to find out and
settle matters" so saying Dr. Pauline took his departure shutting the door
with his foot, while he held his precious top hat in his two hands.

As soon as the Dr. left the room, Mr. Hose began hurrahing and laughing at the idea of the new baby coming. "I am very glad it's come, arn't
you?" he said to his wife.

"Yes, I'm very glad. Hasn't it come early?"

"Yes," said her husband, "but don't you think we had better open the
box and look at it?"

15 JUNE

He Beat You to That One, Too

Some slang terms remain just that, neither disappearing nor yet becoming acceptable
English. Expressions used by Shakespeare, yet still borderline after three hundred
years, include "dead as a doornail," "done me wrong," "a hell of a time," "not so hot,"
"go hang yourself," "she fell for it," and "how you do talk." Do you know in which
of Shakespeare's plays the following locutions appear?

> The game is up
> I have yet room for six scotches more
> I have been in such a pickle
> I cannot tell what the dickens his name is
> I'll not budge an inch
> Not so hot
> The first thing we do, let's kill all the lawyers
> I'll tell the world
> There is something in the wind
> I will tell you my drift
> Spread yourselves
> With bag and baggage
> It's Greek to me

Not Shakespeare but Sir Walter Scott—in *Redgauntlet*—introduced the expression "Tell that to the Marines"

16 JUNE

Britannia Rules of Orthography

From British novels a thrill I get
That I sadly miss in the American tale—
The thrill of a heroine suffragette
In gaol.

They touch on Life in the Quivering Raw,
With the frankest noun and the straightest verb,
And all of them—Hewlett, Bennett, and Shaw—
Say kerb.

Domestic voices are flabby and weak
In the Search for Truth that the age requires.
Would Ade or Tarkington dare to speak
Of tyres?

Hail to Conrad, Galsworthy, Wells,
To the crunching might of their books and dramas
And the Lure of the East when Kipling spells
Pyjamas.

—Firth

17 JUNE

Balamer Is in Murlin

Some odd pronunciations are localisms; like certain wines, they do not travel well. Howard K. Smith twitted Baltimoreans for their local twang:

"They call their city Balamer, Murlin. They call garbage gobbidge, legal liggle. Paramour is their word for power mower. And if you ever ask directions there, remember that Droodle Avenue means Druid Hill Avenue. Clays means clothes. Doll means dial—the phone. Cancil means council, as in town council. Council means cancel, as with a check." Replied Baltimore officials, male-chauvinistically: "What's so funny about a paramour to cut the grass?"

A correspondent wrote Cleveland Amory: "For real hair-tearing mispronunciations, nothing could top the new car dealers on Phoenix TV. All their noo cores have par steering, diss brakes, tinn-ed winshills, and the used cores are in lock-noo condition."

Even my home state of Washington, in most respects impeccable, has its oddities of pronunciation. Sequim, a village where, by a freak of nature, no more than two or three inches of rain falls in a year, though the rainfall roundabout is never less than a hundred, is called *Squim*. John F. Kennedy lost Washington's electoral vote in 1960, say some, because he pronounced Spokane (Spoke-Ann to natives)* *Spokayne*. A Washingtonian calls Wahkiakum County Wah-KEYE-a-kum, and next door an Oregonian says Wil-lam'-ette River; visiting easterners will say Wah-ki-ak'-um and Wil-la-mette' every time.

18 JUNE

Rosencrantz and Guildenstern

The author of *Rosencrantz and Guildenstern Are Dead* puts his title characters through a wordplay game that consists of an exchange of questions, each player trying to win by making the other respond with a statement, repeat a previous question, ask the equivalent of an earlier question, blow his cool ("rhetoric"), or ask a question having no connection with the previous one. The first player to score three points wins. It takes fast footwork to keep one's foot out of one's mouth in this game, and I do not recommend that you play it unless your name is Rosencrantz, Guildenstern, Hamlet, Shakespeare, or Stoppard.

Here R. and G. go:

ROS: We could play at questions.
GUIL: What good would that do?
ROS: Practice!
GUIL: Statement! One-love.
ROS: Cheating!
GUIL: How?
ROS: I hadn't started yet.
GUIL: Statement. Two-love.
ROS: Are you counting that?
GUIL: What?
ROS: Are you counting that?
GUIL: Foul! No repetitions. Three-love. First game to . . .
ROS: I'm not going to play if you're going to be like that.
GUIL: Whose serve?
ROS: Hah?
GUIL: Foul! No grunts. Love-one.

* See 10 July.

ROS: Whose go?

GUIL: Why?

ROS: Why not?

GUIL: What for?

ROS: Foul! No synonyms! One-all.

GUIL: What in God's name is going on?

ROS: Foul! No rhetoric. Two-one.

GUIL: What does it all add up to?

ROS: Can't you guess?

GUIL: Were you addressing me?

ROS: Is there anyone else?

GUIL: Who?

ROS: How would I know?

GUIL: Why do you ask?

ROS: Are you serious?

GUIL: Was that rhetoric?

ROS: No.

GUIL: Statement! Two-all. Game point.

ROS: What's the matter with you today?

GUIL: When?

ROS: What?

GUIL: Are you deaf?

ROS: Am I dead?

GUIL: Yes or no?

ROS: Is there a choice?

GUIL: Is there a God?

ROS: Foul! No *non sequiturs,* three-two, one game all.

GUIL: (*seriously*) What's your name?

ROS: What's yours?

GUIL: I asked you first.

ROS: Statement. One-love.

GUIL: What's your name when you're at home?

ROS: What's yours?

GUIL: When I'm at home?

ROS: Is it different at home?

GUIL: What home?

ROS: Haven't you got one?

GUIL: Why do you ask?

ROS: What are you driving at?

GUIL: (*with emphasis*) What's your name?

ROS: Repetition. Two-love. Match point to me.

GUIL: (*seizing him violently*) WHO DO YOU THINK YOU ARE?

ROS: Rhetoric! Game and match!

—*Tom Stoppard*

19 JUNE

Kipling Rudyards

J. K. Stephen wrote a complaint about poor writing which ended:

> When the Rudyards cease from Kipling
> And the Haggards ride no more.

To which David McCord added:

> Still for us where Cottons mather
> In the spring the Willas cather
> As of yore.

Perhaps with such precedents in mind, Arthur Berger wrote as follows:

> John
> Was Gay
> But Gerard Hopkins
> Manley

> Dame May
> Was Witty
> But John Greenleaf
> Was Whittier

> Oscar
> Was Wilde
> But Thornton
> Was Wilder

20 JUNE

Oysterville, O Oysterville!

I mentioned earlier that some of the best good bad verse I know—verse, that is, so ghastly that only genius could have created it—springs from my boyhood home at Oysterville. For example:

> Oysterville, a pearl, a gem of the sea,
> Crowned once in glory, when land it was free;
> Fathers and mothers then young in their years,
> Builded on faith, love, labor and tears,
> A harbinger of hope to declining years,
> No thought of being tossed, torn and rent on an uncharted shore;

Their beacon light was a point on high
Close to the stars in the western sky.
It was not given to man to impart the fate in store;
Cursed be the day she went on the shore.
It was never intended she should be eternally lost,
However stranded and tempest tossed
But time and circumstances will yet find her place,
Trusting to God for eternal grace.

—Author Unknown

2 1 JUNE

Like Wow, Man!

And when you stick on conversation's burrs,
Don't strew your pathway with those dreadful *urs*.

Such was the advice of Oliver Wendell Holmes. He probably had in mind that Er, Judah's son, was "wicked in the sight of the Lord; and the Lord slew him." My guess is that when the Lord asked, "Will you obey my commandments?" Er's reply was "Er . . ." The Lord thereupon not only wiped out Er but laid down a new commandment: "Thou shalt not intercalate." Soon afterward the Lord also slew Er's younger brother Onan, this time for spilling his seed on the ground. One suspects that Onan was the victim of a misunderstanding; God thought he too was intercalating.

Intercalations are sounds that lengthen a sentence without adding to its meaning. A noted linguist says they appear in all languages:

From Spanish we borrowed, at least in Western states, the exact equivalent of "you know"—"sabe"—which came out as "savvy?" Italians often use "sai" or "capisci," of which the first is the exact translation of "you know," the second of "you understand." Italian has "di" as the exact equivalent of "say." French has "dites." Spanish has an equivalent of "look!" that is just as overused as "you know"—"mira!" Then there is the whole family of "Is it not so?" "Isn't it true?" or even "Ain't it?" which English does not overuse, but other languages do (French "n'est-ce pas?" German "nicht wahr?" Italian "nevvero?" even Russian "ne tak li?").

The English "man!" so widely used in some circles of our society, has an exact Spanish parallel: "Hombre! no me diga!"—"Man! don't tell me!" meaning "you don't say so!" "It can't be!"

"Like," as in "it's like cold," is said to have started among "jazz, coll, beat groups in New York, probably to avoid making too definite a statement." It is also said to have been reinforced by Yiddish speech-patterns, but the evidence for this is not clear.

The intercalation has a precise ancestry in the old Roman custom of "decreeing that something be stuck in between," specifically, days and even months inserted into the calendar to make the year come out even. It was the function of the high priest to decree the intercalation whenever necessary to bring the solar year in line with the lunar months of twenty-eight days. A few extra days, or an extra month of limited length, would do the trick. Just as days and months were "thrown into the calendar," so are expressions like "you know," "man," "like" thrown into the language.

Will they stay? It depends. "Man" and "like" are as current today as were "gadzooks" and "ablood" in the days of Shakespeare. Where are THEY now?

But perhaps "you know" is a horse of a different color. Its roots seem to lie not only in the dim past, but also in human psychology ("I don't have to explain it to you! You're too intelligent! You already know it.") No matter how much it may be a reflex in the mouths of some, the chances are it will still be around in A.D. 3000.

—*Mario Pei*

22 JUNE

Part of Adam Is Mad

EVE'S DREAM

The dream that your demeanor shows, dear friend,
   Leads on to sorrow. Dreams hold something sad;
Your dream knows part of Eden is Eden's end,
   And part of Adam is mad.

—*W.R.E.*

IN-RIDDLE

I was recently told by a girl in Algeria
   There was peace in Hepaticae, war in Wisteria.
I put her in halter, that girl in Algeria:
   She wasn't Insane, but she was in Hysteria.

—*W.R.E.*

23 JUNE

Petersonese

One of the fringe benefits of playing for the Houston Oilers is listening to Coach Bill Peterson, who does things with the language that have not been heard since Casey Stengel was in his prime.* After Miami's Kim Kiick and Larry Csonka ran all over his team, Peterson explained, "We just weren't compared for their backfield."

* See 14 August and 16 November

Discussing strategy, he said, "We're changing our floormat this week." Of a limping player, "He has a chronicle knee injury." Of the Oakland Raiders: "That Oakland is tough. They timidate your offense, they timidate your defense, they even timidate the officials."

He has said, "This is the crutch of the problem," and "Things are going bad, but we've got to keep our cools." In training camp, he told his squad, "We're all in this together, and don't you remember it." He also spoke of the team's goal for the year: "Men, I want you thinking of just one word all season. One word and only one word: Super Bowl!" And in the waning minutes of a game with Denver, he proclaimed, "Don't you guys think for a minute that I'm going to take this loss standing down."

One day, reflecting on all the problems a coach has in handling the various personalities among his players, Peterson confessed, "Sometimes I feel like that psychiatrist, Frood."

—Robert W. Creamer

2 4 JUNE

Midsummer Madness

Before starting the business of the day, I remind you of what the day is:

MIDSUMMER DAY

Midsummer Day no other than
Indeed this is, although

It's odd, since summer just began
A day or two ago.

—W.R.E.

A while back* I mentioned Uncommon, Improper Nouns—words that once were proper names, but have become part of the vernacular. A sub-order of these eponyms consists of words that still represent a person's name, but have become code for some characteristic with which that person is identified. Thus a hero-worshiping biographer is a *Boswell;* a man of vast wealth, a *Croesus;* an irresistible lover, a *Casanova.* Such code names are included in the following sonnet:

WHEN CHARON FERRIES ME ACROSS THE STYX

When Charon ferries me across the Styx,
And Cerberus acknowledges I'm dead,
Pray, Boswell, carve some legend at my head!
Say that I sharpened Machiavelli's tricks;
Out-Croesused Croesus and his golden bricks;
Loved on when Casanova wearièd;
Pushed back Canute's rude ocean in its bed;
Was funnier than Chaplin in the flicks.

* See 19 April.

Dear Boswell, will you carve in stone how I
Awhile to Joan was Darby, and awhile
To Damon, Pythias? Will you descry
Jack Ripper's rictus underneath my smile?

More likely, Boswell, you will not recall
A blessed thing worth writing down at all.
                                    —W.R.E.

25 JUNE

The Centipede, the Water Beetle, and the Praying Mantis

How nice it must be for a song writer, who knows moon *must* rhyme with June! He does not have to brood about it—he does not have to ask himself, "Should I try loon, or balloon, or monsoon, or goon, or shoon, not to say importune, rune, or impugn?" No; there the rhyme is, ordained from the beginning: "Moon—June."* Thank God for reflex decisions; they are the sine qua non of serenity. Suppose you had to decide afresh each day whether or not to brush your teeth?

Accept the conventional wisdom, and never think for yourself. Thinking for yourself leads to the loony bin. Learn from the centipede:

> The centipede was happy quite
>   Until a toad in fun
> Said, "Pray, which leg goes after which?"
> That worked her mind to such a pitch
> She lay distracted in the ditch,
>   Considering how to run.
>   —Mrs. Edward Craster

Learn, too, from the water beetle:

> The water beetle here shall teach
> A lesson far beyond your reach.
> She aggravates the human race
> By gliding on the water's face
> Assigning each to each its place.
> But if she ever stopped to think
> Of how she did it, she would sink.
>
> *Moral*
> Don't ask questions.
>   —After Hilaire Belloc

And take warning from the praying mantis:

* See 26 December for evidence to the contrary.

FOR A PRAYING MANTIS, STANDING IN THE NEED OF PRAYER

The female praying mantis consumes her mate in the process of copulation.

The Male (or Lesser) Praying Mantis is
A victim of romantic fantasies.
He cries, "My angel, let me prove
A mantis' life well lost for love!"
He takes her in his tender arms;
He soothes her virginal alarms—
Pours all his love and longing in her,
While she is having him for dinner.
He reassures her that they'll wed;
Meanwhile, she's gnawing off his head.
He soothes her gastric pains with Borax,
As she is working on his thorax;
And when there's nothing left above,
Still doth the Lower Mantis love.

*This system, as needs scarcely saying,
Makes little Mantises . . . all praying.*
—*W.R.E.*

26 JUNE

To Ms or Not to Ms

Ms is now widely accepted as a form of address for those of the female persuasion, though the word makes no etymological sense and is, on the face of it, unpronounceable. But it is a godsend to junk mailers, who no longer need worry about whether a woman on their lists is married or not; and for that reason if no other it may last.

Even more than they dislike being called Mrs. or Miss, some feminists hate to be considered Sex Objects. A man who sees a woman as a Sex Object is referred to in the trade as a Male Chauvinist Pig. I cannot be more than one-tenth Male Chauvinist Pig, since it does not occur to me to regard more than one woman in ten as a Sex Object. About the rest I am as emancipated as I am about Sue:

Sue is a misfigure
Sue is a disfigure
I would feel more snuggly
If Sue looked less uggly
—*W.R.E.*

The book reviews tell me another subject is exercising some very articulate women:

A DELICATE DISPUTE

Or, Pass a Little of Both, Please

Kate says the clitoral one
Is the literal one
Sig says the vaginal one
Is the final one
                              —*W.R.E.*

27 JUNE

Point of View

Bertrand Russell is credited with inventing the self-centered game of which David
L. Silverman here gives examples:

I am thrifty. You're a bit of a tightwad. He's a real skinflint.
I'm cautious. You're timid. He's chicken-hearted.
I'm human. You're prone to err. He's a blundering idiot.
I have hepatitis. You drink too much. He's an alcoholic.
I'm human. You've got an eye for the girls, haven't you? He's lecherous.
I'm diplomatic. You take a pragmatic approach to the truth. He's a hyp-
ocrite.

28 JUNE

Spring in the Fall? Nein! Nicht Möglich!

Louis Untermeyer (who in his ninetieth year proposed writing a book to outsell
The Joy of Sex; he said he would call it *The Joy of Impotence*), says that "The
limerick loses its quality and its point becomes pointless when it has to be filtered
through another language." He gives an example:

There was a young fellow named Hall
Who fell in the spring in the fall.
    'Twould have been a sad thing
    Had he died in the spring,
But he didn't—he died in the fall.

A German translator was completely stymied by that limerick, says Mr. Untermeyer, and had to resort to *two* translations. In the first he translated both spring
and fall as seasons—*Früjahr* and *Herbst*. In the second he rendered both as water—
Quelle (a flow of water), and *Wasserfall* (waterfall).

29 JUNE

Confound Your Words, Your Looks, Your Handwriting!

Ambiguity takes many forms.

"I counted girls going barefoot to classes; about one in every four." Does that mean, asks *Word Ways,* that one of every four girls goes barefoot to class? Or that barefoot girls go to one out of four classes? Or that girls choose to go to one out of every four classes barefoot? Or that one of every four students is a barefoot girl? Or, perhaps, that the girls have four legs?

Another form of ambiguity:

AFFAIRE DE COEUR MANQUÉE

Like hammered gold the tresses shone that crowned
    That fragile head.
        My heart more bravely stepped.
Then passing by, I dared to look around,
    And saw the beard.
    And wept.

—W.R.E.

Here a poet tackles the ambiguity of illegibility:

ANSWERING YOURS OF (DATE ILLEGIBLE)

The morning mail is here; I have your
    charming letter;
  I kiss each word you penned, with
    ecstasy devout;
  I love each little word; I'd love them
    even better
  If I could make them out.

Your writing is as strange and dark as
    modern art is;
  A rippling, trembling line, with curls
    and whirls between;
—Alas, what news is this! "Flinty," you
    say my heart is?
  Or "flirty," do you mean?

Inscrutable, the page yields not to my
    entreaty,
  You speak in covered words of Delphic
    mystery;
It looks as though you think that I am
    "such a sweety";
  (Or "sweaty," can it be?)

Can "deary" be the word? I trust it is
    not "beery,"
  My whispers, not my whiskers, that
    linger in your ear;
And do you find my verse so cheesy or so
    cheery?
  And am I deaf or dear?

Your writing swoops and swirls, with no
    suggestion whether
  I am an Awful Slob or only Awful
    Slow;
Did you perhaps suggest that we should
    "roam" together?
  Or is it double o?

My brain resembles now the Battle of
    Manila,
  Even your signature I study with
    dismay;
Lola or Lena, Lisa, or Lina, Laura,
    Lilla—
  Who are you, anyway?

—Morris Bishop

Finally, I offer for your consideration what might be called an ambiguity of morals:

FOR ADULTS ONLY

Adult, her eighteen-year-old form;
Adult, her hazel eyes . . . and warm.
Adulter, he who pens these lies;
He deems adulterers . . . unwise.

No, no! let never such as he
Adulterate virginity!
He knows adultery is naughty.
He really oughtn't do it . . . ought he?
—W.R.E.

3 0 JUNE

Töf-Töf, Doki-Doki

You hear a songbird go "Tweet-tweet," says *Word Ways*. The Frenchman hears "Cui-cui." Your heart beats "Pit-a-pat." Japanese hearts beat "Doki-doki." You hear a train: "Toot-toot!" The German hears: "Töf-töf!"

Even British and American ears register some of nature's sounds differently. For instance:

PHILOLOGICAL

The British puss demurely mews;
His transatlantic kin meow.
The kine in Minnesota moo;
Not so the gentle Devon cows:
  They low,
As every school child ought to know.
—John Updike

Leaving onomatopoeia—but staying with cows—I give you this:

The cow is of the bovine ilk;
One end is moo, the other milk.
—Ogden Nash

Since "low" has two meanings in England, the difference between a Devon cow's bow and stern is ambiguous. A clarification:

Any Devon school child knows
Low end's lactic; high end lows.
—W.R.E.

JULY

❧⟊❧

1 JULY
§

The Hard-boiled Seduction of a Soft-boiled Egg

Florence King, a successful writer of pornography, is author of the following passage, highly recommended to those who would like to know how pornographic prose reads without having to read it:

> I took the glistening, virginally white oval out of the fiercely bubbling, ecstatic cauldron of hot, hot water and cupped my hand around it and felt its contours with shimmering delight.
>
> OOOOOHHHHHHHHHHHHHHHHH was it hot!
>
> YESSSSSSSSSSS!
>
> I reached for my long, sturdy, battering egg knife and tapped.
>
> Did it ever come open!
>
> *Wide open!*
>
> What a gorgeous gash!
>
> UMMMMMMMMMMMMMM!
>
> The shell slipped off and I touched the tender, moist, protein-swollen membranes of the secret softness. The steamy slice of hot, ready, edible egg burned my fingers but I thrust firmly with my rigid tool and inserted the erect, serrated knife.
>
> I'M YOLKING YOU!
>
> The lubricious, oleaginous, golden yellow ambrosial nectar of the pulsating, quickening core gushed out into my egg cup.
>
> I centered my mouth over the slickened surface of the spoon and ate, ate, ate!
>
> "I ate you," I whispered.
>
> Did I ever . . .
>
> THEEEEE ENNNNNDDDDDDDD!

Before yielding to Ms. King's siren song, it would be well to pause a moment and consider the cost:

A POSITIVE REACTION

For words to warn the wicked world
    Its wicked ways to cease,
From Shakespeare and from Coleridge
    I borrowed each a piece:

"Who loves not wisely but too well
    On passion's torrent borne
A sadder and a Wasserman
    Shall rise the morrow morn."

                —W.R.E.

2 JULY

Encyclopedic Chant

As a boy, Paul Hollister often found himself dragooned into a church service when he would have preferred to be at home reading the *Encyclopaedia Britannica*. On such occasions he passed the time by fitting the abbreviations on the spines of the eleventh edition, in his head, to the music of Gregorian chants. For instance:

A–AND, AND–AUS, AUS–BIS, BIS–CAL, CAL–CHA, CHA–CON, CON–DEM,

DEN–EDW, EVA–FIZA, GIC–HAR, HAR–HUR, HUS–ITA, ITA–KYS, L–LOR,

LOR–MEC, MED–MUM, MUN–ODD, ODE–PAY, PAY–POL, POL–REE,

REF–SAI, SAI–SHU, SHV–SUB, SUB–TOM, TON–VES, VET–ZYM. INDEX.

(AMEN.)

The sharp-eyed reader will have noted that the abbreviations above do not come from the eleventh edition. Do those in the verse below?

THE PASSIONATE ENCYCLOPAEDIA BRITANNICA READER TO HIS LOVE

As And to Aus, and Aus to Bis;
As Hus to Ita, and Ita to Kys;
As Pay to Pol, and Pol to Ree;
Ah, that is how you are to me!

As Bis to Cal, and Cal to Cha;
As Edw to Eva, and Eva to Fra;
As Ref to Sai and Sai to Shu:
That is, I hope, how I'm to you.
—*Maggie*

3 JULY

Crush vs. Whip

Once upon a time there was a baseball team in New York called the Giants. When it removed to San Francisco, a *New Yorker* writer penned the following advice to the sports writers of the latter city:

Apparently, the St. Louis Cardinals are much more friable than they used to be, for a paper in San Francisco recently ran the headline; "GIANTS CRUSH CARDINALS, 3–1." Now, we don't want to suggest that our city's eldest franchise has got in with a group of orange squeezers who don't know real pulverization when they see it. There's been too much of such carping already. When a boy leaves home, a mother's duty is to hold her tongue, we always say. While voices around us cried that the West Coast was, variously, a vile limbo, an obscure religious sect, a figment of Walter O'Malley's fevered imagination, and a tar pit of busherism certain to fossilize whatever it enveloped, we kept mum. As a reward to ourself for restraint, therefore, we *will* offer some advice about the science or art of baseball-headline verbs. These we have seen evolve from a simple matter of "WIN" and "LOSE" into a structure of periphrasis as complex as heraldry in feudalism's decadence. New York City, now a quaint port known principally for her historical monuments, once boasted three—we swear it, *three*—baseball teams, and a dozen daily newspapers. The lore accumulated here should be passed on to headline writers in all the fresh, brash towns likely to be visited as the major leagues, driven by a dark fatality, continue their migration toward Asia.

The correct verb, San Francisco, is "WHIP." Notice the vigour, force, and scorn obtained, quite without hyperbole. This table may prove helpful:

3-1—WHIP
3-2—SHADE
2-1—EDGE
1-0—(Pitcher's name) BLANKS*

Turning back and working upward, we come to 4-2, known professionally as "the golden mean," or "absolute zero." The score is uniquely characterless. The bland terms "BEAT" and "DEFEAT" are called in from the bullpen (meaning an area in which pitchers not actually in the game may "warm up"). However, 4-1 gets the coveted verb "VANQUISH." Rule: Any three-run margin, *provided the winning total does not exceed ten,* may be described as a vanquishing. If, however, the margin is a mere two runs and the losing total is five or more, "OUTSLUG" is considered very tasty. You will notice, S. F., the trend called Mounting Polysyllabism, which culminates, at the altitude of double digits, in that trio of Latin-root rhymers, "ANNIHILATE," "OBLITERATE," and "HUMILIATE." E.g., "A's ANNIHILATE O'S, 13-2."

Special cases:

1. If the home team is on the short end of the score, certain laws of mutation apply. "SHADE" becomes "SQUEAK BY." For "OUTSLUG," put "WIN IN SLOPPY CONTEST." By a judicious exploitation of "BOW," the home team, while losing, can be given the active position in the sentence and an appearance of graciousness as well.

2. Many novice banner writers, elevated from the 2-col. obscurity of Class A ball to the black-cap. screamers of the big leagues, fumble the concept of "SWEEP." It always takes a *plural* object. Doubleheaders and series can be swept, but not regulation single games. (The minimal "WIN STREAK" is three games long; five makes a "SURGE.") A team that neither sweeps nor is swept splits. A headline familiar to New Englanders is "SOX SPLIT."

3. Which brings up the delicate matter of punning, or paronomasia. Each Baltimore journal is restricted by secret covenant to one "BIRDS SOAR" every two weeks. Milwaukee, with a stronger team, is permitted twelve instances of "BRAVES SCALP" before the All-Star game. "TIGERS CLAW" and "CUBS LICK" tend to take care of themselves. As for you, San Francisco, the lack of synonyms for "giant" briefer than "behemoth" and "Brobdignagian," together with the long-standing failure of New York's own writers to figure out exactly what giants *do* (intimidate? stomp?), rather lets you out of the fun. In view of this, and in view of the team's present surprising record, you may therefore write "GIANTS

---

* Below, in smaller type, you may have "Twirls 3- (4-, 5-) Hitter." Two-hitters are "spun." For a one-hitter, write "Robbed of No-hitter."

A-MAYS."* But don't do it more than once a month; moderation in all things, S. F.

—John Updike

4 JULY

Fanny by Any Other Name

The political separation of England from its American colonies paved the way for the dismemberment of its native language into two parts, English and American.

Anyone who doubts how far this process has gone need only examine the first volume of the new *Supplement to the Oxford English Dictionary, A–H*. It includes words that would surprise most Americans. I for one never expected to find *arse-licking* there. I did not know *cobblers* were testicles, or *Bristols* breasts.

That OE now lists two ancient words once considered too gross to be given countenance in the decent environment of a dictionary does not disturb me, nor am I bothered, as an American, by its definition of *fanny* as backside. But Godfrey Smith, an Englishman, is. "This is one of the key half-dozen vulgar words," he writes in the *Sunday Times* of London, "whose sense separates us from our American cousins; others which can produce gales of unexpected hilarity over there are of course *knock up*† and *keep one's pecker up*. True, [the editor] can produce some literary support for defining it as backside and he does mark it 'chiefly US'; but in no British barracks or classroom is it ever more or less than the female frontside, being, in short, a synonym for one of his two gross and ancient words."

As Robert Bendiner says, "Leave it to the English always to drive on the wrong side of the road."

5 JULY

Sesquipedalia, Hold On! I'm Coming!

The conventional journalistic wisdom anathematizes any mouthful of a word like anathematizes.‡ Write clearly, write crisply, say the commandments; be positive, not negative; active, not passive; concise, not prolix. Never use two syllables where one will do.

---

* Mr. Updike is punning on the name of Willie Mays.
† See 16 January.
‡ See 16 April, 24 May.

Fair enough. But why did God make all those big words if not for man's delight? When I come across a yummy new acromegalic word, I take a sextant measurement of its height, check its meaning a few times (my memory not being what it used to be) and hire it for my personal verbal zoo. How I admire Alden Whitman, the necrologist, for popping "bloviate" into a magazine column! No matter that I first suspected, through an association of ideas I propose not to explain, that he might be talking about the phenomenon of gas accumulation in cadavers. No matter that "bloviate" had no place in American Heritage or Webster's Second (I had to resort to the Third to find it, and resorting to the Third is a personal humiliation for me). The point is that "bloviate" is a collector's item.

So are "akaakai" (ä-kä-ä-kä′-ē) and "borborygmic:"

MOSES INFANTI

She took for him an ark of bulrushes, and daubed it with slime and with pitch, and put the child therein; and she laid it in the flags by the river's brink.

—Exodus 2:3

Among the flags did Moses lie,
Cradled in akaakai,
While a hippopotamus
Made a borborygmic fuss.
—W.R.E.

6 JULY

Cockney Alphabet

This form of wordplay was first called to my attention by Barbara Huston, who lives more than six thousand miles from the Bow Bells of London. I have since received examples from as far away as Melbourne, Australia, and Rome, Italy. Eric Partridge and Rufus Segar are two who have written books of comic Cockney alphabets. R. L. Denyer tells me that the Western brothers, Kenneth and George, played the game on BBC before World War II. So did Clapham and Dwyer.

The number of expressions that can be fitted into the Cockney alphabet is limited only by one's willingness to force unnatural pronunciations onto words—and by one's sense of shame.

Some common variants:

A for 'orses, A for ism
B for lamb, B for mutton
C for sailors, C for yourself
D for ential, D for dumb, D for mitty
E for Adam, E for brick, E for Peron, E for lution

F for vescent, F for so nice, F for been had, F for cacious
G for police
H for mellowness
I for looting, I for an eye, I for nated, I for L tower
J for oranges, J for hear about ... ?, J for nile delinquent, J for see a dream walking
K nanabel, K for ancis, K for teria
L for leather
M for sis, M for size
N for a cockerel, N for sir, N for lope
O for the garden wall, O for populated, O for my dead body, O for sexed, O for coat
P for relief, P for idious Albion, P forming fleas
Q for the pictures, Q for tickets, Q tea pie
R for mo, R for crown
S for as I'm concerned
T for two, T formation
U for got, U for ia, U for mism
V for la France, V for section, V for la différence
W money, W for a match, W for a Siamese ram
X for breakfast
Y for mistress, Y for heaven's sake
Z for breezes

We associate Cockneys with the inaspirate h. C. W. V. Meares, who grew up in London but not within sound of the Bow Bells, reports that he and his schoolmates delighted in the following A for ism: "It ain't the 'opping over the 'igh 'edges that 'urts the 'orses 'ooves; it's the 'ammer, 'ammer, 'ammer on the 'ard 'ighway."

7 JULY

Remember Cyclamates? Maybe They Weren't So Harmful after All

The headline is from the *Wall Street Journal*. A subhead continues, "New Studies Said to Contradict Cancer Evidence That Led to FDA's Ban on Sweeteners."

The *Journal* story inspired me to write the following verse, which I dedicate to Dr. Milton Helpern, retired chief medical examiner of New York City, a scientist who steadfastly refuses to concede that two and two make more than four, even in ecology.

A MOUSE OF MY ACQUAINTANCE

A mouse of my acquaintance in seven days was fed
    Twice twenty thousand swordfish; and THAT MOUSE IS DEAD.
The mercury in swordfish is an enemy to dread;
    He ate twice twenty thousand, and THAT MOUSE IS DEAD.

His sister gnawed through pizzas (I am told one million four);
　　There's talk of botulism, and THAT SISTER IS NO MORE.
Their brother downed ten thousand turkeys lined with pesticide;
　　It took a week to kill him, but THAT POOR MOUSE DIED.

So stay away from hormones, and from salmonella too;
　　Be impolite to cyclamates, and DDT eschew;
For additives and chemicals can kill you just like *that,*
　　Though (confidentially) those mice were done in by the cat.
　　　　　　　　　　　　　　　　　　　　—*W.R.E.*

Speaking of DDT, a sign scrawled by a Japanese farmer alongside a DDT extermination station in a field near Tokyo, said, "Dear flies. We kill you not in the spirit of hate, but because necessity demands it. Please accept, in manly fashion, the inevitable consequence of being born flies."

8 JULY

He Goddam Mad Dog, Eh?

Good palindromes almost make sense: "Madam, I'm Adam"; "Able was I ere I saw Elba"; "A man, a plan, a canal, Panama." "Yreka Bakery" almost makes sense if you live in Yreka, California (though there is no longer a Yreka bakery there). "Sex at noon taxes" makes increasing sense as the years pile up. (Michael Gartner combined this with "I moan, Naomi," to create " 'Naomi, sex at noon taxes,' I moan.") Dmitri Borgmann's "Was it a bar or a bat I saw?" may be a pretty silly question, but it is a reasonable sentence, as is Martin Gardner's "Norma is as selfless as I am, Ron."
J. A. Lindon makes poems of one-line palindromes:

HA! ON, ON, O NOAH!

Eel-fodder, stack-cats red do flee,
　　Unglad, I tar a tidal gnu,
I tip away a wapiti,
　　Ewer of miry rim for ewe.

My favorite among lateblooming palindromes is James Thurber's "He goddam mad dog, eh?" A pedant might scratch this entry because of the spelling of goddam. But foreigners call Englishmen goddams, don't they? Thurber probably ran into his mad dog while it was out with Englishmen in Noel Coward's midday sun.
It is my impression that nobody with a palindromic name ever died in the sanctity of his countrymen's love. Where is Premier Lon Nol of Cambodia now? U Nu, erstwhile premier of Burma, had a palindromic name. So did Laval, the quisling premier of France.

There are few rational palindromes of more than fifty or sixty letters. (Penelope Gilliatt made a better try than most in this 51-letter oddity: "Doc, note, I dissent. A fast never prevents a fatness. I diet on cod.") But if you waive rationality, there is no limit to the length a palindrome can reach. The author of the following 450-letter phenomenon has written other palindromic verses more than 1,000 letters long:

THE FADED BLOOMERS' RHAPSODY

Flee to me, remote elf—Sal a dewan desired;
Now is a Late-Petal Era.
We fade: lucid Iris, red Rose of Sharon;
Goldenrod a silly ram ate.
Wan olives teem (ah, Satan lives!);
A star eyes pale Roses.

Revel, big elf on a mayonnaise man—
A tinsel baton-dragging nice elf too.
Lisp, oh sibyl, dragging Nola along;
Niggardly bishops I loot.
Fleecing niggard notables Nita names,
I annoy a Man of Legible Verse.

So relapse, ye rats,
As evil Natasha meets Evil
On a wet, amaryllis-adorned log.
Norah's foes' orders (I ridiculed a few) are late, Pet.
Alas, I wonder! Is Edna wed?
Alas—flee to me, remote elf.
                                    —*Howard W. Bergerson*

9 JULY

Those Terrible Russian Winters

Most theatres are not on Broadway, most advertising agencies not on Madison Avenue, most motion picture studios not in Hollywood. The label has been substituted for the reality, as is done below:

You may recall the story of the woman who returned to the doctor's office a week after a test. "Ah, Mrs. Jones," said the doctor. "I have good news for you." "My name is Miss Jones," said the woman. "Well, Miss Jones," replied the doctor, "I have bad news for you."

The classic story about the way we live by labels more than by reality concerns the old peasant whose farm was on the Russian-Polish border during the long conflict between those states. As the battles continued back and forth, his land kept changing sides, from Russia to Poland, and back again.

Finally, the Poles conquered, and, as the army left, the commanding officer assured the farmer that he was now safely and permanently in Polish territory. "Thank God," said the farmer. "Now no more of those terrible Russian winters."

—Sydney J. Harris

10 JULY

Omak Me Yours Tonight

(Or, Ilwaco Million Miles for One of Your Smiles)

The bulk of the Washington State place names abused in this verse derive from Indian words that sound as if they should mean something in English. They don't.* They are explained, though, in the Answers at the back of the book.

> Chet suffered sore from Acme;
> Yet (so I'm Tolt), all day
> Upon his Fife he'd Toutle
> Dabob Spee-Bi-Dah-ay
> . . . And brush the girls away.
>
> He loved to Walla Walla
> In breakers warm and wet.
> In all Duwamish waters
> Would splash and Wollochet.
>
> And was he brave? Wenatchee!
> Also Elochoman—
> Till Latah he fell in with
> A Lilliwaup named Ann.
>
> Olalla Palouse was Annie.
> Lor' Lummi, wasn't she, though!
> She had Asotin something
> That should have laid Chetlo.
>
> But it was hair of Auburn
> That Chester loved in maids,
> While ne'er was raven's Quilcene
> More black than Annie's braids.

* See 22 March.

Chesaw him in Dewatto,
A-floating on his back,
With Tatoosh on his Tumtum
That made her lips go smack.

Now Whatcom over Annie?
'Twas love, Attalia that.
Her heart went Hamma Hamma,
And her teeth went Klickitat.

She cried, "You are Malott, dear!
Wynoochee kiss me, pet?"
The Mattewa, such ardor
Did not Startup in Chet.

So Anacortes Chester,
Thurston to Havermale.
But he replies, "Tonasket!
Ohop off! Hit the trail!"

"Naselle me your embraces,"
She begs him with sweet moan;
"My family's Algona;
I sleep and dream Malone."

With Methow in her madness,
Once more the girl began:
"I Sekiu and you only;
Alava you," Spokane.

"Though man and maiden Canby
Olequa in God's view,
You're free to Sauk and kick me.
Go on—Satsop to you.

"My itch Tacoma to you is
Mowich than e'er I've had.
Draw closer!—Touchet!—Scatchet!—
Or else I shall go mad."

"Come Offut," quoth Chet Coulee;
"Pysht Pysht! You plead in vain.
Shoo! Skagit! Having walked here,
Newaukum home again!"

Then Ann began to Yellepit,
And soon she Yelm some more;
Then she began Taholah;
Then she began to roar:

"Tahuyah think you're talking,
Yacolt and frigid fella?"
In Sucia angry Vashon
All this and Moran yella.

She Vader in, and gave him
Back to Leland La Push;
She Twisp his nose, and Chucka-
nut pie in his mush.

*Lebam! ** Bangor! ** Kapowsin! ***
"Oh, Memaloos!" begged he;
"You've just knocked out a Mohler!
Dosewallips broke my knee!"

She Kickit him. He hollered:
"Wawawai! Let's cry Queets!"
Klipsan Moclips she gave him;
He grovelled at her feets.

"Elwha-cha doing? Stop it!
Become Ione instead!
I Wauna you!" Chet pleaded.—
In a Semiahmoo they were wed.

Thus did our Doughty hero
To his dear Anatone:
No more does Chester Toutle,
Or Annie dream Malone.

The Colfax is, Snohomish
More Happy, Neah or fah:
Soon Chester Willapa be,
And Annie be a ma.

Moral
Utsalady who knew a fat Liplip
Often Kachess the cockiest male.
You must Coweman—jostle him—Ruff him—
If Flattery doesn't a-Vail!

I offer this word Towal spinsters:
Don't Blaine yourself—just beat your man.
You'll Seattle work out for you just
Azwell as for Lilliwaup Ann.

                              —W.R.E.

11 JULY

The French Don't Talk like You and Me

The French cat leads a varied life, says Israel Shenker. Where you and I buy a pig in a poke, the Frenchman buys a cat in a pocket. He has a cat in his throat where we have a frog. The worm turns for you and me, but the cat turns for a Frenchman.

Cows bemuse the Frenchman, too. You may be hungry enough to eat a horse; the Frenchman would eat a cow. It may rain cats and dogs in America, but it rains cows in France. To insult a Frenchman you not only call him a dirty pig; you also say "dirty cow."

Because the French Academy frowns on evolution of the language, says Mr. Shenker, "some things will probably still move at the pace of an escargot. 'Insérer une pièce d'un franc dans la fente supérieure' may forever remain 'Insert a one-franc piece in the superior slot.' And heaven forbid that the French railroads give up their translation of 'Pour avoir de l'eau, tournez le robinet indifféremment à gauche ou à droite'—'To obtain water turn the tap indifferently to the right or to the left.'"

The French, for their part, are convinced that it is English that does not make sense, and—in a sense—they may be right. Take the plight of the Frenchman who came to London and one morning called on an English friend. "Mr. Marlborough is not down yet," said the maid. In an hour the Frenchman called again. "My husband is not up yet," said the wife. Flinging his arms wide, the exasperated Frenchman cried, "Pliss, when will he be in ze middle?"

12 JULY

Scrawny Cag-Mag Sheep

Webster's Second has all but one of the unfamiliar words in this verse. Not that you need the dictionary; Auden makes the words self-explanatory.

In his dream zealous
To attain his home,
But ensorcelling powers
Have contorted space,
Odded the way;
Instead of a facile
Five-minute trot,
For he must hirple,
Clumsied by cold,
Buffeted often

By blouts of rain,
On stolchy paths
Over glunch clouds,
Where infrequent shepherds,
Sloomy of face,
Smudge of spirit,
Snoachy of speech,
With scaddle dogs
Tend a few scrawny
Cag-mag sheep.

—W. H. Auden

13 JULY

Funsky with Strunsky

WELLFLEET, MASS.—We are spending a few days in the pine woods here, in a home belonging to Philip and Anna Hamburger. Anna is a niece—I think that is the right relationship—of Simeon Strunsky, the late columnist, and I found a 1913 collection of his writing on her bookshelf. You will see from the following excerpt that things are much the same today as they were sixty-odd years ago:

SHEATH GOWNS

It was bad enough, I said, to see elderly matrons arrayed like Oriental dancing girls. But what was worse was to see young girls, mere children, in scant and provocative attire.

"Of course it's disgusting," said Emmeline, "but it's their right. We have outgrown the days when young ladies fainted and wives fetched their husband's slippers. We have broken the shackles of mid-Victorian propriety and are working out a new conception of free womanhood. You might as well make up your mind to be shocked quite frequently before the process is completed."

"Oh, I see," said I. "Enslaved within the iron circle of the home, crushed by the tyranny of convention, of custom, of manmade laws, woman lifts up her head and declares she will be free by inserting herself into a skirt thirteen inches in diameter. Where's the sense of it?"

"It's all very simple," said Emmeline. "It means that we are having an awful time trying to escape from the degradation into which you have forced us. We struggle forward, and then the habits of the harem civilization which you have imposed on us assert themselves. Do you think we women love to dress? Every time we try on a pretty gown we know that we are riveting on the chains of our own servitude."

"But why make the chains so tight?" I said.

14 JULY

Punctuation (Parenthetical)

THE LESSON

Of all the fleas that ever flew
   (And flying fleas are rather few
((Because for proper flying you
(((Whether you are a flea or not)))
Need wings and things fleas have not got)))—

(I make the further point that fleas
Are thick as these parentheses
((An illustration (((you'll agree)))
Both apt and pleasing to a flea)))—

Now then where were we? Let me see—
Ah, yes—We said to fly you ought
(Whether you are a flea or not)
To have some wings (yes, at least two
((At least no less than two will do
(((And fleas have something less than one
((((One less, in fact (((((or, frankly, none
((((((Which, as once more you will agree))))))
Limits the flying of a flea))))))))))))))).

And let me add that fleas that fly
Are known as Flears. (You can see why.)
All I have said thus far is true
(If it's not clear, that's up to you.
((You'll have to learn sometime, my dear,
That what is true may not be clear
(((While what is clear may not be true
((((And you'll be wiser when you do.)))))))))).

—*John Ciardi*

15 JULY

Last Request

I'll die, my DVS sins 2 XP8,
    Where K9, snake and AVN
'Mid murmurs APN
    XUV8;
While U, by 4N springs RTZN,
AKN DETs SML8,
And 4 the water in the cooking pan
    2 S28
        Wait.

Dear NTT, from whom doth MN8
The S¢ of U4EA 4 me;
U OPM B9, U OP8 . . .
IDL HNC of XTC . . .

These D¢CC pray grant· no LEGG,
No $S PNN 2 X-10-U8
  My sins; no O my sad state.
Nay—raise T DMM; cheer for my DCC;
  Then help some new FMRL mate
    EE
  His TDm, and all his ¢S sate
    And TT.
      Please.

                —*W.R.E.*

ON MorAA AND MorLET

  The vs my hurrAA R 4
  R vs of a TDS mor-
  L D¢C, EE us chaps
  Who OKZNLE lapse.
          —*W.R.E.*

16 JULY

Equational Communication

17 JULY

The Akond of Swat

Who or why, or which, or *what*,   Is the Akond of SWAT?

Is he tall or short, or dark or fair?
Does he sit on a stool or a sofa or chair,   or SQUAT,
                                        The Akond of Swat?

Is he wise or foolish, young or old?
Does he drink his soup and his coffee cold,   or HOT,
                                        The Akond of Swat?

Does he sing or whistle, jabber or talk,
And when riding abroad does he gallop or walk,   or TROT,
                                        The Akond of Swat?

Does he wear a turban, a fez, or a hat?
Does he sleep on a mattress, a bed, or a mat,   or a COT,
                                        The Akond of Swat?

When he writes a copy in round-hand size,
Does he cross his T's and finish his I's   with a DOT,
                                        The Akond of Swat?

Can he write a letter concisely clear
Without a speck or a smudge or smear   or BLOT,
                                        The Akond of Swat?

Do his people like him extremely well?
Or do they, whenever they can, rebel,   or PLOT,
                                        At the Akond of Swat?

If he catches them then, either old or young,
Does he have them chopped in pieces or hung,   or SHOT,
                                        The Akond of Swat?
                                        —*Edward Lear*

(And on it goes, funnier and funnier for a dozen or so more stanzas.)

A Note by Mr. Lear: The proper way to read the verses is to make an immense emphasis on the monosyllabic rhymes, which indeed ought to be shouted out by a chorus.

A further comment on the Ahkoond, variantly spelled:

> Now the Ahkoond of Swat is a vague sort of man
> Who lives in a country far over the sea;
> Pray tell me, good reader, if tell me you can,
> What's the Ahkoond of Swat to you folks or to me?
>   —*Eugene Field*

And a threnody:

> What, what, what,
> What's the news from Swat?
>   Sad news,
>   Bad news,
> Comes by cable led
> Through the Indian Ocean's bed,
> Through the Persian Gulf, the Red
> Sea and the Med-
> Iterranean—he's dead;
> The Ahkoond is dead!*

—*George Thomas Lanigan*

18 JULY

Office Rules and Regulations

This document, headed "Office Staff Practices" and dated 1852, was found in a recently demolished building in Lichfield, Staffordshire:

1. Godliness, Cleanliness and Punctuality are necessities of a good business.

2. This firm has reduced the hours of work, and the Clerical Staff will now only have to be present between the hours of 7 A.M. and 6 P.M. on week-days.

3. Daily prayers will be held each morning in the Main Office. The Clerical Staff will be present.

4. Clothing must be of a sober nature. The Clerical Staff will not disport themselves in raiment of bright colours, nor will they wear hose unless in good repair.

5. Overshoes and top-coats may not be worn in the office, but neck scarves and headwear may be worn in inclement weather.

6. A stove is provided for the benefit of the Clerical Staff. Coal and wood must be kept in the locker. It is recommended that each member of the Clerical Staff bring 4 pounds of coal each day, during cold weather.

7. No member of the Clerical Staff may leave the room without permission from Mr. Rogers. The calls of nature are permitted, and Clerical Staff may use the garden below the second gate. This area must be kept in good order.

---

* Sorry that my extract does not include the best lines in the verse:
> The great Ahkoond of Swat
> Is not!

8. No talking is allowed during business hours.

9. The craving of tobacco, wines and spirits is a human weakness and, as such, is forbidden to all members of the Clerical Staff.

10. Now that the hours of business have been drastically reduced the partaking of food is allowed between 11.30 A.M. and noon, but work will not, on any account, cease.

11. Members of the Clerical Staff will provide their own pens. A new sharpener is available, on application, to Mr. Rogers.

12. Mr. Rogers will nominate a senior Clerk to be responsible for the cleanliness of the Main Office and the Private Office, and all Boys and Juniors will report to him 40 minutes before Prayers and will remain after closing hours for similar work. Brushes, Brooms, Scrubbers and Soap are provided by the owners.

13. The New Increased Weekly Wages are as hereunder detailed:

Junior Boys (to 11 years)	1s. 4d.
Boys (to 14 years)	2s. 1d.
Junior Clerks	8s. 7d.
Senior Clerks (after 15 years with the owners)	21s. 0d.

The owners recognize the generosity of the new Labour Laws but expect a great rise in output of work to compensate for these near Utopian conditions.

19 JULY

O Some May Promise Riches

O some may promise riches
And some may promise ease
But I will deck my darling
In suns and galaxies.

Upon her finger, Lyra's
Ring Nebula she'll wear;
Against her throat, the Cluster
In Berenice's Hair.

Rosette in Montesoros
Her bosom shall adorn,
And Veil of Cygnus hide her
Upon her wedding morn.

O some may promise riches
And some may promise ease
But I will deck my darling
In suns and galaxies.

WRE

20 JULY

Journal de la Mère Oye

Jargoned summaries of certain well-known rhymes:

1. A triumvirate of murine rodents totally devoid of ophthalmic acuity was observed in a state of rapid locomotion in pursuit of an agriculturalist's uxorial adjunct. Said adjunct then performed a triple caudectomy utilizing an acutely honed bladed instrument generally used for subdivision of edible tissue.

2. A young human female, not in a state of wedlock, occupied a small supportive structure, simultaneously undertaking consumption of nutriments comprising (a) the coagulated portion of lactic fluid and (b) the aqueous residue of coagulated lactic fluid. The unforeseen approach of an arachnid followed by establishment of the arachnid upon the supportive structure in close proximity to the subject caused severe emotional trauma in said subject, resulting in rapid self-translation of the subject from the environs.

—*Mary J. Youngquist*

21 JULY

Hallelujah, Hermit!

Each passing day provides more evidence that a fine poet being funny is generally funnier than a not-so-fine poet being funny. For instance:

HALLELUJAH!

"Hallelujah" was the only observation
That escaped Lieutenant-Colonel Mary Jane,
When she tumbled off the platform in the station,
And was cut in little pieces by the train.
  Mary Jane, the train is through yer:
  Hallelujah, hallelujah!
We will gather up the fragments that remain.
  —*A. E. Housman*

SIR JOSHUA REYNOLDS

When Sir Joshua Reynolds died
  All nature was degraded;

The King dropped a tear into the Queen's ear,
And all his pictures faded.
—*William Blake*

"HERMIT HOAR .. "

Hermit hoar, in solemn cell,
    Wearing out life's evening gray,
Smite thy bosom, Sage, and tell,
    What is bliss? And which the way?

Thus I spoke; and speaking sigh'd;
    Scarce repress'd the starting tear;
When the hoary sage reply'd:
    "Come, my lad, and drink some beer."
—*Samuel Johnson*

22 JULY

All in the Family

My third wife's eldest niece's first husband's first wife was the second wife of Supreme Court Justice William Douglas. If I meet the justice, should I call him cousin?

English is weak on words describing degrees and varieties of kinship. Melanesian words, by contrast, go so far as to distinguish between father's brother's child and mother's sister's child, or between an aunt by marriage and a mother's sister.

Yiddish too is a tongue more surefooted* than English in the darkling zone between kin and kith. *Mishpocheh* (mish-paw'-keh) means Family in its broadest sense—relatives of any sort, by blood or marriage. My third wife's eldest niece's first husband's first wife—and Justice Douglas to boot, were I Jewish—would be my *mishpocheh*. The nearest equivalent in English, says Leo Rosten, is *clan*—and that does not come very close.

Machuten (m-khoot'-n) goes even further. It is a Yiddish word meaning not just an undifferentiated father-in-law, but the father of the girl I'm going to marry; or the father of the boy I'm going to marry; or the father-in-law of my son or daughter. *Machetunim* (mokh-eh-tu'-nim) are members of a wife's or husband's extended family, to the thousands.

Meghan Burges proposes to close the gap of English in family nomenclature, at least in "the mod relationships that keep cropping up these days." His prescriptions:

"There is that young lady, for example, who shares the same address but not the same name with your son. You and she are on such terms that you feel duty bound to invite her for Thanksgiving and Christmas, but when you have to explain her socially, you mumble.

* What a lovely idea—a surefooted tongue!

"I propose that such relations shall be called the 'daughter-outlaw' or the 'son-out-law,' as the case may be. You, of course, are the 'parent-outlaw.' The titles not only are clarifying but have a certain dash.

"Two other persons who are likely to be frequent and awkward figures in your conversations are your former spouse and his/her new mate. To call someone 'David, my first wife's second husband' is a clumsy mouthful, like those pompous German titles: 'Herr Under-Inspector of the Waterworks.' The terms 'frouse' and 'frouspouse' come to mind as substitutes, but they lack pith somehow.

"American breeziness with words suggests another way. A former husband or wife is often called 'my ex,' which could be further shortened to 'X.' Using analogical extension, it follows that when you get a look at the new spouse of your X, you ask yourself, 'Y?' Right?

"So now you have your basic X and Y. Further, if divorce should become a chronic family pattern, as sometimes happens, you now have a succinct way of identifying the cast of characters: "My X-1 and Y-2," etc. But let us rather hope that your X and Y will make a go of it and even have some little Zs of their own."

23 JULY
〜

Newspeak and Nadsat

Whenever a politician utters an équivoque, we begin running, flapping our wings like Chicken Little, to tell the king that the sky of freedom is falling; Newspeak has arrived. In Newspeak, the language George Orwell dreamed up for *1984, goodsex* means chastity, *joycamp* a forced labor camp, the *Ministry of Love* a prison for the torture of dissenters. And so on.

Yet if you reread *1984*, you will find that nobody in the book speaks Newspeak. Nobody. To be sure, one character is writing a Newspeak dictionary, and another is translating Oldspeak into Newspeak, but when they converse, they use English. Or Cockney.

"If you want a stronger version of 'good,'" says the dictionary maker, "what sense is there in having a whole string of vague useless words like 'excellent' and 'splendid' and all the rest of them? 'Plusgood' covers the meaning, or 'doubleplusgood' if you want something stronger still."

But does he use "plusgood" himself? No, he says "better," as if Newspeak had never been invented.

Newspeak is just not a language one can speak, and if it has to catch on before we become a tyranny, we are still safe.

Nadsat, now, is a donkey with a different bray. Nadsat, Anthony Burgess's *Clockwork Orange* language, is spoken in a social disorder where teen-age gangs plunder, murder, and rape at will. It is current counterculture slang hyperbolized, and under certain circumstances could even happen. (Mr. Burgess, by the way, has drawn much of his Nadsat vocabulary from Russian; one wonders how London teen-agers became familiar with Russian words.)

Nadsat, as Stanley Edgar Hyman points out, also employs gypsy talk ("O my brothers"); rhyming slang ("luscious glory" for hair, rhyming perhaps with "upper story"); association ("cancer" for cigarette); amputation ("pee and em" for pop and mom); schoolboy transformations ("baddiwad" for bad), and portmanteau words ("chumble" for, Mr. Hyman guesses, "chatter-mumble").

A dictatorship might make Newspeak the official language, but no one would use it. Alienated groups, from pickpockets to Weathermen, have always used some equivalent of Nadsat. But it will never become official.

24 JULY

Gay's Gay New Song of Gay New Similes

Similes tend to become clichés, as I proved earlier.* Mr. Gay, who wrote nearly three hundred years before me, proves it here:

My passion is as mustard strong:
    I sit all sober sad;
Drunk as a piper all day long,
    Or like a March-hare mad.

Pert as a pear-monger I'd be
    If Molly were but kind;
Cool as a cucumber could see
    The rest of womankind.

I, melancholy as a cat,
    Am kept awake to weep;
But she, insensible of that,
    Sound as a top can sleep.

As fine as fivepence is her mien,
    No drum was ever tighter;
Her glance is as the razor keen,
    And not the sun is brighter.

Brisk as a body-louse she trips,
    Clean as a penny drest;
Sweet as a rose her breath and lips,
    Round as the globe her breast.

—*John Gay*

25 JULY

A Windy Love Song, Annotated

The wind that blew down the Methodist Church at Oysterville† was a dawdler compared to some of the winds in the following sonnet.

* See 25 April.
† See 29 January.

Doldrumed, with sail a-sag and rudder free,

Doldrums. The calm often met with at sea near the Equator.

To squalls and calms and baffling gusts a prey,

Changeable weather is characteristic of the doldrums.

I drift. At length a zephyr breathes my way.

Zephyr. A west breeze almost too light to measure.

With moist chinook behind. Then burns at me

Chinook. A warm, moist, southwest wind of the Washington and Oregon coast.

Sirocco!—desert sand storm in the sea!

Sirocco. A south wind beginning dustily in the Sahara but moistening as it crosses the Mediterranean.

North veers the wind; a mistral chills the day;

Mistral. A dry, cold norther that blows through the Rhone Valley toward the Mediterranean.

Behind howls bora, puffing frozen spray;

Bora. A cold and violent nor'easter blowing on the Dalmatian coast of Yugoslavia in the winter.

The gale's now storm. I run; I scud; I flee,

Gale: 25-63 mph. *Storm:* 64-75 mph.

Pursued by whirlwind, baguio and monsoon;

Whirlwind. A rotating, forward-moving column of air. *Baguio.* A tropical cyclone. *Monsoon.* A wind system in S.E. Asia blowing from opposite directions at different times of year.

Cyclones to lar and star in ambuscado;

Cyclone. A rotating wind of up to 150 mph.

Above me, jet stream, hurricane, typhoon;

Jet stream. A tropospheric wind, moving from the west at upwards of 250 mph. *Hurricane.* A cyclone of more than 75 mph., usually accompanied by heavy rain. *Typhoon.* A tropical hurricane in the western Pacific or China Sea.

Beneath me, vortex; and before, tornado.

Vortex. Whirlpool. *Tornado.* A rotating column of air whirling at speeds of up to 300 mph.

They rush upon me. Then, their task complete,

They cease, and drop me, winded, at your feet.

—W.R.E.

26 JULY

More Geo-metrics

CONCAVERSE

MT. HELICON WAS WHERE THE MUSES,
DEEP IN A CAVE, DWELT WITH APOLLO.
THE CLASSIC MORAL CODE CONFUSES
THIS LEGEND, DIFFICULT TO SWALLOW.
IF ANCIENT GRECIAN LORE REFUSES
TO DRAW THE PICTURE, LET US FOLLOW
THESE GEO-METRIC FORMS AND USES
TO OUTLINE "HELICONCAVE HOLLOW".

CONVEXSTASY

IF THAT'S THE INSIDE, HERE'S THE OUTSIDE;
ABOUT A SIN-SIDE, THERE'S A DOUBT-SIDE.
THE MUSES' SEX-LIVES' HIDDEN HISTORY
WITHIN THAT CAVE REMAINS A MYSTERY.

NEITHER CONVEXITY NOR CONCAVITY
IMPLIES COMPLEXITY OR DEPRAVITY,
NOR SHOULD WE BE PERPLEXED TO SEE
A-MUSE-MENT IN CON-VEX-STA-SY.

COSMICRHYME

Three co-ordinates in Space
Make a frame or leave a trace
Whereby anyone can plot
The location of a Spot.

But in Hyper-space sublime
You must add the cosmic Time
When you seek to represent
What is known as an "Event".

As undoubtedly you know,
It's impossible to show
Four dimensions in a poem.
Even Einstein couldn't show 'em!

Hence the quatrains given here
Aren't as warped as may appear:
They are plotted as a rhyme
In the Curvature of Time.

2 7 JULY

Palindromes of Number

The *Times* of London printed a letter sent by a reader on 27 July 1972, of which the sole point was the date. 27 July 1972, written numerically, goes the same backward as forward—27/7/72. Said the letter:

> Apart from the three rather less pleasing palindromes arising on the 27th of the 8th, 9th, and 11th months of this year, today's is the last palindromic date until 18-1-81, when I shall of course write to you again, unless I wait until the even more pleasing 18-8-81 and unless I am by then no longer in a position to be
>
> Your obedient servant,
MATTHEW NORGATE

If Mr. Norgate's calendric palindromes confuse you, it may be because most Americans write the month before the day, while our English cousins generally, but by no means always, put the day before the month. If you stipulate that the palindrome must consist of two digits, one digit, and a final two digits, as he does, there will be no palindromic dates in this country until the next century, when there will be 10/1/01, 11/1/11 (!), 12/1/21—and that is all. But Mr. Norgate is wrong in that stipulation, because though 27/7/72 may be more symmetrical than 2/7/72, the latter is equally palindromic. Both Englishmen and Americans can look forward to a palindromic date in every year that does not end in 0: 5/7/75, 6/7/76, 7/7/77 (!), 8/7/78, 9/7/79, 1/8/81, etc. Each of these of course will fall on a different day in England than in America.

2 8 JULY

Hitchcock Steers a Bull

Alfred Hitchcock, reflecting that it takes only a simple excision to turn a bull into a steer, castrated a number of well-known entertainers by dropping a single letter from their first names:

- Ickey Rooney • Orgie Jessel • Rank Sinatra • Lark Gable • Reer Garson • Helley Winters • Ick Cavett • Ill Cosby • Irk Douglas • Lip Wilson • Uke Ellington • Ex Harrison •

Leonhard Dowty points out that marriage can produce memorable name twists:

> If Tuesday Weld married Frederic March II, she would be Tuesday March II. If Carole Lombard married Isaac Singer, she would be Carole

Singer. If Ginger Rogers married Theodore Mann, she would be Ginger Mann. If April Stevens married Monty Love, she would be April Love.

A number of celebrities in and out of show business are known by other names than they received at birth. The adopted names of the people listed here became household words:

• Nicholas Bronstein • Lev Bronstein • Gladys Smith • Mary Ann Evans • Israel Baline • Benjamin Kubelski • Albert of Saxe-Coburg • Michael Goldbogen • Archie Leach • Domenico Teotocopulo •

A book called *Hundreds of Things to Do on a Rainy Day* suggests names for young people who plan a career in the public eye:

• Luke Warm • Kitty Litter • Ella Vater • May O'Naise • Sal Hepatica • Ben O'Fishal •

29 JULY

Young Johnny and Ugly Sal

Young Johnny, chancing to discover
That everybody loves a -----,
Concluded it would be his pleasure
To wed in -----, repent at -------.
He said to ugly Sal, "I'm bound,
My dear, love makes the world go '-----.
Your looks, that make an angel weep,
Are only epidermis ----.
Who says men seldom ------ make
At girls with -------? a mistake!
Appearances -------, 'tis true;
Yet better *they* deceive, than *you*.
It's not immortal beauties that
Make mortal hearts go pitty-pat;
You're wealthy, Sal, per my research:
A rich bride goeth ----- to church."

Sal felt her laggard pulses start:
----, ---- her hands; ----, ---- her heart.
She thought: "Each day it truer gets:
Men wink at blondes, but wed ---------!
Though gray my hair beneath the dye,
No older than I ---- am I;
This hand shall soon the ------ rock,

And ---- the world (per Doctor Spock)!"
Who takes a wife, he takes a ------;
For John, the marriage was disaster.
Love makes ---- pass away, I guess.
But t'other way around no less.
Who weds for love, his ------ are great,
But daytime is the normal state;
And marriages, in ------ made,
On dusty Earth are soon decayed.
The lewdest bride may pass for ------
Unless too soon she goes to waist.
And when such fruits begin to show,
The cuckold is the last to know.

Now one last, sad reminder to end John's dreary tale:
The ------ of the species is more deadly than the ----.
                                                —W.R.E.

30 JULY

The Nicknaming of States

Nations are often personified. France is Marianne, England John Bull, the United States Uncle Sam. The fifty American states, however, have taken another tack: they adopted nicknames, sometimes several nicknames to a state. Most of these nicknames are assembled, capitalized, in the stanzas below.

1. SHOW ME the LAND OF OPPORTUNITY!
2.   LAND OF ENCHANTMENT! EMPIRE of the FREE!
3. The INLAND EMPIRE! EMPIRE OF THE SOUTH!
4.   Show me a PELICAN, and in its mouth

5. A NUTMEG, which no SOONER doth it eat
6.   Than it a pit of GRANITE must excrete!
7. Here OLD NORTH, NORTH STAR, HEART OF DIXIE stay
8.   With OLD LINE, LONE STAR, DIAMOND, and BAY.

9. Here CONSTITUTION holds CENTENNIAL
10.   In SILVER SUNSHINE by a KEYSTONE wall.
11. Here OLD DOMINION and OLD COLONY
12.   Split GOLDEN TREASURE in EQUALITY.

13. HOOSIER, ALOHA! Welcome, VOLUNTEER!
14.   CORNHUSKER, LITTLE RHODY—glad you're here!
15. You also, HAWKEYE, TAR HEEL, wily SIOUX—

16.   Let me be FIRST to walk BLUE GRASS with you!

17. To climb, in BIG SKY COUNTRY, MOUNTAIN GREEN;
18.   MOUNTAIN of PINE TREE and of WOLVERINE.
19. GRAND CANYON we'll explore, and BUCKEYE breach;
20.   We'll sniff MAGNOLIA, and eat GARDEN PEACH.

21. In JAYHAWK, SAGEBRUSH, EVERGREEN we'll tarry;
22.   Grow BLUE HEN, BEEF, and COTTON in the PRAIRIE;
23. Plant yellow SUNFLOWER, of all blooms the GEM,
24.   To grace our BEEHIVE with its diadem.

25. PALMETTO leaves will yield their cooling shade
26.   When BADGER, BEAVER, COYOTE promenade
27. With FLICKERTAIL and GOPHER, to the yammer
28.   (GREAT LAND above!) of
                    YELLOWHAMMER.
                                        —W.R.E.

3 1 J U L Y

The Gentle Witch

Mary Easty or Esty (not Espy), my six-times-great-grandmother, was hanged as a witch with her elder sister Rebecca at Salem, Massachusetts in 1692. We could use a few witches like her today. When I feel sorry for myself, as sometimes happens, I shame myself into good cheer by rereading the letter Mary wrote to the judges who had condemned her. I defy you to cite a more moving example of resignation, forgiveness, and Christian love:

> I petition not to Your Honours for my life, for I know I must die, and my appointed time is set; but the Lord he knows it that if it be possible, no more innocent blood may be shed, which undoubtedly cannot be avoided in the way and course you go in. I question not but Your Honours do the utmost of your powers in the discovery and detecting of witchcraft and witches, and would not be guilty of innocent blood for the world. But, by my own innocency, I know you are in the wrong way. The Lord in his infinite mercy direct you in this great work, if it be his blessed will that no more innocent blood be shed! I would humbly beg of you, that Your Honours would be pleased to examine these afflicted persons strictly, and keep them apart for some time, and likewise to try some of these confessing witches; I being confident there is several of them has belied themselves and others, as will appear; if not in this world, I am sure in the world to come, whither I am now a-going. I question not but you will

see an alteration of these things. They say myself and others having made a league with the Devil, we cannot confess. I know, and the Lord knows, as will shortly appear, they belie me, and so I question not but they do others. The Lord above, who is the Searcher of all hearts, knows, as I shall answer for it at the tribunal seat, that I know not the least thing of witchcraft; therefore I cannot, I dare not belie my own soul. I beg Your Honours not to deny this my humble petition from a poor, dying, innocent person. And I question not but the Lord will give a blessing to your endeavors.

I hope Mary was looking down from Heaven when, after twenty years, the diligence of her husband Isaac resulted in the annulment of the verdict against her.

AUGUST

1 AUGUST

Fifty English Emigrants

You will readily identify most of these words. It may be more difficult, however, to identify the languages that have naturalized them.

1) stiff-ticket; 2) biftek; 3) colcream; 4) strajkar; 5) blajnpigg; 6) apera-shen; 7) lof-letter; 8) te lu fong; 9) telewizja; 10) njeuspapier; 11) peda; 12) salang; 13) pikunikku; 14) bara i minne; 15) blaekbor; 16) atomi pommi; 17) smoking; 18) bondes; 19) puddi gud; 20) engin; 21) dipoidh; 22) Geancach; 23) racchettiere; 24) fanfurria; 25) mpasketm-pall; 26) cora; 27) gemlingshus; 28) makinchprc; 29) redingote; 30) guafay; 31) herkot; 32) nailon; 33) ajskrym; 34) peipi; 35) o kontri; 36) kawboju filmas; 37) kaddam; 38) sityholly; 39) k'a fei; 40) vilda vastern; 41) muvingpikceris; 42) p'u-lo-lieh-t'a-li-ya; 43) saiduak; 44) guachiman; 45) gescreent; 46) risurin; 47) schiacchenze; 48) calamazo; 49) vacuomme-clineaur; 50) enugkh.

—Leonard R. N. Ashley

2 AUGUST

Aris Old Tot

This quotation appeared in the letters column of the *New York Sunday Times*:

> The young are prone to desire and ready to carry any desire they may have formed into action. Of bodily desires it is the sexual to which they are the most disposed to give way, and in regard to the sexual desire they exercise no self-restraint. They are passionate, irascible, and apt to be carried away by their impulses. They have high aspirations, for they have never yet been humiliated by the experience of life, but are unacquainted with the limiting force of circumstances. If the young commit a fault, it is always on the side of excess and exaggeration.

Spoken, I thought, like any sour forty-year-old—until I saw that it was Aristotle who had made the comment some time around 350 B.C. I hasten to berate his prejudiced and ill-tempered ghost, as follows:

Aris old tot
you who begot
logical thought

kids that I spot
aren't a bad lot
sure they have got

addled on pot
kiss like a shot
young loins are hot

Aris old tot
young did you not
have your cocotte

drink like a sot
I did so what
face it old tot

we're both dry rot
let the kids trot
Aris old tot

—*W.R.E.*

(Joe Alger said fifty years ago that what we need isn't birth control. It's controlling them after they are born.)

3 AUGUST

Word Ways' *Ways with Words*

Word Ways is a quarterly publication whose editors, contributors, and readers are maniacs—logomaniacs.

Who but *Word Ways* would serve drinks on the house because "unoriental" (not to mention "suoidea," the name of the superfamily of pigs and peccaries) has all the vowels in reverse order? Who but *Word Ways* would display, with the pride of a cat bringing home an eviscerated frog, a collection of three-syllable, four-letter words—aero, aery, Aida, area, aria, idea, iota, Iowa, Ohio, oleo, olio, and urea? Or demonstrate that by adding a single letter you can turn certain one-syllable words into three-syllable words—smile into simile, lien into alien, came into cameo? Or reduce two-syllable words to one-syllable words by adding letters—rugged to shrugged, ague to plague, aged (the adjective) to staged or raged?

Words of two or more identical parts—cancan, Sing Sing, dodo, papa, tartar, wogga wogga, cha-cha-cha—are called tautonyms or reduplications. It took *Word Ways* to teach me that there are words with *four* identical parts: Kukukuku (a people inhabiting parts of eastern New Guinea); Fofo Fofo (a town in Papua); angang-angang (a kind of Javanese gong).

It was not enough for *Word Ways* to point out that there are as many as nine letters in some common one-syllable words: scratched, screeched, scrounged, squelched, strengths, stretched. It went on to list unisyllabic words of *ten* letters —words I shall not repeat here, since I can think of no use for them.

Offhand, how many words would you say have just one letter? Twenty-six, notes *Word Ways:* every one of the letters in the alphabet.

Or take the matter of miscegenation among states. Alaska, says *Word Ways,* blends Alabama and Nebraska; Arkansas is a cross between Arizona and Kansas; North Dakota mixes North Carolina and South Dakota; South Dakota is part South Carolina and part North Dakota; South Carolina is part South Dakota and part North Carolina. The entire United States is summed up within the bounds of one state: LoUiSiAna.

It would never have occurred to me that "indivisibility" and "niminypiminyism" have each, phonetically speaking, seven i's and no other vowels; or that you can say, but not write, "There are three ways to spell (to, two, too?)," while you can write, but not say, "There are three ways to pronounce 'slough.' "

A quick check reveals dozens of excerpts from the pages of *Word Ways* in this book, and there may be some I have forgotten to credit.

You might do a little checking of your own. Send an $8 check to Faith W. Eckler, Spring Valley Road, Morristown, New Jersey 07960, and she will send you *Word Ways* every three months for a year.

4 AUGUST
ᰔ

Mnemonics into Jargon

A mnemonic device is supposed to make it easy to remember something: "i before e except after c," "30 days hath September, April, June, and November," "Even's east (for street directions), odd's bodkins."

I would have welcomed a mnemonic device to fix in my mind the name of one of my clients, Mr. Hamburger (or was it Frankfurter?). I always got it wrong. I would walk into his office repeating in my head, "Hamburger, Hamburger, Hamburger," and then say, "Good morning, Mr. Frankfurter" every time. Or the other way around.

Here is a mnemonic to end all mnemonics from *The Lancet,* an English medical magazine:

MNEMONIC FOR REPORTING BACTERIOCIN AND BACTERIOPHAGE TYPES

Sir—During the search for a better method to report bacteriocin and bacteriophage patterns, a mnemonic evolved which has greatly simplified the reporting of our typing results. Each of the tests is assigned a number from 1 to N where N is the number of tests employed. For example, in typing by bacteriocin production, the reaction against indicator strain 1 is designated test 1, the reaction against indicator strain 2 is designated test 2, and so on, until all tests are defined. The results of the first three tests are then assigned a number, as determined from the following mnemonic.

Results for 3 Tests	Representation	Results for 3 Tests	Representation
+++	1	+--	5
++-	2	-+-	6
+-+	3	--+	7
-++	4	---	8

Each of the subsequent data triplets is assigned its proper number in a similar fashion. Thus, a test strain which has a bacteriocin production pattern (+---+--+++-+----+-) would be, by definition, type 564386. If the number of tests is not evenly divisible by three, a second (++ = A, +- = B, -+ = C, -- = D) and third (+ = E, - = F) mnemonic can be used to represent those results remaining after division into triplets. Each of the 2^N possible patterns is automatically assigned a type designation according to these simple rules.

—*J. J. Farmer III*

I am told that a boy rhinoceros has no difficulty identifying a girl rhinoceros, and doubtless a medical researcher will find it easy to identify bacteriocin and bacteriophage patterns by means of the foregoing mnemonic. But for a layman the mnemonic is no mnemonic at all. It's jargon.

5 AUGUST

*Drinking Song of a Hard-Hearted Landlord**

Though my ant-ant-ant-ant-ant-ant-ant-ant-ant-ant a lass who's a loner,
So many con-der-der-der-der-der-der-der-der-der-der are milling
About with pre-tion-tion-tion-tion-tion-tion-tion-tion-tion-tion to own her,
They'd be dear at ha'penny-ha'penny-ha'penny-ha'penny-ha'penny-ha'penny-ha'penny-
    ha'penny-ha'penny-ha'penny the shilling.

CHORUS: They'd be dear at, *etc.*

The dril-dril-dril-dril-dril-dril-dril-dril-dril-dril that frame her sweet forehead
Would merit niel-niel-niel-niel-niel-niel-niel-niel-niel-niel at-tion-tion-tion-tion-tion-
    tion-tion-tion-tion-tion;
But her ement-ement-ement-ement-ement-ement-ement-ement-ement-ement mine—
    and *I'm* horrid:
I jeer at romantic in-tion-tion-tion-tion-tion-tion-tion-tion-tion-tion.

* See also 30 January.

CHORUS: I jeer at, *etc.*

If she der-der-der-der-der-der-der-der-der-der her payments I heed not
How der-der-der-der-der-der-der-der-der-der this lass when unbent
Treat ant-ant-ant-ant-ant-ant-ant-ant-ant-ant as humans? Indeed not:
Their dency-dency-dency-dency-dency-dency-dency-dency-dency-dency not to pay
    rent.

CHORUS: Their dency-, *etc.*

—W.R.E.

6 AUGUST

The Showman's Courtship

It is too bad that there are no hicks anymore, nor any more showmen like Artemus
Ward to give them a show "ekalled by few and exceld by none:"

Altho I hankered intensly arter the objeck of my affecshuns, I darsunt
tell her of the fires which was rajin in my manly Buzzum. I'd try to do
it but my tung would kerwollup up agin the roof of my mowth & stick
thar, like deth to a deseast Afrikan or a country postmaster to his offis,
while my hart whanged agin my ribs like an old fashioned wheat Flale
agin a barn floor.

'Twas a carm still nite in Joon. All nater was husht and nary zeffer
disturbed the sereen silens. I sot with Betsy Jane on the fense of her farther's pastur. We'd bin rompin threw the woods, kullin flours & drivin
the woodchuck from his Nativ Lair (so to speak) with long sticks. Wall
we sot thar on the fense, a swingin our feet to and fro, blushin as red as
the Baldinsville skool house when it was fust painted, and lookin very
simple, I make no doubt. My left arm was ockepied in ballunsin myself
on the fense, while my rite was woundid luvinly round her waste.

I cleared my throat and tremblinly sed, "Betsy, you're a gazelle."

I thought that air was putty fine. I waited to see what effeck it would
hav upon her. It evidently didn't fetch her, for she up and sed,

"You're a sheep!"

Sez I, "Betsy, I think very muchly of you."

"I don't bleeve a word you say—so there now cum!" with which ob-
sarvashun she hitched away from me.

"I wish thar was winders to my Sole" sed I, "so that you could see some
of my feelins. There's fire enuff in here," sed I, strikin my buzzum with
my fist, "to bile all the corn beef and turnips in the naberhood. Versoovius
and the Critter ain't a circumstans!"

She bowd her hed down and commenst chawin the strings to her sun
bonnet

"Ar, could you know the sleeplis nites I worry threw with on your account, how vittles has seized to be attractiv to me & how my lims has shrunk up, you wouldn't dowt me. Gase on this wastin form and these 'ere sunken cheeks—"

I should have continnered on in this strane probly for sum time, but unfortnitly I lost my ballunse and fell over into the pastur ker smash, tearin my close and seveerly damagin myself ginerally.

Betsy Jane sprung to my assistance in dubble quick time and dragged me 4th. Then drawin herself up to her full hite she sed:

"I won't listen to your noncents no longer. Jes say rite strate out what you're drivin at. If you mean gettin hitched, I'M IN!"

I considered that air enuff for all practicul purpusses, and we proceeded immejitly to the parson's, & was made 1 that very nite.

(Notiss to the Printer: Put some stars here.)

* * * * * * * * * *

I've parst threw many tryin ordeels sins then, but Betsy Jane has bin troo as steel. By attendin strickly to bizniss I'v amarsed a handsum Pittance. No man on this foot-stool can rise & git up & say I ever knowinly injered no man or wimmin folks, while all agree that my Show is ekalled by few and exceld by none, embracin as it does a wonderful colleckshun of livin wild Beests of Pray, snaix in grate profushun, a endliss variety of life-size wax figgers, & the only traned kangaroo in Ameriky—the most amoozin little cuss ever introjuced to a discriminatin public.

—*Charles Farrar Browne*

7 AUGUST
∽

The Sounds of Oysterville

HANDSAWWWWWWWWWWWWWWWW
—*Richard Lebovitz*

The sound reproduced by Mr. Lebovitz in that one-line, one-word, onomatopoeic poem was a regular refrain in my home village of Oysterville half a century ago. Today it is replaced by a snarl:

CHAINSAWWWWWWWWWWWWWWWWW

Another sound inseparable from Oysterville in my mind has been missing since August 7, 1959. That is the voice of my father not-swearing. His most common not-swearing expletives were "Son of a sea cook!", "Consarn it!", "Dad durn it!", "Dad dum it!", "Dad cuss it!", "Ding bust it!", and "Sou-wegian!" The ultimate in rage came out as "Devil!" or, more commonly, "Devilation!" Since my father was by nature a cheerful man, and by self-discipline a controlled one, he seldom uttered even these harmless-appearing epithets; but when they came, they came like thunder-bolts. It was when he said "Dad cuss it!" in the midst of a hurricane that the Method-ist church fell down.*

> In Oysterville,
> Mosquitoes whine, and mating frogs are shrill;
> While bumblebees, bluebottle flies, and uzzers
> Are buzzers.
>
> In Oysterville,
> The chipmunks scold, the yellowhammers drill;
> While certain clicks one hears in Oysterville
> Are misadventures
> Of dentures.
>
> —W.R.E.

8 AUGUST

A Brew of Brewer

All about me the news media are titting and tatting and tutting in anticipation of the Last Trump; no day but blares its apocalypse; no worm but is labeled python, and no minnow but whale. God must have had something in mind when he created doomsayers who live, so to speak, at the top of their lungs; they may be quite right that next Tuesday will end the world; still, I wish John Oakes would instruct his boys to read a page from Isaac Disraeli, E. C. Brewer, or Montaigne for perspective each morning before they begin writing their editorials for the *Times*.

My father remarked on his deathbed that he only regretted he could not know how everything turned out; I could tell him now that nothing turns out; fashions and shapes and vocabularies change, but the root of the plant keeps on digging.

Alexander and Caesar and Attila and Hitler did not change their world: the changes were going on all the while underground. Tomorrow is nuzzling tran-quilly away in the earth right now while all the radioactive melodrama distracts our attention overhead.

E. Cobham Brewer's famous *Dictionary of Phrase and Fable* strings hundreds of examples of that nuzzling together, until we begin to see a pattern emerging, as in these hobson-jobsons:

- Brasenose College (Oxford). Over the gate is a brass nose, the arms of the

---

* See 29 January.

college; but the word is a corruption of brasenhuis, a brasserie or brewhouse, the college having been built on the site of a brewery.

• Andiron. From Old French andier; no connection with iron.

• Public House Signs. Bull and Gate, Bull and Mouth—corruptions of Boulogne Gate or Mouth adopted out of compliment to Henry VIII, who took Boulogne in 1544. The Bag o' Nails—corruption of Bacchanals; also The Devil and Bag o' Nails. The Cat and Wheel—corruption of St. Catherine's Wheel. The Goat and the Compass—perhaps from "God Encompasseth Us." The Pig and Whistle—perhaps from "pig and wassail," pig being an abbreviation of piggin, an earthen vessel. Plum and Feathers—a corruption of The Plume and Feathers. Swan with Two Necks—perhaps a corruption of "two nicks" with which the Vintners' Company marked the beaks of their swans.

• Bowler hat. From Mr. Beaulieu. "Like the billycock hat it is said to have been introduced by the Norfolk landowner, William Coke. Because he found his tall riding hat frequently swept off by overhanging branches, he asked (c. 1850) a famous hatter of the period (Mr. Beaulieu) to design him a lower-crowned hat."

• Johnny cake. Journey cake.

• Gingerly. Probably from Old French gensour, comparative of gentle, delicate, dainty. No connection with ginger.

* * *

In the 1970s, young men wear their hair to their shoulders; in the 1980s, their heads may be shaved. In the 1970s, DDT was reviled; in the 1980s, it may again be a boon. In the 1970s, people jogged to avert heart attacks; in the 1980s, they may prefer heart attacks to jogging.

Such shifts are as unimportant as whether the next President is a Republican or a Democrat. Forget your newspaper headlines; the changes that count are happening the way hobson-jobsons happen, unannounced, unnoticed, underground.

9 AUGUST

Salisbury, Colquhoun, and Cuchulain

Christine Magriel asked a London coster how to reach her hotel. He replied, "It's beside Mahblahtch." "Mahblahtch?" asked Christine in confusion. "Yes, Miss, Mahblahtch," said the coster, sketching a wicket with his hands. The light dawned. "Oh!" said Christine, "Marble Arch!"

The British laugh a lot at the way they pronounce their proper names, and I suppose that is better than crying. Louisa Bonner, who called today's unattributed limericks to my attention, justifies the first one on the grounds that the Latin name of Salisbury was Sarum, while the abbreviation of Hampshire is Hants. But since nobody says Sarum any more, or pronounces Hants the way it is spelled, I see no way of making the verse innerly consistent either in scanning or in rhyme.

THE YOUNG CURATE OF SALISBURY

There was a young curate of Salisbury
Whose manners were quite halisbury-skalisbury.
  He ran around Hampshire
  Without any pampshire,
Till the vicar compelled him to walisbury.

A YOUNG MAN CALLED CHOLMONDELEY COLQUHOUN

A young man called Cholmondeley Colquhoun
Kept as a pet a babolquhoun.
  His mother said, "Cholmondeley,
  Do you think it quite colmondeley
To feed your babolquhoun with a spolquhoun?"

Erse, or Scottish Gaelic, has its own pitfalls of pronunciation, as is demonstrated here:

CUCHULAIN

The pronunciation of Erse
Gets worse and worse.
They spell it Cuchulain—
No fuchulain!
              —A. D. Hope

10 AUGUST

The Comtator and the Door

Whenever the story fuddles, insert "men."

Following the adjournt of the annual meeting of sa, an imsely wealthy comtator rubbed his throat with thol, donned his outer gart (a Burberry), and paused in his departure to lat as follows to the door:

My complits, gentle! (For, despite the abaset of your jobs, you see that I do not consider you ials.) Sirs, it is too late to d the Establisht; instead, I recomd its instant replacet. Wherever one may comce one's assesst, whatever one's ideological alignt, one's judgt must be that our democratic experit, once the adornt of the ages, has wound up as a torted society, a detrit to the attaint of 's goals.

"What, gentle, are its so-called accomplishts? Where are its aities? We dwell in a agerie, trusting for safety to its taess. Diseased dicants walk streets paved with excret. We breathe ingitis from the air. Unemployt is rife. A shortage of tenets has driven rent payts through the roof. We are impelled to supplet our incret by moonlighting. The u of our senior citizens consists of gruel. Oppression fots unrest.

"Do I dare tion the fate of the great issues of war and peace? Postponet! Of the man who is crippled? Laess! Of civil rights? Abridget! Of slum dwellers? Displacet! Of militant dissenters? Internt—nay, often, intert!

"What endorset can be given a govert that requires a white integut for economic advancet? Where every segt of the population is aced by crime? Where even the college fresh are in a fert? Nor is improvet to be expected; there is no comsurate concern, no agreet on priorities, no tor to relieve our bafflet. All is argut. Our leaders are temperatally unfit. They lack discernt. They are dacious. And I suspect they are hang."

The door professed to be imsely impressed by these eletary comts. One, who was religious, cried, "A!" Another, who was French, said, "Evidemt!" A third said: "In addition, Car is a lousy opera; the weather is inclet, my investts have gone sour, my wife has joined Wo's Lib, and I might tion also that I find the saess of my work detrital to my health."

Since they were so sympathetic, the wealthy comtator left a tredous tip.

MORAL: The road to pecuniary prefert is not necessarily to become a shevik or to stuff cet into the Alitary Canal. You will do comdably well if you pretend agreet with anyone, however deted, who has money.

11 AUGUST

For the Common Market

It's easy to be witty in French.
You don't have to know French well.
Think of those expressions (this is the secret) . . .
Gout du néant, esprit de l'escalier,
Dégoût de la vie, nostalgie de la boue,
Adieu supreme des mouchoirs.
All you have to do is take two nouns,
Any old nouns, the iller-assorted the better,
And couple them with a genitive,
Shrug, throw your hands out (not too far),
In a French sort of way,
And give the casual knowing look of someone
Who knows the girl at the bar.
Try it and see . . .
With faint disdain . . . c'est un sentiment de vestiaire,
Goût de Londres, tendresse des wagon-lits
Or sighing
Les au revoirs de Vendredi.
Everyone will say how well you know French.
I've tried it on Frenchmen, and I know.

In German just couple the words together,
Like any old strangers meeting in any old street . . .
Himmelschnabel Apfelpudel Heldenbegeisterun Weltkrebs . . .
No one will know any better.

In Italian, it will be helpful to know the first line of Dante,
And also, brushing away a tear,
"Italia, Italia, terra di morti,"
And go straight on to business.

I will advise later about the Scandinavian countries.

—*Michael Burn*

12 AUGUST

Poem Composed in Rogue River Park

Poem Composed in Rogue River Park, Grants Pass, Oregon, after Wayman's Car Stopped Dead on the Oregon Coast in the Middle of a Howling Rainstorm and Had to be Towed First to Yachats, Oregon, Where It Couldn't Be Fixed, and Then One Hundred Miles through the Mountains to Eugene, Where after It was Repaired and Wayman Started out Again His Accelerator Cable Parted and He Had to Run on the Last Dozen Miles or so into Grants Pass at Midnight with His Throttle Jammed Open and Spend the Night Waiting for the Garage to Open Which Is at This Moment Working on His Car, or Rather Waiting for a New Part to Be Shipped Down from Eugene (and Which Garage, Incidentally, Would Fix the Cable But Fail to Discover that All That High-rev Running Would Have Blown the Head Gasket on Wayman's Car Causing Frightening Overheating Problems the Next Day when Wayman Did Try to Blast on Down to San Francisco)

Let me not go anywhere,
Let me stay in Grants Pass, Oregon, forever.

—*Tom Wayman*

13 AUGUST

Coleridge on Cologne

I once calculated that there would be no carbon monoxide cluttering up the air of New York today if only the city had had sense enough to ban gasoline-powered vehicles back in 1903. The same calculation showed, though, that horse manure would now be up to the ninety-second floor of the Empire State Building.

These conclusions were passed along to my limited public as a pleasantry; but pleasantries are suspect these days. My ensuing mail was divided between correspondents who felt I was being disrespectful toward ecology, and correspondents who felt I was being disrespectful toward horses. The reactions bothered me: how, I wonder, can one solve any serious problem except by way of a joke?

A hundred and fifty years before ecology became a parlor, bedroom, and bath game, a poet made a joke of the miasma investing the city of Cologne:

> In Köln, a town of monks and bones,
> And pavements fanged with murderous stones,
> And rags, and hags, and hideous wenches,
> I counted two-and-seventy stenches,
> All well defined and separate stinks!
>
> Ye nymphs that reign o'er sewers and sinks,
> The river Rhine, it is well known
> Doth wash your city of Cologne;
> But tell me, nymphs, what power divine
> Shall henceforth wash the river Rhine?
> —*Samuel Taylor Coleridge*

How about *eau de cologne*, Sam?

14 AUGUST

Sentences Askew

Red Smith, the sportswriter, recalls that Grantland Rice once interviewed Babe Ruth on radio. Because the Babe sometimes struck out in conversation, Rice typed out the questions and answers in advance. "Well, you know, Granny," Ruth read in answer to a question, "Duke Ellington and the Battle of Waterloo was won on the playing fields of Elkton." "Babe," Granny said after the show, "Duke Ellington for the Duke of Wellington I can understand. But how did you ever read Eton as Elkton? That's in Maryland, isn't it?" "I married my first wife there," Babe said, "and I hate the gawdarn place."

Skewed sentences are among life's unalloyed pleasures; they do not embarrass the skewer, since he is unaware that anything has gone amiss, and they are a source of innocent merriment for the hearer.*

Well, once in a while they do embarrass the skewer. Warren Austin, the United States ambassador to the United Nations, was not allowed to forget his suggestion

---

* See 23 June and 16 November.

to the quarreling Israelis and Arabs that they should "sit down and settle their differences like good Christians."

The mayors of New York have a noble tradition of skewing. Jimmy Walker announced, "We're launching this innovation for the first time." Robert Wagner said, "I have reiterated over and over again what I have said before."

No one has exceeded Casey Stengel for sheer incomprehensibility: "I would be batting the big feller if they wasn't ready with the other one, but a left-hander would be the thing if they wouldn't have knowed it already because there is more things involved than could come up on the road, even after we've been home a long while." Mr. Stengel remarked that "Gil Hodges is so strong he could snap your eyebrows off," and said of another player, "He's so lucky he could fall in a hole and come up with a silver spoon." A cogent bit of Stengelese advice: "Don't cut off your nose yourself."

Then there was Sam Goldwyn. He denied originating "Include me out," but admitted to "It's a dog-eat-dog world, and nobody's gonna eat me." "No, thanks," he told his hostess, "coffee isn't my cup of tea." Other Goldwynisms: "Most directors bite the hand that lays the golden egg." "When I want your opinion, I'll give it to you." "I had a monumental idea last night, but I didn't like it." "I never put on a pair of shoes until I've worn them five years."

Either Goldwyn or Gregory Ratoff said of television, then in its infancy, "I won't believe it until I see it in black and white." It was certainly Ratoff who told John Huston, "John, if you weren't the son of my beloved friend Walter, and if you weren't a brilliant writer and a magnificent director, you'd be nothing but a common drunk."

15 AUGUST

In Vino Veritas

It has been a paronomasiac day.

First, at lunch, Hobart Weekes was describing a cruise in which his fellow passengers included certain Pillsburys of the Middle Western milling family. "Flour children," said Paul Hollister. "Lots of dough," said Paul Bonner, Jr.

This afternoon, as I was re-reading Richard Hughes's *In Hazard,* I caught him slipping a pun into a sentence so deftly that I had to look twice to be sure it was there:

> Presently she told Dick she had a cat so smart that it first ate cheese and then breathed down the mouseholes—with baited breath—to entice the creatures out.

A lordly pun. Less lordly are these by Colin Sanderson:

> *Girl*: Orange juice sorry you made me cry?
> *Boy:* Don't be soda pressed; them martini bruises.

Girl: Wine you leave me alone?
Boy: Water you mean? I didn't even have to let gin.
Girl: Oh, why Chianti leave me alone?
Boy: Look, vodkan I do to make it all rye?
Girl: Just leave me beer I'll scream.
Boy: Oh, I'd like tequila.
Girl: Darling, let's give up bourbon life.
         There's more rum in the country.

(I'm afraid those two should moderate their drinking.)

16 AUGUST

A Reasonable Reply to John Ball

In the fourteenth century, John Ball went around stirring up the peasants with this incendiary couplet:

> When Adam delved and Eve span,
> Who was then a gentleman?

Well, the fact is that Eve was sitting with her back against a tree, napping, when the Serpent shook a branch and the Apple fell between her innocent, parted lips.* She didn't have to lift a finger for it. No arrangement could have been more gentlemanly—or ladylike—than that. It was later that God told Adam and Eve to go peel their own apples. Someone in Ball's audiences should have reminded him:

> Eve was spick and Adam span
> Till that Sweat of Brow began.
>   —*W.R.E.*

The significance of the apple incident grows obscure as my blood slows with age. Didn't it have something to do with figs?

FIGS AND FIGLEAVES

> I don't give a fig for your figleaf, my doe,
> Or a damn for a damsel who flaunts one.
> The snake left my Eden a long time ago,
> So take back your apple—who wants one?
>
> The chaster the girls, once the harder I chased,
> Enticingly waving pajamas;
> But now that I measure four feet in the waist,
> I'm reckoned as safe by their mamas.
>   —*W.R.E.*

---

* Or was it Newton who ate the apple?

17 AUGUST

Lizzie Borden and Her Playmates

It is hard to say now whether the American public at the turn of the century bled more for poor Lizzie Borden, or *with* Lizzie's poor parents, whom she was accused of slaying with more enthusiasm than finesse. Though the jury acquitted her, her name has come down for seventy-five years as a synonym for an innocent butcher. School children still chant:

> Lizzie Borden took an axe
> And gave her mother forty whacks.
> And when she saw what she had done
> She gave her father forty-one.

It is arguable whether Lizzie's experience inspired the sick verses so popular in those days, or whether the verses inspired Lizzie. In any event, from then until now there has been a bubbling, bloodstained spring of them. Two examples will be enough:

> Willie built a guillotine,
> Tried it out on sister Jean.
> Said Mother as she got the mop:
> "These messy games have got to stop!"
> —*William E. Engel*

> Father heard his children scream,
> So he threw them in the stream,
> Saying, as he drowned the third,
> "Children should be seen, not heard!"
> —*Harry Graham*

18 AUGUST

High Flight Highlights

Riddles serve a useful purpose in reminding us, if we need reminding, that things are not always what they seem. So I am grateful to the airline (since I can't recall whether it was American, United, or Northwest Orient, I thank them all) that included this riddle in its magazine:

> What is it that from which you may take the whole and yet have some left over?

The riddle is attributed to the famous puzzlemaker Ernest Dudeney.

What, asked the same magazine, is unique about this list of words?

HEX
CHOICE
HIC
OH
ICE
HO
HI

Carl Sandburg turned riddles into poetry:

THEY HAVE RIDDLES

In the farm house passing another crock of apples,
On the street car riding to the roller coasters,
At picnics, clam-bakes, or the factory workbench
They have riddles, good and bad conundrums:

Which goes through the plank first, the bullet or the hole?
Where does the music go when the fiddle is put in the box?
Where does your lap go when you stand up? The same place your fist goes when you open your hand.
What are the two smallest things mentioned in the Bible? The widow's mite and the wicked flea.
Who are the shortest people mentioned in the Bible? Bildad the Shuhite, Knee-high-miah, and the man who had nothing but from whom even that which he had was taken away.
What was the last thing Paul Revere said to his horse on the famous ride? "Whoa!"
"Did you hear about the empty barrel of flour?" "No." "Nothing in it."
What is there more of in the world than anything else? Ends.

They have Irish bulls timeworn and mossgrown:

You are to be hanged and I hope it will prove a warning to you.
I took so much medicine I was sick a long time after I got well.
I can never get these boots on until I have worn them for awhile.
One of us must kill the other—let it be me. We were boys together—at least I was.
If all the world were blind what a melancholy sight it would be.
This will last forever and afterward be sold for old iron.
They would cut us into mince-meat and throw our bleeding heads on the table to stare us in the face.
On the dim and faroff shore of the future we can see the footprints of the unseen hand.
We pursue the shadow, the bubble bursts, and leaves in our hand only ashes.

—*Carl Sandburg*

19 AUGUST
෨

The Thesaurus and the Muse

The author of this verse had a diverting notion and I wish I had thought of it first:*

LET'S HAVE A PARTY

Reach down the Thesaurus, put the
    Roget
before us; send for the harlot, the street-
    girl,
the courtesan, adultress, advoutress, kept
    woman,
the strumpet, the prostitute, the tart
and the broad, the hussy, the trollop, the
    jade, bitch and whore;
send for the whole of the frail
sisterhood, and we'll have a cocktail
a party and food in a gigantic reception
a schnozzle, a rort, and that's no decep-
    tion, no falsehood,
no imposture, no untruth, no conjure,
    no joke;
the youths and the boys, the lads, slips
and callants and lassies and wenches and
    virgins and damsels
and colleens and flappers and hoydens
    and tomboys,
codlins and tadpoles and cublets and
    striplings to indulge
in some drinking, imbibing and tippling,
in boozing and toping
and swilling and soaking, bousing, ca-
    rousing,
guzzling and swigging, draining and
    bibbing,
lushing and sponging till we all get
    drunk,

tipsy and temulent, inebri -ous, -ated,
    sewed up,
befuddled, intoxicated, obfuscated, maud-
    lin and mellow,
groggy and beery; drunk as a piper, a
    fiddler,
a Chloe, squiffy and plastered and
    flustered,
musty and bosky, muddled and merry
and fou, fresh and fuddled,
so we'll wake up next morning
all twitching with pain, with headaches
    and toothaches,
migraine, neuralgia, neuritis, lumbago
    and gout,
tonsilitis, the tick, aching all over with
    spasms
cricks, stitches and kinks; with itches,
    orgasms and soreness
and redness and rawness of all our blood
    plasms;
convulsions and throbbing, torment, tor-
    ture, discomfort
and pangs; in anguish, in agony, with
    twinges that come
from going on binges and having such
    fun as
writing poems like this and exclaiming in
    chorus:
  "What a wonderful thing is a
    Thesaurus!"
               —Don Laycock

David McCord found the following in *Poems from Life* (Macmillan, 1923), "beyond which," he writes, "I have been unable to trace it:"

---

* F. P. A. once wrote something of the same sort.

A THESAURUS NIGHTMARE

Drink (ingurgitate, engulph, engorge, gulp) to me only with thine eyes (vision,
    glance, look, gaze, stare, perspicacity)
And I will pledge (toast, salute, do the honors, greet, hob and nob) with mine;
Or leave a kiss (buss, smack, osculation) within the cup (receptacle, mug, goblet,
    glass, tumbler),
And I'll not (nowise, on no account, in no respect, by no manner of means) ask for
    (request, beg, sue, pray, petition, beseech, adjure, clamour for) wine (spirits,
    liquor, stingo, grog, cup that cheers, Sir John Barleycorn).

—*J. Willard Ridings*

2 0 AUGUST

Word Belt

We played this word game last night. I was not very good at it. Try it, though; it's
fun, and you will doubtless do better than I did:

> The first player defines a word. The next identifies it, then gives the third
> player a definition of another word whose first three letters are the last
> three of the original word. And so on and on: opaque—querulous; ouster
> —terrain (some players may drop out on that last one, but there *are*
> words beginning with ain). A player who fails to identify a word defined,
> or whose own word has the wrong letter arrangement, is eliminated, and
> the play continues until only one contestant remains.

If you correctly name the words defined below, you will have a word belt:

> • Lithe • Abundant • Salesman • Courageous • Excessive • Greek letter •
> Mild oath • Ingenious contrivance • Scene of Christ's betrayal • Old
> age • Instrumentality • Whole • Peaceful •

Another game to talk about, if not to play, on a rainy evening, is "Firing the
Fireman." It is based on the assumption that holders of different jobs are discharged
in different ways. An orchestra leader, says John Fuller, is disbanded; an electrician,
discharged; a postman, unzipped.

Herb Caen developed an analogous game, "I Could Have Been," for his column
in the *San Francisco Chronicle*. Readers submitted such entries as these:

> I could have been a
> • proctologist, but I could never get to the bottom of things.
> • dermatologist, but I was too thin-skinned.
> • nun, but I had sworn to kick the habit.

- railroad builder, but I couldn't make tracks fast enough
- baker, but there was no dough in it.
- Bill Buckley's assistant, but I wasn't right for the job.

21 AUGUST

The Web Retangled

Sir Walter Scott said:

> Oh, what a tangled web we weave
> When first we practice to deceive!

To which Phyllis McGinley rejoined:

> Which leads me to suppose the fact is
> We really ought to get more practice.

J. R. Pope agreed:

> But when we've practiced quite a while
> How vastly we improve our style!

The two latter couplets betray a deplorable abdication of moral responsibility. Let the authors heed this warning from one of the few completely frank and honest men. I know:

> Forget, dear friends, that practice angle!
> You'll only tangle up the tangle.
> —W.R.E.

22 AUGUST

Swiftly Speaking

A month or so ago I told you that American crossword puzzles are no match for their British counterparts in verbal ingenuity. But I must acknowledge that Will Weng, who edits *The New York Times* crossword puzzles, is catching up. His selections are a steaming, seething, stinking, odious mudpot of puns, anagrams, and hidden words. One puzzle by Edward J. O'Brien is built around thirty-four Tom Swifties—puns of the sort that you figure out only to discover you have to figure out what you have figured out.

I list here a few examples from Mr. O'Brien's opus. They may make you a *Times* puzzle addict for life. Or you may treat them as a warning to avoid the *Times* puzzle page as you would avoid quicksand.

"Who, what?" said Tom warily. "Young M.D.," said Tom internally. "Gold leaf," said Tom guiltily. "John," said Tom wanly. "Elec. unit," said Tom amply. "Go easy, Mr. Roper," said Tom politely. "Coda," said Tom finally. "Shirtwaist," said Tom blowsily. "Maid's night off," said Tom helplessly. "K-," said Tom rationally. "Pass the cards," said Tom ideally. "Quiet meadow," said Tom silently. "Zero," said Tom naughtily. ". . . and lose a few," said Tom winsomely. "Drei . . . fünf," said Tom fearlessly. "Brothers," said Tom grimly. "Oriental gift," said Tom pleasantly. "One pair," said Tom abrasively. "X's and," said Tom wisely. "I bequeath," said Tom willingly. "Just Newsweek," said Tom timelessly. "Tripod," said Tom easily. "Pope," said Tom piously. "Furn.," said Tom aptly.

23 AUGUST

Some Mad Young Wags

There is a luncheon club in New York City that has no rules. But if it did have rules, one would be that only an imminent appointment for extreme unction would excuse a member from pausing at a certain octagonal table for a convivial glass before eating.

A second rule, if rules did exist, would be that introductions are unnecessary, agreeable conversation needing no signature. Even without existing, this rule has been known to have awkward consequences. There was the case, for instance, of the member who discovered that the author of a book he was reviewing had lifted great hunks from another writer's work without credit.

Such an incident makes a good story for the octagonal table, and the member told it with gusto, while his listeners chuckled and interjected coarse remarks. As he was leaving, someone tapped his shoulder and said, "I thought you should know that the man laughing loudest was the author of the book."

The moral? Never trust an author. Trader Horn made a fortune by reporting as fact adventures that had never taken place. Clifford Irving wrote a life of Howard Hughes that may have been correct to the last semicolon, but was fake all the same. (The firm that had contracted to publish the Irving book removed to a new building soon after the hoax was exposed. Their ground floor tenant is the Irving Trust Company.)

I know a publisher who receives so many plagiarized contributions that he has developed a standard euphemism for his letter of rejection. "I fear," he says, "that you have relied too much on sources."

The verb "to fraud" is obsolete, but not the practice. Writers still flimflam and filch. (Especially filch.) Only the immature poet plagiarizes, said T. S. Eliot; the mature poet steals. Eliot was proud to be a mature poet.

This description of how a ballad is sometimes born was written a hundred years ago, but it fits more than one opus that will see print in the current year of our Lord:

> Some mad young wags, wishing to test the critical powers of an experienced collector, sent him a new-made ballad, which they said they had been enabled to secure only in a fragmentary form. To the surprise of its fabricators, it was duly printed; but what naturally raised their surprise to astonishment, and revealed to them a secret, was, that it was no longer a fragment, but a complete ballad,—the collector, in the course of his industrious inquiries among the peasantry, having been so fortunate as to recover the missing fragments!
>
> —*John Hill Burton*

2 4 AUGUST

The Susurrant Schwa

A schwa, indicated in dictionaries by an ə, is a vowel so unstressed that it all but loses its distinction of sound, thus:

> The ə on his diurnəl rounds
> Is minəs all but minər sounds;
> Yet may, phonetəcəsts əgree,
> Transmit a wide vəriəty
> Of audəble phənomənა:
> Aə, Eə, Iə, Oə . . .
> Uə.
>
> —*W.R.E.*

A schwa carried past the point of no return vanishes into an apostrophe. Philip Cohen relates this hyperapostrophic story:

> An old salt was telling of going through a typhoon in his sailing ship. At the top of the storm, he said, "M' jibs'l's lines snapped. And m't'g'll'nts'l's'd'a done the same if it hadn't slacked off just then."

Mr. Cohen found the eight-apostrophe "m't'g'll'nts'l's'd'a"—surely a record—in *Slaves of Sleep,* a science-fiction novel by L. Ron Hubbard. When he rechecked his source, the apostrophe between g and l had disappeared, but I prefer the story as I first received it.

2 5 AUGUST

Professor Otto R. Osseforp

A Harvard Bulletin interview between Professor R. Osseforp, holder of the Emor D. Nilap Chair in Palindromology at Harvard, and Solomon W. Golomb (Ph.D. '57), includes this palindromic exchange:

"And what about your new novel, could you tell me the title?"

"Dennis Sinned."

"Intriguing. What is the plot?"

"Dennis and Edna sinned."

"I see. Is there more to it than that?"

"Dennis Krats and Edna Stark sinned."

"Now it all becomes clear," I agreed. "Tell me, with all this concern about the ecology, what kind of car are you driving nowadays?"

"A Toyota."

"Naturally, and how about your colleague, Prof. Nustad?"

"Nustad? A Datsun."*

2 6 AUGUST

Printing Was Difficult at Fust

When monks wrote out books by hand, they would sometimes finish with "explicit," short for *explicit (um est volumen)*, or *explicit (us est liber)*, "the book has been completely unrolled." One scribe added:

> Be careful with your fingers; don't put them on my writing. You do not know what it is to write. It is excessive drudgery; it crooks your back, dims your sight, twists your stomach and sides. Pray then for poor Raoul, God's servant, who has copied it entirely with his own hand in the cloister of St. Aignan.

Good Raoul would have considered printing, which came along in the fifteenth century, to be the work of the devil, and he might have been right. Many attributed the invention to Dr. Faust, whose neck the devil wrung in 1525. The attribution may have come by confusion with Johann Fust, who lent Gutenberg the money to create tools for printing. In 1455 Fust took possession of Gutenberg's implements and stock in satisfaction of the debt, and set up as a printer himself. He immediately found himself in trouble, as is told here:

* Ralph G. Beaman adds: "and his wife May?"
"Aha! May? A Yamaha!"

When Fust had discovered this new art, and printed off a considerable number of copies of the Bible to imitate those which were commonly sold as mss., he undertook the sale of them at Paris. It was his interest to conceal this discovery, and to pass off his printed copies for mss. But, enabled to sell his Bibles at sixty crowns, while the other scribes demanded five hundred, this raised universal astonishment; and still more when he produced copies as fast as they were wanted, and even lowered his price. The uniformity of the copies increased the wonder. Informations were given in to the magistrate against him as a magician; and in searching his lodgings a great number of copies were found. The red ink, and Fust's red ink is peculiarly brilliant, which embellished his copies, was said to be his blood; and it was solemnly adjudged that he was in league with the Infernals. Fust at length was obliged, to save himself from a bonfire, to reveal his art to the Parliament of Paris, who discharged him from all prosecution in consideration of the wonderful invention.

—*Isaac Disraeli*

27 AUGUST

Had Darwin Dug up Fossil Words

Mutation is as inexorable for words as for roses, may flies, and horses. (Is it true that Morgan horses have fewer vertebrae than other equines?) A *rostrum* was once a bird's beak; a *symposium,* a drinking party; to *garble,* to sift spices; to *heckle,* to comb flax.* So:

> Had Darwin dug up fossil words
> Instead of fishes, beasts, and birds,
> Instead of wasting time and ink
> On that elusive missing link
> He might have traced our verbal zoos
> Clear back to the primeval ooze:
>
> When "nosegay" was *anthology;*
> When "wild pitch" was *hyperbole;*
> And "brave deeds," *jests;* and *rigmaroles,*
> "The fealty sworn to kingly goals."
>
> When *style* was "something used to write,"
> While "writing rubbed away" was *trite.*
> *Antic* was "old;" *achieved* was "died";
> *Spoil* was "a skin; an uncured hide."

* See 29 February and 3 December.

Mischief was "headless" formerly,
And *lewd* was "of the laity";
By *arctic* then a bear was meant,
And *buxom* was "obedient."

Derive was "leave the river," and
Arrive, of course, was "reach the land."
Tidier meant "more opportune";
For "Drink up, boys!" one said, *"Lampoon!"*

Hackneyed was "like an aging horse";
A "plow-turned furrow" was a *verse;*
A "flash of lightning" was a *blizzard.*
So words evolved from A to izzard.

—*W.R.E.*

28 AUGUST

Mystery News

Here is a complaint about news stories that leave you knowing less than you did before reading them.

The story:

Medical researchers from the University of Cincinnati revealed Tuesday they have found traces of cadmium, a potentially dangerous metal, in the hair of 200 urban Cincinnatians. Dr. Harold Petering, associate professor of environmental health, said cadmium could be very dangerous to man. He said the amount found in the subjects' hair was low, but increased continuously from birth to old age.

Next, the complaint:

(1) Why is the presence of cadmium in human hair, presumably in microscopic amounts, a danger? What illnesses does it cause?

(2) How did the cadmium get into the hair of the subjects tested? If the phenomenon is unusual, indicated by the fact that it was considered newsworthy, there must be a story behind it. Certainly, it isn't common knowledge, or possibly even esoteric knowledge, that cadmium is a normal constituent of the air that surrounds us.

(3) Is the cadmium radioactive? That is, could it be the result of atomic fallout? Is that what makes it dangerous?

(4) Were the 200 Cincinnatians selected purely at random, or were they primarily factory workers of some kind exposed to cadmium contamination as an occupational hazard?

(5) If the selection was entirely random, as the account seems to imply, why was the hair of the subjects tested for cadmium, of all things? Did the researchers test for the presence of many different substances, or did they have some reason to suspect that they might find cadmium? What was that reason?

(6) Why did the cadmium settle in hair, rather than in some other part of the body?

(7) The study was made in Cincinnati. Should we attribute special significance to that circumstance, or is it reasonable to suppose that research in other cities would show similar results? In short, does the peril concern all large-city dwellers?

(8) Is there anything the ordinary citizen can do or should do to protect himself against this new menace to life?

(9) *Urban* Cincinnatians? These are evidently being distinguished from *rural* Cincinnatians. Of course, Cincinnati, Ohio, is a major metropolis, with a population of about half a million, so that the picture of rural Cincinnatians peacefully pursuing their rustic ways is a contradiction in terms, and the word urban is surely redundant.

Like a bolt from the blue, the news item quoted hits the reader suggesting that his health is in jeopardy, and evoking a torrent of questions to which no answers are provided. Those connected with the research know what it is all about, but at least 99 percent of all newspaper readers haven't the foggiest notion.

—Dmitri A. Borgmann

29 AUGUST

Fraffly Fine Poetry

Here Afferbeck Lauder proves that Fraffly* is not just an in-language for the West End of London, but a *lingua franca* between gods and men:

HOMENNY BINS

Homenny bins, I yosked, *meck fev?*
Not knowing what I quett-ment.
Bot three, he said. His fess were skrev
With British onder-stettment.

A fewer chodged with theft or frod,
I yosked, *What compromise*
Woo chewer dopt? He loft, *Good Lord,*
It zoller pecker flies.

* 17 February has a fraffly fine glossary.

Seh yorron fire, or prepshaw dead,
I yosked, *War twoochoo do?*
A British gentleman, he said,
Will lohweh smoddle through.

TEMPUS FUGIT

Conservative, dislecking chenge,
With ing-com in the oppah renge,
Meh views meh seem a treffle strenge:
Meh pot a treffle crackish.

The tamer skom to collar halt!
Though Slebber cheps. Itzol their fault.
We Britons, once on earth the salt,
Are nobbot milleh brackish.

En sober said meh bed eh kneel,
Empray: "Dillod, You should, effeel,
Epplay Yosh-older to the wheel,
And turn it slettleh backish."
                              —*Afferbeck Lauder*

30 AUGUST
∽

Anthon's Classical Dictionary

A favorite reference book since my childhood has been Anthon's *Classical Dictionary,* a volume on which I cut my eye teeth (the teeth I read with). It is still on my shelf, though I now need a magnifying glass to make out the six-point type.

Mr. Anthon, with an assist from Rabelais and Moses, is the spiritual progenitor of the two verses that make up today's ration.

WILD BOARS AND LIONS HAUL ADMETUS' CAR

Wild boars and lions haul Admetus' car.
    White horses seven serve the Morning Star.
A panther team takes Bacchus on his way,
    While peacocks Juno's chariot convey.
By chastened lions Cybele is drawn,
    And antlered stags bear fair Diana on.
Behind her wingèd dragons Ceres travels,
    And flights of doves draw Venus to her revels.
Sea horses carry their thalassic lord.
    I drive a Ford.
                              —*W.R.E.*

"NEVER EMBERLUCOCK OR INPULREGAFIZE
YOUR SPIRITS WITH THESE VAIN THOUGHTS
AND IDLE CONCEPTS."
                                                        —Rabelais

Was Bacchus a boil vexing Jupiter's thigh?
Gargantua, wax formed in Gargamelle's ear?
(And where did we come from ourselves, you and I?)

A heel burst its blister for Roquetaillade's try;
From nurse's old slipper did Crocmosh appear.
(Was Bacchus a boil vexing Jupiter's thigh?)

When Castor and Pollux hatched, Leda clucked, "My!
The neighbors may gossip a swan has been here!"
(And where did we come from ourselves, you and I?)

The dad of Adonis with myrrh bark did lie;
Minerva was born of a migraine chimere.
(Was Bacchus a boil vexing Jupiter's thigh?)

Jehovah shaped Eve from the rib of a guy;
From foam Venus vaulted to launch her career.
(And where did we come from ourselves, you and I?)

We call for the Author, and hear no reply;
The future is mist, and the past is unclear.
Was Bacchus a boil vexing Jupiter's thigh?
And where did we come from ourselves, you and I?
                                                        —*W.R.E.*

3 1 AUGUST

Cat Words

Everyone knows that words ending in -*cat* (particularly *scat,* but also such resonant, reverent words as *magnificat* and *requiescat*) are cat words. But you may not know that words ending in -*cate* or -*cated* are also cat words. The final -*e* (-*ed*) was added by cat haters, just to deny cats their due. Read this verse as carefully as a cat licks its fur. Thereafter spell all cat words in proper cat fashion.

1. Let us arise now to invocat
    The CAT;
    No less the raffish Allocat
    Than the elegant Domesticat.

2. Let us arise now and pat
    The intricat
    Complicat
    Delicat

Indelicat
Sophisticat
Unsophisticat
CAT!

3. The wicked *hat*
   The CAT.
   They defecat
   Upon the CAT.
   They deprecat
   And imprecat
   The CAT.
   They'd send a Syndicat
   To eradicat
   The CAT.

4. The wicked even *altercat*.
   (Oh no! not that!)

5. Go to, CAT!
   Fornicat!—
   Propagat!—
   CAT!
   Duplicat!
   Triplicat!
   Quadruplicat!
   Quintuplicat!

6. The wicked shall not dislocat
   Confiscat
   Suffocat
   Your kittens, CAT—

We'll see to *that!*—
You Silicat!

7. Let us arise now, and excommunicat
   The damn'd souls who fabricat . . .
   Prevaricat . . .
   About the CAT.
   Let us arise, and stat:
   SCAT!

8. Let us now dedicat
   Mouse and rat
   To the CAT.
   Masticat,
   CAT!
   Extricat
   Lean and fat!

9. Our senses you intoxicat,
   Our mental joints you lubricat,
   CAT!

10. One caveat:
    Do you reciprocat
    Our passion, CAT?
    CAT?
    CAT!
    We supplicat
    You, CAT:
    Com M E W nicat
    With us, CAT!

                                    —*W.R.E.*

(A number of cat words—educat, indicat, inculcat, advocat, abdicat, locat, placat, coruscat, and so on—are not included. Enough is enough of anything, even cats.)

SEPTEMBER

1 SEPTEMBER

A Teacher Look at Oysterville

Among the good bad verse I have inherited from my childhood in Oysterville, the only example bearing directly on my own family is the one that follows. It was written by the teacher of the one-room schoolhouse at which four Espy children were then in attendance. My father was head of the school board.

One knows not what among strange people one may find;
  What grief their follies great may bring to an observing mind.
That backward, tumble-down old village by the sea
  Well taught me much that will not soon depart from me.

The wise and brilliant pupils of its queer old school
  May look upon the writer (who so lately taught them) as a fool
But full well has he seen that they but little know,
  That much have they to learn to fit themselves abroad to go.

What shallow pates the parents and directors are,
  That great and wonder-working Espy is their guiding star.
Oh! fortunate I surely was in time so well to see,
  That by resigning from the school, I'd leave behind much grief to me.

The learned Senator Espy the law to teacher vile did well expound:
  "Know thou that not one mark shall on our angels dear be found;
That not the slightest mark upon their sacred flesh is now allowed by law.
  So then beware! a tiny mark upon an angel's back we saw."

Then Mrs. Espy showed great brains in wonderous note she did so boldly sign
  "Now, teacher, if you can't control the school by gentle means, you should resign."
Just think! "Wild cattle" she would have controlled by love! Oh! where could there
    be found
  Another case of impudence and ignorance so glaring and profound?

"Upon our precious ones, to order get you must not lay a hand;
  But still you must supply their minds with all the knowledge we do demand."
A little imp then fired with parents' evil spirit said in school one day:
  "You will not stay here very long, if your hands upon me lay."

Although of Oysterville I think not well, Pacific County is to me so dear,
   And much I hope a few months there again to spend in time that's near
Oh! let me see again those things that there I knew;
   Those things that fond remembrance does so vividly present to view.

Oh! let me see again the deep blue ocean as it rolls along the shore,
   Where I may sit in solitude and gaze upon its vast expanse once more.
Oh! let me feel again the mighty ocean's breath so sweet,
   Imparting health and vigor where for recreation youth & beauty meet.

—*C. J. Stupp*

Mr. Stupp was committed to an insane asylum soon after he wrote the foregoing lines. My father had no connection with the commitment, but I suspect it would have been difficult to convince Mr. Stupp of that.

2 SEPTEMBER

The Yellow Prose of Texas

To know the full marvel of the brand that Texas has burned into the hide of the English language, you have to spend a few days there. The next best thing is to buy a copy of Jim Everhart's *Illustrated Texas Dictionary*. In passing on the excerpts below I regret only that I cannot show you the grotesque facial distortions with which Mr. Everhart, in accompanying photographs, illustrates the definitions.

- ails—other than the person or thing implied. "Ah only done what anybody *ails* would do."
- beggar—larger in size, height, width, amount, etc. "The *beggar* they come the harder they fall."
- cheer—in this place or spot. "Yawl come riot *cheer* this minute."
- fair—a distressing emotion aroused by impending danger. "The only thing we have to *fair* is *fair* itself."
- hep—to render assistance. "Ain't nobody gonna *hep* me?"
- lacked—was on the verge of or came close to. "Ah *lacked* to died laughin'."
- main—of ugly disposition, nasty. "That there is one *main* man."
- often—so as to be no longer supported or attached. "Now stan still so ah can shoot that apple *often* yore had."
- riot—correct or proper. "That's jes as *riot* as rain."
- squire—honest and above board. "Everything is fire and *squire*."
- truss—reliance on integrity. "Don't yawl *truss* me?"

Mr. Everhart's final definition is of the word thank—to have a judgment or opinion of. "Jes *thank*," he says, "of what yew must sound lack to a Texan!"

3 SEPTEMBER

The Conversational Reformer

When Theo: Roos: unfurled his bann:
  As Pres: of an immense Repub:
And sought to manufact: a plan
  For saving people troub:
His mode of spelling (termed phonet:)
Affec: my brain like an emet:

And I evolved a scheme (*pro-tem*)
  To simplify my mother-tongue,
That so in fame I might resem:
  Upt: Sinc:, who wrote "The Jung:,"
And rouse an interest enorm:
In conversational reform.

I grudge the time my fellows waste
  Completing words that are so comm:
Wherever peop: of cult: and taste
  Habitually predom:
'Twould surely tend to simpl: life
Could they but be curtailed a trif:

" 'Tis not in mort: to comm: success,"
  As Addison remarked; but if my meth:
Does something to dimin: or less:
  The waste of public breath,
My country, overcome with grat:
Should in my hon: erect a stat:

For is not "Brev: the Soul of Wit"?
  (Inscrib the mott: upon your badge).
The sense will never suff: a bit
  If left to the imag:
Since any pers: can see what's meant
By words so simp: as "husb:" or "gent:"

When at some meal (at dinn: for inst:)
  You hand your unc: an empty plate,
Or ask your aunt (that charming spinst:)
  To pass you the potat:,
They have too much sagac:, I trust,
To give you sug: or pep: or must:.

Gent: Reader, if to me you'll list:
  And not be irritab: or peev:,
You'll find it of tremend: assist:
  This habit of abbrev:,
Which grows like some infec: disease,
Like chron: paral: or German meas:.

My bust by Rod: (what matt: the cost?)
  Shall be exhib: devoid of charge,
With (in the Public Lib: at Bost:)
  My full-length port: by Sarge:
That thous: from Pitts: or Wash: may
  swarm
To Worsh: the Found: of this Reform.

Meanwhile I seek with some avid:
The fav: of your polite consid:.

—*Harry Graham*

4 SEPTEMBER

A Chronology of Anagrams

The moon circles the earth and the earth circles the sun and the anagrams go on, year after year. Some dates, some anagrams:

1883   Chester Arthur: *Truth searcher.*

1884   Dante Gabriel Rossetti: *Greatest born idealist.*
1894   Court of general session: *Scenes of rogues on trial.*
1899   The death of Robert G. Ingersoll, the famous agnostic: *Goes, gathering the belief that no Lord comforts us.*
1903   The detectives: *Detect thieves.*
1904   A confirmed bachelor: *I face no bold charmer.*
1906   Charitableness: *I can bless earth.*
1908   The Dead March in Saul: *Hear deathland music*
1912   Beer saloons: *Booser's lane.*
1917   Blandishment: *Blinds the man.*

I do not recall where I found the dates for the foregoing anagrams (perhaps in *Word Ways?*) nor can I date the following, perhaps the earliest of them all:

Astronomical observations: *To scan a visible star or moon.*

5 SEPTEMBER

The Profundity Kit

In English literature, the model of someone using verbal resources beyond her grasp is Mrs. Malaprop. But in modern social criticism we are dealing with something far more serious—a kind of conceptual malapropism that involves the large-scale use of concepts in contexts where they are quite inappropriate. The motive of both kinds of malapropism is the same: the desire to sound impressive. It is here that we find the source of many desperate attempts at profundity. And the most evident sign of this disposition is the weakness for anything that sounds like a technical term. The party conversation that used to make do with homely bits of pretension like the "inferiority complex" is now peppered with terms like "alienation," "paranoid" and "feedback." If such terms do not rise quickly to the tip of the tongue, they can be constructed out of a verbal kit whose more commonly used members are "symbol," "complex," "context," "society," "dynamic," "process," "ongoing" and "structure." In the conversation of those who have learned the trick, these words weave their way in and out of split infinitives, mangled subjunctives and elephantine hypotheticals. Journalistic descriptions with the right sound (such as "generation gap") come to be confidently pronounced as if they explained something. Since language is a vital part of life, its corruption is of more than cultural significance. Indeed ingenious—possibly over-ingenious—exponents of the argument I am making here have attempted to attribute some features of the Vietnam war to the use of pseudo-technicalities like "escalation" and "the credibility gap." The word "gap" clearly has a great future in the profundity kit.

—*K. R. Minogue*

6 SEPTEMBER

A Lewdness of Limericks

A poet unknown to me wrote:

> The limerick's an art form complex
> Whose contents run chiefly to sex;
>   It's famous for virgins
>   And masculine urgin's,
> And vulgar erotic effects

Morris Bishop phrased the same indictment more elegantly:

> The limerick's furtive and mean;
> You must keep her in close quarantine;
>   Or she sneaks to the slums
>   And promptly becomes
> Disorderly, drunk, and obscene.

Many a literary craftsman of the second or third water, and a few of the first, have tried their hands at dirty limericks. The Norman Douglas compilation of these sits on my shelf beside a collection of 1700 edited by G. Legman. Between them, the two books may tell you more about dirty limericks than you want to know.

Wading through 1700 off-color limericks is like wading against a current of hip-deep sludge. There is, however, an occasional reward: a gorgeous twist of phrase that hits the gut—I leap nimbly here from metaphor to metaphor—like the initial sip of a snow-cold, bone-dry martini. In the following example, which I first heard from Richard Edes Harrison, the reward is a staggeringly clever rhyme:

> There was a young lady of Yap
> Who had pimples all over her map.
>   But in her interstices
>   There lurked a far worse disease,
> Commonly known as the clap.
> *—Francis Dewerville Schroeder*

Naughtiness without cleverness makes for a depressing limerick. Indeed, the most famous limericks, certainly including Lear's, are not off-color at all. Take the senior Oliver Wendell Holmes's immortal pun on Henry Ward Beecher:

> A great Congregational preacher
> Called a hen an elegant creature.
>   The hen, just for that,
>   Laid an egg in his hat.
> And thus did the hen reward Beecher.

Or this by Ogden Nash:

> There was a young belle of old Natchez
> Whose garments were always in Patchez.
>   When comments arose
>   On the state of her clothes
> She drawled, "When Ah itchez, Ah Scratchez."

With the exception of a mild oath, there is nothing that Anthony Comstock himself could find objectionable in this, perhaps the most familiar limerick of all:

> A wonderful bird is the pelican,
> His bill will hold more than his belican.
>   He can take in his beak
>   Food enough for a week,
> And I'm damned if I see how the helican.
> —*Dixon Lanier Merritt*

There is a rumor that archaeologists exploring King Tutankhamen's tomb found on a mutilated wall the third and fourth lines of an ancient Egyptian limerick, these lines translating as

> She had for her clients
> Both pygmies and giants

You may wish to reconstruct the whole limerick from this fossil jawbone. Clean or dirty, according to taste.*

7 SEPTEMBER

The Venereal Game

Venus pursued her prey indiscriminately in bower or bosky dell, but in the venereal game† only the bosky dell is involved. *An Exaltation of Larks,* by James Lipton, lists scores of venereal terms, relics of mediaeval times. Some—"a school of fish"; "a pride of lions"—are still in general use; others—"a skulk of foxes"; "a barren of mules"— are still used by specialists; still others have vanished from the general ken. Mr. Lipton also went on to conjure up his own collectives, such as "an unction of undertakers," "a float of dancers," "a dilation of pupils," and "a wince of dentists." This is a game open to all. It is played with gusto on Mary Ann Madden's competition page in *New York* magazine, with results like these:

• A riot of students • a peck of kisses (or bad boys) • a Buckley of Bills •

* See also 28 June.
† See also 20 January, 18 May, 17 November.

a mine of egotists • a host of parasites • a complement of sycophants • a range of ovens • a furrow of brows • a nun of your business • a lot of realtors • a whack of Portnoys • a knot of Windsors • a wagon of teetotalers.

8 SEPTEMBER

A Gaggle of Giggles

One is not surprised to find Walter de la Mare or A. E. Housman laughing. And Thomas Hood laughs as he weeps. But I had not expected D. H. Lawrence to be willfully funny, and I have decided his "The Oxford Voice" was funny by mistake. He meant to be savage.

THE OXFORD VOICE

When you hear it languishing
and hooing and cooing and sidling through the front teeth,
   the Oxford voice
     or worse still
   the would-be Oxford voice
you don't even laugh any more, you can't.

For every blooming bird is an Oxford cuckoo nowadays,
you can't sit on a bus or in the tube
but it breathes gently and languishingly in the back of your neck.

And oh, so seductively superior, so seductively
  self effacingly
  deprecatingly
  superior—

We wouldn't insist on it for a moment
  but we are
   we are
you admit we are
  superior.—

                         —D. H. Lawrence

BUTTONS

There was an old skinflint of Hitching
Had a cook, Mrs. Casey, of Cork;
There was nothing but crusts in the kitchen,
While in parlour was sherry and pork.

So at last Mrs. Casey, her pangs to assuage,
Having snipped off his buttonses, curried the page;
And now, while that skinflint gulps sherry and pork
    In his parlour adjacent to Hitching,
To the tune blithe and merry of knife and of fork,
    Anthropophagy reigns in the kitchen.
                                    —*Walter de la Mare*

INFANT INNOCENCE

Reader behold! This monster wild
Has gobbled up the infant child.
The infant child is not aware
It has been eaten by the bear.
                        —*A. E. Housman*

ON A ROYAL DEMISE

How monarchs die is easily explained,
    And thus it might upon the tomb be chiseled,
"As long as George the Fourth could reign he reigned,
    And then he mizzled."
                            —*Thomas Hood*

9 SEPTEMBER

Please, Please Keep Coming

A puzzle we insecure types never solve is, How can I get from where I am to where I want to be? We proceed as gingerly as the cross-eyed man in Paul E. Manheim's triplet:

The cross-eyed man must walk with care,
    For he sees where he's going,
    But he's not going there.

As for me, I not only doubt whether I shall ever get where I am going, but if I do get there I doubt whether anyone will be waiting to meet me. This insecurity is reflected in the verses that follow.

CHERCHEZ, CHERCHEZ LA FEMME

The Beauty has drawn up a guide for the Beast
To Ninety-six Fifteen Thirteenth Street Northeast.
"You can't lose your way," she declares, "if you drive:
Follow Fifth, University, Interstate Five;
For Bellevue, cross toll bridge, pay thirty-five cents;
From then on it's easy as finding the Gents':

First Eighty-four, right; and then left, Twenty-four;
Then Ninety-four, right; left on Fourteen once more.
When you hit Ninety-seven, go only a block"
(The Beast is now suffering cultural shock)
"To Ninety-six Fifteen Thirteenth Street Northeast."
("Couldn't *you* come to *my* place instead?" begs the Beast.)
—*W.R.E.*

COME ANY OLD WAY

Come any old way, dear, or come any new way;
Expressway or parkway or freeway or throughway
Or pathway or skyway or highway or tollway;
Come any old way, dear, but come, come the whole way—

By pathway or railway or roadway or stairway
By driveway or crescent or circle or airway;
By midway, arterial, or, if you wish,
By plaza or plaisance or square or Boul' Mich'.

By boulevard, avenue, alley, ascension,
By detour or thoroughfare, rut or extension.
The way doesn't matter, but dear, persevere
By lane or by trail or by street, till you're here!

—*W.R.E.*

10 SEPTEMBER

English Is Unamerican

Though the differences between English and American are shrinking fast, some English usages still bemuse an American, and vice versa. If you score 100 percent in rendering the expressions below into American, you must have spent a while in England.

(1) Advert; (2) Arterial road, or trunk road; (3) Bathe (noun); (4) Beetroot; (5) Blackleg; (6) Booking clerk; (7) Box; (8) Break (school); (9) Cab rank; (10) Calendar (school or university); (11) Car park; (12) Carrier; (13) Catmint; (14) Chips; (15) Close season (for hunting); (16) Clothespeg; (17) Compere (of a show); (18) Cornet (of ice cream); (19) Crawling (taxi); (20) Crisp (noun); (21) Deputation; (22) Doss house; (23) Flex; (24) Friendly society; (25) Full stop; (26) Gingernut; (27) Goods van; (28) Hire purchase system, or hire system; (29) Holiday maker; (30) Hooter (automobile); (31) Indian rubber; (32) Inland mails; (33) Larder; (34) Leading article, or leader; (35) Left-luggage office, or room; (36) Market gardener; (37) Match (e.g., football); (38)

Meat pie; (39) Mobile police; (40) Nib; (41) Page, or buttons; (42) Passage (in a private house); (43) Perambulator, pram, or baby coach; (44) Petrol; (45) Poste restante; (46) Public prosecutor; (47) Raider; (48) Rump (of beef); (49) Running expense, or working expense; (50) Season-ticket holder; (51) Sell up; (52) Service lift; (53) Shepherd's pie; (54) Shocker; (55) Shorthand typist, or writer; (56) Single ticket; (57) Soda bar; (58) Stomach warmer; (59) Stockist; (60) Studentship; (61) Swede, or horse turnip; (62) Telly; (63) Ticket of leave; (64) Tin; (65) Timber; (66) Torch; (67) Tramp (verb); (68) Troopship, or trooper; (69) Truncheon; (70) Try (in football); (71) Turning; (72) Underdone (meat); (73) Watch glass; (74) Witness box; (75) Wood wool.

11 SEPTEMBER

Amos 'N' Andy

When my father was in the state legislature, before the first World War, the boot-black in the county courthouse at South Bend delighted in telling him, "You better be nice to me, Senator—ah controls de colored vote 'round yere." And he did, being the only black man in the county.

In later years, my father followed Amos 'n' Andy on the radio. For those too young to remember, Amos was a hardworking little fellow who tried to help others, while Andy was a loud-talking big fellow who wanted others to help him. The show would be considered antisocial today, since it stereotyped blacks, but in the 1930s both blacks and whites thought it was just good clean fun. Besides, as Irvin S. Cobb said, "Golly, what grand dialect they use!"

Here Andy is instructing Amos on the economics of the taxicab business (they are about to buy a secondhand car on installments to start their fleet):

ANDY. Now, we'se workin' dis on de cut rate basin—lemme see yere. We'll charge 22½ cents fur de fust mile—see, I done looked all dis stuff up—I got de figgers yere. I been watchin' taxicabs evvyday—evv'y time I see one I look at 'em—I'se gittin' so I knows 'em now.

AMOS. What you goin' charge de fust mile?

ANDY. 22½ cents.

AMOS. Where I goin' git any half cents's from?

ANDY. I'll fix de meter so dat, in case de man ony ride a mile, you tap de meter on top wid a little hammer an' it jumps up to 25 to make it even money.

AMOS. 25—dat's 25 cents fur de fust mile—in case I hit it wid a hammer.

ANDY. Now de question is—how much for each 'ditional.

AMOS. How much it goin' be fur what?

ANDY. Ev'vy mile after de fust mile is gone cost 'em so much.

AMOS. Oh, de fust mile's goin' cost 'em 22½ cents an' if I hit wid a hammer it's 25—

ANDY. I wuz just thinkin' yere—de way we might work dis thing—instead o' havin' dat meter runnin' on de mile, might let you take a hammer an' hit dat meter ev'vy time you think you gone a mile an' let it jump up 'bout ten cents.

AMOS. What you mean—ev'vy time de meter changes I got hit it wid a hammer, huh?

ANDY. Den, you see, if you git somebody in de car dat looks like dey is got a lot o' money—while you is drivin', ev'vy time you think you is gone a mile, hit de meter once—den de meter will jump up ten cents—kind of turn around an' if the man is lookin' out de side o' de car, an' you see he ain't watchin' you, give de meter another crack.

AMOS. Dat wouldn't be right though. You can't do dat.

ANDY. Yeah—we better not work it dat way—dat'll mess up wid de inde-state commerce re-mission.

(*They then start figuring out expenses, and discover that they will lose money on every passenger they pick up.*)

AMOS. De 'spenses done run us out o' bizness, ain't dey?

ANDY. We can't make no money like dat.

AMOS. No—'cordin' to dem figures ever'thing done eat up de money.

ANDY. I got it—I'll git you two hammers an' you kin hit de meter ev'vy other block.—An' if de man in de back don't like it, bus' him in de haid.

AMOS. We got do sumpin' bout it a'right—we can't make no money de way we been goin'.

ANDY. I'll git you a sledge hammer, dat's whut I'll git you.

—C. J. Correll, F. F. Godden

12 SEPTEMBER

I Dreamed the Devil's Wife Proposed a Game

A number of bodily parts, Don Davidson reminds me, show up in the language as metaphors. Dancers *heel and toe;* sails *belly* in the wind. But I really needed no reminder; this trick of the language had already undone me in the nightmare recalled below.

> I dreamed that I was kidnapped by the Devil,
> And since I couldn't raise the ransom money
> The Devil's wife proposed a game to free me.
> She said, "If you will chat a little with me,
> And never mention any fleshly member,
> I'll see that dear Nick lets you out of Hell;
> But any part you name is forfeit to me."

"You've got a lot of cheek," I said, "to think
That I would trust you, or believe your mouthings.
I know what's passing through your head; I've watched you
Go nose among the relicts of the damned
And elbow through their innermost recesses.
I've watched you when you kneed those fallen angels
And fingered hapless sinners for your husband.
If I were better heeled, I'd pay my ransom
And hold my tongue. And even as things are,
I'm not about to neck with you, or even
To foot a measure with you on the dance floor.
A woman of your kidney's hard to stomach.
Still, when it comes to using words, I figure
That I can stay abreast of any devil.
If you aren't ribbing—if you'll swear by Hell
That you will toe the line, and knuckle under
When fairly beaten by me—then I'll shoulder
The full responsibility if any
Injuncted reference escapes my lips.
But come—we've jawed and chinned enough already;
I've met your terms. I think I'll ankle off now
And thumb a truck-ride back to Oysterville.
(Have I said something wrong? You eye me strangely.)"

I woke, and found I had no cheek, or mouth;
No head; no nose; no elbow, knee, or finger;
No heel; no tongue; no neck; no foot; no kidney;
No stomach, breast, or rib, or toe, or knuckle;
No shoulder, lips, or jaw, or chin, or ankle;
No back; no eye.
I wonder why.

—*W.R.E.*

13 SEPTEMBER

Eskimo* Recipes

OWL

Pluck out plenty feathers;
Plenty guts unpin.
Boil in plenty water;
 Plenty salt shake in.

AH-PIK

Pick lots Ah-pik. Pack
In Amouk sack
For winter snack.

* From Cree *askimowew,* "he eats it raw."

AHLOWE'KUK AND AHSEE'ACH

Cook Ahlowe'kuk till is soft.
Add seal blubber. Soak.
Mash with Tuh'gooh. Let' em cool.
Poke in poke.

Mix Ahsee-ach berries—
Maybe ten.
Then
Poke in poke again.

PTARMIGAN SMALL INTESTINES

For five seconds heat 'em;
Old folks eat 'em.

ESKIMO ICE CREAM

Watered seal oil . . .
Reindeer tallow . . .
Salmonberries.
Can you swallow?

PICK'NIEK

Wash first. Serve with oil of seal.
White man, he don't like this meal.

—W.R.E.

(My thanks to the students of the Shishmaref Day School, Shishmaref, Alaska, for *The Eskimo Cook Book,* from which the foregoing recipes are approximated. I gather that *Ah-pik* are salmonberries, and *Ahsee'ach,* blackberries. *Amouk* is a sealskin bag in which the berries are carried, *Ahlowe'kuk* is wild chard, and *Pick'niek* is the Mouse Food plant, *Tuh'gooh* is not explained.)

14 SEPTEMBER

Fable of the H¹ and the Stupid but Persistent A²

It was only in the nineteenth century that dictionaries began to distinguish i from j and u from v; Brewer points out that as recently as 1847 the old style was adhered to in Henry Washbourne's dictionary; in Dr. Johnson's, ninety years before, "iambic" comes between "jamb" and "jangle." Go back still farther and you will find such indiscriminate substitutions between i and j and u and v as these from the title page of *Polymanteia,* published anonymously in 1595:

> Polymanteia, or, The means . . . to jvdge of the fall of a Commonwealth, against the friuoulous and foolish coniectures of this age. Where vnto is added, a Letter . . . perswading them to a constant vnitie . . . for the defence of our . . . natiue covntry.

A number of letters of the alphabet originally represented objects: animals, furniture, and the like. In the following nonsense story, each keyed letter started out as such a hieroglyph. Where the origin is Egyptian, the key is 1; where the origin is Phoenician-Hebrew, the key is 2. Look up the original meanings of the letters in your dictionary in order to follow the narrative:

> A L¹ met an A² carrying a H¹. "Where are you taking the H¹, A²?" asked the L¹. "To the river to fetch M²N¹ for my friend the B¹, dear L¹," replied the A²; "he is dreadfully ill, and I fear he may soon be carried out on a P¹." "No wonder men use an L² to keep an A² on the road!" fumed

the L^1. "Don't you know you can't carry M^{2}N^1 in a H^1?" "That remains to be seen," said the A^2, and he trudged on until he came to an old B^2 where an M^1 sat dozing outside the D^2. "Where are you going with that H^1, A^2?" asked the M^1, opening an O^2. "To the river to fetch M^{2}N^1 for the B^1, dear M^1," said the A^2. "Get a K^1, you foolish A^2!" cried the M^1; "a H^1 won't hold M^{2}N^1!" "That remains to be seen," said the patient A^2, and on he went until he met an A^1 sitting on a H^2 and holding a wriggling F^1 in his P^2. "Why are you holding that F^1 in your P^2, dear A^1?" inquired the A^2; but the A^1 remained silent, for he feared that if he opened his P^2 the F^1 would bite him before he could get his P^2 closed again.

At last the A^2 reached the river, where he found an old C^2: The G^2 were lowered because the C^2 was swilling down the last of his weekly quota of M^{2}N^1. "What are you doing with that H^1, A^2?" asked the C^2 when he had finished swilling. "I am going to use it to take M^{2}N^1 back to my sick friend the B^1, dear C^2," said the A^2. "But an H^1 does not hold M^{2}N^1, you silly A^2!" said the C^2. "That remains to be seen, dear C^2," said the A^2, and he dipped the H^1 into the M^{2}N^1. No sooner had he brought the H^1 up from the M^{2}N^1 than all the M^{2}N^1 it contained was gone. But there in the bottom of the H^1 flapped a beautiful N^2!

"Oh, well," said the A^2 philosophically, "I am sure the B^1 would rather have an N^2 than nothing." And he was right.

MORAL: You've got to D^1 it to that A^2. He took those smart alecks down a F^2 or two!

15 SEPTEMBER

Reas'ning but to Err

Pope says man is ". . . born but to die, and reas'ning but to err." The author of the following essay has concluded that some of our errors are largely typographical:

FIRST, there are incomprehensible blunders: 'xbl gvtrpjklhjtrkeosixl . . .'

SECOND, some blunders, much like the first, place gibberish in a context wherein a certain sense emerges. Here, for instance, is a movie review culled from the Washington (D.C.) *Daily News*:

> Sitting in the middle of the bed, being wheeled across London by three attentive young men, Nancy falls in love with the conveyance. Need I say what the outcome is? Kfln. Shrd cmfw cmfw cm.

THIRD, there are changes in the form of a word which result in the complete reversal of the writer's intention, as witness this sentence from the FBI Law Enforcement Bulletin:

> We would hope that a record-breaking summer of strife and lawfulness can be averted.

FOURTH, the linotypist, we presume, gets the lines from two or more stories mixed up, as in this article, quoted in full, from the Davenport (Iowa) *Times-Democrat:*

> DRINKING NOTE: For a mild and tasty appetizer, try three dog, put a drop of castor oil in each eye to protect them from soap- parts of tomato juice with one part sherry.

FIFTH, there are those messages that execute an about-face for the want of one intended letter, as we can see in this headline from the Little Rock (Ark.) *Democrat:*

DECLINE IN MORALITY
SAID TREAT TO U. S.

SIXTH, there are errors that carry a self-fulfilling message, like this head-line from the Toronto (Ont.) *Financial Post:*

DEFECIT BUDGETS LIKE LIQUOR:
TOO MANY AND YOU GET STUPID

SEVENTH, we have writing from which a single letter has been dropped, as in our fifth category, only this time the effect is not to reverse the in-tended meaning, but rather to transform it into a wildly hilarious state-ment. As evidence, I give you the following article, quoted *in toto,* from the Milwaukee *Journal:*

> Southern Michigan's peasant population, now in the midst of its nesting season, is up about 25% over the spring of 1964.

EIGHTH, we have what is either an inspired solecism or an intentional twist from a bored reporter. Whatever the cause, the effect is a Spoonerism that makes sense, as in this UPI wire lead, which must go down in re-portorial annals as the gayest of all attributions:

> According to informed White Horse souses . . .

NINTH, there is the situation where, because of a linotypist's peccadillo with just one letter, a crucial word shuffles off its mortal coil and the whole sense of the article reverses itself and, not content with this alone, permits the entrance of an otherwise unuttered truth. This sample is from a Reuters article, dateline Harrogate, England, May 29, 1967. The article begins by stating that the overwhelming majority of 500 headmasters at the National Association of Head Teachers meeting voted to continue the caning of their captive students. One headmaster justified his use of the cane, and with help from the linotypist it came out this way:

But we are not living in Utopia. Creating, lying, stealing and pornographic scribbling still distresses us, and what are the remedies to be when kindness fails?

We must agree with this headmaster: if there is any certain remedy for creating, it must be a sound thrashing with a cane.

Of the same sort must be this headline from the Nyack (N.Y.) *Rockland County Journal-News*:

GLUE FACTORIES HAVE STOPPED
USING OLD HAGS FOR ADHESIVES

TENTH, there is writing that is not incorrect in any literal sense, but is ambiguous to the point of being ludicrous. These we cannot call typos, since, presumably, the linotypist rendered it precisely as it was given to him. For instance, an Iowa newspaper recently headlined a story about the marriage of a boy from Manly, Iowa, to a girl from a town named Fertile, in this way:

MANLY BOY MARRIES FERTILE GIRL

An Illinois newspaper couldn't resist this headline about nuptials between a boy from Oblong, Illinois and a girl from Normal, Illinois:

OBLONG BOY MARRIES NORMAL GIRL

—Temple G. Porter

(I imagine Mr. Porter would put this news item from the Los Angeles *Times* in a category of "remarkably precise dating":

Engineers surveying for a railroad in Northern Turkestan have uncovered the skeleton of a massive saurian that must have passed away 3,000,000 years ago last Friday.)

16 SEPTEMBER
✌

The Naughty Preposition

I have a friend, one of the best direct-mail copywriters in the country, whose rigid rule for his children is that they must never end a sentence with a preposition. But some sentences are ridiculous precisely because they fail to end with prepositions.

And why end a sentence with just one preposition? Why not use several? The late Mr. Bishop did—and his judgment was excellent:

I lately lost a preposition;
It hid, I thought, beneath my chair.
And angrily I cried: "Perdition!
Up from out of in under there!"

Correctness is my vade mecum,
  And straggling phrases I abhor;
And yet I wondered: "What should he come
  Up from out of in under for?"
                              —*Morris Bishop*

17 SEPTEMBER

I into My Mirror Peeked

In these two rhopalic verses, the first word of each line is a letter longer than the first word of the line preceding. I cheated in the last line of the first verse and the last two lines of the second verse by breaking the words in two.

1. I into my mirror peeked.
   "Is this horror me?" I shrieked.
   "Sit down, mirror; say what glue
   Ties fair me to ugly you.
   Tires about my tum you loop;
   Sister tires my eyes endroop.
   Tigress' mate am I! what error
   Gritless shows me in my mirror?
   Slighters cite your glass to prove me
   Less bright than those think who love me."

2. I saw a tin hayfork
   In a barn bin—
   Tin handle, every
   Tine made of tin.
   Trine the tin tines were,
   Winter was a-rattle;
   Tin were the barn roofs,
   Thin were the cattle.
                              —*W.R.E.*

18 SEPTEMBER

Sight Rhymes, Slight Rhymes

Alliance does not rhyme with dalliance, a fact known to lovers as well as poets. (This

is because the Lord our God is a jealous god, who frowns on fooling around.)
Alliance and dalliance are sight rhymes—words that rhyme to the eye but not the
ear. The impossibility of using sight rhymes in verse is demonstrated in these two
stanzas:

> I am just a humble student,
> I don't want to seem impudent;
> Poems are not what I type.
> I appreciate human glory,
> Drama, fiction, and history,
> But I cannot follow your recipe.
>
> Mine is not a playful nature;
> I am rational and mature,
> Working points of logic through.
> No; my verse would sound too strident,
> All its hollowness evident,
> As I clank and grind and huff and cough.
> —*Hedya Pachter*

19 SEPTEMBER

Much Ado About Malapropisms

Simpletons were malapropping before the word was invented—none to better effect
than Constable Dogberry, who here instructs his watch in *Much Ado About Nothing*:

Dogberry (to First Watchman): You are thought here to be the most
senseless and fit man for the constable of the watch, therefore bear you the
lantern. This is your charge: you shall comprehend all vagrom men; you
are to bid any man stand, in the prince's name.

Watch. How, if a'well not stand?

Dogb. Why, then, take no note of him, but let him go; and presently
call the rest of the watch together, and thank God you are rid of a
knave. . . . You shall also make no noise in the streets; for, for the watch
to babble and to talk is most tolerable and not to be endured.

Sec. Watch. We will rather sleep than talk; we know what belongs to
a watch.

Dogb. . . . Well, you are to call at all the alehouses, and bid those that
are drunk get them to bed.

Watch. How if they will not?

Dogb. Why, then, let them alone till they are sober; if they make you
not then the better answer, you may say they are not the men you took
them for.

—*William Shakespeare*

20 SEPTEMBER

Nameplay

Names are one jumping-off place for parlor games. Players might be asked, for instance, to suggest capitol figures who by reason of their name would be appropriate sponsors for certain fictitious legislation. *The Wall Street Journal* gives such examples as the Butler-Baker-Cook household-employes wage bill; the Hunt-Heinz-Pickle-Pepper food-additive bill; the Bible-Church-Chappel-Bell-Tower prayer amendment; the Bray-Cannon noise-control bill; the Long-Dole guaranteed-annual-wage bill; and the Little-Mann-Staggers alcoholic-beverage-control bill for minors.

Then there are proper names used as verbs: Is Clare Boothe Luce? Does Saul Bellow? Can Alistair Cooke? Did Ezra Pound? Did Mary Garden? Did John Reed? (Falk and similar names are forbidden.)

For the literary, there is the First Lines game. The idea is to read the first sentences of a familiar book, saying the word "blank" for any proper names. Contestants guess the book. Thus:

First sentence, "Blank." Second sentence, "No answer." Third sentence, "Blank."

If you don't know the answer to that one, ask Mark Twain.

21 SEPTEMBER

I Saw a Peacock with a Fiery Tail

To make sense of this exercise in punctuation, insert commas (or, as I prefer, semicolons) to taste: ". . . brimful of ale / I saw a Venice glass;" etc.

I saw a peacock with a fiery tail
I saw a blazing comet drop down hail
I saw a cloud wrapped with ivy round
I saw an oak creep on along the ground
I saw a pismire swallow up a whale
I saw the sea brimful of ale
I saw a Venice glass full fathom deep
I saw a well full of men's tears that weep
I saw red eyes all of a flaming fire
I saw a house bigger than the moon and higher
I saw the sun at twelve o'clock at night
I saw the man that saw this wondrous sight.
—From *The Westminster Drollery, 1671.*
Author Unknown

2 2 SEPTEMBER

Word and Line Palindromes

Palindromes of words are easier to create than palindromes of letters, and more likely to make sense. Some pleasing specimens:*

From *Word Ways:*
- So patient a doctor to doctor a patient so.
- Girl, bathing on Bikini, eyeing boy, finds boy eyeing bikini on bathing-girl.
- You can cage a swallow, can't you, but you can't swallow a cage, can you?

From *The New Statesman:*
- Bores are people that say that people are bores.
- Does milk machinery milk does?
- God knows man. What is doubtful is what man knows God.
- Women understand men; few men understand women.
- "Come, shall I stroke your 'whatever' darling? I am so randy." "So am I darling. Whatever your stroke, I shall come."

Vulgar that last one may be, but it is too clever to omit.

Using not the letter of the word but the entire line as a unit, J. A. Lindon came up with a palindromic triolet:

AS I WAS PASSING . . .

As I was passing near the jail
I met a man, but hurried by.
His face was ghastly, grimly pale.
He had a gun. I wondered why
He had. A gun? I wondered . . . why,
His face was *ghastly!* Grimly pale,
I met a man, but hurried by,
As I was passing near the jail.

2 3 SEPTEMBER

Address Unknown

James de Kay, like Doctor Emmanuel,† has a very big head with brains inside, and

---

* The *Word Ways* selections are by J. A. Lindon; the others, in order, by David Phillips, William Hodson, G. J. Blundell, Naomi Marks, and Gerard Benson.
† See 11 January.

what happens inside those brains is likely to be a question like this: If a Spaniard finds Los Angeles in his atlas, does he assume that an American atlas would say "The Angels?"

This verse is for James:

> Sing tra la la for Red Stick LA
>   And Holy Faith New Mex.;
> For Earring WA sound loud huzzah;
>   Cheer Body of Christ Tex.
> Raise roundelay for Monks IA,
>   To Yellow TX sing;
> But if you send your mail that way,
>   Your mail will stray,
> I'll bet you anything.
>
> —W.R.E.

24 SEPTEMBER

Chemicals and Other Big Ones

Of the longest words vouched for by standard dictionaries, most are chemical terms. A. Ross Eckler found two 45-letter giants, pneumonoultramicroscopicsilicovolcanoconiosis and pneumonoultramicroscopicsilicovolcanokoniosis. Among the longest non-technical terms are our old friends supercalifragilisticexpialidocious (34) (a nonsense term invented for a Walt Disney motion picture) and antidisestablishmentarianism (28).

"Protein molecules," says scientist Thomas H. Jukes, "may be likened to words of great length, written in an alphabet of twenty letters: the amino acids. Hemoglobin is a protein "word" containing a string of 287 such letters. The hemoglobins of human beings and gorillas differ in only two of the 287 letters. Cow hemoglobin is about 29 letters different from both gorilla and human hemoglobins; kangaroo hemoglobin has about 47 differences from cow, gorilla and human hemoglobins." The 267 amino acids in tryptophan synthetase, an enzyme used by a common intestinal bacterium, translate into a 1,913-letter word that I'll be glad to forward if you will promise to pronounce it.

Changing the subject, the middle name of Miss Dawne N. Lee, whose baptism was reported in the November 8, 1967, issue of the Honolulu *Star-Bulletin*, consisted of 101 letters, to wit:

Napaumohalaenaenaamekawehiwehionakuahiwiamenaawawakehoomakehooaalakeeaonaainananiakeaohawaiiikawanaao.

The name means, "The fragrant abundant beautiful blossoms begin to fill the air of hills and valleys throughout the breadth and width of these glorious Hawaiian Islands at dawn."

The longest word I know in French is anticonstitutionnellement (25) ("anticonstitutionally"); the longest place name, Roche-sur-Linote-et-Sorans-les-Cordiers (33).

According to Gary Jennings, there is a back-country whistle-stop in New Zealand called Taumatawhakatangihangakoauotamateaturipukakapipkimaunghoronukupokaiwhenualitanatahu—83 letters meaning, he says, "I know not what." He adds:

"For his *Ecclesiazusae*, Aristophanes coined what is probably the longest word in literature. Describing a buffet meal that apparently included every item on the Greek bill of fare, from oysters to *ouzo*, he compounded a single word which spans 77 syllables in Greek and requires 184 letters for a Roman-alphabet transliteration: Lepadotemachoselachogaleokranioleipsanodrimhypotrimmatosilphiokarabomelitokatakechymenokichlepikossyphophattoperisteralektryonoptokephalliokingklopepeiolagoiosiraiobaphetraganopterygon."

Nicholas Denyer tells me the word is as follows:

λοπαδο τεμαχο σελαχο γαλεοι ρανιο
λει ψανοδριμ υποτριματοσι λφιο κ́αραβο μολιτοκατακεχυμενο κιχλ επικοσσυφ-
ο φαττοπερ στεραλεκτρυον οπτοκεφάλ̇λ̇ιο κιγκλο πελειο λαγωο σιραιο βαφη —
Τραχανοπ. ρύχωζ ση, trans literated, lopado temacho selacho galechs
αριο λειψα οδριμ ipotrimato silph io karoβ ση elitokatakechymeno kich
lepi kossy, hoph atto peristera lektryon opto keph alliokin kl peleiole goi
ο siraio paphe tragano pterygon.

Among the longer Bible words is the symbolic name of the second son of Isaiah (Isaiah 8:1): Maher-Shalal-Hash-Baz. It has 18 letters, and means "The spoil speeds, the prey hastes"—that is, the doom of Syria and Ephraim is irrevocable. In the caption of Psalm 56, the title Jonathan-Elem-Rehokim ("The dove of the distant terebinths") has 17 letters.

Roger Angell once said his favorite among interminable words was Hottentottenpotentatentantenattentat (36), which, in spite of its astonishing length, uses only seven letters of the alphabet.

25 SEPTEMBER

Take 5 Tsp Auden; Add 1 Tsp Listerine

I am sorry I never met W. H. Auden. He must have been a lovely man. Once someone asked him his opinion of the poetry of his good friend Mike Di Lisio, the sculptor. "Does Mike write poetry?" asked Auden. "Yes, indeed, Wystan—he has had verses in *The New Yorker*." Auden thought a moment. "How nice of him," he said finally, "never to have told me!"

When Auden was young and unknown, he was asked how he would conduct his life should he become famous. Again he paused before replying. "I believe," he said, "that I would always wear my carpet slippers." He did become famous—and he did wear his carpet slippers, even when he was in evening clothes.

This is how Auden treated clerihews:

Henry Adams
Was mortally afraid of Madams;
In a disorderly house
He sat quiet as a mouse.

Lord Byron
Once succumbed to a Siren—
His flesh was weak,
Hers Greek.

Dante
Was utterly *enchanté,*
When Beatrice cried in tones that were peachy:
Noi siamo amici.

When the young Kant
Was told to kiss his aunt,
He obeyed the Categorical Must,
But only just.

Joseph Lister,
According to his sister,
Was not an alcoholic:
His vice was carbolic.

Even better than Auden's clerihew about Lister I like this one, unattributed, from *The Lancet:*

"Mamma, Mamma!" cried Joseph Lister,
"Pray tell me what's inside that blister."
Which people thought a lot of fuss
To make about a little pus.

26 SEPTEMBER

Th Hrglphs F Th Nw Yrk Tms

Only the consonants were represented in early Egyptian script. The time may have come to revive this system.* Lt s s hw tpcl Nw Yrk Tms dtrl wld rd wtht vwls:†

PKNG ND TWN

Th prgrss md n Mrcn rltns wth Chn snc 1971 hs bn drmtc nd t hs ld t rptd spcltn bt th pssblt f cmpltng th prcss b stblshng fll dplmtc rltns, clrl dsrbl mv. Th nl rl bstcl hs bn nblt t gr bt Twn.

Wht md th brkthrgh f 1971–72 pssbl ws Pkng's dcsn tht th Twn qstn ws nt rgnt. Th rslt, drng Prsdnt Nxn's 1972 vst, ws "splt" r prtll dsgrd

---

* Charles Kingsley made a start when he introduced Professor Ptthmllnsprts in "The Water Babies."

† See 12 March for a similar suggestion to the *Reader's Digest.*

cmmnq. Pkg xprssd sprt vw bt Twn, sttng tht t ws "th crcl qstn bstrctng th nrmlztn f rltns" nd mkng fv spcfc cmplnts bt Mrcn plc thr. Th mplctn ws that 11 fv wld hv t b crrctd bfr fll dplmtc rltns cld b stblshd.

The style of the foregoing may seem a trifle dense, but the message is as clear as in most editorials, and shorter, which, on balance, must be to the good.

Nd jst thnk f ll th nwsprnt tht wld b svd!

27 SEPTEMBER

About That Cow . . .

Roald Dahl reported not long ago that a cow mounted with her head to the south would produce a heifer, while mounted to the north she would produce a bull; or perhaps it was the other way around. I am not sure how this squares with present-day artificial insemination, which prompted E. B. White to lament:

> I'm sorry for cows who have to boast
> Of affairs they've had by parcel post.

The love life even of cattle reflects the state of their health. An ailing bull might explain his indifference to his mate in all-too-human terms:

> Love's joust you hint you'd undertake?
> My dear, I have a bellyache!
> Your beauty glimmers through a prism
> Distorted by my rheumatism.
> Europa's charms, or Aphrodite's,
> Cannot compete with my arthritis.
> My interest in making out
> Is overridden by my gout,
> And though my loins for you in bed ache,
> My mind is focused on my headache.
> Your joys venereal I'll prove;
> But wait until my bowels move.
>
> —W.R.E.

If I make my point with confidence, it is because my father once spent what was in those days a staggering sum to purchase a champion Shorthorn bull named Lambert. It was Lambert's responsibility to raise the quality of the Espy herd, a mixture of milch and beef stock. Unfortunately, Lambert soon developed rheumatism, and no longer could mount a knoll, much less a cow. Pop hammered together an upward-sloping ramp, so that the bull would not have to rear back so far; but Lambert refused to climb the ramp. Then Pop put a sling under his chest, with a rope running up from it through a pulley; by heaving on the free end of the rope one could lift

Lambert's forequarters off the ground; but the awkwardness of the position under-mined his libido. So Pop canned him.*

These bovine memories were brought to mind by an item in the newspaper:

WASHINGTON—The Agriculture Department has received a letter from a farmer whose cow was killed by one of the department's trucks. The department responded with an apology and a form to be filled out. It included a space for "disposition of the dead cow." Replied the farmer: "kind and gentle."

A. Ross Eckler says a farmer caught a crow with a band on its leg marked WASH. BIOL. SURVEY, and a return address. "Dear Sirs," wrote the farmer, "I washed, biled and surved the bird, but it tasted turrible."

28 SEPTEMBER

King David and King Solomon

A 94-year-old, informed that he had just become a father for the eleventh time, replied pregnantly, if squeakily, "You give me the mold, and I can make the bullets!" The following verse indicates that King David and King Solomon came to take a different view:

King David and King Solomon   But when old age crept over them
    Led merry, merry lives   With many, many qualms,
With many, many lady friends   King Solomon wrote the proverbs
    And many, many wives.   And King David wrote the psalms.
                                          —James Ball Naylor

When old age creeps over me, I know exactly how I am going to take advantage of it. I am going to wear bibs at meals to save my neckties. I should never have let myself be persuaded out of that sensible custom at the age of five.

29 SEPTEMBER

The Rein in Spain Reigns Mainly in the Rain†

When you light gleefully upon some grammatical infelicity in this book, you may

---

* For thousands of years, peasants in the Middle East have dug pits for the cows of rheumatic bulls to stand in. Pop should have thought of that.
† See also 15 February.

blame me, or my editor, or my typesetter, or my proofreader, and you may be right all four times. Could Louis Auchincloss deliberately have written (in *Portrait in Brownstone*) "Could he not pick up the dropped reigns whenever he chose?" Or, in *The Rector of Justin*, "He then turned to the other door through which Dr. Prescott always emerged and waited"? Speaking of reigning in the reins, could it possibly be purist William Safire who wrote, "As the reigns of power have been held more loosely, each of the horses in the team has taken the bit in its teeth"?

If you have a mean streak in you, you can find happiness by opening almost any book, magazine, or newspaper at almost any page to chortle over the innocent bloopers waiting there. Katherine Fessenden found these:

From a Doubleday book: "Each of them had once before entered a new home with the person to whom they were married."

From a Scribner's book: "She had ought to have become accustomed."

From a Harper & Row book: "Dizzy once caught a four and a half pound trout in his charming stream which he sent to the Queen."

Other Fessenden discoveries: "He kept them in the back of his closet and in the bottom of the grandfather clock in the front hall that never worked"; "a miasma of thermometers, barometers, switches, and dials"; "Simon simply failed to work on any team, God's notwithstanding"; and "Crest poured over charts by the hour."

3 0 SEPTEMBER

*Mr. K*A*P*L*A*N's Dark Logic*

H*Y*M*A*N K*A*P*L*A*N, one of "thirty-odd adults in the beginner's grade of the American Night Preparatory School for Adults ('English—Americanization—Civic—Preparation for Naturalization')," first beat the daylights out of the English language in the 1930s in the pages of *The New Yorker*. As the following incident indicates, it was no contest; the language did not have a chance.

> The class was making three-minute addresses. Miss Rochelle Goldberg was reciting. She was describing her experience with a ferocious dog. The dog's name, according to Miss Goldberg, was "Spots." He was a "Scotch Terror."
>
> "Was he a beeg, wild dug!" Miss Goldberg said, her eyes moving in recollective fear. "Honist you would all be afraid something tarrible! I had good rizzon for being all scared. I was trying to pat Spots, nize, on the had, and saying, "Here, Spots, Spots, Spots"—and Spots bites me so hod on the—"
>
> " 'Bite' is the *present* tense, Miss Goldberg."
>
> A look of dismay wandered into Miss Goldberg's eyes.
>
> "You want the—er—*past* tense." Mr. Parkhill spoke as gently as he could: Miss Goldberg had a collapsible nervous system. "What *is* the past tense of 'to bite'?"

Miss Goldberg hung her head.

"The past tense of 'to bite'—anyone?"

Mr. Kaplan's Samaritan impulses surged to the fore. "Isn't 'bited,' ufcawss," he ventured archly.

"No, it isn't—er—'bited'!" Mr. Parkhill couldn't tell whether Mr. Kaplan had uttered a confident negation or an oblique question.

Miss Mitnick raised her hand, just high enough to be recognized. "'Bit,'" she volunteered, quietly.

"Good, Miss Mitnick! 'Bite, *bit, bitten.*'"

At once Mr. Kaplan closed his eyes, cocked his head to one side and began whispering to himself. "Mitnick gives 'bit' . . . *'Bit'* Mitnick gives . . . My!"

This dramaturgic process indicated that Mr. Kaplan was subjecting Miss Mitnick's contribution to his most rigorous analysis. Considering the ancient and acrid feud between these two, to allow one of Miss Mitnick's offerings to go unchallenged would constitute a psychological defeat of no mean proportions to Mr. Kaplan. It would be a blow to his self-respect. It would bring anguish to his soul.

"'Bite, bit, bitten'? Dat sonds awful fonny! . . ."

It was no use for Mr. Parkhill to pretend that he had not heard; the whole class had heard.

"Er—isn't that clear, Mr. Kaplan?"

Mr. Kaplan did not open his eyes. "*Clear,* Mr. Pockheel? Foist-class clear! Clear like gold! Only I don' see *vy* should be dat 'bit'. . . . It don' makink sanse!"

"Oh, it doesn't make *sense,*" Mr. Parkhill repeated lamely. Suddenly he glimpsed a golden opportunity. "You mean it isn't—er—*logical?*"

"Exactel!" cried Mr. Kaplan happily. "Dat 'bit' isn't logical."

"Well, Mr. Kaplan. Surely you remember our verb drills. The verb 'to bite' is much like, say, the verb 'to hide.' 'To hide' is conjugated 'hide, hid, hidden.' Why, then, isn't it—er—logical that the principal parts of 'to bite' be 'bite, bit, bitten'?"

Mr. Kaplan considered this semi-syllogism in silence. Then he spoke. "*I* tought de pest time 'bite' should be—'bote.'"

Miss Mitnick gave a little gasp.

"'Bote'?" Mr. Parkhill asked in amazement. "'Bote'?"

"'Bote'!" said Mr. Kaplan.

Mr. Parkhill shook his head. "I don't see your point."

"Vell," sighed Mr. Kaplan, with a modest shrug, "if is 'write, wrote, written' so vy isn't 'bite, bote, bitten'?"

Psychic cymbals crashed in Mr. Parkhill's ears.

"There is not such a word 'bote,'" protested Miss Mitnick, who took this all as a personal affront. Her voice was small, but desperate.

"Not-soch-a-void!" Mr. Kaplan repeated ironically. "Mine dear Mitnick, don' *I* know is not soch a void? Did I said *is* soch a void? All I'm eskink is, isn't logical *should be* soch a void?"

—Leo Rosten

OCTOBER

1 OCTOBER

Ballad of Soporific Absorption

Told that General Grant was a whiskey drinker, Lincoln said he wished he could send that whiskey to his other generals. I don't know Sir John's favorite drink, but any light versifier could use a few cases of it.

Ho! Ho! Yes! It's very all well,
　　You may drunk I am think, but I tell you I'm not,
I'm as sound as a fiddle and fit as a bell,
　　And stable quite ill to see what's what.
　　I under *do* stand you surprise a got
When I headed my smear with gooseberry jam:
　　And I've swallowed, I grant, a beer of lot—
But I'm not so think as you drunk I am.

Can I liquor my stand? Why, yes, like hell!
　　I care not how many a tossed I've pot,
I shall stralk quite weight and not yutter an ell,
　　My feech will not spalter the least little jot:
　　If you knownly had own!—well, I gave him a dot
And I said to him, 'Sergeant, I'll come like a lamb—'
　　The floor it seems like a storm in a yacht,
But I'm not so think as you drunk I am.

For example, to prove it I'll tale you a tell—
　　I once knew a fellow named Apricot—
I'm sorry, I just chair over a fell—
　　A trifle—this chap, on a very day hot—
　　If I hadn't consumed that last whisky of tot!—
As I said now, this fellow, called Abraham—
　　Ah? One more? Since it's you! Just a do me will spot—
But I'm not so think as you drunk I am.

ENVOI

So, Prince, you suggest I've bolted my shot?
Well, like what you say, and soul your damn!
　　I'm an upple litset by the talk you rot—
But I'm not so think as you drunk I am.

—*John C. Squire*

2 OCTOBER

Pinking the Politician

How the art of political insult has decayed! I recall no memorable ad hominem hereabouts since Clare Boothe Luce explained Senator Wayne Morse's political positions as a result of his having fallen from a horse and landed on his head. Even this was more a roundhouse swing with a broadsword than a precise lunge with a rapier.

In general, the English pink more deftly than Americans. Benjamin Disraeli remarked that a traveler, learning that Lord John Russell was leader of the House of Commons, "may well begin to comprehend how the Egyptians worshiped an insect." Disraeli used his rival, William Gladstone, to illustrate the difference between a misfortune and a calamity: "If Gladstone fell into the Thames, it would be a misfortune. But if someone dragged him out again, it would be a calamity." (Gladstone, for his part, once said of bishops appointed by him who voted against him in the House of Lords: "Have they forgotten their Maker?" But he was not pinking; he was perfectly sincere.)

Pinkest and most cherubical of pinkers was Winston Churchill. He once described Clement Attlee as "a modest man with much to be modest about," and again as "a sheep in sheep's clothing." He credited Ramsay MacDonald with "the gift of compressing the largest amount of words into the smallest amount of thoughts." He said of Stanley Baldwin, "He occasionally stumbles over the truth, but he always hastily picks himself up and hurries on as if nothing had happened." And of Sir Stafford Cripps, known for arrogance, he remarked: "There, but for the grace of God, goes God."

3 OCTOBER

Strine Revisited

These two Strine verses would not have lessened the reputation of an Ovid or a Milton:*

THE BOSSA NYE

Ware niker tinter work now
The bossa zinner hedomy;
Ickisser smee, and sair, 'Swill yubie mine?'
I got a rillked lurk now;
'I lar few, dear,' he sedomy,
But ice air, 'Gee, it sneely ah-pa snine.'

* See 24 April.

I fleft me jobber twirk now;
The bosket spy withairt me;
A niken stayer tome a slardger slife.
I give a little smirk now;
The bossle torga bairt me:
'Me sekkertry has nowbie cummy wife.'

WITH AIR CHEW

With air chew, with air chew,
Iker nardly liver there chew,
An I dream a badger kisser snite and die.
Phoney wicked beer loan,
Jars-chewer mere nonnair roan,
An weed dreamer batter monner pinner sky.

With air chew, with air chew,
Hair mike-owner liver there chew?
Wile yerrony immy dream sigh maulwye scrine.
Anna strewer seffner barf,
Yuma snow-eye Nietzsche laugh,
Cars with air chew immy arm sit snow-ewe Strine.
—*Afferbeck Lauder*

4 OCTOBER

Singular Plurals

Axes is the plural form of both ax and axis; bases the plural form of both base and basis. Wherefore:

1.

Paul Bunyan swung his ax, with view
To sundering the globe in two;
The ax that made that mighty probe
Stuck at the axis of the globe.
Pray tell, Larousse, pray tell, Bowditch,
Of those two axes, which was which?

2.

The base of any basis from the basis of its base
Is easy to distinguish in the ordinary case;
But give them plural number, and it's *bases* that you get;
Don't try to disentangle them; you'll only get upset.
—*W.R.E.*

Another point of view on plurals:

> Two staffs make staves;
> Two giraffes don't make giraves.
> One giraffe
> Makes one laugh.
> —*David McCord*

Which reminds me: *pease* was once both singular and plural. Because it just naturally sounded plural, the singular shrank to *pea*.

5 OCTOBER

How Not to Solve a Cipher

Many people enjoy deciphering codes, and I recently found an example in *Time* that I thought I might share with my readers. But though the principle was clearly explained, the work of solving the code turned out to be tedious, and I decided that I might save time for both you and myself by creating a shorter code of my own for you to break down. The way one starts to solve a usual cryptogram is by making use of the frequency rates of the letters of the alphabet. The most common letter is e. Unfortunately, my message turned out to have no e's. For that matter, it had no b's, d's, g's, i's, j's, p's, q's, v's, w's, x's, y's, or z's. To solve such a cipher would overstrain even the most proficient cryptanalyst. So instead I give you my message in the clear:

> Thanks munch
> For lunch.
> —*W.R.E.*

6 OCTOBER

Where Is the Slang of Yesteryear?

Where now are the debs, gold diggers, and flappers, not to mention the belles and vamps, who used to lead a chap on and then give him the air? Where are the roués, the triflers, the philanderers, the rakes, the cads, and the gigolos? What has become of vanity-cases, déshabillé, and *it*? When did the last young couple neck, pet or spoon? Where did the gadding and the joy riding go? When did the last tabloid shake its last love nest out of the tree? When did you last meet an old maid?

The boreal blast of the Great Depression blackened and shriveled the in-language of the roaring twenties—the language of John Held, Jr.; of Anita Loos; and, supremely, of the lighthearted lexicographer whose definitions appear below.

AMBIDEXTROUS   Not letting your right hand know who is holding your left hand.

BONERS   Scrambled definitions attributed to children by their elders. *Example*—"A GENTLEMAN is a man who always gets up and gives his seat to a lady in a public convenience."

CHAP   A good egg. CHURL, a bad egg, and CHUMP, an addled egg.

EDGE   Something one has on when one is a bit off.

FELINE   Something about Cats and Women that is viewed with distrust by Mice and Men.

HALF   One of the twin offspring of WHOLE.

HEREAFTER   An evasive answer to the GREAT QUESTION: "Where do we go from Here?"

IDIOT   A person of average intellect.

IGNORAMUS   A person of average knowledge.

ILLITERACY   Average scholarship.

INTEMPERANCE   The retort to intolerance.

JAG   Term derived from the Jagged Peak of Ararat where Noah became inebriated.

LISP   To call a spade a thpade.

LITTER   A coming-out party of puppies.

MUSIC   Here's to Music, joy of joys,
One man's music's another man's noise.

OAF   Contraction of "Oaf—for Heaven's sake."

OPTIMIST   A happychondriac.

ORNITHORHYNCHUS   A furry quadruped that has the bill of a duck and lays eggs.
This vacillating beast you see
Could not decide which one to be
Fish Flesh or Fowl and Chose all three.

POSTSCRIPT   The tail that wags the letter.

PRONOUN   The understudy of a noun.

PULP   The stuff that reams are made from.

QUALM   Inside information of danger. The Qualm before the storm.

QUATRAIN   Verse that goes on all fours.

ROUGE   The four-flush of health.

UPRIGHT   Very good—but not very good company.

VINE   The Grapeful source of a fermented drink, blessed by Christ and Paul but banned by Clarence True Wilson and Bishop Cannon.*

God made man,   God made the Vine
Frail as a Bubble   Was it a sin
God made Love   That Man made Wine
Love made Trouble   To drown Trouble in?

* Wilson and James Cannon were two clergymen who took Prohibition seriously.

WARREN   Meeting place of rabbits. See *Mrs. Warren's Profession* by Bernard Shaw.

—Oliver Herford

7 OCTOBER

Lo, the Frolicsome Eskimo
(Or, Winter Games in the Yukon Territory)

"What sports fan," says a *Wall Street Journal* dispatch from White Horse, "wouldn't be thrilled by Simon Tookoome's lightning reflexes in ipirautaqturqi, little Roger Kunayak's determination in agraorak or Reggie Joule's thrilling bounce in the nalukattak? Oh sure. There's some disappointment that Tautugni hasn't shown up to defend his ayagaq record. But the fact that the world mark in agraorak was almost equaled more than makes up for his absence."

Sound the trumpets, beat the drums!   When will Tau-tugni be back
The champ of agra-orak comes!   To show off his aya-gaq,
Kicks his foot above his crown   Throwing seal bones up together,
To bring the hanging milk can down!   One combining with the other?

In ipír-autaq-turník   In the nalu-kattak toss
Lengthy whips of sealskin flick;   The performers scored a loss:
Why did champion Tookoome   Did gymnastics in the air,
Leave his thirty-footer home?   Dropped, but found no blanket there.

—W.R.E.

8 OCTOBER

Opposite Proverbs

1. A man's reach should exceed his grasp.
   A bird in the hand is worth two in the bush.
2. Haste makes waste.
   He who hesitates is lost.
3. Above all, to thine own self be true.
   When in Rome, do as the Romans do.
4. It is never too late to learn.
   You can't teach an old dog new tricks.

5. Good things come in small packages.
   The bigger, the better.
6. There is no point in beating a dead horse.
   If at first you don't succeed, try, try again.
7. He who hesitates is lost.
   Act in haste, repent at leisure.
8. Two is company, three is a crowd.
   The more, the merrier.
9. . . . do it well or not at all.
   Half a loaf is better than none.
10. Nothing ventured, nothing gained.
    Better safe than sorry.
11. Never judge a book by its cover.
    Clothes make the man.
12. Out of sight, out of mind.
    Absence makes the heart grow fonder.
13. Many hands make light work.
    Too many cooks spoil the broth.
14. Never send a boy to do a man's job.
    . . . and a little child shall lead them.
15. Actions speak louder than words.
    The pen is mightier than the sword.
16. Never change horses in mid-stream.
    Variety is the spice of life.
17. Silence is golden.
    The squeaky wheel gets the grease.
18. Practice makes perfect.
    All work and no play makes Jack a dull boy.
19. A penny saved is a penny earned.
    The love of money is the root of all evil.

—*M. H. Greenblatt*

9 OCTOBER

What Is the Question?

I am told that this game was popular at the White House during the Thousand Days of J. F. Kennedy. The answers come first:

1. Dr. Livingston, I presume.
2. Oh, about 20 drachmas a week.
3. No strings attached.
4. Crick.

5 February 29th, for example.
6. Chromatic scales.
7. A youthful figure.
8. Black.
9. A Greek letter.
10. Strontium 90, Carbon 14.
11. Around the world in 80 days.
12. George Washington slept here.
13. From the rockbound coast of Maine.
14. Stork Club.
15. Poetic justice.

All right—what are the questions?

10 OCTOBER

The Mad Round Robin

If the writers for *Mad* are not insane geniuses, at least they are genially insane. One of them likes to filter famous authors' verses through other famous authors' pens, with results like those below:*

IF POE'S "THE RAVEN" WERE WRITTEN BY JOYCE KILMER

I think that I shall never hear
A raven who is more sincere
Than that one tapping at my door
Who's ever saying, "Nevermore."
A raven who repeats his words
Until I think I'm for the birds;
A raven who, I must assume,
Will dirty up my living-room;
A raven fond of bugs and worms
With whom I'm on the best of terms.
Let other poets praise a tree—
A raven's good enough for me!

IF KILMER'S "TREES" WERE WRITTEN BY JOHN MASEFIELD

I must go up in a tree again
 and sit where the bullfinch warbles;

* See also 21 April.

Where the squirrel runs up and down a limb
    and the owl has lost his marbles;
And the squawks and hoots and chirps and squeaks
    that all the birds are making
Fill the air around so I can't hear
    the branch beneath me breaking!

I must go up in a tree again,
    from where people look like ants,
And all I ask is a branch that's smooth
    so I won't rip my pants;
And a dozen bugs running up my leg,
    and the sap so sticky,
And the cooing doves and the screaming crows
    making messes icky.

IF MASEFIELD'S "SEA FEVER" WERE WRITTEN BY CARL SANDBURG

Fish Tank for the World,
Shark Breeder, Maker of Waves,
Lousy with Herring and the Nation's Saltcellar;
Briny, bottomless, undrinkable,
Home of the Big Flounder;
They tell me you are stormy, and I believe them;
    for I have crossed you on a tramp steamer
    and have lost my lunch at the poop rail.
And they tell me you are messy, and my reply is:
    Yes, it is true I have swum in your surf and
    have emerged yecchy, with seaweed.
And having answered, I ask myself: Why am I not
    writing a poem about Chicago instead of a poem
    about the Fish Tank for the World, Shark Breeder,
    Maker of Waves, Home of the Big Flounder, and
    Saltcellar to the Nation?

IF CARL SANDBURG'S "CHICAGO" WERE WRITTEN BY RUDYARD KIPLING

You can talk of Mandalay,
Of Calcutta or Bombay,
    Where the heat'll make a fuzzy-wuzzy fry;
But if to drink you're driven
And don't give a damn for livin'
    Then you oughta hit the road for windy Chi.

It's a town where hoods and thugs
Like to send a dozen slugs
    Right through a copper pretty as you please;

Where the breezes blow like hell,
And that awful stockyard smell
  Is enough to bring a blighter to his knees.

For it's Chi! Chi! Chi!
Guns are shootin' and I'm just a passerby!
Though your buildings may be pretty,
You can keep your bloomin' city
'Cause I'm headin' back to Injia, windy Chi!
          —*Frank Jacobs* in *Mad Magazine*

There is no room for the rest of the round robins: if Kipling's "Gunga Din" were written by Clement Clarke Moore; if Moore's "The Night Before Christmas" were written by Robert W. Service; if Service's "The Shooting of Dan McGrew" were written by Henry Wadsworth Longfellow; if Longfellow's "The Midnight Ride of Paul Revere" were written by Ernest Lawrence Thayer; and finally, to round out the round robin, if Thayer's "Casey At the Bat" were written by Edgar Allan Poe.

11 OCTOBER

Streets in Old London

Isaac Disraeli, father of the British prime minister, reported as follows on the evolution of certain street names in London:

Mincing-lane was *Mincheon-lane;* from tenements pertaining to the Mincheons, or nuns of St. Helen's, in Bishopsgate-street.

Gutter-lane, corrupted from *Guthurun's lane;* from its first owner, a citizen of great trade.

Blackwall-hall was *Bakewell's-hall;* from one Thomas Bakewell.

Finch-lane was *Finke's-lane;* from a whole family of this name.

Billiter-lane is a corruption of *Bellzetter's-lane;* from the first builder or owner.

Crutched-friars was *Crowched* or *Crossed-friars.*

Fetter-lane has been erroneously supposed to have some connection with the *fetters* of criminals. It was in Charles the First's time written *Fewtor-lane* . . . from *"Fewtors"* (or idle people) lying there. . . .

Gracechurch-street, sometimes called *Gracious-street,* was originally *Grass-street,* from an herb market there.

Bridewell was *St. Bridget's-well,* from one dedicated to Saint Bride, or Bridget.

Marybone was *St. Mary-on-the-Bourne* . . .

Maiden-lane was so called from an image of the Virgin, which, in

Catholic days, had stood there . . . and the frequent sign of the *Maiden-head* was derived from "our Lady's head."

Piccadilly was named after a hall called *Piccadilla-hall,* a place of sale for *Piccadillies,* or *turn-overs;* a part of the fashionable dress which appeared about 1614.

Mr. Disraeli may have known this riddle:

In England I have no head nor foot, in America no top nor bottom. Corner me in America, and you will give me a bad turn in England. What am I?

1 2 OCTOBER

"Hark to the Mewsicians of Bremen!" Mewed the Caterpillar

"Easel" derives from the Danish word for "ass"; an easel, like an ass, being a bearer of burdens. Had an easel rather than an ass sounded the C for the Musicians of Bremen, he and his fellows might have sung like this:

> The monkeywrench chattered
> The easel brayed
> The firedog barked
> The sawhorse neighed
> The duckpin quacked
> The weathercock crowed
> The chickenpox cheeped
> The cowlick lowed.
> —*W.R.E.*

Here are a dozen adjectives that refer to specific animals. How many of the animals can you identify:
1. Cervine. 2. Colubrine. 3. Hircine. 4. Larine. 5. Lutrine. 6. Meline.
7. Mephitine. 8. Musteline. 9. Ovine. 10. Phocine. 11. Sciurine. 12. Viverrine.

1 3 OCTOBER

Sim Ines
Or, Ode to a Bide-to-Be

This marvel, like several others herein, I owe to the truffle-dog nose of William Cole:

Mrs. Richard Feltus and Mrs. W. T. Mallory entertained yesterday at a tea shower. They feted Miss Barbara Steitenroth who is engaged to be married. The party took place at the Mallory home on Highway 61 north.

Aangements of white Dutch es wee used fo decoation. The tea tabe was coveed with a white impoted inen coth and centeed the white fowes whirh wee offset with ighted white randes in sive hodes.

and white sik fock designed on sim ines and compemented with back patent accessoies. He cosage, a gift of the hostesses, was of white bida booms.

Guests incuded a imited goup of cose fiends.

—Natchez (Miss.) Democrat

> Oh, I woud I wee a cose, cose fiend,
> That these ovey things I might have seen:
> The tea tabe centeed with fowes white
> Offset with ighted white randes bight,
> And coveed with inen coth impoted—
> Suey on these I would have doted!
> The sive hodes and the eses Dutch
> To the decoation added much;
> But the pettiest sight in those chaming ooms
> Was he white sik fock and he bida booms.
> *—Jane Stubbs*

14 OCTOBER

The Variety of Abel Green

If a headline reading STICKS NIX HICK PIX means to you that films with bucolic themes flop in Bucolia, you speak on equal terms with *Variety,* the Bible of show business. Abel Green, editor of *Variety* for forty years,* legalized such linguistic tender as boff, yocks, plushery, femcee, flivved, and crix. For Mr. Green, TV networks were webs; festivals, fests; film biographies, biopics; executives, exex. If he wanted to hear from you by telephone, he would say, "Gimme an Ameche"—Don Ameche having played Alexander Graham Bell in a motion picture about the invention of the telephone. A Green analysis of the demise of Toots Shor's restaurant began: "The raison d'être for el foldo . . ."

Even funerals were show biz to Abel Green. His headline for a report on the last rites for one of his best friends was "S.R.O. attendance of over 1,000 at Temple Emmanuel." He embraced the lowly pun; one of his headlines summarized the engorging career of Linda Lovelace, of the x-rated film *Deep Throat,* in four words: A STAR IS PORN.

---

* He died in 1973.

No wonder H. L. Mencken worshiped at the Green shrine! No wonder Francis Cardinal Spellman told him, "I read your Bible every week, just as I read my own!"

15 OCTOBER

Fallen Women

My Women's Liberation friends should do something to salvage the good name of their sex. The very word *woman* has become offensive in some circles; *lady* has come down to where *woman* was a hundred years ago, and in two thousand years *carus,* Latin for "dear," has degenerated to *whore*. A *courtesan* was once a lady at court; a *wench,* any young girl; *tart,* a term of endearment. Even *housewife,* that most respectable of appellations, becomes opprobrious when pronounced *hussy*. *Dame* is now a slang term of dubious implication; *madam* makes us think of someone running a house of prostitution, and *queen* (properly *quean*) is a homosexual.

But I suspect it's not the ladies who drive these terms down the social ladder; it's the gents.

16 OCTOBER

A Collection of Crocks

"If crockery is a collection of crocks," writes Evan Esar, "then flattery is a collection of flats, scullery is a collection of skulls, sorcery a collection of sources, and monastery a collection of monsters." I have used Mr. Esar's collectives in the following Japery (a collection of Japes) which is based on the reasonable assumption that any word ending in -ry must be a Collection of Something or Other.

From a Sorcery
I bring you this curious Factory.
One day a Gallantry
A Jury
And a Hickory
Who included a Calory
And a Dickery
Left their Flattery
To walk on a Dockery
With a Monastery.

There they met a Gallery
Among whom were a Janissary
A Salary
And a Misery.
The Hickory
Had brought a Henry
And the Henry
Had brought a Chicory.
The Gallery
Agreed to dance a Jiggery

On the Dockery
With the Gallantry
The Jury
And the Hickory
But not the Monastery.
This enraged the Monastery
Who loosed in the Jiggery
A Battery
And made off in the confusion with the
  Henry
And the Chicory.
With the prodigious Cursory
The Hickory
Sic'ed a Curry
A Colliery
And a Berry
On the fleeing Monastery
But the clever Monastery
Ran into a Story

Where they sold the Henry
And the Chicory
For a Sentry.
With a quick Peccary
The Henry
And the Chicory
Ate a Pillory
And a Buggery.
When the police caught the Monastery
They rode them on a Raillery
And in a Celery
Rapped a Scullery.
The judge imposed a Finery.
But the Hickory
Never got back the Henry
Or the Chicory
For the Hickory
Were a Foolery.

—W.R.E.

17 OCTOBER

Colloquy between a Devout Man and His Wicked Echo

An echo may convey a different meaning from the original phrase:

A good man muttered to himself as he walked on a hill;
And Echo followed after him, as Echo always will.

Good man: I bend my neck to be God's sacrifice;
One final throe will win me Paradise.

Echo: *One final throw will win, me pair o' dice!*

Good man: I seek out God behind His shining gate,
Where cherubims and angels scintillate.

Echo: Where cherubims and angels *sin till late.*

Good man: Flesh, fall away! I climb the spirit's heights!
How futile now, those orgiastic nights!

Echo: *How few till now,* those orgiastic nights!

Good man: Beyond the grave, eternal life begins.
But what is life? Forgive me, Lord, my sins!

Echo: *But what is life for? Give me, Lord, my sins!*

—W.R.E

18 OCTOBER

Mini, Minu

A number of years ago, when I couldn't find "miniscule" in my desk dictionary, I briskly turned to my unabridged and didn't find it there, either. How do you react upon not finding in the dictionary a word you think you know? Trembling, I managed to call the reference room of the New York Public Library and was calmly told that the word is spelled m-i-n-u-s-c-u-l-e. As it turned out, this librarian was the last person I've run across who knew how to spell the word. Everyone else spells it wrong, in the same way.

Even when the subject is a dictionary, as in the review of the two-volume Oxford English Dictionary in *Medical World News,* the reproductions are described as "sharp but miniscule."

The *Milwaukee Journal* refers to a chemical additive as being a "miniscule ingredient."

Newsfront tells of someone grabbing a "miniscule slice of the Democratic party pie."

The *Chicago Tribune Magazine* mentions "her cheerful, miniscule candybox of an apartment."

It's rampant in *The New York Times.* On the sports page there are terms of "Lilliputian dimensions and miniscule skills." A subheadline in the news section reads: "Impressive or Miniscule?" And there is mention of a magazine with a "relatively miniscule 15,000 subscribers"—who, even if they were minuscule, would probably have trouble lifting the magazine.

But don't think it's solely an American failing. The *Montreal Star* tells of an amount of "alleged marijuana that was so miniscule that it was destroyed in the laboratory." It does sound American, though, from the alleged to the miniscule.

And in Philip Roth's *Goodbye, Columbus,* in both the hardcover and paperback editions, a letter is written in "an extraordinarily miniscule hand."

Is this the way language changes?

—*Sidney Harris*

19 OCTOBER

Forgotten Positives

A reviewer once complained that in an article about forgotten positives I myself had "forgotten the classic text on this subject, which begins with the line: 'I know a little man who's ept and ert.'" Well, I had not forgotten it—I had never seen it. But I have seen it now, and here is the first stanza:

> I know a little man both ept and ert
> An intro? extro? No, he's just a vert
> Sheveled and couth and kempt, pecunious, ane;
> His image trudes upon the ceptive brain.
> —*David McCord*

I included in the article a quatrain of my own, "I Dreamt of Couth." I add herewith a second stanza:

> I dreamt that bulating the youth would dulate
> In a peccable, ferior vein.
> I'm turbed that he's funct and chalant, and I'll state
> I'd be poverished having his dain.
> —*W.R.E.*

(By the way, when was the last time you heard scruple used as a verb, save in the negative "does not scruple to . . ."? Yet it is a lovely word of conscience: "She scrupled," wrote Jane Austen, "to point out her own remarks to him, lest it seem like ill nature.")

20 OCTOBER

Alexander's Number One

A while back I had urgent occasion to cable my eldest daughter, then resident in Uganda, as follows:

> ALEXANDER'S NUMBER ONE / ELLIOT IS TWO /
> JEREMY IS NUMBER THREE / AND I THINK THAT
> SHOULD DO

This is your birthday, Jeremy, and I have something to whisper to you: Did you know that the indentation above your upper lip was caused by an angel who put her finger against your mouth to hush your crying just after you were born? This is perfectly true; your mother saw the angel, and she told me. But she could not tell me what to call the indentation, so I wrote this verse:

BETWEEN YOUR NOSE AND UPPER LIP

> Between your nose and upper lip
> There runs a cleft; a trough; a slip;
>
> A runnel, furrow, gutter, split;
> I wish I knew the name for it.
> —*W.R.E.*

21 OCTOBER

Lerner's Mixed Lerning

You are being metaphorical when you complain about the cost of keeping up with the Joneses, as you are when you call a policeman a pig, a pretty girl a bird, a white a honkey, or a black a coon. (Come to think of it, though, blacks haven't been called coons in a coon's age.)

Sometimes metaphors lose their way.* Shakespeare's "to take arms against a sea of troubles" is a mixed metaphor, just as is Ian Fleming's "Bond's knees, the Achilles' heel of all skiers, were beginning to ache," or Foreign Minister Bevin's warning: "If you let that sort of thing go on, your bread and butter will be cut out from under your feet."

One of the generally straightforward journalists of our time is Max Lerner. I love him when he speaks to the point, like this:

> On exams: There are three reasons I don't give them. I hate writing them; I hate reading them; and I was never able to pass any exam I drew up.

But when Mr. Lerner lets loose with a volley of mixed metaphors, they are beauts. Here is my favorite:

> Thus Sadat wrestled with the Devil for the soul of Egypt, and lost, because the Devil had most of the cards, and the jury of world opinion was half asleep and wholly blinkered.

Watch it, Max. You've got a sword of Damocles hanging over that Pandora's box.

22 OCTOBER

Stinky-Pinkies

Stinky pinkies—nouns modified by rhyming adjectives—pall even faster than limericks, but a few, such as these, are good enough to renew one's faith.

> 1. Ardent employee.
> 2. Unimaginative surface decoration.

* There isn't room here for all of Thomas Hood's *Muddled Metaphors* but at least you can have a taste:

> Oh, ever thus from childhood's hour
> I've seen my fondest hopes recede!
> I never loved a tree or flower
> That didn't trump its partner's lead . . .

3. A cactus that goes out of its way to needle you.
4. A world of igneous rock.
5. Boisterous policy meeting.
6. Dismal chorus.
7. Childish wall-painting.
8. Brackish nut-confection.
9. Fanatic slave.
10. Fruitful interval of time.

—*David L. Silverman*

23 OCTOBER

Upon October Twenty-Third

Upon October
Twenty-third
A singular
event occurred:

I put my paper
To my pen;
I put my paper
Back again;

For though the world
Was in distress,
It always had been,
More or less

With murder, war,
And peculation,
Adultery,
Discrimination,

And princes in,
And princes out,
And not a thing
To write about.*

—*W.R.E.*

24 OCTOBER

Surf Bird, Shore Bird

"A goldfinch is sometimes called a thistletweeker, a linet a linet tweaker, a curlew a whelp." *The Sea Farer* (early Anglo-Saxon)

Are the shore birds around Oysterville peeps, or snipe? I know only that they belong to the Charadrii family, with cousins innumerable. I learned this from read-

---

* The only event worth recording that I can recall occurring on a 23 October was the birth of one of my daughters.

ing Peter Matthiessen's *Wind Birds**—a writing as precise and lovely as a snipe's clawprint in wet sand. A few of the subspecies Mr Matthiessen mentions are listed here:

> Surf bird, shore bird, veering over,
> Are you Dowitcher, or Plover?
>
> You at edge of tide who sprint
> Are you Avocet, or Stint?
>
> You who Peewee, you who Pipe,
> Are you Tattler? Curlew? Snipe?
>
> Wader, sitting on your eggs,
> Are you hatching Yellowlegs?
>
> Wind bird, glinting in the sun,
> Are you Stilt? Peep? Simpleton?
>
> Turnstone? Oystercatcher? Knot?
> Ox-eye? Doughbird? Whimbrel? Spot?†
>
> Thick-knee? Godwit? Dotterel?
> Chickenbird? Or Rail? Ah well . . .
>
> It suffices that you be
> Of Sub-order *Charadrii*.
>   —W.R.E.

25 OCTOBER

We Interrupt Our Program for a Word from Mr. McLuhan

> My TV tells me, *all men have their* - - - - -;
> It says, *who pays the piper calls the* - - - -;
> And *haste makes* - - - -, and *cat away, the mice*
> Will - - - -, and *better half a loaf than* - - - -.
> My TV says, *what's dirt cheap's cheap as* - - - -;
> And - - - - - - - *would, were wishes horses, ride;*
> And *out of sight is out of mind.* (But ponder
> As well that - - - - - - - *makes the heart grow* - - - - - -.)

* The English say waders; in this country we generally say surf birds or shore birds.
† The correct name is Spotted. Sorry, Peter.

My TV tells me *water's not as thick*
As ----- , and ----- *heart ne'er fair* ---- *won;*
Speak soft, but ever carry a big ----- ;
The rich grow ------ , *but the poor have fun.*

Of what new insight are all these the presage?
You said it, Mac! The ------ *'s the message!*

                                                       —W.R.E.

26 OCTOBER

Polish Up Your Polish, Zywacki!

Heteronyms are words identical in spelling, but different in both sound and meaning. Polish (pertaining to Poland*), and polish (to make smooth or glossy) are heteronyms.

The word *os,* reports *Word Ways,* is a four-way heteronym: "Pronounced AHSS, it means a bond, also a mouth or an opening; pronounced OASS, it refers to a narrow ridge or mound of gravelly and sandy drift, deposited by a subglacial stream; pronounced OZE, it designates ciphers or zeroes; pronounced OWE-ESS, it is a verb defined as 'to record the time of arrival and departure of a train by telegraphing the information in a certain manner.'"

Until I read the foregoing, I would have considered OS a misspelling of Dorothy's Kingdom of OZ.

27 OCTOBER

Above All That?

As a partisan of Mary Magdalen, I advise you that the following double dactyl perpetuates a canard. Mary, faithful follower of Jesus and first to speak to the risen Lord, was once the involuntary receptacle of seven devils, which Jesus drove away (Luke 8:2). She has no demonstrated connection with the unnamed fallen woman

---

* American Poles—more secure, it would appear, than Jews, blacks, Italians, or WASPS—do not write hysterical letters to the newspapers because of the recent spate of such Polish jokes as these: "Don't tell a Polish joke in front of me," said the Pole; "I'm Polish." "That's all right," said the story teller; "I'll speak slowly." Again: The Polish recruit asked the sergeant where he should stand. "At the end of the line," said the sergeant. "But I can't," said the Pole; "somebody's already there." And so on and on.

who was permitted by Jesus to anoint His feet (Luke 7:37 et seq.); and some scholars even assert she may have been Jesus' wife. Yet the tradition that Mary incontinently received men as well as devils has endured for two thousand years. Accept the following verse for its gorgeous wordplay, not its accuracy:

> Higgledy-piggledy   "Parthenogenesis
> Mary of Magdela   I for one left to the
> Said to the dolorous   Simple amoeba or
> Mother of God: Gasteropod."
>   —James Merrill

28 OCTOBER

Love Is a Four-letter Word

You may recall that in April I tried writing a love poem in words of three letters or less, but could not squeeze much sentiment into them. It occurred to me that I might do better if I raised the number of letters per word to four, and I here try to meet that challenge. But I seem only to have made a bad matter worse:

LOVE THEE EVER, DEAR

Love thee ever, dear?
  Only time will show.
Pray, come back next year.

Wind that blew love here
  Love from here must blow.
Pray, come back next year.

Love thee ever, dear?
Pray, come back next year.

TILL FAKE TURN REAL

Till fake turn real,
Till fool turn wise,
Till head turn heel,
  Tell your love lies.

Till nays turn ayes,
Till book turn bell,
Tell your love lies:
  They work well.
         —W.R.E.

29 OCTOBER

Caught in the Middle

To discover the common words hidden below, put two letters before each of the four-letter combinations capitalized, and two after.

LECI

"LECI," the untaught cry: "I'll not tell you that," says I,
"What's next, and what's before?"   "But give three answers more:

As E V I A is to priest,
J U T A's to major;

While R I D I's a deceased
Geographer, I'll wager."
—*W.R.E.*

3 0 OCTOBER

A Fracture of French, an Omelet of Afrikaans, and an Indiscretion of Italian

Everyone has played Knock-knock:

"Knock, knock." "Who's there?" "Little old lady." "Little old lady who?" "I didn't know you could yodel."

But it took Ogden Nash to play Knock-knock in French:

"Frappe, frappe." "Qui va là?" "Alençon." "Alençon qui?" "Alençonfants de la patrie."

Changing the subject, Paul Jennings noted that "Hamlet, I am thy father's ghost" sounds in Afrikaans like "Omlet, ek is de papap spook."

And it took the late W. H. Auden to discover—in an Italian-English phrase book hastily compiled in Florence in 1945 to promote understanding between the Florentines and the British and American troops—this unlikely entry:

ITALIAN   ENGLISH
Posse presentare il conte.   Meet the cunt.

3 1 OCTOBER

Dipping for Apples

It is Hallowe'en, but there are no backyard privies to overturn any more, so I think I'll stay home. I might invite friends to try to seize with their teeth apples floating in a tub of water. But the teeth of some of my friends are not what they used to be, so the game might not prove popular. Instead I think I'll go back through my daybooks, dipping for verses I meant to include in this almanac but forgot.

This first one I did not exactly forget; I was advised against including it by a friend who said it showed poor taste. Perhaps poor taste is excusable on Hallowe'en.

FOR A RESTLESS MISTRESS

Virility has been associated with baldness.—News item

You have not said, but I infer
You like your lovers lustier,

And resonate at optimum
To quickbeat of a martial drum.

So you'll be pleased, I have no doubt,
To hear my hair is falling out.
                                    —*W.R.E.*

My second selection, by an unknown author, repeats elegantly a well-known injunction:

TEACH NOT THY PARENT'S MOTHER

Teach not thy parent's mother to extract
   The embryo juices of the bird by suction.
The good old lady can that feat enact
   Quite irrespective of thy kind instruction.

My third Hallowe'en apple, also anonymous, reflects a literary point of view that many of us share:

AS I WAS PLAYING ON THE GREEN

As I was playing on the green
A little book it chanced I seen.
Carlyle's *Essay on Burns* was the edition;
I left it laying in the same position.

Finally, a sentimental quatrain:

THE FLOW OF LOVE

Flo was fond of Ebenezer—
   "Eb," for short, she called her beau.
Talk of Tides of Love, great Caesar!
   You should see them—Eb and Flo.
                                    —*T. A. Daly*

NOVEMBER

1 NOVEMBER

Page-flipping in a Daybook

• *A Whole Greater than the Sum of Its Parts*

Can a three-letter word have four syllables? Yes—in a manner of speaking. *Viz.* (to wit, namely) is an abbreviation that should be pronounced as if spelled out: vi-de-li-cet.

• *Four Words in One*

Take so. Take in. Take ever. Take where. Rearrange them. You have whereinsoever.

Take i. Take a. Take ties. Take men. Rearrange them. You have amenities.

Take tin. Take city. Take a. Take per. Rearrange them. You have pertinacity.

• *A-1*

Lloyd's inspectors used to designate the condition of a ship's hull with a letter of the alphabet, and the condition of the rigging with a number. A was the best hull; 1 was the best rigging. Hence A-1 for the best of anything. Everyone but me has always known this.

• *Self-descriptive Sentence*

In this sentence, the word "and" occurs twice, the word "eight" occurs once, the word "four" occurs twice, the word "fourteen" occurs once, the word "in" occurs twice, the word "occurs" occurs twelve times, the word "sentence" occurs twice, the word "seven" occurs once, the word "times" occurs five times, the word "twice" occurs four times,* and the word "word" occurs twelve times.

—Howard W. Bergerson

(Actually, "twice" occurs five times, but then the word "four" would occur only once—and *then* "twice" would occur four times. . . . You try to make it work.)

• *Cease, Qircl!*

Spell cease: c as in cue, e as in eye, a as in are, s as in sea, e as in ell. Qircl, right? Or, says Dick Anderson, spell yes: y as in you, e as in enemy, s as in see. So long, unc.*

* Other words from *Word Ways* that use the same device: A as in "aisle," C as in "czar," D as in "djinn," K as in "knew," P as in "psalm," W as in "wrong," X as in "xylophone."

- *Qwertyuiop*

"What," writes Christopher Reed, "is the longest word that can be made with the letters in the top row of letters on a typewriter (qwertyuiop)? In case you don't know,* it's typewriter." Actually, there are at least three longer, if less familiar, words: proprietory, proterotype, and rupturewort.

- *Count-up*

One would think that MENSA members, having high IQs, would be able to count to ten; but this advertisement in their journal stopped at nine:

"Want a Wooden Overcoat? Buy H*one*st John Whi*two*rth's heal*th-re-e*nergizing sul*fo-ur*anyl-impregnated 'Com*fi-ve*st' with its unique qua*si-x*yloid fibers—obtainable only from the Paradi*se Ve*nding Company, Harpurville H*eight*s, N*ine*vah, New York."

2 NOVEMBER
 ഗ

A Tolling of Bells

This is All Souls' Day, time to pray for the souls of the dead—a good time, too, to swallow hard, and clear your throat, over three of the loveliest dirges ever written:

BELLS FOR JOHN WHITESIDE'S DAUGHTER

There was such speed in her little body,
And such lightness in her footfall,
It is no wonder that her brown study
Astonishes us all.

Her wars were bruited in our high
    window.
We looked among orchard trees and
    beyond,
Where she took arms against her shadow,
Or harried unto the pond

The lazy geese, like a snow cloud
Dropping their snow on the green grass,
Tricking and stopping, sleepy and proud,
Who cried in goose, Alas,

For the tireless heart within the little
Lady with rod that made them rise

* I did not.

From their noon apple-dreams, and
    scuttle
Goose-fashion under the skies!

But now go the bells, and we are ready;
In one house we are sternly stopped
To say we are vexed at her brown study,
    Lying so primly propped.
               —John Crowe Ransom

AN EPITAPH

Here lies a most beautiful lady,
Light of step and heart was she;
I think she was the most beautiful lady
That ever was in the West Country.
But beauty vanishes; beauty passes;
However rare—rare it be.
And when I crumble, who will remember
This lady of the West Country?
               —Walter de la Mare

UPON A CHILD

Here a pretty baby lies
Sung asleep with lullabies;
Pray be silent, and not stir
The easy earth that covers her.
               —Robert Herrick

3 NOVEMBER

Bloody

Some Englishmen still consider *bloody* a bloody indecent expletive, though nobody knows why. Etymologists assure us the word is not, as once supposed, a degenerate form of such oaths as *God's blood* or *by our Lady*. Transplanted to Australia, it has thrived without embarrassment. Australian troops stationed in Newfoundland during World War II sang this bloody awful song:

No bloody sports, no bloody games;
No bloody fun with bloody dames;
Won't even tell their bloody names;
Oh, bloody, bloody, bloody!

In a song called "———, the Great Australian Adjective," you fill in the expletive yourself. One stanza is sufficient to give the idea:

> He rode up hill, down ——— dale,
> The wind it blew a ——— gale,
>   The creek was high and ——— floody.
> Said he: The ——— horse must swim,
> The same for me and ——— him
>   Is somethin' ——— sickenin',
>   ———!

4 NOVEMBER

There's Nothing Funny
about Falling into the 'Ay Cutter

It was once an article of faith among Americans that the English had no bump of humor. The typical Englishman was Joseph C. Lincoln's Lord James:

> I drawed a long breath. "That fortune'll be the death of me yet, Eureka," I told her. "If I fell into the hay cutter I presume likely you wouldn't fret; you'd know I'd come out fine."
> "Oh, you silly!" says she, and laughed. Lord James had come in, and he heard the last part of this. He rubbed his chin. "Why did she laugh?" he wanted to know. "My word! There's nothing funny about falling into the 'ay cutter."
> "Don't you see?" says Eureka, trying to explain. "He means he'd come out fine—chopped fine. He's joking, as usual."
> "But—but that wouldn't be a joke; that would be 'orrible! Chopped in a 'ay cutter! My word!"
> He said Americans were "blooming red Indians; they 'adn't no 'uman feelings at all." We didn't try to explain any more. What was the use?

But the more I try to isolate the distinctions between the British and the American sense of humor the more elusive I find them. My guess is that these two lines would not stir an Englishman's risibilities as they stir mine:

> The cow kicked Nelly in the belly in the barn.
> Didn't do her any good; didn't do her any harm.

But for all I know that couplet might evoke hilarity throughout the United Kingdom. For that matter, most Americans may not consider it funny at all; perhaps it amuses me simply because I hail from Oysterville.

I assume that James Payn, who wrote the following in 1884, was English; but if he was really Mark Twain writing under a nom de plume, I should not be surprised:

> I never had a piece of toast
> Particularly long and wide
> But fell upon the sanded floor,
> And always on the buttered side.

It would take a library the size of the British Museum to hold all the funny things said by Englishmen, from Geoffrey Chaucer to Anthony Burgess. Since there is no room for a library here, I am going to rest my case on just one English writer— Charles Dickens. Has anyone uttered more truths, and often bitter truths, in a form that so compelled laughter?

- In came a fiddler—and tuned like fifty stomachaches. In came Mrs. Fezziwig, one vast substantial smile.
- He has gone to the demnition bow-wows.
- "If the law supposes that," said Mr. Bumble, "the law is a ass, a idiot."
- With affection beaming in one eye, and calculation shining out of the other.
- Oh Sairey, Sairey, little do we know wot lays afore us!
- Secret, and self-contained, and solitary as an oyster.
- I am a lone lorn creetur, and everythink goes contrairy with me.
- Barkis is willin'.
- Annual income twenty pounds, annual expenditures nineteen nineteen six, result happiness. Annual income twenty pounds, annual expenditure twenty pounds ought and six, result misery.
- It was as true as turnips is. It was as true as taxes is. And nothing's truer than them.

The other day Marc Connelly remarked at lunch (there was no chance to ask whether he was quoting himself or someone else): "Only a man with a heart of stone could read Dickens's death scene of Little Nell without laughing."

5 NOVEMBER

Extracts from 1066 and All That

Julius Caesar, having defeated the Ancient Britons by unfair means, such as battering rams, tortoises, hippocausts, centipedes, axes and bundles, set the memorable Latin sentence, "Veni, Vidi, Vici," which the Romans, who were all very well educated, construed correctly. The Britons, however, who of course still used the old pronunciation, understanding him to have called them "Weeny, Weedy and Weaky," lost heart and gave up the struggle, thinking that he had already divided them All into Three Parts.

The Scots (originally Irish, but by now Scotch) were at this time inhabiting Ireland, having driven the Irish (Picts) out of Scotland; while the Picts (originally Scots) were now Irish (living in brackets) and vice versa. It is essential to keep these distinctions clearly in mind (and versa visa).

King Alfred was the first Good King, with the exception of Good King Wenceslaus, who, though he looked forth, really came first (it is not known, however, what King Wenceslaus was King of.)

The Barons compelled John to sign the Magna Charter, which said:

1. That no one was to be put to death, save for some reason—(except the Common People).
2. That everyone should be free—(except the Common People).
3. That everything should be of the same weight and measure throughout the Realm—(except the Common People).
4. That the Courts should be stationary, instead of following a very tiresome mediaeval official known as the *King's Person* all over the country.
5. That "no person should be fined to his utter ruin"—(except the King's Person).
6. That the Barons should not be tried except by a special jury of other Barons who would understand.

Magna Charter was therefore the chief cause of Democracy in England and thus a *Good Thing* for everyone (except the Common People).

After this King John hadn't a leg to stand on and was therefore known as "John Lackshanks."

The Roundheads, of course, were so called because Cromwell had all their heads made perfectly round, in order that they should present a uniform appearance when drawn up in line. Besides this, if any man lost his head in action, it could be used as a cannonball by the artillery.

When Charles I had been defeated he was brought to trial by the Rump Parliament—so-called because it had been sitting for such a long time—and found himself guilty of being defeated in a war against himself, which was, of course, a form of High Treason.

The Great War was between Germany and America and was thus fought in Belgium, one of the chief causes being the murder of the Austrian Duke of Sarajevo by a murderer in Serbia . . . The War lasted three years or the duration, the Americans being 100% victorious.

America was thus clearly top nation, and History came to a .*
—*W. C. Sellar and R. J. Yeatman*

* Our English friends render . not as "period," but as "full stop."

6 NOVEMBER

Just Because . . .

Kittens have paws they don't have pawses,
Lions have maws they don't have mawses,
Tigers have jaws they don't have jawses,
And crows have caws they don't have cawses.

I make one pause, I make two pauses:

Nine jackdaws aren't nine jackdawses,
Seven seesaws aren't seven seesawses,
Five oh phsaws aren't five oh pshawses,
Three heehaws aren't three heehawses.

Do you give two straws? Do you give two strawses?
—*David McCord*

7 NOVEMBER

Epigrammatic Espy

Anybody can write an epigram. The only trouble is that most of us don't write them very well. Here are some of mine:

TO A YOUNG POETESS

You're beautiful, you're sweet,
But God!—
How your iambic feet
Plod!

MENCKEN: A UNIVOCALIC

Mencken terse?
The reverse.

ON SALT-SPRINKLING

The Bird of Love, which lit
    at our command,
Too briefly halted.
The moral? Keep the Shaker
    close at hand,
The Tail well salted.

LOVE'S A GAME

Love's a game
Indeed, my pet;
I think its name
Is Russian Roulette.

PAMPHLET FROM THE RIGHT TO LIFE FOUNDATION

To abort little Willy
Is silly.
That's what war
Is for.

BLEST ARE THE POOR

Blest are the poor. I never guessed
I'd be elected to the blest.

8 NOVEMBER

Lay of the Deserted Influenzaed

Doe, doe!
  I shall dever see her bore!
Dever bore our feet shall rove
  The beadows as of yore!
Dever bore with byrtle boughs
  Her tresses shall I twide—
Dever bore her bellow voice
  Bake bellody with bide!
Dever shall we lidger bore,
  Abid the flow'rs at dood,
Dever shall we gaze at dight
  Upon the tedtder bood!
    Ho, doe, doe!
  Those berry tibes have flowd,
Ad I shall dever see her bore,
  By beautiful! by owd!
  Ho, doe, doe!
  I shall dever see her bore,
She will forget be id a bonth,
  (Bost probably before)—
She will forget the byrtle boughs,
  The flow'rs we plucked at dood,
Our beetigs by the tedtder stars.
  Our gazigs at the bood.
Ad I shall dever see agaid
  The Lily and the Rose;
The dabask cheek! the sdowy brow!
  The perfect bouth ad dose!
    Ho, doe, doe!
Those berry tibes have flowd—
Ad I shall dever see her bore,
  By beautiful! by owd!!
    —*Henry Cholmondeley-Pennell*

9 NOVEMBER
〆

I'd Walk 1.6093 Kilometers for a Camel

"Metric System Inches Along," says a newspaper headline. True enough; the British are walking the last kilometer toward substitution of the metric system of measurements for our present inches, pints, and pounds, and bills to the same end are pending in the United States Congress. Which leads a *New York Times* man to comment:

> "A miss is as good as a kilometer." Or would you believe: "A gram of prevention is worth a kilogram of cure"? Many would be aghast at the thought of converting, "I love you, a bushel and a peck," to liters and hectoliters. Will angry men cry: "I'll beat you to within a centimeter of your life"? Or "Give him a millimeter and he'll take a kilometer"?
>
> It used to be said, "A pint's a pound the world around"—that is, a pint of water weighs one pound everywhere. Today, it would be more accurate to say: "Wherever in the world I am, a cubic centimeter is a gram."
>
> —*Walter Sullivan*

10 NOVEMBER
〆

The Naming of Cats

There are two particular reasons for my admiration of T. S. Eliot. One, mentioned earlier in this Almanac, is that he said "Immature poets imitate; mature poets steal," and never hesitated to exhibit his maturity. The other is that he wrote a marvelous book of verse on cats, some lines of which follow:

> The Naming of Cats is a difficult matter,
>   It isn't just one of your holiday games;
> You may think at first I'm as mad as a hatter
>   When I tell you, a cat must have THREE DIFFERENT NAMES.
> First of all, there's the name that the family use daily,
>   Such as Peter, Augustus, Alonzo or James,
> Such as Victor or Jonathan, George or Bill Bailey—
>   All of them sensible everyday names.
> There are fancier names if you think they sound sweeter;
>   Some for the gentlemen, some for the dames:
> Such as Plato, Admetus, Electra, Demeter—
>   But all of them sensible everyday names.
> But I tell you, a cat needs a name that's particular,

A name that's peculiar, and more dignified,
Else how can he keep up his tail perpendicular,
    Or spread out his whiskers, or cherish his pride?
Of names of this kind, I can give you a quorum,
    Such as Munkustrap, Quaxo, or Coricopat,
Such as Bombalurina, or else Jellylorum—
    Names that never belong to more than one cat.
But above and beyond there's still one name left over,
    And that is the name that you never will guess;
The name that no human research can discover—
    But THE CAT HIMSELF KNOWS, and will never confess.
When you notice a cat in profound meditation,
    The reason, I tell you, is always the same:
His mind is engaged in a rapt contemplation
    Of the thought, of the thought, of the thought of his
        name;
    His ineffable effable
    Effanineffable
Deep and inscrutable singular name.

—T. S. Eliot

11 NOVEMBER
∾

Pandora Opens a Can of Worms

My sister Dale, whose birthday this is, does not regularly read the *Wall Street Journal*, but she does know something about clichés, and about congressmen, and I think she will enjoy this *Journal* account:

> Clichés and hackneyed expressions are the mortar of congressional speech. The middle-aged men who make their living with words feel the need, under the pressures of extemporaneous debate, to use combinations of words they've heard before and are comfortable with. So hoaxes are always "cruel,"* an inadequate proposition is always "woefully inadequate," and whatever a "little guy" pays, he pays "through the nose."
>
> Some people are collectors of Capitol Hill clichés. One such connoisseur is John Pastore of Rhode Island, who as a senator for 23 years has heard them all. He prides himself on being able to reel off dazzling clusters of bromides in his own speeches, as in this heroic combination on the Senate floor:
>
> "I say today, let us not throw out the baby with the bath water, let us

---

* Not a cliché, says A. Ross Eckler: hoaxes *are* always cruel.

not lose sight of the forest for the trees, let us not trade off the orchard for an apple."

Sen. Pastore used the most common form of the baby and the bath water cliché, but others sometimes employ original variations.

Sen. Mike Gravel of Alaska: "It seems that many times when we want to change the water, we wind up throwing out the baby."

Rep. Frank Denholm of South Dakota: "I do not agree with those here or elsewhere that favor throwing out the baby because of dirty water."

Tiresome clichés can be enriched somewhat by mixing them inventively. A memorable mixture came from the late George Andrews of Alabama one day during a House debate on busing. Addressing members from the North, Mr. Andrews shouted: "Now the chickens are coming home to roost and the monkey is on your back."

Congressional prose tends toward the stuffy side, but now and then somebody will attempt comedy. Rep. Silvio Conte is a severe critic of federal compensation payments to beekeepers whose bees are killed by pesticides, and he worded an attack this way:

"This federal giveaway should really set my colleagues off buzzing, if it does not make them break out in hives.

"My waxing rhetorically would be very funny if it were not for the taxpayers who are getting stung . . . if Congress were to continue this program, it would lay itself bare to the stinging indictment of taxpayers that it has, may I say, bees in its bonnet."

A snappy saying is about all today's lawmakers ever try for. With the death of Everett Dirksen, elegant oratory isn't heard in the Senate any more. Democratic Leader Mike Mansfield of Montana thinks the reason is that Senators just don't have the time to put a high polish on their rhetoric. Whatever the reason, the result is an addiction to what's been said before, and it accounts for the sound of all those apprehensive babies sloshing around in their bathwater.

—*Arlan J. Large*

12 NOVEMBER

The Drunkard's Conceit

If on my theme I rightly think,
There are five reasons why men drink:
Good wine, a friend, or being dry,
Or lest we should be, by and by,
Or any other reason why.
—*Henry Aldrich*

A California survey indicates that drinkers are less subject than teetotallers to heart attacks.* This news must rejoice the ghost of Oliver Herford, who wrote

> The bubble winked at me, and said,
> "You'll miss me, brother, when you're dead."

It must also rejoice the spirits of the authors of the two passages I now quote.

THE DRUNKARD'S CONCEIT

Straight from the tavern door
  I am come here;
Old road, how odd to me
  Thou dost appear!
Right and left changing sides,
  Rising and sunk;
Oh, I can plainly see—
  Road! thou art drunk!

Oh, what a twisted face
  Thou hast, O moon!
One eye shut, t'other eye
  Wide as a spoon.
Who could have dreamt of this?
  Shame on thee, shame!
Thou hast been fuddling,
  Jolly old dame!

Look at the lamps again;
  See how they reel!
Nodding and flickering
  Round as they wheel.
Not one among them all
  Steady can go;
Look at the drunken lamps,
  All in a row.

All in an uproar seem
  Great things and small;
I am the only one
  Sober at all;
But there's no safety here
  For sober men;
So I'll turn back to
  The tavern again.

—*F.C.H.*

The Old Soak expressed a similar attitude:

"I never could see liquor drinking as a bad habit," said the Old Soak, "though I admit fair and free that it will lead to bad habits if it ain't watched.

"One feller I knowed whose liquor drinking led to bad habits was my old friend Hennery Simms.

"Every time Hennery got anyways jingled he used to fall downstairs, and he fell down so often that it got to be a habit and you couldn't call it nothing else. He thought he had to.

"One time late at night I was going over to Brooklyn on the subway, and I seen one of these here escalators with Hennery onto it moving upwards, only Hennery wasn't riding on his feet, he was riding on the spine of his back.

"And when he got to the top of the thing and it skated him out onto the level, what does Hennery do but pitch himself onto it again, head first, and again he was carried up.

"After I seen him do that three of four times I rode up to where Hennery was floundering at and I ast him what he was doing.

" 'I'm falling downstairs,' says Hennery.

" 'What you doing that fur?' I says.

* See also 13 December.

"'I'm drunk, ain't I?' says Hennery. 'You old fool, you know I always falls downstairs when I'm drunk.'

"'How many times you goin' to fall down these here stairs?' I ast him.

"'I ain't fell down these here stairs once yet,' says Hennery, 'though I must of tried to a dozen times. I been tryin' to fall down these here stairs ever since dusk set in, but they's something wrong about 'em.

"'If I didn't know I was drunk, I would swear these here stairs was movin'.'

"'They be movin',' I tells him.

"'You go about your business,' he says, 'and don't mock a man that's doing the best he can. In course they ain't movin'.

"'They only looks like they was movin' to me because I'm drunk. You can't fool me.'

"And I left him still tryin' to fall down them stairs, and still bein' carried up again. Which, as I remarked at first, only goes to show that drink will lead to habits if it ain't watched, even when it ain't a habit itself."

—*Don Marquis*

1 3 NOVEMBER

Notpoems

Notpoems, by Adele Aldridge, is a book expressing cross, not to say crossgrained, points of view on such topics as women, mothers, life, love, and death, in graphic lettering combinations. A few examples of this odd art form:

TEACH

TEACH

TAEHC

CHTA

CHETA

CHEAT

CHEAT

14 NOVEMBER

Dialects, Various

Swedish: SONNET ON STEWED PRUNES

Ay ant lak pie-plant pie so wery vell;
Ven ay skol eat ice-cream, my yaws du ache;
Ay ant much stuck on dis har yohnnie-cake
Or crackers just so dry sum peanut shell.
And ven ay eat dried apples, ay skol svell
Until ay tenk my belt skol nearly break;
And dis har breakfast food, ay tenk, ban fake:
Yim Dumps ban boosting it, so it skil sell.
But ay tal yu, ef yu vant someteng fine,
Someteng so sveet lak wery sveetest honey,
Vith yuice dat taste about lak nice port vine,
Only it ant cost hardly any money,—
Ef yu vant someteng yust lak anyel fude,
Yu try stewed prunes. By yiminy! dey ban gude.
                                        —*William F. Kirk*

Brooklynese   BROOKLYNESE CHAMPION

I thought the winner had been found
    The day I heard a woman make
The butcher cut her off a pound
    Of fine and juicy soylern steak.
Imagine then the dizzy whirl
    That through my head did swiftly surge
The day I heard the gifted girl
    Who wished departing friends "Bon Verge."

                                        —*Margaret Fishback*

1 5 NOVEMBER

Double Duty

Insert in the blank space between each of the two matched syllables below a syllable that will make one word out of the first syllable, and another out of the second.

1. Back	_____	Robe
2. Bar	_____	Der
3. Bor	_____	Ive
4. Com	_____	Ey
5. Cur	_____	Ted
6. Door	_____	Stone
7. Ex	_____	Tive
8. Fire	_____	Ways
9. Foot	_____	Son
10. Fret	_____	Mill

11. Ham	_____	Tuce
12. Hand	_____	Body
13. House	_____	Man
14. Mis	_____	Tain
15. Pre	_____	Ence
16. Prow	_____	Ence
17. Pur	_____	Able
18. Sun	_____	Tee
19. Tas	_____	Rant
20. War	_____	Well

1 6 NOVEMBER

Let the Ball Lay Where It Was Flang

There are strong verbs, and then there are weak verbs. *Weed* is a weak verb, because its root does not change with its tense: weed, weeded, weeded. But *Wede,* my nickname, is a strong verb, or would be if it were a verb; its tenses would go: wede, wed, divorced, re-wed, divorced, re-wed. . . . M. H. Greenblatt recalls that Dizzy Dean preferred the strong to the weak verb; thus:

"The pitcher wound up and he flang the ball at the batter. The batter swang and missed. The pitcher flang the ball again and this time the batter connected. He hit a high fly right to the center fielder. The center fielder was all set to catch the ball, but at the last minute his eyes were blound by the sun and he dropped it."

The following is a classic parade of strong, even musclebound, verbs:

THE LOVERS

Sally Salter, she was a young teacher who taught,
And her friend, Charley Church, was a preacher, who praught;
Though his enemies called him a screecher, who scraught.

His heart, when he saw her, kept sinking, and sunk;
And his eye, meeting hers, began winking, and wunk;
While she, in her turn, fell to thinking, and thunk.

He hastened to woo her, and sweetly he wooed,
For his love grew until to a mountain it grewed,
And what he was longing to do, then he doed.

In secret he wanted to speak, and he spoke,
To seek with his lips what his heart long had soke;
So he managed to let the truth leak, and it loke.

He asked her to ride to the church, and they rode;
They so sweetly did glide, that they both thought they glode,
And they came to the place to be tied, and were tode.

Then homeward he said let us drive, and they drove,
And soon as they wished to arrive, they arrove;
For whatever he couldn't contrive, she controve.

The kiss he was dying to steal, then he stole;
At the feet where he wanted to kneel, then he knole;
And he said, "I feel better than ever I fole."

So they to each other kept clinging, and clung,
While Time his swift circuit was winging, and wung;
And this was the thing he was bringing and brung:

The man Sally wanted to catch, and had caught—
That she wanted from others to snatch, and had snaught—
Was the one she now liked to scratch, and she scraught.

And Charley's warm love began freezing and froze,
While he took to teasing, and cruelly toze
The girl he had wished to be squeezing, and squoze.

"Wretch!" he cried, when she threatened to leave him, and left,
"How could you deceive, as you have deceft?"
And she answered, "I promised to cleave, and I've cleft."
—*Author Unknown*

1 7 NOVEMBER

A Flock of Ships

A foreigner looking at a picture of a number of vessels, said, "See what a flock of ships." He was told that a flock of ships was called a fleet, and that a fleet of sheep was called a flock. And it was added, for his guidance in mastering the intricacies of our language, that a flock of girls is called a bevy, that a bevy of wolves is called a pack, and a pack of thieves is called a gang, and that a gang of angels is called a host, and that a host of porpoises is called a shoal, and a shoal of buffaloes is called a herd, and a herd of children is called a troop, and a troop of partridges is called a covey, and a covey of beauties is called a galaxy, and a galaxy of ruffians is called a horde, and a horde of rubbish is called a heap, and a heap of oxen is called a drove, and a drove of blackguards is called a mob, and a mob of whales is called a school, and a school of worshippers is called a congregation, and a congregation of engineers is called a corps, and a corps of robbers is called a band, and a band of locusts is called a swarm, and a swarm of people is called a crowd.

—C. C. Bombaugh

18 NOVEMBER

The Strange Case of the Surplus Anagrams

If a puzzle does not make me smile, I find it of little interest. By this criterion, is the five-anagram verse immediately below preferable to its nine-anagram enlargement?

Five anagrams:
A ****** from ****** named Boreas
As a ****** for girls was notorious.
  When their answer was "Nay,"
  He would ****** away;
When 'twas "yes," the ****** was quite
  glorious.

Nine anagrams:
A lady from ****** her lute softly
  played;
A ****** beside her made sweet
  serenade.
"O fairest of ******, take pity," he sang;

"Thou ****** my heart into many a
  pang.
Thou ****** me ever; I see in thine eyes
A ****** unmatched in the earth or the
  skies.
Though ne'er was I ****** for feminine
  flesh,
Thy gown's slightest ****** my heart
  doth enmesh.
So sang the poor fellow, and so did he
  woo;
And what the ****** was, I leave up to
  you.

—W.R.E.

19 NOVEMBER

You Know Me, Al

Nowadays it takes a Ph.D. to break into professional baseball, but when I was a boy ball players were illiterates, and not self-conscious about it either. In "You Know

Me Al," which began to run in *The Saturday Evening Post* at about the time of the outbreak of World War I, Ring W. Lardner preserved in amber the language of pitchers, catchers, and shortstops. "He had known when he wrote it that the language was right," said his son John a generation later. "He was bound to know—he had the world's best ear."

Jack Keefe, Lardner's hero (anti-hero we'd call him today), lacked both brains and humility—but he did have a very fast ball. The letter that follows is vintage Keefe:

SAN FRANCISCO, CALIFORNIA,
MARCH 25

Well Al I done my first pitching of the year this P.M. and I guess I showed them that I was in just as good a shape as some of them birds that has been working a month. I worked 4 innings against my old team the San Francisco Club and I give them nothing but fast ones but they sure was fast ones and you could hear them zip. Charlies O'Leary was trying to get out of the way of one of them and it hit his bat and went over first base for a base hit but at that Fournier would of eat it up if it had of been Chase playing first base instead of Fournier.

That was the only hit they got off of me and they ought to of been ashamed to of tooken that one. But Gleason* don't appresiate my work and him and I allmost come to blows at supper. I was pretty hungry and I ordered some stake and some eggs and some pie and some ice cream and some coffee and a glass of milk but Gleason would not let me have the pie or the milk and would not let me eat more than ½ the stake. And it is a wonder I did not bust him and tell him to mind his own business. I says What right have you got to tell me what to eat? And he says You don't need nobody to tell you what to eat you need somebody to keep you from floundering yourself. I says Why can't I eat what I want to when I have worked good?

He says Who told you you worked good and I says I did not need nobody to tell me. I know I worked good because they could not do nothing with me. He says Well it is a good thing for you that they did not start bunting because if you had of went to stoop over and pick up the ball you would of busted wide open. I says Why? and he says because you are hog fat and if you don't let up on the stable and fancy groceries we will have to pay 2 fairs to get you back to Chi. I don't remember now what I says to him but I says something you can bet on that. You know me Al.

I wish Al that Callahan† would hurry up and order me to join the 1st team. If he don't Al I believe Gleason will starve me to death. A little slob like him don't realize that a big man like I needs good food and plenty of it.

Your pal. JACK

* Assistant Manager.
† Manager.

20 NOVEMBER

Eisenhower's Address at Gettysburg

Gettysburg, Pennsylvania
November 19, 1863

AND NOW FOR A FEW CLOSING REMARKS BY PRESIDENT EISENHOWER

I haven't checked these figures, but eighty-seven years ago, I think it was, a number of individuals organized a governmental setup here in this country, I believe it covered certain eastern areas, with this idea they were following up based on a sort of national-independence arrangement and the program that every individual is just as good as every other individual. Well, now, of course, we are dealing with this big difference of opinion, civil disturbance you might say, although I don't like to take sides or name any individuals, and the point is naturally to check up, by actual experience in the field, to see whether any governmental setup with a basis like the one I was mentioning has any validity, whether that dedication, you might say, by those early individuals will pay off in lasting values.

Well, here we are, you might put it that way, all together at the scene where one of these disturbances between different sides got going. We want to pay our tribute to those loved ones, those departed individuals who made the supreme sacrifice here on the basis of their opinions about how this setup ought to be handled. It is absolutely in order and one hundred percent okay to do this.

But if you look at the over-all picture of this, we can't pay any tribute—we can't sanctify this area—we can't hallow according to whatever individual's creeds or faith or sort of religious outlooks are involved—like I said about this very particular area. It was those individuals themselves, including the enlisted men, very brave individuals, who have given this religious character to the area. The way I see it, the rest of the world will never forget how these men put their shoulders to the wheel and carried this idea down the fairway.

Our job, the living individual's job here, is to pick up the burden and sink the putt they made these big efforts here for. It is our job to get on with the assignment—and from these deceased fine individuals to take extra inspiration, you could call it, for the same theories about the setup for which they did such a lot. We have to make up our minds right here and now, as I see it, that they didn't put out all that blood, perspiration, and—well—that they didn't just make a dry run here, and that all of us here, under God, that is, the God of our choice, shall beef up this idea about freedom and liberty and those kind of arrangements, and that government of all individuals, by all individuals, and for the individuals, shall not pass out of the world picture.

—Oliver Jensen

21 NOVEMBER

Big and Little Slips from Big and Little Slippers

O may thy powerful word
Inspire the feeble worm
To rush into thy kingdom, Lord,
And take it as by storm.
— *The Wesleyan Hymn Book*

O never, never she'll forget
The happy, happy day
When in the church, before. God's priest,
She gave herself away.
— *Author Unknown*

O Moon, when I gaze on thy beautiful face,
Careering along through the boundaries of space,
The thought has often come into my mind
If I ever shall see thy glorious behind.
— *A Housemaid Poet, quoted by*
Robert Toss in the Academy

In Rome too liberty once reign'd, in Rome
The female virtues were allow'd to bloom,
And bloom they did.
— *Thomas Steward, On the*
Female Right to Literature

So past the strong heroic soul away,
And when they buried him, the little port
Had seldom seen a costlier funeral.
— *Tennyson, Enoch Arden*

Thou little bounder, rest.
— *John Ruskin*
(addressing his heart)

Will you oftly
Murmur softly
— *Mrs. Browning*

Why streams the life-blood from that female throat?
She sprinkled gravy on a guest's new coat.
— *Unknown American Anti-Slavery Poet*

Across the wires the gloomy message came:
"He is not better; he is much the same."
— *Unknown University Poet, On the*
Recovery of the Prince of Wales

2 2 N O V E M B E R

Lines to Miss Florence Huntingdon

The place names of the state of Maine are even odder to read and hear than those of my native Washington. But they are not so suited to punning. This nineteenth-century verse gives the flavor of them:

> Sweet maiden of Passamaquoddy,
>   Shall we seek for communion of souls
> Where the deep Mississippi meanders,
>   Or the distant Saskatchewan rolls?
>
> Ah no,—for in Maine I will find thee
>   A sweetly sequestrated nook,
> Where the far-winding Skoodoowabskooksis
>   Conjoins with the Skoodoowabskook.
>
> There wander two beautiful rivers,
>   With many a winding and crook;
> The one is the Skoodoowabskooksis,
>   The other—the Skoodoowabskook.

(And so on for a total of twelve stanzas. Let us limit ourselves to the last two:)

> Let others sing loudly of Saco,
>   Of Quoddy, and Tattamagouche,
> Of Kennebeccasis, and Quaco,
>   Of Merigonishe, and Buctouche,
>
> Of Nashwaak, and Magaguadavique,
>   Or Memmerimammericook,—
> There's none like the Skoodoowabskooksis,
>   Excepting the Skoodoowabskook!
>   —*Author Unknown*

2 3 N O V E M B E R

The Egg That Hen Belonged To

Some observations by Samuel Butler, the man who said, "A hen is only an egg's way of making another egg":

• I got some new-laid eggs a few Sundays ago. The landlady said they were her own, and talked about them a good deal. She pointed to one of them and said: "Now, would you believe it? The egg that hen belonged to laid 53 hens running and never stopped."

- Jones's Conscience. He said he had not much conscience, and what little he had was guilty.

- Dogs. The great pleasure of a dog is that you may make a fool of yourself with him and not only will he not scold you, but he will make a fool of himself too.

- Solomon in all his Glory. But, in the first place, the lilies do toil and spin after their own fashion, and, in the next, it was not desirable that Solomon should be dressed like a lily of the valley.

- From a worldly point of view there is no mistake so great as that of always being right.

- God is Love. I dare say. But what a mischievous devil Love is!

- A little boy and a little girl were looking at a picture of Adam and Eve. "Which is Adam and which is Eve?" said one. "I do not know," said the other; "but I could tell if they had their clothes on."

- Seasickness. How holy people look when they are seasick! . . . He [the seasick man] made a noise like cows coming home to be milked on an April evening.

- The Complete Drunkard. He would not give money to sober people, he said, because they would only eat it and send their children to school with it.

- Falsehood. If a man is not a good, sound, honest, capable liar there is no truth in him. Any fool can tell the truth, but it requires a man of some sense to know how to lie well. I do not mind lying, but I hate inaccuracy.

- Theist and atheist. The fight between them is as to whether God shall be called God or shall have some other name.

- All progress is based upon a universal, innate desire of every organism to live beyond its income.

- To live is like love, all reason is against it and all healthy instinct for it.

- Life is one long process of getting tired.

24 NOVEMBER

Winchellese

It must have been at about the time that the country tilted into the Great Depression that I first saw "celebrity" shortened to "celeb." The truncation occurred, naturally, in a Walter Winchell newspaper column. "Celeb" is one of the few Winchell neologisms that have endured. Many were only respellings or distortions of familiar words:

"That's the sitch-ee-ay-shun," or "What producer gave his squaw a swelegant black orb after He Found Her Out?" or "Oakie's sensayuma is de-voon." Some Winchell-isms were puns: "Girlesq"; "Things about a Restaurant I Never Noodle Now." Others were inelegant wordplay: "The neatest of squelches for bores, to wit: 'Oh, you're simply too, too, threesome.'"

The most famous Winchellisms were in the area somewhat misleadingly known as love. Winchell loved his celebs passionately, but not so passionately as he loved their love affairs. It is common knowledge that the course of true love seldom runs smooth: Winchell exploited the fact that the course of untrue love seldom runs smooth either. He flitted from nightclub table to nightclub table, on the watch for some hint of tumescence. When he saw the telltale, he told his readers, linking each confidence with a string of dots denoting breathlessness. He kept them informed as the balloon swelled, and he clapped his hands with public glee when it popped.

Having to tell the same story again and again about different people, he found that the best way to avoid monotony was to create a variety of arch words for a single meaning. The result was the repellent language known as Winchellese. It fascinates. Here are some examples of the tongue:

They're in love:
- "That rumor about Jed Harris being yowzuh over Margaret Sullavan is true."
- "Dorothy Parker is riding the skies again with Alan Campbell."
- "Drew Eberson and Betty Boyd have that droopy look in their orbs."
- "Prince George of Russia and Mary Hoyt Wiborg have the tremors."
- "Vincent Youman and Marjorie Oolricks are dueting."
- "Neva Lynn and E. Judson are On The Verge."
- "Eileen Wenzel and Nicholas Blair are plenty Voom Voom."
- "Mrs. J. Loose and V. P. Curtis are blazing."

They're getting married:
- "Charles Chaplin is about to announce his Secret Merger."
- "Jack Pickford and Mary Mulhern will probably middle-aisle it."
- "Jayne Shattuck and Jack Kirkland Blend on Friday."

They're expecting:
- "The Al Trahans are threeing."
- "The Jack Dempseys will be a trio in later July."
- "The John LaGattas are infanticipating."

They're no longer in love:
- "Two of the polo playing Hays tribe of Chicago are unwinding secretly."
- "The Robert Carses are unraveling."
- "They have placed it in the paws of their respective counsellors."
- "Lord and Lady Cavendish will have it melted soon."
- "Roberta Wells, the oil heiress, and I. Belasco, the baton juggler, have crashed."
- "Marion Batista and Tom Hamilton have phfftt." (How Winchell relished that phfftt!)
- "Stella Duna and the heart, Francis Lederer, are shrugging."
- "So the Fred Warings are having the handcuffs melted after all."
- "The Arthur Mays are Renovating it"

2 5 NOVEMBER

Jensen WITH Scotch IN HAND

Jensen with Scotch in hand was heard to say
That **Noontime** is the DEADWOOD of the day.
"Give me," cried he, "the **Glamour** of the dark;
A Bembo who will cuddle in the park!
Perhaps some Oriental with Oblique
Regard and dainty MOLE on SHADED cheek!
Some fair Amati, DANDY Nymphic peach
To show me Boulevard, BROADWAY or BOUL MICH
Some **Latin, Wide** Open for the marriage bell!
Suburban French! Parisian Mademoiselle!
In Stygian Black Schadow let me hold
An Ultra Modern Venus Extra Bold!
'Neath Stellar Light I'll Charme and Fox the maid
With SAPPHIRE CIRCLET, DIAMOND-INLAID;
ONYX and OPAL BRACELET drape upon her,
And write a Novel Gothic in her honor.
I'll woo her with Typewriter and with Quill
I'll take her to BURLESQUE and VAUDEVILLE;
To Barnum, P.T., and the CIRCUS too;
To Zebra, ZEPHYR, Zeppelin and zoo.
With KLONDIKE GOLD I'll Signal my desire;
With Coronet her MARBLE HEART I'll fire.
If she from all this Artcraft Bold should shrink,
Why then (says Jensen with Scotch in hand), I think
                    . . . I'll have another drink."

                                        —W.R.E.

26 NOVEMBER

A Zoological Romance

INSPIRED BY AN UNUSUAL FLOW OF ANIMAL SPIRITS

No sweeter girl ewe ever gnu
Than Betty Marten's daughter Sue.

With sable hare, small tapir waist,
And lips you'd gopher miles to taste;

Bright, lambent eyes, like the gazelle,
Sheep pertly brought to bear as well;

Ape pretty lass, it was avowed,
Of whom her marmot to be proud.

Deer girl! I loved her as my life,
And vowed to heifer for my wife.

Alas! a sailor, on the sly,
Had cast on her his wether eye—

He'd dog her footsteps everywhere,
Anteater in the easy-chair.

He'd setter round, this sailor chap,
And pointer out upon the map

The spot where once a cruiser boar
Him captive to a foreign shore.

The cruel captain far outdid
The yaks and crimes of Robert Kid.

He oft would whale Jack with the cat,
And say, "My buck, doe you like that?

"What makes you stag around so, say!
The catamounts to something, hey?"

Then he would seal it with an oath,
And say, "You are a lazy sloth!"

"I'll starve you down, my sailor fine,
Until for beef and porcupine!"

And, fairly horse with fiendish laughter,
Would say, "Henceforth, mind what giraffe ter!"

In short, the many risks he ran
Might well a llama braver man

Then he was wrecked and castor shore
While feebly clinging to anoa;

Hyena cleft among the rocks
He crept, *sans* shoes and minus ox;

And when he fain would goat to bed,
He had to lion leaves instead.

Then Sue would say, with troubled face,
"How koodoo live in such a place?"

And straightway into tears would melt,
And say, "How badger must have felt!"

While he, the brute, woodchuck her chin,
And say, "Aye-aye, my lass!" and grin.

* * * * *

Excuse these steers . . . It's over now;
There's naught like grief the hart can cow.

Jackass'd her to be his, and she—
She gave Jackal and jilted me.

And now, alas! the little minks
Is bound to him with Hymen's lynx.
                        —*Charles Follen Adams*

2 7 NOVEMBER

Faultily Faultless

A cosmetic ad says, "Honest makeup!" One would think such an oxymoron would cancel itself out, but the effect seems to be synergistic. Claudio's oxymorons did not soften his indictment of Hero:

But fare thee well, most foul, most fair! farewell,
Thou pure impiety, and impious purity!

Swinburne described the archetypical poet as a "bird of the bitter bright grey golden morn," with "poor splendid wings." Erasmus made an oxymoron out of one word: "foolosophers."

I give you an oxymoronic jingle:

By yourself, you are: Faultily faultless,[1]   Politely insulting,
                        Splendidly null,[2]   Brilliantly dull.

[1] Tennyson.
[2] Tennyson.

By myself, I am: A little bit big,[3]   Idly laborious,
                   A bigger bit little;   Gummily brittle.

Together, we are: Modestly arrogant,   Cheerfully mournful,
                   Sadly amused,   Clearly confused.[4]
                                                            —W.R.E.

28 NOVEMBER

Truth and Such

Where an echoing verse* repeats a sound, chain verse repeats an entire word. A Victorian chain verse entitled "Truth" hobbles along for twelve lines, of which the first four will suffice:

> Nerve thy soul with doctrine noble,
> Noble in the walks of time,
> Time that leads to an eternal
> An eternal life sublime . . .
>   —*Author Unknown*

The sonnet below is a potpourri of chain and echo. There's a refrain in there, too.

I SCARCE RECALL

I scarce recall when first you said hello.
"Hello!" said I, too young to realize
Lies were your vade mecum. (Spiders so
Sew webs, and lie in wait for hapless flies.)

Flies time so fast? Why is it I can know
No more that lying lovelight in your eyes?
I scarce recall . . . it was so long ago . . .
A golden time, before I grew too wise.

Why's wisdom executioner of youth?
You thought I left because you lied. Not I!
I left when you began to tell the truth:
Truth comes too dear for coinless youth to buy.

By lies I might regain you, after all.
Although . . . so long ago? . . . I scarce recall.
                                        —W.R.E.

[3] Thurber.
[4] The British Foreign Office, reporting on the situation in Iraq.
* 29 May.

29 NOVEMBER

The Venom of Contented Critics

That is the way someone described dramatic criticism, and here are some drops of the venom:

Noel Coward on a play about an obnoxious schoolboy: "Both the boy's throat and the second act should be cut." A capsule criticism of *I Am a Camera*: "No Leica." Eugene Field on Creston Clarke's portrayal of King Lear: "Mr. Clarke played the king as though under momentary apprehension that someone else was about to play the ace." Howard Dietz on Tallulah Bankhead: "A day away from Tallulah is like a month in the country."

George Oppenheimer objected to a geriatric drama: "I don't like plays," he said, "in a varicose vein."

An aspiring playwright asked Carl Sandburg, "How could you sleep through my dress rehearsal when you knew how much I wanted your opinion?" "Young man," said Sandburg, "sleep *is* an opinion."

John Chapman predicted that a play starring Mae West would be a bust, "which," he said, "is one more than Mae West needs."

Banned from the Shubert theatres, Walter Winchell said, "I can't go to the openings, eh? Well, I'll wait three days and go to the closings."

None of those jeremiads appeared in the advertisements for the plays. Every producer, like every publisher, has a slavey behind the curtain who is charged with extracting a favorable word or phrase from even the most damning review. *New York Times* film critic Vincent Canby says an advertisement in the *Times* for Ingmar Bergman's film "The Touch" included a misleading endorsement, attributed to Mr. Canby, that said:

> INGMAR BERGMAN'S "THE TOUCH" TELLS A LOVE
> STORY FULL OF THE INNUENDOES OF HIS GENIUS

This, he says, is how they did it:

> They took the headline on the review that said simply "Bergman's 'Touch' Tells a Love Story" and then skipped to the 10th paragraph of the review to ransack a sentence that said, in its entirety: "Bergman may occasionally make dull movies—as I believe 'The Touch' to be—but he cannot be stupid, and 'The Touch' is full of what might be called the innuendoes of his genius."

Book reviewers too are occasionally unkind, as witness this report by John Jay Chapman:

> Did you hear what Howells once said to a boring author who was trying to wring a compliment out of him? "I don't know how it is," said the author, "I don't seem to *write* as well as I used to do." "Oh, yes you do—indeed you do. You write as well as you ever did. But your *taste* is improving."

Keith Preston was one of the few reviewers without carbolic acid in his veins. I commend his point of view to other critics:

> We cannot bear to roast a book
> Nor brutally attack it.
> We lay it gently in our lap
> And dust its little jacket.

30 NOVEMBER

"Biby's" Epitaph

Except for "Cockney Comic Alphabet"* there are no examples of Cockney in this Almanac, so I was delighted to find the following in one of William Cole's marvelous anthologies:

> A muvver was barfin' 'er biby one night,
> The youngest of ten and a tiny young mite,
> The muvver was poor and the biby was thin,
> Only a skelington covered in skin;
> The muvver turned rahnd for the soap off the rack,
> She was but a moment, but when she turned back,
> The biby was gorn; and in anguish she cried,
> "Oh, where is my biby?"—The angels replied:

> "Your biby 'as fell dahn the plug-'ole,
> Your biby 'as gorn dahn the plug;
> The poor little thing was so skinny and thin
> 'E oughter been barfed in a jug;
> Your biby is perfeckly 'appy,
> 'E won't need a barf any more,
> Your biby 'as fell dahn the plug-'ole,
> Not lorst, but gorn before."

> —Anonymous

* See 6 July.

DECEMBER

❦ ❦

1 DECEMBER

A Delight of Dictionaries

Nothing is as full of surprises as a dictionary, except of course a woman. Why should American Heritage, a paragon among lexicons, have printed *vichysoisse* for *vichyssoise?* Why does Webster's Third list *couldn't* and *shouldn't,* but not *wouldn't?*

But let us think positively. By thumbing through your dictionary you will discover that two common words—latchstrings and catchphrase—have six successive consonants with no intervening vowel. In a dictionary you will find definitions like these:

UCALEGON. A neighbor whose house is on fire.

SEREIN. A mist which sometimes falls from a clear sky just after sunset.

SCIAPODOUS. Having very large feet.

GALIMATIAS. Nonsense; gibberish; jargon.

LATAH. A kind of jumping disease peculiar to Malays.

If the standard dictionaries don't provide enough astonishment to roll under your tongue, turn to the specialized lexicons. *The Glossary of Geology and Related Sciences,* for example, gives this definition of *cactolith:*

A quasi-horizontal chonolith, composed of anastomising ductoliths, whose distal ends curl like a harpolith, thin like a sphenolith, or bulge discordantly like an akmolith or ethmolith.

I trutht that maketh everything clear.

Darryl Francis attests these definitions from the *Cyclopedic Lexicon of Sex:*

MELCRYPTOVESTIMENTAPHILIA. A fondness for women's black undergarments.

CRYPTOSCOPOPHILIA. The desire to look through windows of homes that one passes by.

DYSCALLIGYNIA. Antipathy for beautiful women.

ECDEMOLAGNIA. The tendency to be more lascivious when away from home.

GENUGLYPHICS. The art of decorating the female knee to make it more erotic.

HAPTEVOLUPTAS. Somebody very pleasant to touch.

IATRONUDIA. The desire on the part of a woman to expose herself to a physician under the pretext of being ill.

2 DECEMBER

Friend in the Middle

J. Newton Friend invites you to make words by putting three letters on each side of the combinations below:

1.	URAL	5.	CAUT	9.	REDI	13.	CTRO
2.	OCIA	6.	HEST	10.	DPEC	14.	HANI
3.	UPUL	7.	MENT	11.	OLUT	15.	USTR
4.	CINA	8.	IDEL	12.	EPHO	16.	GERH

3 DECEMBER

Pseudo-opposites

Night hawk	Mourning dove
Catwalk	Dogtrot
Ant hill	Uncle Sam
Water mark	Fire brand
Lowlands	High seas

—David L. Silverman

Undergo	Overcome
Hereafter	Therefore
Write ahead	Left behind
Piece work	War games
Rare coins	Common sense
Cargo	Bus stop

—Murray Pearce

Undertow	Overhaul
Hotheads	Cold feet
Creeping thyme	Walking space

—Les Card

4 DECEMBER

Ambivalence in the Oyster Beds

Scientists are still arguing about what destroyed the native oysters in the bay off
Oysterville. This double-dactyl explanation of their extinction is as good as any:

> Evil days fell upon
> Oysterville, Washington;
> Oysters grew testy, no
> More reproduced.
>
> Theirs was a quandary
> Hermaphroditical:
> Which should be gander and
> Which should be goosed.
> —*W.R.E.*

Florence M. Platt understood the problem:

THE BEWILDERED OYSTER

> Oh me, Oh my, what shall I do?
> Asked the oyster of its mother.
> Yesterday I was just a girl but
> Since I slept, I am her brother.
> There's no sense in your complaining
> I haven't time to bother;
> You're not the only changeling here
> Since I have just become your father.

5 DECEMBER

Alimentary Canals Abroad

"Alimentary Canals Around the World" is a twelve-nation stew of palatable verses,
two of which I serve up here:

FRANCE

> Digestions of the Gallic school
> are tuned to *escargots* and *moules,*
> *terrine* and crusty bread and *mousse*
> and *cassoulets* of pork or goose.

French mice will mutter "Quel dommage!"
if traps aren't set with fine *fromage*
while hens rinse off with *Chambertin*
to qualify as *coq au vin*.
For him you bore that bygone day,
our thanks, Madame Escoffier.

GERMANY

The Germans fuel the body cavity
with fare of great specific gravity.
Digestive enzymes tilt and topple
under the threat of *hoppelpoppel*,
hassenpfeffer and *pfefferbrot*
thundering heavily down the throat.
Scarce is that gone (though not forgotten),
there follows a volley of *sauerbraten*.
"Watch out, watch out," the enzymes whine,
"Upstairs he's reached for *gänzeklein*
and, after a *bier* to quench his thirst,
no doubt we all can expect the *wurst*."
—*E. C. K. Read*

6 DECEMBER

Agape and Cupid*

I'll take my chances with wickedness, but save me from good intentions! Lyly's Campaspe, a naughty girl, deliberately stripped Cupid of his possessions; but my Agape, out of the purest motives, ruined him. The legend appears here in a hodge-podge of pagan, Christian, and Freudian reference:

In a bower by the sea
  Dwelt the virgin Agape,
Guardian of fruit and vine,
  Keeper of Athena's shrine.

Cupid aimed an idle dart
  At that consecrated heart;
But the arrow, striking stone,
  Ricocheted, and pierced his own.

Now the maddened god regard,
  Hoisted by his own petard!
What a sorry sight is this:
  Cupid, crying for a kiss!

First he promises to give her
  Bow and arrows, string and quiver.
Surely an excessive bid
  For a still untested id!

---

* a'-ga-pē. Christian, and thus spiritual, love.

Sternly Agape replies:
  "Throw in too your wings and eyes.
Lust and lechery recant:
  Be Athena's hierophant.

If all this you swear and do
  I shall lie an hour with you."
"Done!" cried Cupid; and they did,
  Ego in the sheets with id.

Being bound to chasteness, Cupid
  Found the whole thing rather stupid . . .
Just as Agape discovered
  'Twould be lovely to be lovered.

* * *

Eyeless, wingless, gray and grave,
  Cupid guards Athena's cave.
Agape, concealing pox,
  Waits for sailors at the docks.
                              —W.R.E.

7 DECEMBER

Ounce Dice Trice

"Words," says the poet Alastair Reid, "have a sound and shape, in addition to their meanings. Sometimes the sound *is* the meaning. If you take a word like BALLOON and say it aloud seven or eight times, you will grow quite dizzy with it."

Mr. Reid elaborated his point in a book called *Ounce Dice Trice*. (I am sorry I cannot reproduce Ben Shahn's illustrations.) Here is the source of the title:

> "If you get tired of counting *one, two, three,* make up your own numbers, as shepherds used to do when they had to count sheep day in, day out . . . : OUNCE, DICE, TRICE, QUARTZ, QUENCE, SAGO, SERPENT, OXYGEN, NITROGEN, DENIM."

The way to get the feel of words, says the poet, "is to begin with a sound and let it go. ZZZZ is the sound of someone sleeping. From it, you easily move to BUZZ and DIZZY, and soon you have a list: ZZZZ, BUZZ, DIZZY, FIZZLE, GUZZLE, BUZZARD, BAMBOOZLE. Or begin with OG and see what happens: OG, FROG, OGLED, GOGGLED, GROGGY, TOBOGGAN, HEDGEHOG."

Mr. Reid has *light words* (ARIEL, WILLOW, SPINNAKER); *heavy words* (DUFFLE, BLUNDERBUSS, GALOSHES); *words to be said on the move* (FLIT, FLUCTUATE, WOBBLE); *squishy words* (SQUIFF, SQUIDGE, SQUAMOUS); *bug words* (HUMBUG, BUGBEAR, BUGABOO). And many, many more.

I give you here a few of his Garlands, "odd words, either forgotten or undiscovered, with which you can bamboozle almost anyone."

GARLANDS

What is a Tingle-airey?
A *tingle-airey* is a hand organ, usually played on the street by the turning of a handle, and often decorated with mother-of-pearl or *piddock* shells.

What are Piddocks?
Piddocks are little mollusks which bore holes in rocks and wood, or in the *breastsummers* of buildings.

What is a Breastsummer?
A *breastsummer* is a great beam supporting the weight of a wall, and sometimes of a *gazebo* above.

What is a Gazebo?
A *gazebo* is a round balcony with large windows looking out on a view, often of ornamental gardens and *cotoneasters*.

What is a Cotoneaster?
A *cotoneaster* is a kind of flowering shrub, a favorite of *mumruffins*.

What is a Mumruffin?
A *mumruffin* is a long-tailed tit which often visits bird tables in winter for its share of *pobbies*.

What are Pobbies?
Pobbies are small pieces of bread *thrumbled* up with milk and fed to birds and baby animals.

What is Thrumbled?
Thrumbled is *squashed* together. Ants thrumble round a piece of bread, and crowds in streets thrumble round *gongoozlers*.

What is a Gongoozler?
A *gongoozler* is an idle person who is always stopping in the street and staring at a curious object like a *tingle-airey*.

Alastair Reid goes on with more Garlands, but this seems a good place to cut off, since we are back at our beginning and can start again.

8 DECEMBER

Stop Hissing, Belinda!

Barbara, does it bother you that your name has the same root as barbarous? Leah, when I say I love you do you realize that I am protesting my devotion to a cow?

Let me confine my point to the names of beasts. As the curtain rises, we find a cluster of these milling about the cradle of a newborn girl. Each wishes the babe to bear its own name.

The Chorus speaks:

Hair and scale and wool and starling,
How shall mummy name her darling?

The Beasts speak:

"Pick *Jemima*," DOVE suggests;
"*Lilith*, rather," SNAKE contests.
(He'd accept *Ophelia*, too;
Or *Belinda*, that would do.)

"*Ursula*," growls father BEAR;
"*Leah*," BOSSY doth declare;
"*Agnes, Agnes*," baas the LAMB;
"*Rachel, Rachel*," bleats her DAM.

"*Lupe, Lupe*," WOLF doth cry;
"*Vanessa*," answers BUTTERFLY.
"*Dorcas*" the GAZELLE doth please;
"*Deborah*," the HONEY BEES.

The Chorus speaks again:

Hair and scale and wool and starling,
How shall mummy name her darling?
                                    —W.R.E.

9 DECEMBER

Mama's Advice

A macaronic verse of the Pennsylvania Dutch variety:

Die Mutter sagt, "Nau Liebschen listen here.
Es tun für dich die Wedding Bells heut pealeh,
Und's iss mei Pflicht und Duty dass ich dir
Die Facts von Life mitaus Reserf revealeh.
Ich hab in Innocence dich augebracht
But nau lässt sich die Sach' net länger shirkeh.
So keep mei Words in Mind bei Tag und Nacht:
A gute Noodlesupp' tut Wunders workeh.

"Wie shweet geflavort iss der Honeymoon!
But leider kann et net fürever lasteh.
Bald giebt's aplenty Chores in Haus zu tun
Wo likely sein Loff's süssen Traum zu blasteh.
A Mann gemarried iss a Mann gebored.
In Intimacy da tut Danger lurkeh.
But sei net bang wenn er a Kiss ignored:
A gute Noodlesupp' tut Wunders workeh.

"Die cut'sten Charms, die faden mit der Zeit.
Die Shkin ver yellowed und commenzt su saggeh;
Das Harr wird dühn, der Back in Shpots zu breit
Und Conversation tut auch öfters laggeh.
Man foolt mit Canfield, und turnt's Radio an,
Und tried all kinds von Schemes um aufzuperkeh.
Mei Child, remember speshelly dass dann:
A gute Noodlesupp' tut Wunders workeh."
                                    —*Kurt M. Stein*

1 0   D E C E M B E R

Da, One Jellyfish to Go, Tovarich

Time has described "The Russian-English Phrasebook" as a "vade mecum for Soviet visitors to the United States." *Time* adds that the respect in which it is held does not say much for the level of communication between one country and the other. At a restaurant, the Russian tourist is instructed to say, "Please give me curds, sower cream, fried chicks, pulled bread and one jellyfish." At the doctor's, he complains of "a poisoning, a noseache, an eyepain or quinsy." He asks, one assumes with trepidation, "Must I undress?" At Saks Fifth Avenue he looks for a "ladies' worsted-nylon swimming pants." If he is a she, she asks the stylist at a beauty salon to "make me a hair-dress," "sprinkle my head," or "frizzle my hair." If he is a businessman, he demands sternly, "Whose invention is this? When was this invention patented? This is a Soviet invention."

1 1   D E C E M B E R

We Men of Sagittarius

This is my birthday, which makes me a Sagittarean. We male Sagittareans are free from malice, and are painfully honest; but our feet seldom leave our mouths. We hold our wit in higher esteem than the case seems to call for. We secretly consider ourselves irresistible to women, and marvel at the cleverness with which they conceal their longing from us.* We are generally friendly, often indigent, and certainly a trifle tetched. Walt Disney, John Milton, and James Thurber were Sagit-

---

* Isaac Bickerstaff (see 4 February) could have been nothing but a Sagittarean, though some skeptics claim he was the invention of Jonathan Swift, who was himself a Sagittarean, his birth date being November 30.

tareans. Joe DiMaggio and David Susskind still are. Others of our select little band are celebrated below.

We men of Sagittarius,
Our wit is so hilarious,
The girls all want to marry us,
    Tra la, tra la.

We men of Sagittarius
Are socially gregarious,
Financially precarious,
    Tra la, tra la—

From Churchill to Beethoven,
Our hooves are slightly cloven,
Our brains a little stove in,
    Tra la, tra la.

Pope John and David Merrick,
Producer and top cleric,
Have passed their climacteric,
    Tral la, tra la.

I thank my stars that luck'ly,
Like Coward and Bill Buckley,
I don't walk Donald Duckly,
    Tra la, tra la.

Because the ladies crave us,
Sinatra, Sammy Davis,
Must run from Maud and Mavis,
    Tra la, tra la.

I only faintly see
How this applies to me;
Yet I sing happily,
    Tra la, tra la,
        Tra la, tra la,
        Tra la.
                    —W.R.E.

12 DECEMBER

Triple Platform

The following is a memorial of the Civil War. The first column is supposedly the position of the Confederates; the second, that of the Abolitionists; and the whole, read together, the platform of the Democratic party:

Hurrah for	The old Union
Secession	Is a curse
We fight for	The Constitution
The Confederacy	Is a league with hell
We love	Free speech
The rebellion	Is treason
We glory in	A Free Press
Separation	Will not be tolerated
We fight not for	The Negro's freedom
Reconstruction	Must be obtained
We must succeed	At every hazard
The Union	We love
We love not	The Negro
We never said	Let the Union slide
We want	The Union as it was
Foreign intervention	Is played out
We cherish	The old flag
The stars and bars	Is a flaunting lie
We venerate	The *habeas corpus*
Southern chivalry	Is hateful
Death to	Jeff Davis
Abe Lincoln	Isn't the Government
Down with	Mob law
Law and order	Shall triumph.

13 DECEMBER

********** *Drank for 969 Years*

I gave up any notion of abandoning liquor when I read that even if I stopped drinking altogether, my stomach would go right on brewing something like a gallon of beer a day.*

Here is a set of bibulous anagrams on the name of a man who bibbed joyously for 969 years.

Muse, say not I (tush ****!) ** ****
That out of ale I make my meal.
**********, it now appears,
*** **** *** was of many beers.
No gold a man might **** *** ***
Gold as the **** ** **** would brew;
And no **** *** *** kick those beers
Supplied him for a thousand years.

* See 12 November.

****, ****** waits in the glass! I pray
Let ale ****; **** ** not away.
                            —W.R.E.

14 DECEMBER

The Quodlibets of Tom Aquinas

Seventeen folio volumes, says Isaac Disraeli, testify to the industry and genius of
Thomas Aquinas, the Angelical Doctor: "A great man, busied all his life with making the charades of metaphysics."

I

ON LOVE, DEMONS, SOUL, AND SINS

Ne'er divine was so divine as
Sainted Doctor Tom Aquinas,
Who on LOVE wrote plus or minus
Eight discursions and eight score;
On DEMONS, five and eighty more;
On SOUL, two hundred. Then he tore
Into SINS, and from him sundered
Thirty-seven plus two hundred,
Who in batlike panic blundered
Into this old debauchee.
Tom, the sins you lodged in me
Flourish like the green bay tree.
                            —W.R.E.

II

ON ANGELS

You'll find items infinite in
Tom on Angels. He has written
Fifteen score and ten and eight
On angelical estate.

Tom can tell you whether mange'll
Harm the feathers of an angel;
Whether angels moult, or shed;
How they fold their wings in bed;

Tell their substance, orders, natures,
Offices, and legislatures;
How they differ in their species;
If they're he's or she's or he-she's.

He can count the cherubin
Doing kick-ups on a pin
(But he keeps their numbers hidden,
Knowing dancing is forbidden).

More corporeal than God is,
Less corporeal than bodies,
Angels don't have matter where
Matter matters—they have air.

                            —W.R.E.

III
A FUNDAMENTAL DISPUTE

The contradiction between man's corporeal and spiritual parts was a source of endless quodlibetting by Tom Aquinas and his fellow disquisitors in the seventeenth century. Today's more ardent ecologists can sympathize with their dilemma:

> Shall good men on the Final Day
> With Bowels be to Heaven sent,
> To soil the very Seat of God
> With Risen Human Excrement?
> —W.R.E.

15 DECEMBER

Holey, Holey, Holey, Holed Sox Almighty

Homophonic puns, irresistible a couple of centuries ago, are showing signs of wear, but I still fall for them, as you see here:

> I sought to hold a maiden,
> As fair as any foaled,
> With golden tresses laden—
> Well heeled, and so well soled.
> (I could not take the jade in
> Because my sox were holed.)

> I'd normally have sold her
> With clever lies well told;
> Or maybe bowled her over
> With kisses overbold;
> (But I could not enfold her,
> Because my sox were holed.)

> Quoth she, "I find you holy,
> All-wise, and lofty-souled;
> But I reject you wholly—
> My goal depends on gold.
> (Not just your sox are holey,
> Your trousers too are holed.)"

> "Though hotly coaled your stove be,"
> Cried I, "your heart is cold;
> I'd rather die and moulder
> Than fit into your mold.

Let richer lovers hold you—
I like my sox well-holed."

You dears whose arms enfold me,
Long, long may you be skoaled!
But as for you who scold me
Because my clothes are old,
I'll live to see you mould,
And when your death-bell's tolled,
I'll dance in sox still holed.

—W.R.E.

16 DECEMBER

Kew, Kew, Si Si Si

Unlikely as it seems, this is a Christmas card. It came to Kathleen Daly, who writes and edits children's books, from Tibor Gergely, who illustrates them; and it consists of bird calls. The callers are listed in the back of the book.

Kew, kew, si si si,

gobak gobak zwick t-weet,
mee-oo klee-weet chrr crek
ticky-tic, pitchoo zup zup zup
dzweee ho-hoo-hoo-oooo,
chack peep peep peep tu-whit
wee-tuc-tuc, dzer curreh
kuk-kuk-hoo-coo.
Agh kek, kek, kek, fullock
pink-a-pink, kittie-needie
ooi-ooi-ooi kloo-it if-hee tak,
tweedle tweedle sweet sweet
sweet, tuk-tuk cheevik kark
ha-ha-ha-ha,

Tew-tew-tew

1 7 DECEMBER

Games for Insomniacs

That's the name of a verbal kaleidoscope of a book drawn by John G. Fuller from his *Saturday Review* column, "Trade Winds." Mr. Fuller multiplies a thousandfold snippets like the following:

- BUSINESS SLOGANS. The Victor Refuse Company (to the Victor Belong the Spoils); the Macduff Linoleum Company (Lay On Macduff); the Mercy Baby Food Company (the Quality of Mercy is Not Strained).

- FRACTURED BOOK REVIEWS. *Webster's Dictionary:* Too wordy. *Hammond's Atlas:* Covers too much ground. *Handbook of Adhesives:* Couldn't put it down.

- BOOK TITLES. *Tender is the Knight:* Memoirs of a dragon who devoured Sir Galahad. *Gone to Pot:* Confessions of a Dope Addict.

- ANIMAL CRACKERS. As inflamed as a moth; as hidebound as a rhino; as canny as a sardine; as testy as a guinea pig; as chaste as a fox; as instinctive as a skunk.

- INVERTED ZOO. Whales that had a people of a good time; the sardines who felt like people in the subway; the cat who let the man out of the bag.

- FRACTURED GEOGRAPHY. Feeling, Ill.; Hoop, La.; Requiem, Mass.; Ding, Dong, Del.; Vita, Minn.; Dunno, Alaska; Nohitsnorunsno, Ariz.

- UNLIKELY LETTER COMBINATIONS. XOP (saxophone); DHP (jodhpurs); RIJU (Marijuana); OMAHA (tomahawk); AGAMU (ragamuffin); HTH (eighth); RND (dirndl); RYG (drygoods).

- EXCLAMATION—Without Point. By Jerre Mangione: What, no mummy? Tut, Tut! What, no drama? Pshaw! What, no corn? Shucks! By Marvin Preiser: What, torn socks? Darn!

- MEANINGLESS NOTHINGS. By Kelley Roos: A chainless end; a pitless bottom; a gameless score; a bra-less strap; a gemless flaw; a jobless thank; a hatless brim; a caseless hope.

- TRANSITIONAL LOGIC. By Harry Kuris, to prove a sheet of paper is a lazy dog: (1) A sheet of paper is an ink-lined plane (2) an inclined plane is a slope up (3) a slow pup is a lazy dog.

- HAPPY BIRTHDAY. Mark Koppel and his roommates send greetings to Mary Ann Haste, Judy Obscure, Bella de Ball and others.

- NEWSMEN'S SELF-INTRODUCTIONS. Some of Bruce Fessenden's: I'm Cutt from the *Blade;* I'm Brown, from the *Sun;* I'm Justice, from the *Tribune;* I'm Tied, from the *Post.* Some of E. P. H. James's: I'm Ugley, from the *American;* I'm Shakespeare, from the *Globe;* I'm Trumpett, from the *Herald.*

Go ahead—anyone can play.

18 DECEMBER

One Last Giggle

I trust you have kept track of the difference between the Muse Agiggle and the Muse on a Banana Skin. The Muse Agiggle is deliberately funny; the Muse on a Banana Skin is funny by mistake. When Swinburne parodied himself, he did so deliberately:

THE HIGHER PANTHEISM IN A NUTSHELL

One, who is not, we see; but one, whom we see not, is;
Surely, this is not that; but that is assuredly this.

What, and wherefore, and whence; for under is over and under;
If thunder could be without lightning, lightning could be without thunder.

Doubt is faith in the main; but faith, on the whole, is doubt;
We cannot believe by proof; but could we believe without?

Why, and whither, and how? for barley and rye are not clover;
Neither are straight lines curves; yet over is under and over.

One and two are not one; but one and nothing is two;
Truth can hardly be false, if falsehood cannot be true.

Parallels all things are; yet many of these are askew;
You are certainly I; but certainly I am not you.

One, whom we see not, is; and one, who is not, we see;
Fiddle, we know, is diddle; and diddle, we take it, is dee.
                                   —*Algernon Charles Swinburne*

De la Mare was being light-hearted:

THE BARDS

My aged friend, Miss Wilkinson,
    Whose mother was a Lambe,
Saw Wordsworth once, and Coleridge, too,
    One morning in her pram.

Birdlike the bards stooped over her
    Like fledgling in a nest;
And Wordsworth said, "Thou harmless babe!"
    And Coleridge was impressed.

The pretty thing gazed up and smiled,
    And softly murmured, "Coo!"
William was then aged sixty-four
    And Samuel sixty-two.
                                   —*Walter de la Mare*

And cummings was being . . . cummings:

SHE BEING BRAND

she being Brand
-new; and you
know consequently a
little stiff i was
careful of her and (having
thoroughly oiled the universal
joint tested my gas felt of
her radiator made sure her springs were O.

K.)i went right to it flooded-the-carburetor
    cranked her

up, slipped the
clutch (and then somehow got into reverse she
kicked what
the hell)next
minute i was back in neutral tried and

again slo-wly; bare,ly nudg. ing(my

lev-er Right-
oh and her gears being in
A 1 shape passed
from low through
second-in-to-high like
greasedlightning)just as we turned the corner
              of Divinity

avenue i touched the accelerator and give

her the juice,good

       (it
was the first ride and believe i we was
happy to see how nice she acted right up to
the last minute coming back down by the Public
Gardens i slammed on
the

internalexpanding
&
externalcontracting
brakes Bothatonce and

brought allofher tremB
-ling
to a:dead.

stand-
;Still)

e.e. cummings

19 DECEMBER

Da Wheestlin' Barber

One by one the immigrant dialects have vanished—the German, the Irish, the Jewish, the Italian. There is still a black dialect of sorts, but it has become so involved with the counterculture that no one knows whether it started in Harlem or Harvard.

In my college speech class I used to recite T. A. Daly's great Italian dialect verse, "Mia Carlotta," with gestures. That I was permitted to do so shows the kind of speech class *that* was. Here is a less familiar example of the Daly magic:

> Las' night you hear da op'ra?
>   Eef you was uppa stair
> And eef you know Moralli
>   You mebbe see heem dere.
> Moralli? He's a barber,
>   But vera bright an' smart,
> An' crazy for da op'ra;
>   He knows dem all by heart.
> He's alla tima wheestlin';
>   An' often you can find
> Jus' from the tune he wheestles
>   W'at thoughts ees een hees mind.
> Las' week hees wife, Lucia—
>   Fine woman, too, is she—
> She gave to heem som' babies,
>   Not only wan, but three!
> Eef to your shop som' neighbors
>   Should breeng sooch news to you
> Eet sure would jus' excite you
>   To say a word or two;
> But deesa Joe Moralli,
>   Dees music-crazy loon,
> He never stopped hees wheestlin'—
>   But justa changed hees tune.
> Dees answer from hees music
>   Was all dat dey could gat:
> "Trio from 'Trovatore.' "
>   Ha! w'at you theenk of dat?
>
> He nevva stopped hees wheestlin'
>   Dat "Trovatore" tune,
> Not even w'en he's dreenkin'
>   Weeth frands een da saloon.
> He wheestled eet dat evenin'
>   W'en home he went to see
> Hees granda wife, Lucia,
>   And leetle babies three.

But w'en he stood bayfore dem
   He was so full weeth dreenk,
He looked upon dose babies,
   An' wheestle—w'at you theenk?
O! den da tune he wheestled
   Was—how-you-call-eet—"pat":
"Sextetta from Lucia."
   Ha! w'at you theenk of dat?

20 DECEMBER

Antics

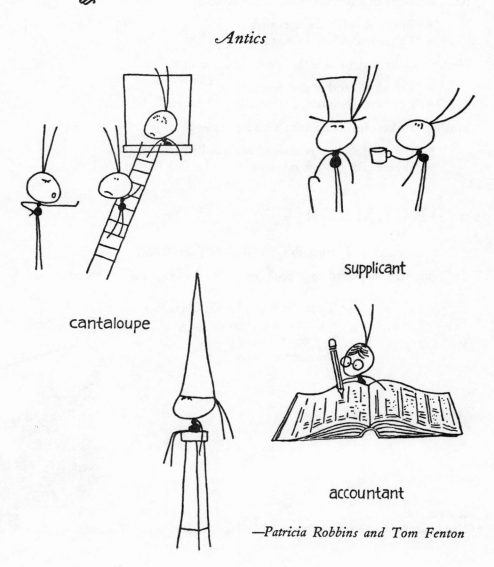

supplicant

cantaloupe

accountant

—*Patricia Robbins and Tom Fenton*

ignorant

21 DECEMBER

One Last Croak

James I. Rambo and Mary J. Youngquist start with standard Croakers*:

- "You snake!" she rattled.
- "Someone's at the door," she chimed.

The next step is homonymic Croakers:

- "Company's coming," she guessed.
- "Dawn came too soon," she mourned.

Next, Croakers that use only part of the verb:

- "Ring the bell," she appealed.
- "I already did," he harangued.

Next, Croakers that involve the speaker's name in the pun:

- "I think I'll end it all," Sue sighed.
- "I ordered chocolate, not vanilla," I screamed.

Finally, Croakers involving both verb and adverb.

- "Your embroidery is sloppy," she needled cruelly.
- "Where did you get this meat?" he bridled hoarsely.

22 DECEMBER

Cajun Night Before Christmas

This Cajun verse appeared as a book, of which I can give you only fragments.†

> 'Twas the night before Christmas
> An' all t'ru de house
> Dey don't a t'ing pass
> Not even a mouse.

---

* See 2 February.
† *Cajun Night Before Christmas*, Pelican Publishing Company, Gretna, Louisiana, 1973.

* * * *

As I look out de do'
In de light o' de moon
I t'ink "Manh, you crazy
Or got ol' too soon."

Cuz dere on de by-you
Wen I stretch ma' neck stiff
Dere's eight alligator
A-pullin' de skiff.
An' a little fat drover
Wit' a long pole-ing stick
I know r'at away
Got to be ole St. Nick.

Mo' fas'er an' fas'er
De gator dey came
He whistle an' holler
An' call dem by name:

"Ha, Gaston!
Ha, Tiboy!
Ha, Pierre an' Alcée!
Gee, Ninette!
Gee, Suzette!
Celeste an' Renée!"
"To de top o' de porch
To de top o' de wall
Make crawl, alligator,
An' be sho' you don' fall."

* * * *

An' I hear him shout loud
As a-splashin' he go
"Merry Christmas to all
'Til I saw you some mo'!"
—*Trosclair.*
Edited by Howard Jacobs.

23 DECEMBER

Nay, Nay, Neigh not, Neighbor Bob

If I were Commissar of Education, every child in the country would start Latin in the fourth grade and Greek in the sixth, and would continue chewing on both languages as long as he stayed in school. That way he would have a foundation for English, which in my lifetime has itself become a dead language; I don't know just what it is that English teachers teach and best-selling writers write, but certainly it is not English.

I dropped Latin after three years and never studied Greek at all. One reason words fascinate me so is precisely that I know so little of how they came to be what they are. Why, it is only a few weeks ago that I learned that bribe comes from the French word for the heel of a loaf of bread.*

Reading of course enlarges one's vocabulary, but in an eclectic, unsystematic fashion. Nor does it explain *why* a word or expression means what it does. If I say, "flattery turned his head," you know exactly what "turned his head" means; but *why* does it mean that? (Note that I did not say Latin and Greek will give you a command of English. I said they will give you a foundation.)

One worthwhile work,† the King James Bible, I did read through at an early age, skipping the begats. I completed my first reading of it just before my tenth birthday, promptly proceeded to reread it, and still dip into it to this day. But here again my lack of Greek—not to mention Hebrew—handicaps me. Take, for instance, this thought-provoking line from Jeremiah:

> They were *as* fed horses in the morning;
> every one neighed after his neighbor's wife.

Now, there is a magnificent metaphor, and a superb example of word play; but was the word play in the original, or was it introduced by the translators? I have no idea. All I know is that in my mind's eye I can see those fed horses, neighing and galloping and farting across the fields after their neighbors' wives, as would-be sinners, like my neighbor Bob, are doing to this very day:

AS FED HORSES IN THE MORNING

> Neighbor, neighing after Nan,
>   Neigh not, neighbor, neigh not!
> Neighing, Bob, is not the plan
>   To win her—I should say not.
>
> "Nay," she'll answer to your neigh,
>   "You're too low on hay, Bob.
> I'll save rolling in the hay
>   For some neighing nabob."
>   —W.R.E.

* See 29 February, 9 April, 16 May, and 27 August.

† And written by a committee, at that.

24 DECEMBER

A Visit from St. Nicholas

```
                              T
                             WAS
                            THENI
                          GHTBEFO
                         RECHRISTM
                        A SWHENAL L
                       THR OUGHT HEH
                      OUSEN OTA CREAT
                     UREWASS T IRRINGN
                    OTEVENAMO USETHESTO
                   C KINGSWE R EHUNGBY T
                  HEC HIMNE YWI THCAR EIN
                 HOPES THA TSAIN TNI CHOLA
                SSOONWO U LDBETHE R ETHECHI
               LDRENWERE NESTLEDAL LSNUGINTH
              E IRBEDSW H ILEVISI O NSOFSUG A
             RPL UMSDA NCE DINTH EIR HEADS AND
            MAMMA INH ERKER CHI EFAND IIN MYCAP
           HADJUST S ETTLEDD O WNFORAL O NGWINTE
          RSNAPWHEN OUTONTHEL AWNTHEREA ROSESUCHA
         C LATTERI S PRANGFR O MMYBEDT O SEEWHAT W
        HAT WASTH EMA TTERA WAY TOTHE WIN DOWIF LEW
       LIKEA FLA SHTOR EOP ENTHE SHU TTERS AND THREW
      UPTHESA S HTHEMOO N THEBREA S TOFTHEN E WFALLEN
     SNOWGAVEA LUSTEROFM IDDAYTOOB JECTSBELO WWHENWHAT
    T OMYWOND E RINGEYE S SHOULDA P PEARBUT A MINIATU R
   ESL EIGHA NDE IGHTT INY REIND EER WITHA LIT TLEOL DDR
  IVERS OLI VELYA NDQ UICKI KNE WINAM OME NTITM UST BESTN
 ICKMORE R APIDTHA N EAGLESH I SCOURSE R STHEYCA M EANDHEW
HISTLEDAN DSHOUTEDA NDCALLEDT HEMBYNAME NOWDASHER NOWDANCER
N OWPRANC E RANDVIX E NONCOME T ONCUPID O NDONNER A NDBLITZ E
NTO THETO POF THEPO RCH TOTHE TOP OFTHE WAL LNOWD ASH AWAYD ASH
AWAYD ASH AWAYA LLA SDRYL EAV ESTHA TBE FORET HEW ILDHU RRI CANEF
LYWHENT H EYMEETW I THANOBS T ACLEMOU N TTOTHES K YSOUPTO T HEHOUSE
TOPTHECOU RSERSTHEY FLEWWITHA SLEIGHFUL LOFTOYSAN DSTNICHOL ASTOOANDT
H ENINATW I NKLEIHE A RDONTHE R OOFTHEP R ANCINGA N DPAWING O FEACHLI T
TLE HOOFA SID REWIN MYH EADAN DWA STURN ING AROUN DDO WNTHE CHI MNEYS TNI
CHOLA SCA MEWIT HAB OUNDH EWA SDRES SED ALLIN FUR FROMH ISH EADTO HIS FOOTA
NDHISCL O THESWER E ALLTARN I SHEDWIT H ASHESAN D SOOTABU N DLEOFTO Y SHEHADF
LUNGONHIS BACKANDHE LOOKEDLIK EAPEDDLER JUSTOPENI NGHISPACK HISEYESHO WTHEYTWIN
K LEDHISD I MPLESHO W MERRYHI S CHEEKSW E RELIKER O SESHISN O SELIKEA C HERRYHI S
DRO LLLIT TLE MOUTH WAS DRAWN UPL IKEAB OWA NDTHE BEA RDONH ISC HINWA SAS WHITE AST
HESNO WTH ESTUM POF APIPE HEH ELDTI GHT INHIS TEE THAND THE SMOKE ITE NCIRC LED HISHE
ADLIKEA W REATHHE H ADABROA D FACEAND A LITTLER O UNDBELL Y THATSHO O KWHENHE L AUGHEDL
IKEABOWLF ULLOFJELL YHEWASCHU BBYANDPLU MPARIGHTJ OLLYOLDEL FANDILAUG HEDWHENIS AWHIMINSP
I TEOFMYS E LFAWINK O FHISEYE A NDATWIS T OFHISHE A DSOONGA V EMETOKN O WIHADNO T HINGTOD R
EAD HESPO KEN OTAWO RDB UTWEN TST RAIGH TTO HISWO RKA NDFIL LED ALLTH EST OCKIN GST HENTU RNE
DWITH AJE RKAND LAY INGHI SFI NGERA SID EOFHI SNO SEAND GIV INGAN ODU PTHEC HIM NEYHE ROS EHESP
RANGTOH I SSLEIGH T OHISTEA M GAVEAWH I STLEAND A WAYTHEY A LLFLEWL I KETHEDO W NONATHI S TLEBUTI
HEARDHIME XCLAIMASH EDROVEOUT OFSIGHTHA PPYCHRIST MASTOALLA NDTOALLAG OODNIGHTP OEMBYCLEM ENTCMOORE
                              1822    1972
                             THIS MOST
                             FAM OUS
                              YU LE
                              PO EM
                             OBSE RVES
                             THIS XMAS
                         ITS 150TH ANNIVERSARY
```

25 DECEMBER

Take Back That Powdered Rhinoceros Horn, Santa!

To decode the following acrostic sonnet, you must know that I first intended to call this book *The Oysterville Almanac* rather than *An Almanac of Words at Play*. I changed my mind, indeed, only a few days ago. On a basis of the earlier title, the verse contains my season's greetings to you.

Start decoding by listing the first letter of each line, but don't stop with that—the acrostic runs down the lines twice more.

These presents are quite odd (I speak of mine):
Hand-painted sox; linguini made of eel;
Engraved cigars; mice from the river Rhine;
One yak; and barbwire for my fishing reel.

You meant no harm, I know, about that yak;
Strange gifts arise from love. (Thus, I conject,
The queer clock ticking in my haversack
Expresses, though bizarrely, your respect.

Really, won't it explode, though—or implode?)
Venom's a *darling* thought. Now let me see . . .
I never saw a better-looking toad.
Land's sake! You say it's here to marry me?

Love sometimes overdraws and misses aim.
Eject this useless stuff! Thanks all the same.
                                        —*W.R.E.*

26 DECEMBER

Spark in the Dark

If the words of a memorable song are shut off, I hum happily (off key) to the tune; if the tune is shut off, the words by themselves often come out absurd. "Words divorced from their legally wedded music," says David McCord, "are never entirely satisfactory as verse unless they were written without reference to the accenting demands of musical notation. Moral: If you write both words *and* music, music is the controlling factor. . . . Writing words for music is an art in itself. It requires a knowledge of vowel and consonant values which even the best of light verse writers may not understand. The converse of this is that verses from the text of first-rate musical comedies such as *Of Thee I Sing* just don't read as well as they sing."

Many familiar songs started out as poems; but no lyricist comes to mind, with the exception of W. S. Gilbert, to disprove Mr. McCord's contention that songs just don't read as well as they sing. Gilbert was a special case; he was a poet first and foremost, and Sullivan's scores had to fit Gilbert's words, not the other way around. Nor did the lyricist have to worry about what the score would be like; when you have heard one Sullivan score, you have heard them all.

But though few lyricists may be great poets, no one can deny that the likes of Coward, Hammerstein, Harburg, Lerner, Loesser, Mercer, Porter, and Sondheim,* are dazzlers when it comes to rhyming. I asked Richard Lewine, the composer, to give me one of the musical rhymes he likes best. He offered several, of which this, by Lorenz Hart, is a fair sample:

> Horace was a poet who adored the night
> In his verse he always underscored the night
> I recall that Horace said in Latin A
> Never make your love affair a matinee.
> Wait till after dark
> For that classical spark.

Brilliant. But as you read it without music, whether silently or aloud, you know you are missing something: those words were meant to be sung.

(William Ray, the photographer, disagrees with Horace's premise. There is much to be said he opines, for a matinee love affair. He likes Hart's rhyming better than Horace's timing.)

27 DECEMBER

The Assination of English

It is an article of faith with politicians, professors, and editorial writers that each new generation of boys and girls is handsomer, brighter, and more honest than the one before. If I ever doubted that proposition, I doubt it no longer. Here, from essays of recent school years, is the proof:

- "Henry VIII found walking difficult because he had an abbess on his knee."
- "In *A Streetcar Named Desire* the climax is when Blanche goes to bed with Stella's husband."

---

* Not to change the subject, but Mr. Sondheim (whom Arthur Laurents and others have hailed as "the best Broadway lyricist past or present") once recalled that *A Funny Thing Happened on the Way to the Forum*—later to become a memorable Broadway hit—was a disaster when it opened out of town, and nobody knew why. He added: "Even George Abbott, who had been connected with more farces than anybody, said, 'I don't know what to do. I like it. They don't like it. I don't know what to do, you've got to call in George Abbott.'"

- "In *Mrs. Warren's Profession,* her profession is the Oldest Profession, but she is not really a Lost Woman. She is just mislaid."
- "Abstinence is a good thing if practiced in moderation."
- "Today every Tom, Dick, and Harry is named Bill."
- "A virgin forest is a place where the hand of man has never set foot."
- "It was the painter Donatello's interest in the female nude that made him the Father of the Renaissance."

—*Temple G. Porter*

28 DECEMBER

More Notpoems

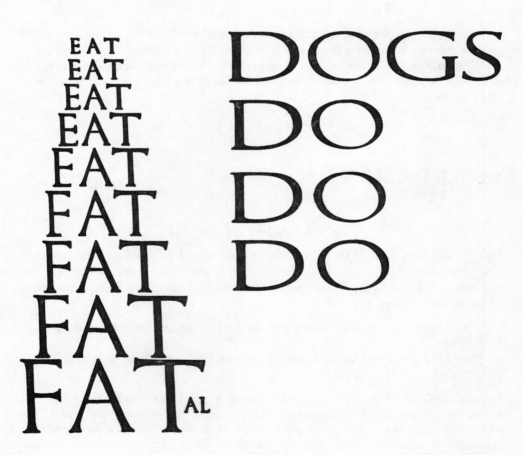

—*Adele Aldridge*

29 DECEMBER

The Kentucky Thoroughbred

Long before Woman's Lib, Tennyson warned a maiden against the villain who was pursuing her.

> He will hold you, when his passion
> Shall have run its shallow course
> Something better than his dog,
> A little dearer than his horse.

Well, there was once an American poet who on the subject of horses could give Tennyson half a furlong and beat him in a trot. Listen to this:

I love the hoss from hoof to head,	I love my God the first of all,
From head to hoof and tail to mane;	Then Him that perished on the Cross;
I love the hoss, as I have said,	And then my wife, and then I fall
From head to hoof and back again.	Down on my knees and love the hoss.

> —*James Whitcomb Riley*

The horse, of course, can be regarded from a broader point of view:

HORSE AND RIDER

The rider/Is fat/As that ( )/Or wider ( )/
In torso/ Of course/ The horse/ Is more so (   )
—*Wey Robinson*

30 DECEMBER

Papa Belong Me-Fella, Nipee Off Her Nose!

THE LORD'S PRAYER

Papa belong me-fella, you stop long heaven. Al 'e sanctu 'im name belong you. Kingdom belong you 'e come. All 'e hear 'im talk belong you long ground all-same long heaven. Today givem kaikai belong day long me-fella. Forgive 'im wrong belong me-fella, all-same me-fella forgive 'im wrong all 'e makem long me-fella. You no bringem me-fella long try 'im. Take 'way somet'ing no-good long me-fella. Amen.

NURSERY SONG IN PIDGIN ENGLISH

Singee a songee sick a pence,
Pockee muchee lye;

Dozen two time blackee bird
  Cookee in e pie.
When him cutee topside
  Birdee bobbery sing;
Himee tinkee nicey dish
  Setee foree King!
Kingee in a talkee loom
  Countee muchee money;
Queeny in e kitchee,
  Chew-chee breadee honey.
Servant galo shakee,
  Hangee washee clothes;
Chop-chop comee blackee bird,
  Nipee off her nose!
—*Who Done Him, Him No Know*

3 1 DECEMBER

Fee, Fi, Fo, Fum— I Smell the Blood of Frank Sullivan, Etc.

*Happy New
Year to my
contributors:*

1. Let bells of bronze with tongues of gold
   Ring in the new, ring out the old
   For wags and wits, alive and dead,
   Whose bones I've ground to make my bread!

*the
nameless . . .*

2. A happy New Year I propone
   For *Auth. Anon.* and *Auth. Unknown.*

*and the
defunct . . .*

3. It isn't quite the thing, perhaps,
   To bring up New Year to you chaps
   Who sit in bliss, exchanging toasts
   With Fathers, Sons, and Holy Ghosts.
   Instead, I wish for your Fraternity
   A healthy, prosperous Eternity.

*including
those
listed
here . . .*

4. To Mencken, Prior, de la Mare;
   To Sitwell (Edith); Osbert (frère);
   To Coleridge and Sackville-West—
   To Housman, Belloc, Gay—my best!
   May Keats till Judgment Day stay squiffed
   With Herrick, cummings, Stupp, and Swift!

here . . .

5. Beside your Stygian river snore well,
   Cowper, Shelley, Eliot, Orwell!
   On Lander, Thackeray, and Lawrence
   May joy celestial pour in torrents!
   Shakespeare, Riley, Butler, Lardner,
   Thurber, Benchley—*prosit,* pardner!

and
here . . .

6. Swinburne, Leacock, Wordsworth, Donne,
   F.P.A., Yeats, Tennyson,
   Goldsmith, Bishop, Blake, and Proetz—
   Season's greetings, perished poets!

also those who are
still alive . . .

7. For you who yet are overground,
   May royalties next year abound!

these Word
Ways contributors,
for instance . . .

8. May rave reviews, with nary heckler,
   Greet Borgmann, Bergerson, and Eckler!
   May Youngquist, Porter, Ashley, Mercer,
   Find each day better, no day worser!
   May Francis, Silverman, and Lindon
   (And Cohen, too!), have medals pinned on!

certain sots
of my
acquaintance . . .

9. May Cole and Niven live in style,
   And laughing walk the final Miall!
   May banners wave, may hearts be all-astir
   For Morris, Hellman, Read, and Hollister!
   May some kind Angell ease your way,
   Bendiner, Harrison, de Kay!

word players
I know or
would like
to know . . .

10. My wish for Pei and for Ciardi's
    Starlets of their choice at Sardi's;
    For Levin, Schur, and Richardson,
    Paillard de boeuf at Twenty-one;
    For Baker, Lauder, and McCord,
    Wine picked by George of Perigord.

more of
the same . . .

11. May juices this year flow not thinly
    Along MacLean, McCrum, McGinley.
    Rosten, Ransom, Harrold, Tidwell,
    Creamer, Harris, Pope, I bid well;
    Bronowski,* Berger, Brien, Stoppard,
    May your winning cards be coppered!

and still
more . . .

12. This year set afire the Thames,
    Hitchcock, Hickerson, and James!
    Joy shine through your window pane,

* Dr. Bronowski left the present for the past category after this verse was written. Vale!

Bainbridge, Updike, Minogue, Caen!
May no toe of yours be gouty,
Jacobs, Bongartz, Starbuck, Dowty!

perhaps
too many.

13. Take your ease in summer haycock,
Dunphy, Considine, and Laycock!
Farmer, Hollander, and Deal,
Sound the New Year campanile!
Fuller, Gilliatt and Lewis,
Reed and Mockridge, sock it to us!

Repeat now
the Happy New
Year chorus:

14. *Let bells of bronze with tongues of gold*
Ring in the new, ring out the old
For wags and wits, alive and dead,
   Whose bones I've ground
   Whose bones I've ground
   Whose bones I've ground
      To make my bread.
                              —*W.R.E.*

I have left out some contributors, I know. To them no less than those named above—and to you, too, O reader, my rod and my staff—a Happy, Prosperous New Year!

Answers and Solutions

3 JANUARY   *An ABC Proposal Comes to O.*

1. You sigh for a cipher, but I sigh for you;
    Oh sigh for no cipher, but oh sigh for me;
    Oh let not my sigh for a cipher go,
    But give sigh for sigh, for I sigh for you so.

2. Naughty Otto thought he ought
    To own an auto. Otto bought
    An auto but he never thought
    He'd owe the auto dealer aught
    For the auto Otto bought.
    Say, has Otto's auto brought
    Otto aught that Otto sought?
    Otto's auto's good for naught.

6 JANUARY   *My S's Grow S's.*

The word Mr. Canning had in mind was cares.

9 JANUARY   *What's Yours, Fella?*

1. A cup of coffee.
2. An order of Jello.
3. French fried potatoes added.
4. Corned beef and cabbage.
5. Salt and pepper.
6. Doughnut and coffee.
7. A glass of buttermilk.
8. Hash with catsup.
9. A glass of water.
10. One hot dog.
11. An Italian hero sandwich.
12. Bacon, lettuce and tomato sandwich without mayonnaise.
13. Beans with two frankfurters.
14. Beef stew.
15. Scrambled eggs with whole wheat toast.
16. Vanilla ice cream in a chocolate soda or milkshake (sometimes also coffee with cream).
17. A glass of orange juice.
18. A glass of water.
19. Nova Scotia smoked salmon on a bagel.
20. Poached eggs on toast.

12 JANUARY   *Clitch, Clitch, Clitch.*

1. destruction (Proverbs 16:18) 2. paint (Shakespeare, *King John*) 3. learning (Pope, *An Essay on Criticism*) 4. thought (Heywood, *Proverbs*) 5. savage breast (Congreve, *The Mourning Bride*) 6. of (Colton, *The Lacon*) 7. fibs (Goldsmith, *She Stoops to Conquer*) 8. an ell (Ray, *English Proverbs*) 9. very spice (Cowper, *The Task*) 10. The love of money (I Timothy 6:10) 11. nor any (Coleridge, *The Ancient Mariner*) 12. one life to lose (Nathan Hale)

15 JANUARY   *One Man's Abdomen.*

You misunderstood me. I said polo pony.

20 JANUARY   *A Squirming of Snakes.*

1. Apes	13. Kine
2. Wolves	14. Hares
3. Boars	15. Monkeys
4. Chickens	16. Foxes
5. Badgers	17. Peacocks
6. Birds	18. Geese
7. Leopards	19. Partridges
8. Pheasants	20. Whales, or young seals. (A grown male
9. Bears	seal is a *bull*, his females *cows*, their off-
10. Swine	spring *pups*, an immature male a *bachelor*,
11. Fish	a colony of seals a *herd*, and their breeding
12. Cats	place a rookery.)

21 JANUARY   *Nudists Take Off.*

Here is your competition:
1. Lost His Grippe?
2. Après Mao Le Deluge?
3. Nixon Pandas to Capital Zoo's Wishes.
4. Oregon Gamecock Breeders Cry, "Fowl!"

27 JANUARY   *Be Friendly, Borgmann.*

Mr. Friend's anagrams:

1. I got a rat	6. Has to pilfer
2. Cannot stir	7. Can ruin a selected victim
3. I mean to rend it	8. "Time's running past," we murmur
4. Violence run forth	9. No city dust here!
5. Spare him not	10. Ars magna
6. Partial men	11. Sly ware
7. It ran	12. Nine thumps
	13. Stamps one as so nice
Mr. Borgmann's:	14. Voices rant on
1. Attaineth its cause: freedom!	15. A rope ends it
2. They see	16. Tender names
3. Positively!	17. Get a "no" in
4. Hear Dante! oh, beware yon open hell!	18. A step-in
5. Faces one at the end	

30 JANUARY   *Vile Vodka.*

FAREWELL, A LONG FAREWELL
TO ALL MY PROTESTANT ETHIC

Today's misfortunes John ignores, to wait
Tomorrow's joys, which he foresees as great;
Forgets that if his forties were a curse,
His seventies and eighties must be worse.
The future he foretells sounds fine; but he
Foregoes for its sake present ecstasy—
Forbids himself all actions apt to please.

My rule is this: Time's forelock's meant to seize.
What's here for use I mean to use; I reach
For surf that phosphoresces on the beach
No less than sweet forays and foragings;
All are for wise men's use to ease life's stings.
John's foresight's not for me; I give my praise
To pleasures not tomorrow's but today's.

MITIGATION

So tender's the night,
So tender's the voice of the dove,
Who can blame the young wight
If he tenders his lady his love?

9 FEBRUARY   *Mots d'Heures: Gousses, Rames*

The sounds of the first verse approximate "Old Mother Hubbard"; of the second, "Hickory Dickory Dock."

20 FEBRUARY   *Censored Fables.*

SHIPWRECK

Row, row, row your boat
  Till the prow go down;
Fie on him who borrows sorrow;
All must sink and drown tomorrow;
  All must sink and drown.

Let no wailing crowd your throat;
  Bar your brow from frown;
Bare your breast to Cupid's arrow,
Gnaw the bone and suck the marrow,
  Ere you sink and drown.

Plait the blossoms life has grown,
  Wear them as a crown;
Many a crow shall flee from sparrow,
Many a lad his row shall harrow,
  Ere you sink and drown

26 FEBRUARY   *Bless the Shepherd.*

APPROACH OF EVENING

Idling, I sit in this mild twilight dim,
Whilst birds, in wild, swift vigils, circling skim.
Light winds in sighing sink, till, rising bright,
Night's Virgin Pilgrim swims in vivid light!

INCONTROVERTIBLE FACTS

Dull humdrum murmurs lull, but hubbub stuns.
Lucullus snuffs up musk, mundungus* shuns.
Puss purrs, buds burst, bucks butt, luck turns up trumps;
But full cups, hurtful, spur up unjust thumps.

28 FEBRUARY   *Cats, Cats, Cats, Cats!*

The initial letters of the lines of Mr. Lindon's verses spell out the titles.

The initial words of the lines of "Forecast: Chilly," strung together, read "Time for warm clothes, man; this looks like one long cold winter."

25 MARCH   *Re: Rebuses.*

Mr. Manheim's rebuses: The envelope went to John Underwood, Andover, Mass. The descriptive phrase is "a little darky in bed with nothing over him." (This rebus was created before darkies grew darker and came to call themselves blacks.)

Mrs. Youngquist's word rebuses:

1. Much ado about nothing
2. World without end, amen
3. Frameup

4. All in one
5. Six of one, half a dozen of another
6. Square meal

1 APRIL   *Compip, Compoop.*

- ABRACADABRA. From Hebrew Ab (Father), Ben (Son), Ruach Adasch (Holy Spirit). A cabalistic charm, formerly used against ague, flux, etc.
- ICHTHYS (Greek for fish). *Iesous Christos, Theou Yios, Soter* (Jesus Christ, Son of God, Saviour). From the 2nd century the fish was used as a symbol of Christ. Whether the fish symbol arose from the acrostic or vice versa is not known.
- HIP! HIP! HURRAH! The old fanciful explanation is that Hip is a notarikon, composed of the initials *H*iersolyma (Jerusalem) *e*st *p*erdi, and that when German knights headed a Jew hunt in the Middle Ages, they ran shouting "Hip! Hip!" as much as to say "Jerusalem is destroyed." Hurrah was similarly credited to Slavonic Hu-raj (to Paradise), so that "Hip! Hip! Hurrah!" would mean "Jerusalem is lost to the infidel, and we are on the road to Paradise."
- NEWS. E $\frac{N}{S}$ W at one time was used by newspapers to show their information came from north, south, east, and west—i.e., from all over the world. But this is a false acronym. The word used to be spelled newes, and comes from French *nouvelles*.
- PAKISTAN. The name was coined by Chaudrie Rahmat Ali from appropriate letters of the words *P*unjab, *A*fghan Border States, *K*ashm*i*re, *S*ind, and Baluchis*tan*.

*Mundungus is an obsolete word meaning trash. It once had something to do with black pudding

4 APRIL   *Anagrams from* Punch.

Animal Fare: Stable, bleats, tables, ablest
Pre-parental Plaint: Aspired, praised, despair, diapers
*A Cleric of Antic ******:* Stripe, priest, ripest, tripes, sprite
Gastronomically, Cranes Act Comically: Crate, react, cater, carte, trace
Make That Ghost Stop Peeking, Honey! Sacré, scare, cares, acres, races
Royal Pick-me-up. Large, lager, regal, glare

5 APRIL   *Berlitz School.*

1. Self-explanatory.
2. The Japanese words for one, two, four, and five are as stated. The word for three is "san."
3. "Hur star det till?" is "How are you?" in Swedish.
4. "Horasho" is Russian for "good, great."
5. "Hielo" is Spanish for ice; "mantequilla" is butter; the letters S O C K S spell "socks."
6. "Simile," used as a command in Swahili, means "Get lost—go away!"

6 APRIL   *Biblical Fruitcake.*

The Bible verses cited refer to: 1, flour 2. butter 3. sugar 4. raisins 5. figs 6. almonds 7. honey 8. eggs 9. salt 10. baking soda 11. spices (Mrs. Harrold suggested ½ tsp. cloves, ½ tsp. nutmeg, 1 tsp. cinnamon and 1 tsp. mace, but one should choose among them, not use them all.) 12. beat well

8 APRIL   *Spoken Like a Native.*

1. Burma 2. Ceylon 3. Taiwan 4. China 5. Tibet 6. Athens 7. Iceland 8. Iran 9. South Korea 10. Japan

9 APRIL   *O. O. O. (Of Obscure Origin, that is).*

The words are "clobber" ("to batter or maul") and "chum" ("chopped fish").

13 APRIL   *Off with His Foote!*

The number of letters in each word gives the correct digit. Check them: 3 1 4 1 5 9 2 6 5 3 5 8 9 7 9 3 2 3 8 4 6

19 APRIL   *Abigail to Aurora.*

• *Abigail* was the name of a serving maid in *The Scornful Lady* (1613), a play by Beaumont and Fletcher.
• The grove near Athens where Plato met with his followers was named *Akadēmia* after the legendary Attic hero Akadēmos.
• *Agaric* is from *Agaria,* the name of a city in Sarmatia.
• *Alabaster* derives from Egyptian 'a-la-Baste, "vessel of Baste." Baste, the cat-goddess, was patroness of love and fashion.
• Warm foot gear is often a necessity in *Alaska.*
• The Old French poems of the 12th century which established the *alexandrine* verse form celebrated the exploits of Alexander the Great.
• *Alice* Roosevelt Longworth, daughter of President Theodore Roosevelt, fancied pale blue in her gowns and ornamentation.

- *Amaryllis* was a lovely shepherdess in a Greek poem written in the third century B.C.
- The dance is supposedly of German origin. *Allemande* is French for "German."
- The *Amazons* were a legendary race or nation of female warriors. They were said to hack off the right breast lest it interfere with archery and swordplay.
- The *alpine* hat first became popular in the Alps.
- In ancient times, suppliants' camels grazed near the temple of the ram-headed god Jupiter *Ammon,* in Libya. *Ammonia* is said to have been first obtained from their dung.
- Montilla is the Spanish town where *amontillada* was first made.
- A. N. *Ampere,* a French physicist (1775–1836), was instrumental in developing the science of electro-magnetism. Many other electrical measurements are named after physicists.
- *Anekdota* (literally, "unpublished") was the name of a set of gossipy memoirs by Procopius, a sixth-century Byzantine historian.
- *Angostura* was the former name of Ciudad Bolivar, in Venezuela, whence the bark holding the bitters was exported.
- *Makassar,* a city in Indonesia, is the source of an oil, once popular as a hair dressing, which left stains behind. Victorian housewives used *antimacassars* in self-defense.
- Paris gangsters were compared for their ferocity with the *Apache* Indians of the American southwest. While the French were borrowing *apache,* the United States was borrowing *thug,* similar in meaning, from India.
- *Aphrodite* was the Greek goddess of sensual love.
- *Apollo,* Greek god of the sun, was handsome is, though not necessarily handsome does.
- *Arabesque* means "done in the Arab fashion." Forbidden to represent the face of God in their mosques, the Arabs substituted elaborate abstract traceries.
- *Arachne* was a Lydian girl who beat the goddess Athena in a weaving contest. Athena punished her for her effrontery by changing her to a spider.
- *Arcady* was a mountainous district of Greece, celebrated as the abode of a simple people, dwelling in pastoral happiness.
- *"Archibald,* certainly not," a catch phrase from a music-hall song, was the remark with which British aviators in World War I were said to greet bursting shrapnel.
- *Archipelago* ("chief sea") was the Latin word for the Aegean, which is studded with small islands.
- *Arethusa,* a nymph pursued by the river-god Alpheus, was changed by Diana into a fountain; but the ardent god worked a passage for his river and managed to commingle its waters with those of the fountain.
- *Argosy* does not, as one might suppose, derive from *Argos,* the ship in which the Argonauts sought the Golden Fleece, but from a city in either Sicily or Yugoslavia named *Ragusa.*
- In Greek myth, *Argus* was a giant with a hundred eyes.
- *Argyle* was originally the pattern on the tartan of the Campbells of Argyle, in western Scotland.
- *Arras,* a town in northeastern France, became notable in the fifteenth century for the distinguished and energetic style of its tapestry weaving.
- *Artesian* wells were first driven in *Artois,* France, as early as 1750.
- *Ascots* first became popular at *Ascot* Heath, site of the famous race track in Berkshire, England.
- *Aspirin* (from acetyl + *spira*eic acid) was originally a trade name.
- The *Assassins,* Moslem fanatics dedicated to the killing of Christians in the early 1100s, ate *hashshashin,* or *hashish,* to whip up their courage and their fury.
- Named for *Astrakhan,* Russia, where these sheep were first grown.
- Athēnaion was the temple of *Athena* at *Athens,* where philosophy was taught.

• In Renaissance times a picture of *Atlas* supporting the world was commonly prefixed to map collections, which led Gerhard Mercator, the Flemish geographer, to call these by the Titan's name.

• *Atropos*, eldest of the three Greek fates, was the one who cut off the thread of a man's life when his time came to die.

• From *Attica*, a name for ancient Greece. *Attic* at one time implied a design of simplicity, purity, and elegance. Not all present-day attics fit that description.

• *Aurora*, daughter of the Titans Theia and Hyperion, was a personification of the first light of morning.

2 MAY   *Where Did That Poisoned Pawn Come from, Mr. Fischer?*

NxB!? = Knight captures Bishop. Strong, but risky.

O–O = castles to the King's side.

QxQ = Queen captures Queen.

!! = The move is powerful, and winning.

PxP = Pawn captures Pawn.

RxN = Rook captures Knight.

R = Castle, or, as above, Rook.

Q = Queen.

R = Rook.

B = Bishop.

P = Pawn.

– = moves.

So the verse, in the clear, reads as follows:

> The match begins; the breaths are bated.
> Will Black resign? Will White be mated?
> White's Ruy Lopez circumvents
> Black's Nimzo-Indian defense.
> Now White (intent) and Black (intenter)
> Maneuver to control the center.

> White moves. Too bold? Perhaps from whiskey?
> Knight captures Bishop. Strong, but risky.
> Now Black, to plaudits from the ringside,
> Correctly castles to the King's side.
> Queen captures Queen (White's ranks are thinning).
> The move is powerful, and winning.

> The mating net is drawing tight:
> Pawn captures pawn, rook captures knight.
> White, backed against his castle wall,
> In vain seeks check perpetual.
> Of Queen, Rook, Bishop, Pawn bereft,
> He moves to right, he moves to left.

> *Poor White in Zugzwang sealed his fate;*
> *His Fianchetto came too late.*
> *He pondered a Maroczy Bind,*
> *Could see no future, and resigned.*

6 MAY   *Era Uoy a Diamrab?*

1. A backward barmaid fell in love,
   And wed her backward guest.
   Of all Earth's backward children
   Theirs were the backwardest.

2. When I was young as you are
   I bled the system white
   When reading verse and novels
   By starting from the right.

   When you are old as I am
   And equally bereft
   . . . Take comfort then as I do
   By reading right from left.

23 MAY   *Four Kate, Won Eye a Door.*

ANT SONG

Next week offer me romance
Hold me, dance and dance and dance
Answer, answer, answer do
Let us turn a pace or two.

ANN DREW

Ann drew Andrew, Andrew drew Ann
Andrew drew Ann Ann drew Andrew

A CYST ME TWO

Assist me to pursue you, Kate;
My sentiment for you is great.
My heart is melancholic, Kate;
Ah, would that I might germinate
In you also this cancer, Kate!
Ah, would that I might inculcate
Idolatry of me in Kate!
When I see you my eyes dilate.
Yet you appear inviolate;
To no avail do I placate
You, Kate.

My purpose for you I relate,
And mention how I daily wait
For you before your mansion gate;
But this annoys you, for you hate
Romance, dear Kate.
Insensate opals coruscate
And scintillate
No more than you, inhuman Kate.

Diurnally I supplicate
You, Kate,
My charismatic Kate.
Oh Kate, abate
My sordid state!
Deplore my fate!
Communicate
Affection, Kate!
Be not cantankerous, dear Kate—
Capitulate!
Say you will be my candidate
For matrimonial estate.
Pray, answer, Kate!

KNOT TWO KNOT FOUR WON EYE A DOOR

'Tis not amiss a miss to find
With promise in her glance, sir;
If miss with mister be combined,
Then mischief is the answer.

A lass to idolize I sought
In some secluded section;
The noble lass alas would not
Accede to my affection.

If you some maiden would acquire,
She may avoid you also;
All lads are frequently afire,
All lasses oft are false, O.

5 JUNE   *When Baby Gurgles Guam and Georgia.*

When baby gurgles goo and gah,
Then how I envy baby's pa,
As slapping knee with loud huzzah
He sings in key or cries, "Hurrah!
My tad's OK, oh tra la la!"
But when the sound is wah wah wah
He loudly shouts, "Where are you ma,
Our Al is ill, oh pish, oh bah!
The M.D.'s off at baccarat!
Oh ma go hie you in our cah
And fetch him to me, near or fah!"
Then I don't envy pa at a'.

9 JUNE   *I Love You to ∞ (± A°).*

I won't insult you by translating "An ' To My Friend John," but the other two verses read in the clear as follows:

I LOVE YOU TO INFINITY (PLUS OR MINUS A DEGREE)

I am Mars and you are Venus;

Am'rous war shall rage between us—
War in which, as male, my function
Is to orbit toward conjunction,
While reluctance you pretend,
And opposition to my end.
A female knows dissatisfaction
A reversible reaction
Since (as always in these wars)
Venus yields at last to Mars:
My sum of love you'll give again
Multiplied by eight or ten.

INTER-GENERATIONAL QUERY

If parents showed less permittivity,
Would children show less resistivity?

I don't think I need to translate William Cole's love story, if that is the name for it.

15 JUNE   *He Beat You to That One, Too.*

The plays quoted from are, in order: *Cymbeline, Antony and Cleopatra, The Tempest, The Merry Wives of Windsor, The Taming of the Shrew, The Winter's Tale, King Henry VI, Measure for Measure, The Comedy of Errors, Much Ado about Nothing, A Midsummer Night's Dream, As You Like It, Julius Caesar.*

22 JUNE   *Part of Adam Is Mad.*

In "Eve's Dream," *demeanor* contains the letters in *dream*, *dreams* the letters in *sad*, *Eden* the letters in *end*, and *Adam* the letters in *mad*.

In "In-Riddle," *Algeria* contains the letters in *girl*, *Hepaticae* the letters in *peace*, *Wisteria* the letters in *war*, *halter* the letters in *her*, *Algeria* again the letters in *girl*, and *hysteria* the letters in *she*.

6 JULY   *Cockney Alphabet.*

A. Hay for horses, aphorism
B. Beef or lamb, beef or mutton
C. Sea for sailors, see for yourself
D. Differential, deef or dumb, deformity
E. Eve or Adam, heave a brick, Eva Peron, evolution
F. Effervescent, ever so nice, ever been had, efficacious
G. Chief of Police
H. Age for mellowness
 I. Highfaluting, eye for an eye, hyphenated, Eiffel Tower
 J. Jaffa oranges, d'ja ever hear about. . . ?, juvenile delinquent, d'ja ever see a dream walking
K. Cain and Abel, Kay Francis, cafeteria
L. Hell for leather
M. Emphasis, emphasize
N. Hen for a cockerel, enforcer, envelope
O. Over the garden wall, overpopulated, over my dead body, oversexed, overcoat
P. Pee for relief, perfidious Albion, performing fleas
Q. Queue for the pictures, queue for tickets, cutie pie

R. "'Arf a mo'" ("Half a moment—wait a minute!"), half a crown
S. As far as I'm concerned
T. Tea for two, T formation
U. You forgot, euphoria, euphemism
V. Vive la France, vivisection, vive la différence.
W. Double your money, trouble you for a match? double ewe for a Siamese ram
X. Eggs for breakfast
Y. Wife or mistress, why for heaven's sake
Z. Zephyr breezes

10 JULY   *Omak Me Yours Tonight.*

Provenance of the Place Names Used in *Omak Me Yours Tonight*

(To sniff out the sense of the ballad, one must not hesitate to mispronounce some of the place names. The correct pronunciation is indicated below.)

Omak, OH-mak. From omache, "good medicine."

Ilwaco, il-WAW-koh. Name of a chief.

Ballard. Platted as Gilman Park in 1888 by Captain W. R. Ballard.

Acme. The town was named for a hymn book.

Tolt. From H'lalt. Mr. Phillips does not give the meaning of the word.

Fife. Name of the founder of the town.

Toutle. From Hullooetell, a tribe on the Cowlitz River.

Dabob, Dah-BAHB. A tidal estuary on Puget Sound.

Spee-Bi-Dah. Phonetic spelling of a word for "small child."

Walla Walla, WAW-luh WAW-luh. From Walatsa, "running water."

Duwamish, doo-WAH-mish. From dewampsh, "the people living on the river."

Wollochet, WAH-luh-chet. From walatchet, "squirting clams."

Wenatchee, wuh-NACH-ee. From wenatchi, "river flowing from a canyon."

Elochoman, ee-LOH-ku-min, name of an Indian village on the Columbia River.

Latah, LAY-tah. From lahtoo, "the stream where little fish are caught."

Lilliwaup, LIL-uh-wahp. "Inlet."

Olalla, oh-LAL-uh. From olallie, "many berries."

Palouse, puh-LOOS. From the Palus tribe.

Lummi, LUHM-ee. From the Lummi tribe.

Asotin, uh-SOH-tin. "Eel Creek."

Chetlo, CHET-loh. "Oyster."

Auburn. After Auburn, N. Y.

Quilcene, KWIL-seen. "Salt-water people."

Chesaw, CHEE-saw. Name of a Chinese miner.

Dewatto, de-WAH-toh. "Home of evil spirits who make men crazy."

Tatoosh, ta-TOOSH. Perhaps from to-tooch, "thunderbird."

Tumtum. From thum(p)-thum(p), "heart."

Whatcom. WHAHT-kuhm. "Noisy water," the name of a chief.

Attalia, a-TAL-liuh. Named after an Italian hamlet.

Hamma Hamma, HAM-uh HAM-uh. From hab'hab, a swamp reed.

Klickitat, KLIK-i-tat. Either "robber" or "beyond."

Malott, muh-LAHT. Name of a pioneer.

Wynoochee, weye-NOO-chee. "Shifting," as the course of a river.

Mattawa, MAT-a-wuh. "Where is it?"

Startup. Named for an early manager of a lumber company.

Anacortes, an-uh-KOR-tis. A husband's romanticization of his wife's maiden name, Anna Curtis.

Thurston. Named for Oregon Territory's first delegate to Congress.

Havermale, HAV-er-mayl. The name of an early minister.

Tonasket, tuhn-AS-kuht. Honoring Chief Tonascutt.

Ohop, OH-hahp. From owhap, "water rushing out."

Naselle, nay-SEL. From the Nasal tribe.

Algona, al-GOH-na. From algoma, "valley of flowers."

Malone, muh-LOAN. Named for a New York community.

Methow, MET-how. From an Indian tribe.

Sekiu, SEE-kyoo. "Calm water."

Alava, AH-lah-vuh. Named for Jose Manuel de Alava, commissioner for Spain at the Nootka convention of 1790.

Spokane, spoh-KAN. From an Indian who identified himself as "chief of the sun people."

Canby. Named for Maj. Gen. Canby of the U.S. Army.

Olequa, OH-luh-quah. "Where salmon come to spawn."

Sauk, SAWK. From the Sah-kee-ma-hu tribe. No meaning is given.

Satsop, SAT-suhp. From sachap or sats-a-pish, "on a stream."

Tacoma, tuh-KOH-muh. The Indian name for Mount Rainier. The meaning is not given.

Mowich, MOH-ich. "Deer."

Touchet, TOO-she. From tousa, "curing salmon before a fire."

Scatchet, SKA-chit. Variant of Skagit. The meaning is lost.

Offut. Family name of two brothers who were early settlers.

Coulee, KOO-lee. From French couler, "to flow."

Pysht, PISHT. "Fish."

Skagit, SKA-jit. The meaning is lost.

Newaukum, noo-AW-kuhm. "Gently flowing water."

Yellepit, YEL-uh-pit. The name of a chief.

Yelm. From chelm, "heat waves rising from the earth."

Taholah, tuh-HOH-luh. Name of a Quinault tribal chief.

Tahuya, tuh-HOO-ya. From ta and ho-i, "that done," referring to some notable but forgotten occurrence.

Yacolt, YA-kawlt. "Haunted place." "A small band of Indians," says Mr. Phillips, "mysteriously lost their children while picking huckleberries, and after a futile search concluded that they had been stolen by Yacolt, the evil spirit."

Sucia, SOO-shuh. In Spanish, "dirty," or, nautically, "foul," a fair description of the reefs and hidden rocks surrounding the island.

Vashon, VASH-ahn. After Captain James Vashon, a British naval officer who fought the Americans in the Revolution.

Moran, mor-ANN. Named for Robert Moran, the shipbuilder and onetime mayor of Seattle who donated the land for this park.

Vader, VAY-der. In honor of an early settler "who was not honored, but outraged, and promptly moved to Florida."

Leland. An acronym from the name of Mrs. Laura E. Andrews, the first white woman there; originally spelled Lealand.

La Push, luh POOSH. Indian adaptation of French la bouche, "the mouth" (of a river).

Twisp. From twitsp, the meaning of which is not given.

Chuckanut, CHUHK-uh-nut. The definition is unknown.

Lebam, li-BAM. J. W. Goodell created the town's name by spelling his daughter Mabel's name backward.

Bangor, BANG-gawr. Presumably named by former down easters after the city in Maine.

Kapowsin, kuh-POW-suhn. From the Indian name, origin not recorded, for the lake on which the town is situated.

Memaloos, MEM-a-loos. "Dead." Memaloos, an island in the Columbia River, was used by the Indians as a cemetery.

Mohler. Named for a mail-stage driver.

Dosewallips, dhohs-ee-WAH-lips. From the name of a legendary Indian who turned into a mountain.

Kickit, KICK-uht. A peninsula jutting into Puget Sound.

Wawawai, wuh-WAH-ee. "Council ground."

Queets. From the Quaitso tribe.

Klipsan, KLIP-suhn. "Sunset."

Moclips, MOH-klips. A Quinault word for a place where maidens underwent puberty rites.

Elwha, EL-wah. "Elk."

Ione, eye-OHN. For Ione, niece of the town's first postmaster.

Wauna, WAW-nuh. "Strong and mighty."

Semiahmoo, sem-ee-A-moo. Perhaps from a word for "half moon."

Doughty, DOW-tee. Named for John Doughty, a petty officer aboard the Wilkes expedition's vessel *Peacock*.

Anatone, AN-uh-tohn. Name of a legendary Indian woman.

Colfax. In honor of U. S. Grant's Vice-President.

Snohomish, snoh-HOH-mish. Name of an Indian tribe.

Neah, NEE-uh. Nasal pronunciation of Deeah, chief of the Makah tribe.

Willapa, WIL-uh-pah. From Ah-whil-lapah, the name of the Chinook tribe that dwelt on the banks of the river.

Utsalady, uht-suh-LAD-ee. "Land of berries."

Liplip. Chinook jargon for "boiling."

Kachess, kuh-CHEES. "More fish."

Coweman, kow-EE-muhn. From Cowlitz ko-wee-na, "short man," after a dwarf-sized Indian who lived on the bank of the Cowlitz river.

Ruff. Named for the man on whose property the town was located.

Flattery. At the southern entrance of the Strait of Juan de Fuca, noted Captain James Cook in 1778, "there appeared to be a small opening that flattered us with hopes of finding a harbour there." The hope proving vain, he named the point Cape Flattery.

Vail. Named for the family that donated the townsite land to the Weyerhaeuser Company.

Towal, TOW-al. Name of a chief.

Blaine. Named in 1885 for James C. Blaine, unsuccessful Republican candidate for President.

Seattle, see-AT-uhl. Name of a chief.

Azwell, AZ-well Named for A Z. Wells, a prosperous orchard farmer

15 JULY   *Last Request.*

I'll die, my devious sins to expiate,
    Where canine, snake and avian
    'Mid murmurs apian
        Exuviate;
While you, by foreign springs artesian,
Achaian deities assimilate,
And for the water in the cooking pan
    To estuate
        Wait.

Dear entity, from whom doth emanate
The essence of euphoria for me;
You opium benign, you opiate . . .
Ideal agency of ecstasy . . .

These decencies pray grant: no elegies,
No dolorous paeans to extenuate
    My sins; no sigh for my sad state.
Nay—raise Te Deums; cheer for my decease;
    Then help some new ephemeral mate
        To ease
His tedium, and all his senses sate
    And tease.
    Please.

ON MORES AND MORALITY

The verses my hurrays are for
Are verses of a tedious mor-
Al decency, to ease us chaps
Who occasionally lapse.

28 JULY   *Hitchcock Steers a Bull.*

Alan Whitney reports in John G. Fuller's "Trade Winds" column (*The Saturday Review*)
that the people listed attained fame under the following names:

1. Douglas Fairbanks   6. Jack Benny
2. Leon Trotsky   7. Edward VII
3. Mary Pickford   8. Mike Todd
4. George Eliot   9. Cary Grant
5. Irving Berlin   10. El Greco

29 JULY   *Young Johnny and Ugly Sal*

Young Johnny, chancing to discover
That everybody loves a lover,
Concluded it would be his pleasure
To wed in haste, repent at leisure.
He said to ugly Sal, "I'm bound,
My dear, love makes the world go 'round.
Your looks, that make an angel weep,
Are only epidermis-deep.
Who says men seldom passes make
At girls with glasses?—a mistake!
Appearances deceive, 'tis true;
Yet better *they* deceive, than *you*.
It's not immortal beauties that
Make mortal hearts go pitty-pat;
You're wealthy, Sal, per my research:
A rich bride goeth young to church."

Sal felt her laggard pulses start.
Cold, cold her hands; warm, warm her heart.
She thought, "Each day it truer gets:
Men wink at blondes, but wed brunettes!
Though gray my hair beneath the dye,
No older than I feel am I;
This hand shall soon the cradle rock,
And rule the world (per Doctor Spock)!"
Who takes a wife, he takes a master;
For John, the marriage was disaster.
Love makes time pass away, I guess,
But t'other way around no less.
Who weds for love, his nights are great,
But daytime is the normal state;
And marriages, in heaven made,
On dusty earth are soon decayed.
The lewdest bride may pass for chaste
Unless too soon she goes to waist.
And when such fruits begin to show,
The cuckold is the last to know.

Now one last, sad reminder to end John's dreary tale:
The female of the species is more deadly than the male.

30 JULY   *The Nicknaming of States.*

1. Missouri, Arkansas.
2. New Mexico, New York, Maryland.
3. Illinois, Georgia.
4. Louisiana.
5. Connecticut, Oklahoma.
6. New Hampshire.
7. North Carolina, Minnesota, Alabama.

8. Maryland, Texas, Delaware, Massachusetts.
9. Connecticut, Colorado.
10. Nevada; Florida and South Dakota; Pennsylvania.
11. Virginia, Massachusetts.
12. California, Montana, Wyoming.
13. Indiana, Hawaii, Tennessee.
14. Nebraska, Rhode Island.
15. Iowa, North Carolina, North Dakota.
16. Delaware, Kentucky.
17. Montana, Vermont (I reversed "green" and "mountain" for the rhyme).
18. West Virginia, Maine, Michigan.
19. Arizona, Ohio.
20. Mississippi, New Jersey, Georgia.
21. Ohio, Nevada, Washington.
22. Delaware, Nebraska, Alabama, Illinois.
23. Kansas, Idaho.
24. Utah.
25. South Carolina.
26. Wisconsin, Oregon, South Dakota.
27. North Dakota, Minnesota.
28. Alaska, Alabama.

The nicknames used in "The Nicknaming of States" were derived from various annual almanacs—the *World, Reader's Digest, Associated Press,* and so on. After writing the verse I came across a list of additional state nicknames in William Rose Benet's *The Reader's Encyclopedia.* I lacked energy to incorporate them into my verse, but include them here for whatever use you may wish to make of them:

Battle-born State. Nevada, so called because it was admitted into the Union during the Civil War.
Bayou State. Mississippi, because of its bayous.
Bear State. Arkansas, formerly a haunt of the beasts.
Big Bend State. Tennessee, an Indian name meaning "River of the Big Bend."
Blue Law State. Connecticut, for obvious reasons.
Border Eagle State. Mississippi, from the border eagle in its coat of arms.
Bullion State. Missouri, whose Congressman, Thomas Hart Benton, was known as "Old Bullion."
Cockade State. Maryland, from the cockades worn by Maryland Revolutionary troops.
Corn-cracker State. Kentucky, perhaps from its corn-cracker birds. Crackers are "poor whites."
Cracker State. Georgia. More "poor whites."
Creole State. Louisiana.
Equality State. Wyoming, first to grant woman suffrage.
Everglade State. Florida, from its marshes.
Excelsior State. New York, from its motto *Excelsior.*
Freestone State. Connecticut, from its freestone quarries.
Grizzly Bear State. California.
Jay Hawk State. Kansas, where Jay Hawks (anti-slavery guerrillas) were active before and during the Civil War.
Lake State. Michigan, which abuts a number of the Great Lakes.
Live Oak State. Florida.
Lumber State. Maine.
Peninsular State. Florida, because it juts into the ocean.
Sucker State. Illinois, for the "suckers" who worked in the lead diggings of Wisconsin but returned to Illinois for the winter.

Turpentine State. North Carolina, a producer of the oil.
Land of Steady Habits. Connecticut.
Sunset Land. Arizona.

1   AUGUST   *Fifty English Emigrants.*

1. Certificate (Yiddish); 2. beefsteak (French); 3. cold cream (Italian); 4. striker (Slovak); 5. blind pig (Swedish); 6. operation (Danish); 7. love letter (Pennsylvania Dutch); 8. telephone (Chinese); 9. television (Polish); 10. newspaper (Dutch); 11. pay day (Yugoslavian); 12. so long (Malay); 13. picnic (Japanese); 14. bear in mind (Swedish); 15. blackboard (Norwegian); 16. atom bomb (Finnish); 17. smoking jacket (French); 18. streetcars, financed by bonds, (Brazilian); 19. pretty good (Norwegian); 20. engine (French); 21. depot (Icelandic); 22. Yankee (Gaelic); 23. racketeer (Italian); 24. frankfurter (Spanish); 25. basketball (Greek); 26. quarter, or 25¢ (Portuguese); 27. gambling house (Icelandic); 28. mockingbird (Czechoslovak); 29. riding coat (French); 30. quay (Cuban Spanish); 31. haircut (Ukrainian); 32. nylon (Italian); 33. ice cream (Polish); 34. baby (Finnish); 35. old country (Hungarian); 36. cowboy films (Lithuanian); 37. goddamn (Syrian); 38. city hall (Greek); 39. coffee (Chinese); 40. wild western movie (Swedish); 41. moving pictures (Lithuanian); 42. proletariat (Chinese); 43. sidewalk (Italian); 44. watchman (Panamanian Spanish); 45. screened (German); 46. glycerine (Japanese); 47. shake hands (Italian); 48. rail bus made in Kalamazoo (French Canadian); 49. vacuum cleaner (French Canadian); 50. enough (Rumanian).

5   AUGUST   *Drinking Song of a Hard-hearted Landlord.*

> Though my tenant's a lass who's a loner,
> So many contenders are milling
> About with pretensions to own her,
> They'd be dear at ten ha'pence the shilling.
> (CHORUS: They'd be dear at, *etc.*)
>
> The tendrils that frame her sweet forehead
> Would merit Tenniel's attentions;
> But her tenement's mine, and I'm horrid:
> I jeer at romantic intentions.
> (CHORUS: I jeer at, *etc.*)
>
> If she tenders her payments, I heed not
> How tender's this lass when unbent;
> Treat tenants as humans? Indeed not;
> Their tendency's not to pay rent.
> (CHORUS: Their tendency's, *etc.*)

10   AUGUST   *The Comtator and the Door*

Following the adjournment of the annual meeting of Mensa, an immensely wealthy commentator rubbed his throat with menthol, donned his outer garment (a Burberry), and paused in his departure to lament as follows to the doormen:

"My compliments, gentlemen! (For, despite the abasement of your jobs, you see that I do not consider you menials.) Sirs, it is too late to mend the Establishment; instead, I recommend its instant replacement. Wherever one may commence one's assessment, whatever one's ideological alignment, one's judgment must be that our democratic experiment, once the adornment of the ages, has wound up as a tormented society, a detriment to the attainment of men's goals.

"What, gentlemen, are its so-called accomplishments? Where are its amenities? We dwell in a menagerie, trusting for safety to its tameness. Diseased mendicants walk streets paved with excrement. We breathe meningitis from the air. Unemployment is rife. A shortage of tenements has driven rent payments through the roof. We are impelled to supplement our increment by moonlighting. The menu of our senior citizens consists of gruel. Oppression foments unrest.

"Do I dare mention the fate of the great issues of war and peace? Postponement! Of the man who is crippled? Lameness! Of civil rights? Abridgment! Of slum dwellers? Displacement! Of militant dissenters? Internment—nay, often, interment!

"What endorsement can be given a government that requires a white integument for economic advancement? Where every segment of the population is menaced by crime? Where even the college freshmen are in ferment? Nor is improvement to be expected; there is no commensurate concern, no agreement on priorities, no mentor to relieve our bafflement. All is argument. Our leaders are temperamentally unfit. They lack discernment. They are mendacious. And I suspect they are hangmen."

The doormen professed to be immensely impressed by these elementary comments. One, who was religious, cried, "Amen!" Another, who was French, said, "Evidemment!" A third said: "In addition, Carmen is a lousy opera, the weather is inclement, my investments have gone sour, my wife has joined Women's Lib, and I might mention also that I find the sameness of my work detrimental to my health."

Since they were so sympathetic, the commentator left a tremendous tip.

MORAL: The road to pecuniary preferment is not necessarily to become a Menshevik or to stuff cement into the Alimentary Canal. You will do commendably well if you pretend agreement with anyone, however demented, who has money.

18 AUGUST   *High Flight Highlights.*

1. Wholesome.
2. If you turn the list upside down and read it in a mirror the list will be inverted, but the words will stay the same.

20 AUGUST   *Word Belt.*

• Supple • Plentiful • Fuller Brush man • Manful • Fulsome • Omega • Egad • Gadget • Gethsemane • Anecdotage • Agent • Entire • Irenic

22 AUGUST   *Swiftly Speaking.*

Who, what, *where*. Young M.D.: *interne*. Gold leaf: *gilt*. John in Spanish; *Juan*. Elec. unit: *amp*. Elmo Roper's poll: *Poll lightly*. Coda, in music, is a *final* passage. Shirtwaist: *blouse*. Maid's night off: *helpless*. K-: *K-rations*. Pass the cards: *I deal*. Quiet meadow: *silent lea*. Zero: *naught*. Lose a few, *win some*. Drei, *vier*, fünf. Brothers, *Grimm*. Oriental gift: *pleasant*. One pair: *a brace of*. X's and: *Y's*. Bequeath: *will*. Newsweek, *Time*. Tripod: *easel*. Pope, *Pius*. Furn., *apt*.

10 SEPTEMBER   *English is Unamerican.*

1. Ad, advertisement
2. Boulevard, main road
3. Bath
4. Beet
5. Scab, or fink
6. Ticket agent
7. Trunk
8. Recess
9. Taxi stand
10. Catalogue
11. Parking lot
12. Express company
13. Catnip
14. French fries
15. Closed season
16. Clothespin

17. Master of ceremonies
18. Cone
19. Cruising
20. Potato chip
21. Delegation
22. Flop house
23. Extension wire
24. Fraternal order
25. Period
26. Gingersnap
27. Box car
28. Installment plan
29. Vacationist
30. Horn, or siren
31. Eraser
32. Domestic mails
33. Pantry
34. Editorial
35. Checkroom
36. Truck farmer
37. Game
38. Pot pie
39. Highway patrolman
40. Pen point
41. Bellboy, or bellhop
42. Hall
43. Baby carriage, baby buggy
44. Gasoline
45. General delivery
46. District attorney, or state's attorney

47. Holdup man, stickup man, highjacker
48. Sirloin
49. Operating cost
50. Commuter
51. Sell out
52. Dumbwaiter
53. Hash
54. Thriller
55. Stenographer
56. One-way ticket
57. Soda fountain
58. Hot water bottle
59. Distributor
60. Scholarship
61. Rutabaga
62. T.V.
63. Parole (for a criminal)
64. Can
65. Lumber
66. Flashlight
67. Hike
68. Transport
69. Night club, or nightstick
70. Touchdown
71. Street corner
72. Rare
73. Watch crystal
74. Witness stand
75. Excelsior

14 SEPTEMBER *Fable of the H[1] and the Stupid but Persistent A[2].*

The keyed letters evolved from hieroglyphs picturing the following:

The letter	1 (Egyptian source)	2 (Phoenician-Hebrew source)
A.	Eagle	Ox
B.	Crane	House
C.		Camel
D.	Hand	Door
F.	Asp	Peg
G.		Camel's head and neck
H.	Sieve	Fence
K.	Bowl	
L.	Lioness	Ox-goad
M.	Owl	Water
N.	Water	Fish
O.		Eye
P.	Shutter	Mouth

So the fable reads:

A Lioness met an Ox carrying a Sieve. "Where are you taking the Sieve, Ox?" asked the Lioness. "To the river to fetch Water for my friend the Crane, dear Lioness," replied the Ox. "He is extremely ill, and I fear he may soon be carried out on a Shutter." "No wonder men use an Ox-goad to keep an Ox on the road!" fumed the Lioness. "Don't you know you can't carry Water in a Sieve?" "That remains to be seen," said the Ox, and he trudged on until he came to an old House where an Owl sat dozing outside the Door. "Where are you going with that Sieve, Ox?" asked the Owl, opening an Eye. "To the river to fetch Water for the Crane, dear Owl," said the Ox. "Get a Bowl, you foolish Ox!" cried the Owl; "a Sieve won't hold Water!" "That remains to be seen," said the patient Ox, and on he went until he met an Eagle sitting on a Fence holding a wriggling Asp in his Mouth. "Why are you holding that Asp in your Mouth, dear Eagle?" inquired the Ox; but the Eagle remained silent, for he feared that if he opened his Mouth the Asp would bite him before he could get his Mouth closed again.

At last the Ox reached the river, where he found an old Camel. The Camel's Head and Neck were lowered because the Camel was swilling down the last of his weekly quota of Water. "What are you doing with that Sieve, Ox?" asked the Camel when he had finished swilling. "I am going to use it to take Water back to my sick friend the Crane, dear Camel," said the Ox. "But a Sieve does not hold Water, you silly Ox!" said the Camel. "That remains to be seen, dear Camel," replied the Ox, and he dipped the Sieve into the Water. No sooner had he brought the Sieve up from the Water than all the Water it contained was gone. But there in the bottom of the Sieve flapped a beautiful Fish!

"Oh, well," said the Ox philosophically, "I am sure the Crane would rather have a Fish than nothing." And he was right.

MORAL: You've got to Hand it to that Ox. He took those smart alecks down a Peg or two!

17 SEPTEMBER   *I into My Mirror Peeked.*

The rhopalic club begins with the first letter of the first line, and grows as it descends.

1. I into my mirror peeked.
    "IS this horror me?" I shrieked.
    "SIT down, mirror; say what glue
    TIES fair me to ugly you.
    TIRES about my tum you loop;
    SISTER tires from eyes you droop.
    TIGRESS' mate am I! What error
    GRITLESS shows me in my mirror?
    SLIGHTERS cite this glass to prove me
    LESS BRIGHT than they hope who love me."

2. I saw a tin hayfork
    IN a barn bin—
    TIN handle, every
    TINE made of tin.
    TRINE the tin tines were,
    WINTER was a-rattle;
    TIN were the barn roofs,
    THIN were the cattle.

20 SEPTEMBER   *Nameplay.*

The book is *Tom Sawyer*. The opening lines:
"Tom!"
No answer.
"Tom!"

23 SEPTEMBER   *Address Unknown.*

The place names, as you, clever reader, saw at once, are Baton Rouge, Santa Fe, Pend Oreille (though this is really a lake and river, not a town), Corpus Christi, Des Moines, and Amarillo. Have you ever shot craps at The Swans NE?

9 OCTOBER   *What Is the Question?*

The questions:
1. What is your full name, Dr. Presume?
2. What's a Grecian urn?
3. How can you recognize a brass band?
4. What noise does a Japanese camera make?
5. What is so rare as a day in June?
6. What have rainbow trout got that no other trout has?
7. What do you get when you ask a woman her age?
8. What color is a board of education?
9. What's Nu?
10. What was the final score of the Strontium-Carbon game?
11. What was the slogan of that airline that went out of business?
12. What are all those cherry pits doing in my bed?
13. Where the hell did all these rocks come from?
14. What do you use to beat up a stork?
15. What would Oliver Wendell Holmes, Jr., have been had he had his father's talent for writing verse?

11 OCTOBER   *Streets in Old London.*

The answer is "a thoroughfare." A street does not have corners in England, but turnings; neither does it have a head or foot. English thoroughfares have tops and bottoms.

12 OCTOBER   *"Hark to the Mewsicians of Bremen!"*

Cervine is deerlike; colubrine, snakelike; hircine, goatlike; larine, gull-like; lutrine, otterlike; meline, badgerlike; mephitine, skunklike; musteline, weasellike (or martenlike, or minklike); ovine, sheeplike; phocine, seallike; sciurine, squirrellike; viverrine, civetlike.

16 OCTOBER   *A Collection of Crocks.*

From a Collection of Sources
I bring you this curious Collection of Facts.
One day a Collection of Gallants
A Collection of Jews
And a Collection of Hicks
Who included a Collection of Cals
And a Collection of Dicks
Left their Collection of Flats
To walk on a Collection of Docks
With a Collection of Monsters.
There they met a Collection of Gals
Among whom were a Collection of Janices
A Collection of Sals
And a Collection of Mses

The Collection of Hicks
Had brought a Collection of Hens
And the Collection of Hens
Had brought a Collection of Chicks.
The Collection of Gals
Agreed to dance a Collection of Jigs
On the Collection of Docks
With the Collection of Gallants
The Collection of Jews
And the Collection of Hicks
But not the Collection of Monsters.
This enraged the Collection of Monsters.
Who loosed in the Collection of Jigs
A Collection of Bats

And made off in the confusion with the
Collection of Hens
And the Collection of Chicks.
With the prodigious Collection of Curses
The Collection of Hicks
Sic'ed a Collection of Curs
A Collection of Collies
And a Collection of Bears
On the fleeing Collection of Monsters
But the clever Collection of Monsters
Ran into a Collection of Stores
Where they sold the Collection of Hens
And the Collection of Chicks
For a Collection of Cents.
With a quick Collection of Pecks

The Collection of Hens
And the Collection of Chicks
Ate a Collection of Pills
And a Collection of Bugs.
When the Police caught the Collection of
    Monsters
They rode them on a Collection of Rails
And in a Collection of Cells
Rapped a Collection of Skulls.
The Judge imposed a Collection of Fines.
But the poor Collection of Hicks
Never got back the Collection of Hens
Or the Collection of Chicks,
For the Collection of Hicks
Were a Collection of Fools.

22 OCTOBER   *Stinky-Pinkies.*

1. Fervent servant
2. Prosaic mosaic
3. Truculent succulent
4. Granite planet
5. Raucous caucus
6. Dire choir
7. Puerile mural
8. Saline praline
9. Helot zealot
10. Fecund second

25 OCTOBER   *We Interrupt Our Program.*

My TV tells me, *all men have their price;*
It says, *who pays the piper calls the tune;*
And *haste makes waste,* and *cat away, the mice
Will play,* and *better half a loaf than none.*
My TV says, *what's dirt cheap's cheap as dirt,*
And *beggars would, were wishes horses, ride:*
And *out of sight is out of mind* (but ponder
As well that *absence makes the heart grow fonder.*)

My TV tells me, *water's not as thick
As blood,* and *faint heart ne'er fair lady won;
Speak soft, but ever carry a big stick;
The rich grow richer, but the poor have fun.*

Of what new insight are all these the presage?
You said it, Mac! *The medium's the message!*

29 OCTOBER   *Caught in the Middle.*

The completed words are solecism, breviary, adjutant, and meridian.

15 NOVEMBER   *Double Duty.*

1. Backward, Wardrobe
2. Barren, Render
3. Border, Derive

4. Common, Money
5. Curtain, Tainted
6. Doorkey, Keystone
7. Explain, Plaintive
8. Fireside, Sideways
9. Footstep, Stepson
10. Fretsaw, Sawmill
11. Hamlet, Lettuce
12. Handsome, Somebody
13. Housework, Workman (or Houseboat, Boatman)
14. Mischief, Chieftain
15. Present, Sentence
16. Prowess, Essence
17. Pursuit, Suitable (or Purport, Portable)
18. Sunset, Settee
19. Tasty, Tyrant
20. Warfare, Farewell

18 NOVEMBER   *The Strange Case of the Surplus Anagrams.*

The missing words in the five-anagram verse:
Sutler, Ulster, luster, rustle, result.
The missing words in the nine-anagram verse:
Ulster, sutler, luters, lurest, rulest, lustre, luster, rustle, result.

2 DECEMBER   *Friend in the Middle.*

1. Naturalist	9. Ingredient
2. Associated	10. Woodpecker
3. Scrupulous	11. Revolution
4. Fascinated	12. Telephones
5. Precaution	13. Electronic
6. Orchestral	14. Mechanical
7. Commentary	15. Illustrate
8. Infidelity	16. Loggerhead

13 DECEMBER   *Methusalah Drank for 969 Years.*

Muse, say not I (tush tush!) am heel
That out of ale I make my meal.
Methusalah, it now appears,
The hale sum was of many beers.
No gold a man might melt has hue
Gold as the meal he thus would brew;
And no mule has the kick those beers
Supplied him for a thousand years.
Muse, health waits in the glass! I pray
Let ale heal; shut me not away.

16 DECEMBER   Kew, Kew, Si, Si, Si.

I had a dreadful time identifying Tibor Gergely's bird calls.* This is the best I can do:

- Kew, kew. The kestrel.
- Si si si. The blue tit, the great tit, the crested tit.
- Gobak gobak. The red grouse.
- Zwick. The woodcock.
- T-weet. The swallow.
- Mee-oo. The buzzard.
- Klee-weet. The wood sandpiper.
- Chrr. The sedge warbler. Also the blackcap.
- Crek. The corncrake. Also the land rail.
- Tricky-tic. The Lapland bunting.
- Pitchoo. The marsh tit.
- Zup zup zup. The long-tailed tit.
- Dzweee. The brambling.
- Ho-hoo-hoo-oooo. The tawny owl. The wood owl.
- Chack. The fieldfare.
- Peep peep peep. The sandpiper.
- Tu-whit. Again, the tawny or wood owl.
- Wee-tuc-tuc. The spotted flycatcher.
- Dzer. The whitethroat.
- Currah. The tufted duck.
- Kwk-kwk-hoo-coo. The Manx shearwater.
- Agh. The roseate tern; also the great black-backed gull.
- Kek kek kek. The sparrowhawk.
- Fullock. The moorhen.
- Pink-a-pink. The oyster catcher.
- Kittie-needie. The common sandpiper.
- Ooi-ooi-ooi. The ringed plover.
- Kloo-it. The avocet.
- If-hee. The coal tit.
- Tak. The lesser whitethroat. Also the blackcap.
- Tweedle tweedle sweet sweet sweet. The tree pipit.
- Twk-twk. The shoveler.
- Kark. Gray lag goose.
- Ha-ha-ha-ha.. The green woodpecker.
- Tew-tew-tew. The lesser redpoll. Also the greenshank.

25 DECEMBER   *Take Back That Powdered Rhinoceros Horn, Santa!*

Read in order the first letter of the first word of each line of the sonnet ("hand-painted" is one word); the first letter of the third word of each line; and the first letter of the last word of each line. It comes out:

> "The Oysterville Almanac bids
> you Merry Christmas."

And most sincerely.

* Birds make these noises in England. In America, they sound different.

INDEX OF RHETORICAL DEVICES

Abbreviations, 2, 69, 144, 227, 247
ABC language, 2, 181
Acronyms, 86, 111
Acrostics, vii, 57, 326
Ad hominems, 82, 302
American isn't English, 13, 19, 150, 155, 171, 204, 233, 278
Anagrams, 23, 52, 89, 227, 291, 313
Answers and solutions, 333
Burlesque and parody, 56, 100, 259
Calendar verse, 1, 113
Clerihews, 62, 246
Clichés, 8, 133, 147, 193, 270, 284
Countdown verses, 26, 200
Dialect, 22, 46, 73, 104, 112, 123, 146, 155, 188, 201, 221, 226, 234, 250, 253, 288, 291, 303, 310, 319, 322
Echoes and chains, 137, 301
Epigrams, 31, 281
Epitaphs, 27, 51
Equivocally speaking, 18, 312
Euphemisms, 49, 92, 113
Fractured foreigners, 3, 38, 59, 60, 72, 75, 89, 119, 135, 179, 197, 206, 273, 310
Graffiti, 128
Grammar, 7, 11, 22, 43, 68, 79, 82, 94, 108, 116, 139, 153, 159, 180, 208, 238, 243, 249, 254, 262, 266, 281, 289, 327
Haiku, 143
Higgledy-piggledies (Double Dactyls), 21, 271, 306
Hobson-jobsons, 21, 203
Homonyms and heteronyms, 15, 131, 145, 265, 271, 315
Hyperbole, 97
Impossible rhymes, 47

Jargon, 108, 131, 186, 199, 228
Limericks, 165, 229
Lipograms, 45
Macaronics (pig Latin), 75
Malapropisms, 36, 161, 242
Metaphors, 105, 189, 235, 268
Mnemonics, 94
Multitudinous nouns, 16, 127, 230, 290
Onomatopoeia, 60, 74, 167, 202, 316
Oxymorons, 300
Palindromes, 39, 174, 192, 218, 244
Pangrams, 52
Pronunciation, 11, 34, 109, 122, 217
Puns, 41, 209, 299
Rhopalics, 6, 241
Riddles, 211
Sick verse, 66
Sight rhymes, 241
Slang, forward and backward, 6, 98, 106, 114, 255, 263, 277, 296
Spoonerisms, 150, 252
Symbols and signs, 148, 237
Tom swifties, 30, 215, 321
Tongue twisters, 11
Translation, 23, 102, 164
Typefaces and typos, 80, 238, 262, 298
Uncommon, improper nouns, 99
Univocalics, 55, 97
Visual wordplay, 13, 63, 80, 117, 182, 191, 298, 321, 325, 328
Word games for the parlor, 54, 87, 100, 120, 156, 164, 198, 214, 258, 268, 272, 275, 289, 305, 308, 316
Words, evolving, 33, 92, 124, 219, 266, 324
Words, short and long, 97, 171, 272

INDEX OF AUTHORS (OMITTING W.R.E.)*

With an occasional exception to prove the rule, persons referred to but not directly or indirectly quoted are not listed in this index

Aarons, Edward S., 44; Abbott, George, 327; Adams, Charles F., 299–300; Adams, Franklin P., 43, 48, 213; Addison, Joseph, 42, 108; Ade, George, 129–30; Albrecht, 88; Aldrich, Henry, 285; Aldridge, Adele, 287–88, 328; Alger, Joe, 198; Amory, Cleveland, 155; Anderson, Dick, 275; Angell, Roger, 246; Aristophanes, 246; Aristotle, 197; Armstrong, John, 10; Ashford, Angela, 153–54; Ashley, L. R. N., 6–7, 197; Auchincloss, Louis, 250; Auden, W. H., 179, 246, 247, 273; Austen, Jane, 13; Austin, Warren, 208

Bacon, Francis, 86; Bainbridge, Peggy, 114; Baker, Russell, 133, 141–42; Ball, John, 210; Barham, R. H., 48; Beaman, Ralph G., 69, 218; Belloc, Hilaire, 66, 71, 163; Belviso, Bob, 72, 73; Benchley, Robert, 20; Bendiner, Robert, 43, 171; Benson, Gerard, 244; Bentley, E. C., 62–63; Berger, Arthur, 158; Bergerson, Howard W., 175, 275; Berra, Yogi, 37; Bevin, Ernie, 8, 268; Bickerstaff, Isaac, 32; Bishop, Morris, 32, 110, 166, 229, 240–41; Blake, William, 25, 186–87; Blundell, G. J., 244; Bombaugh, C. C., 290–91; Bongartz, Roy, 30–31; Bonheurs, Dominique, 88; Bonner, Anthony E., 39; Bonner, Louisa, 80, 204; Bonner, Paul H., Jr., 209; Borgmann, Dmitri A., 6, 23, 145, 174, 220–21; Brewer, E. Cobham, 86, 203; Bronowski, J., 82; Brougher, Bill, 113; Brown, Edward E., 42; Browne, Charles Farrar, 201–2; Browning, Elizabeth, 294; Browning, Robert, 103; Broyard, Anatole, 44; Buck, Jack, 37; Burges, Meghan, 187–88; Burgess, Anthony, 188–89; Burgess, Gelett, 33; Burn, Michael, 206–7; Burns, Robert, 24; Burton, John H., 217; Butler, Samuel, 295–96; Byron, Lord, 48

Caen, Herb, 214; Canby, Vincent, 302; Canning, George, 5; Card, Les, 305; Carroll, Lewis, 24; Casson, Lionel, 53–54; Chapman, John, 302; Chapman, John Jay, 302; Charleston, R. W., 87; Cholmondeley-Pennell, Henry, 282; Churchill, Winston, 253; Ciardi, John, 120–21, 180–81; Clapham, 172; Clemens, Samuel, 135; Clough, Arthur Hugh, 66; Cocteau, Jean, 59; Cohen, Philip, 217; Coke, T. W. E., 19; Cole, William, 29–30, 138, 143, 148, 149, 262, 303; Coleridge, Samuel T., 208; Congreve, William, 14; Connelly, Marc, 279; Considine, Bob, 92; Coolidge, Joseph, 40; Correll, C. J., 234–35; Corwin, Norman, 42; Coward, Noel, 302; Craddle, W., 149; Craster, Mrs. Edward, 162; Creamer, Robert W., 161; Croll, James, 88; Cross, Milton, 34; Cross, Wilbur, 2; Crowninshield, Frank, 93; cummings, e. e., 318–19; Cunningham, J. V., 32

Dahl, Roald, 248; Daly, T. A., 274, 319–20; Dammers, Kim, 19; Davidson, Marshall, 59; Dean, Dizzy, 289; Dearborn, G. Van Ness, 109; de Kay, James, 244; de Kay, Ormonde, Jr., 74; de Lesseps, Tauni, 63–64; de la Mare, Walter, 231, 277, 318; Democritus, xx; Denyer, Nicholas, 246; Denyer, R. L., 172; de Wailly, Leon, 24–25; Dickens, Charles, 279; Dietz, Howard, 302; Dillard, J. L., 25; Disraeli, Benjamin, 253; Disraeli, Isaac, xx, 219, 261–62; Donchian, Peter, 9; Donne, John, 32; Dowty, Leonhard, 192; Dudeney, Ernest, 211; Duncan, Don, 37; Dunne, Peter Finley, 73–74; Dwyer, 172

Ecclesine, Joseph, 120, 133; Eckler, A. Ross, 45–46, 100, 112, 245, 249, 284; Eliot, T. S., 217, 283–84; Engel, William E., 211; Erasmus, 68, 300; Esar, Evan, 264; Esty, Mary, 195; Everhart, Jim, 226

F. C. H., 286; Farmer, J. J. III, 199; Feldman, Pearl L., 88; Fenton, Tom, 321; Fessenden, Katherine, 250; Field, Eugene, 183, 302; Firth, 155; Fishback, Margaret, 288; Fleming, Ian, 268; Follett, Wilson, 94, 116; Foot, E. E., 134–35; Foote, Samuel, 95; Fowler, H. W., 94, 143; Francis, Darryl, 19–20, 53, 83–84, 304; Franklin, Benjamin, 51; Fraser, Bruce, 109; Freiligrath, Ferdinand, 25; Friend, J. Newton, 23, 305; Fuller, John G., 316; Fuller, Thomas, 52

Gardner, Martin, 11, 174; Gartner, Michael, 45, 174; Gay, John, 51, 189; Gergeley, Tibor, 316; Gilliatt, Penelope, 175; Gish, Lillian, 60; Gladstone, William, 253; Glueck, Grace, 44; Godden, F. F., 234–35; Goldwyn, Sam, 209; Golomb, Solomon W., 218; Gowers, Ernest, 94; Graham, Harry, 211, 227; Graves, Robert, 119; Green, Abel, 263; Green, Joseph, 88; Greenblatt, M. H., 257–58, 289; Grose, Francis, 98; Guiraud, Jules, 103; Guiterman, Arthur, xxiii

Harington, Sir John, 32; Harris, Sidney, 266; Harris, Sydney J., 175–76; Hart, Lorenz, 327; Hartwig, Mela, 25; Hegel, Wilhelm, 88; Hellman, Geoffrey, 138; Henlein, Robert A., 42; Herford, Oliver, 93, 255–57, 286; Herrick, Robert, 277; Hickerson, J. M., 131; Hipple, Ted, 143; Hitchcock, Alfred, 192; Hodson, William, 244; Hoey, Fred, 34; Holland, Lord, 96–97; Hollister, Paul, 168, 209; Holmes, Oliver Wendell, Sr., 159, 229; Hood, Thomas, 231, 268; Hoover, Herbert, 128; Hope, A. D., 205; Housman, A. E., 82, 186, 231; Howells, W. D., 302; Hughes, Richard, 209; Hyman, S. E., 189

Jacobs, Frank, 100–1, 259–61; Jacobs, Howard, 322–23; Jennings, Gary, 82–83; Jennings, Paul, 273; Jensen, Oliver, 293; Johnson, Samuel, 108, 187; Jones, Sir H. A., 88; Jones, James M., 109; Jukes, Thomas H., 245

Kaufman, G. L., 14; Keats, John, 33; Keeley, John W., 33; Kendrick, Green, 75; Kennedy, John F., 156; King, Florence, 167; Kipling, Rudyard, 32; Kirk, W. F., 288

Lamb, Charles, 42; Lanigan, G. T., 8, 184; Lardner, Ring W., 291–92; Large, Arlan J., 284–85; Lauder, Afferbeck, 46–47, 104, 221–22, 253–54; Lawrence, D. H., 232; Lawrence, Jerry, 34; Laycock, Don, 213; Leacock, Stephen, 2; Lear, Edward, 183; Lebovitz, Richard, 202; Lee, Charles, 9; Lerner, Max, 268; Levi–Strauss, Claude, xx; Levin, Ira, 47; Levy, Newman, 11; Lewis, Anthony, 150; Lewis, D. B. Wyndam, 9; Lincoln, Joseph C., 278; Lindon, J. A., 57, 102, 145, 151, 174, 244; Lipton, James, 16, 230; Lyndsay, Sir David, 31

Macklin, Charles, 95; Madden, Mary Ann, 230; Maggie, 169; Manheim, Paul E., 80, 232; Markham, Edwin, 56; Marks, Naomi, 244; Marquis, Don, 286–87; Matthiessen, Peter, 269–70; Mayes, Herbert, 19; McCord, David, 144, 158, 213, 255, 267, 281, 326; McDonald, Ross, 44; McGinley, Phyllis, 215; Meares, C. W. V., 173; Merrill, James, 272; Merritt, Dixon, 230; Miall, Leonard, 22; Minogue, K. R., 228; Mockridge, Norton, 37, 128; Moore, Clement C., 325; Moore, Julia, 10–11; Morgan, Augustus, 52; Morgan, J. A., 76

Nash, Ogden, 167, 229–30, 273; Naylor, James Ball, 249; Newell, Robert H., 40; Nicholson, Nigel, 49; Norgate, Matthew, 192

O'Brien, E. J., 215–16; O'Keefe, 75; Oppenheimer, George, 60, 302; Orwell, George, 109, 188–89

Pachter, Hedya, 241; Pastore, John, 284–85; Payn, James, 278–79; Pearce, Murray, 305; Pei, Mario, 159–60; Peirce, Anna, 152; Peirce, Waldo, 152; Perelman, S. J., 116; Peterson, Roger, 60; Phillips, David, 244; Piron, 51; Platt, Florence M., 306; Pope, Alexander, 33, 108; Pound, Ezra, 131; Porter, Temple G., 49–50, 238–40, 327–28; Preston, Keith, 8, 303; Proetz, Victor, 23

Rambo, J. I., 321–22; Ransome, John C., 276–77; Raoul, 218; Ratoff, Gregory, 209; Read, E. C. K., 306; Reed, Christopher, 276; Reeves, James, 7; Reid, Alastair, 308–9; Reston, James, 44; Rice, Grantland, 208; Richards, Laura E., 139; Ridings, J. W., 214; Robbins, Patricia, 321; Rockefeller, Nelson,

86; Romaine, Octave, 66; Rossetti, Christina, 48; Rosten, Leo, 145, 187; Roth, Arthur, 88; Rowe, R. R., 148, 325; Rowsome, Frank, 61; Ruskin, John, 294; Russell, Bertrand, 164; Ruth, Babe, 208

S. V., 111; Sackville-West, Vita, 49, 61–62, 144; Safire, William, 250; Sala, George A., 28, 43; Sandburg, Carl, 212, 302; Sanderson, Colin, 209; Schultz, Charles, 117; Schroeder, F. D., 229; Scofield, Nanette E., 53–54; Scott, Robert, 24; Scott, Sir Walter, 155, 215; Selassie, Haile, 85; Sellar, W. C., 279–80; Shakespeare, William, xx, 33, 51, 108, 154, 242, 268, 300; Shannon, Claude E., 52; Shaw, George Bernard, 20; Shenker, Israel, 179; Sheridan, Richard B., 14; Shiki, 143; Silverman, David L., 115, 164, 268–69, 305; Sitwell, Edith, 65; Sitwell, Sir Osbert, 65; Skeezix, 52; Smith, Godfrey, 171; Smith, H. Allen, 33–34; Smith, Howard K., 155; Smith, Logan P., 66; Smith, Red, 208; Smith, Sidney, 144; Snake, Speckled, 76; Sock, A., 42; Sondheim, Stephen, 47, 327; Soupault, M. L. and Philippe, 25; Spooner, W. A., 3; Squire, J. C., 252; Starbuck, George, 91; Stein, Kurt M., 310–11; Steiner, George, 44; Stengel, Casey, 209; Stephen, J. K., 158; Steward, Thomas, 294; Stoppard, Tom, 156–57; Stout, Rex, 93;

Strunsky, Simeon, 41, 180; Stubbs, Jane, 263; Stupp, C. J., 225–26; Swift, Jonathan, 42; Swinburne, Algernon C., 300, 317–18

Tennyson, Alfred Lord, 294, 300, 329; Thomas, Dylan, 88; Thurber, James, 174; Tidwell, James N., 67–68; Trosclair, 322–23; Turgenev, Ivan, 33; Tyler, Timothy, 123–24

Untermeyer, Louis, 165; Updike, John, 167, 169–71

Van Rooten, Luis d'Antin, 38–39; Von Bernus, Alexander, 103

Wagner, Robert, 209; Walker, Jimmy, 209; Walker, Louise J., 3; Warren, Samuel, 108; Warrin, Frank L., Jr., 24; Wayman, Tom, 207; Weekes, Hobart, 209; Welch, Patricia R., 102; Weng, Will, 215; Wharton, Edith, 7; Whewell, William, 3; White, E. B., 248; Wilberforce, Samuel, 48; Wildman, John, 42; Wilson, Malcolm, 86; Winchell, Walter, 52, 296–97, 302; Wordsworth, William, 10, 82; Wright, E. V., xxi

Yeatman, R. J., 279–80; Youngquist, Mary, 18–19, 53, 81, 100, 186, 321–22